SPORT DEVELOPMENT

At a time of profound change in the economic, social, political and sporting landscape, sport development faces some important challenges. Now in a fully revised and updated third edition, *Sport Development: Policy, Process and Practice* is still the most detailed, authoritative and comprehensive guide to all aspects of contemporary sport development.

The book examines the roles of those working in and around sport development and explores the most effective methods by which professionals can promote interest, participation or performance in sport. Combining essential theory with practical analysis, the book covers key topics, themes and issues found on the sport development curriculum, including:

- sport policy
- developing 'Sport for All'
- addressing inequality in sport
- community sport development
- partnerships in sport
- PE and school sport
- sport and health
- resources for developing sport
- voluntary sports clubs and sport development
- sport development and sport coaching
- disability and sport development
- researching and evaluating sport development
- sport development and the Olympic/Paralympic Games
- international sport and development.

Each chapter contains a full range of pedagogical features to aid learning and understanding, including revision questions and case studies, while a new companion website provides additional teaching and learning resources, including useful weblinks for students, and PowerPoint slides and a test bank for lecturers. *Sport Development: Policy, Process and Practice* is an invaluable resource for all students, researchers and professionals working in sport development.

Kevin Hylton is Professor of Social Sciences in Sport, Leisure and Education, Carnegie Faculty, Leeds Metropolitan University, UK. Kevin's research interests focus on diversity, equity and inclusion in sport, leisure and education. Kevin has been heavily involved in community sport development and works with equality bodies such as the Runnymede Trust. Kevin's publications include *Sport Development: Policy, Process and Practice* (2001; 2008), *'Race' and Sport: Critical Race Theory* (2009) and *Atlantic Crossings: International Dialogues on Critical Race Theory* (2011).

Visit the companion website at www.routledge.com/cw/hylton-9780415675802/

SPORT

Policy,

EDITED B

Routledge
Taylor & Francis Group
LONDON AND NEW YORK

Third edition first published 2013
by Routledge
2 Park Square, Milton Park, Abingdon, Oxon OX14 4RN

Simultaneously published in the USA and Canada
by Routledge
711 Third Avenue, New York, NY 10017

First edition first published by Routledge 2001
Second edition first published by Routledge 2008

Routledge is an imprint of the Taylor & Francis Group, an informa business

British Library Cataloguing in Publication Data
A catalogue record for this book is available from the British Library

Library of Congress Cataloging in Publication Data
Sports development : policy, process and practice / edited by Kevin Hylton. — 3rd ed.
pages cm
1. Sports—Great Britain. 2. Sports administration—Great Britain. 3. Sports— Social aspects—Great Britain. 4. Sports and state—Great Britain. I. Hylton, Kevin, 1964–
GV605.S76 2013
796.06′9—dc23
2012030482

ISBN: 978-0-415-67579-6 (hbk)
ISBN: 978-0-415-67580-2 (pbk)
ISBN: 978-0-203-08282-9 (ebk)

Typeset in Melior and Univers by Prepress Projects Ltd, Perth, UK

Printed and bound in Great Britain by
TJ International Ltd, Padstow, Cornwall

CONTENTS

1 INTRODUCTION   1

KEVIN HYLTON

2 SPORT POLICY   11

CHRIS WOLSEY AND JEFFREY ABRAMS

9 VOLUNTARY SPORTS CLUBS AND SPORT DEVELOPMENT 213

GEOFF NICHOLS

10 SPORT DEVELOPMENT AND SPORT COACHING 231

JOHN LYLE (WITH THOMAS DOWENS)

FIGURES

TABLES

CONTRIBUTORS

Jeffrey Abrams is Academic Staff Lead for Sport Management and Development at Leeds Metropolitan University. Before becoming a full-time academic, he spent many years as a senior manager in the sport and leisure industry, both in community leisure and in facility management. He also taught Physical Education in the USA. Jeff is co-author of *Human Resource Management in the Sport and Leisure Industry* (Routledge, 2012).

Kevin Hylton is Professor of Social Sciences in Sport, Leisure and Education, Carnegie Faculty, Leeds Metropolitan University. Kevin has been heavily involved in community sport and race equality and has worked with marginalised groups and representative bodies in different settings. Kevin has published extensively in peer-reviewed journals and high-profile book projects in sport, leisure and education. Kevin's publications include the previous two editions of this essential book (2001, 2008). Kevin also wrote *'Race' and Sport: Critical Race Theory* (Routledge, 2009). Kevin's research interests focus on the development of Critical Race Theory (CRT), diversity, equity and inclusion in sport, leisure and education. He is a member of the Runnymede Trust Academic Forum and Advisory Board Member for the *Sociology* journal.

Hayley Fitzgerald is Reader in Disability and Youth Sport at Leeds Metropolitan University. Prior to this she was a researcher at Loughborough University and managed a range of projects supporting young disabled people in physical education and youth sport. Hayley has also worked for a number of disability sport organisations in England. Hayley is known for her data collection methods that enable people experiencing learning and multiple disabilities to be meaningfully included in research. Currently, Hayley is Chair of the UK Disability Sport Coaching, Learning and Leadership Group and is Co-convener of the BERA Physical Education and Sports Pedagogy Group. Hayley is also an editorial board member of *Physical Education and Sports Pedagogy* and *Adapted Physical Activity Quarterly*.

Anne Flintoff is Professor in Physical Education and Sport at Leeds Metropolitan University. Her teaching, research and consultancy centres on issues of equity and social inclusion, particularly gender, in physical education and sport. She publishes widely in both academic and professional journals and textbooks.

Vassil Girginov is Reader in Sport Management/Development at Brunel University and Visiting Professor at the Russian International Olympic University. Vassil has worked with and consulted sport organisations in Bulgaria, Canada and England as well as the Trim and Fitness International Sport for All Association. His research interests, publications and industry experience are in the field of the Olympic movement, sport development, comparative management and policy analysis. Vassil's most recent projects include the UK National Governing Bodies' (NGBs) leveraging of the 2012 London Olympic Games for capacity building and the relationship between the culture of NGBs and participation in sport. His most recent edited and authored books include *Handbook of the London 2012 Olympic and Paralympic Games* (Routledge, 2012), *Sport Management Cultures* (Routledge, 2011), *The Olympics: A Critical Reader* (Routledge, 2010), *Management of Sports Development* (Elsevier, 2008) and *The Olympic Games Explained* (Routledge, 2005, the book has been translated in five languages).

Jonathan Long is a professor in the Carnegie Research Institute at Leeds Metropolitan University. He has now directed some fifty research projects for external clients. His experience embraces all stages of the research process from design to dissemination and his research uses both quantitative and qualitative research techniques. Jonathan's major research interests centre around leisure policies and practices related to social change and issues of social justice. Recent research in sport and leisure has been involved with racial equality, social capital and social inclusion. He is the author of *Researching Leisure, Sport and Tourism: The Essential Guide* (Sage, 2007), was a founding member of the Editorial Board of *Leisure Studies*, and is now on the board of both *Managing Leisure* and the *Journal of Policy Research in Tourism, Leisure and Events*. He is an Academician of the Academy of Social Sciences.

John Lyle is Adjunct Professor of Sports Coaching at the University of Queensland and former Professor of Sports Coaching at Leeds Metropolitan University. He is a consultant specialising in programme evaluations, workforce planning and sports coaching policy. He established the first professional diploma in Sports Coaching and the first Masters degree in Coaching Studies in the UK, and has played a significant role in the development of sports coaching as an academic field of study. He is the author of the influential textbooks *Sports Coaching Concepts* (2002) and *Sports Coaching: Professionalisation and Practice* (2010). John has contributed widely through publications, presentations, master classes, working groups and other media to academic and professional developments in sports coaching. John's academic experience is complemented by considerable personal experience as a volleyball coach, and engagement in consultancy, policy and the delivery of coach education.

Jim McKenna has been Professor of Physical Activity and Health and head of the centre of Active Lifestyles research in the Carnegie Faculty of Leeds Metropolitan University since 2005, joining after eighteen years at the University of Bristol. He has an extensive portfolio of peer-reviewed publications and grants covering interventions and community evaluations, spanning schools through to workplaces and working with older adults. Jim is currently working with colleagues from across the university evaluating the Premier League Health intervention for young men, which is being run through the Football Premier League in England, and in evaluating a staged recovery intervention targeted on wounded injured and sick service personnel, based around adapted sport and adventure education.

Oscar Mwaanga is Senior Lecturer and course leader of the MA Sport and Development at Southampton Solent University (UK). Oscar holds a PhD in the Sociology of Sport from Leeds Metropolitan University and an MSc in the Social Psychology of Sport from the Norwegian University of Sport Science. Oscar is a renowned international Sport for Development and Peace (SDP) activist who has focused his work on promoting sport empowerment for marginalised groups in Sub-Saharan Africa and the UK. Oscar is also recognised as an indigenous leader of the Sub-Saharan Africa SDP movement of the last decade, especially after founding EduSport Foundation, which is the first SDP organisation in Zambia. Oscar is also the founder and Chairman of the Zambian Institute of Sport and also the pioneer of a number of world renowned SDP initiatives including Kicking AIDS Out, SDP peer leadership, Go Sisters and recently the Fair Game Football programme in Zambia.

Geoff Nichols is Senior Lecturer at Sheffield University Management School. His main research interests are volunteers in sports clubs and events, management of sports clubs run by volunteers and the volunteering legacy of sports events. His research has included the volunteering legacy of the 2002 Commonwealth Games (with Rita Ralston, Manchester Metropolitan University), a national survey of sports clubs in the UK and research into how sports clubs recruit new volunteers (both with Peter Taylor and colleagues at Sheffield Hallam University). Since 2009 he has chaired the Sports Volunteering Research Network which promotes research into sports volunteering through symposia and a newsletter. His previous work on the relationship between sport and crime reduction, especially for young people, was summarised in his 2007 book *Sport and Crime Reduction: The Role of Sports in Tackling Youth Crime*. He has worked as a sports development officer with Tameside Council and as an outdoor pursuits instructor, using these activities in personal development programmes for young people.

Janine Partington is Senior Lecturer in Sport Development at Leeds Metropolitan University. Prior to this appointment, she worked in sport development for ten years for both local authorities and voluntary sector organisations. She has managed a range of successful community sports projects and initiatives that were developed by, and built upon, successful partnerships. Her academic interests include the strategic management of sport development, partnerships in sport and community sports development. Janine has written on community sport, community empowerment and partnership working.

Stephen Robson is a former local authority sport development professional who works as Senior Lecturer in Sport Development at Leeds Metropolitan University. As well as heading up the Sport Development degree, he leads the teaching of strategic management. Stephen has extensive experience of working on national-level projects related to employability and continuing professional development in sport development, including the development of bespoke National Occupational Standards for Sports Development and the first professional degree endorsement scheme for the sector. He is a co-editor and author of *Strategic Sport Development* (also published by Routledge), the first textbook to focus the strategic management of sport development services. He has contributed to both previous editions of this book.

Peter Taylor is Professor of Sport Economics at Sheffield Hallam University; co-director of the Sport Industry Research Centre; founding editor of *Managing Leisure: An International Journal*; and a board member of 7 Hills Leisure Trust, which owns a number of sports facilities in Sheffield. Peter's publications include *Economics of Sport and Recreation*, with Chris Gratton, and *Torkildsen's Sport and Leisure Management*. His research has included analyses of the economics of sport and leisure; the financing of excellence in sport; the economic impact of the Edinburgh Festivals; volunteers in sport; graduate employment in the sport and recreation industry; demanding physical activity programmes for young offenders; and performance indicators and national benchmarks for local authority sports centres and swimming pools. Peter has been technical consultant to Sport England's National Benchmarking Service (NBS) for Sports and Leisure Centres since its beginning in 2000. The NBS has provided performance measurement data to over 400 individual sports centres from over 160 organisations, on one or more occasion. Peter has led many workshops with practitioners on performance measurement and management, both generally and in relation to specific NBS reports.

Mick Totten is Senior lecturer in Community Leisure and Recreation at Leeds Metropolitan University. He started his working life in community theatre, sport, youth and social work. He completed his Masters Degree in Leisure and Human Potential. He then worked for five years in further education teaching sport and drama courses before joining Leeds Metropolitan University in 1995. Since then he has taught mainly on the Sport Development course in community sport, community development, sociology and politics. He has been involved in consultancy work in community leisure and sport and has published in the areas of community sport, alternative sport, fan power and sport activism. Mick has spent many years coordinating amongst a network of alternative sports teams.

FOREWORD

DERRICK ANDERSON

The world in which we live is changing rapidly. Since the 2008 edition of this book we have experienced a worldwide banking crisis, a general election and the formation of a coalition government for the first time in the history of the UK. As a consequence, there has been a seismic shift in the UK political terrain which has brought with it major consequences for sports in general and for the sport development profession in particular. Whilst all this has been going on, in 2012 the UK witnessed the most successful Olympic Games to date. This was achieved amidst great expectation that the sport development profession will deliver the legacy promised by the nation in 2005, when the right to stage the games was won under what one can only describe as dramatic circumstances. Now is of course the time to deliver upon that commitment.

The third edition of this book sustains the previous arguments about the linkage between sport development, wider social and economic policy and the need to adjust development processes to reflect the reality of the world we now live in. However, with all that has happened in recent times it also draws commentary about how the profession has proactively responded to this fast changing agenda. In so doing the commentary has gathered the perspectives of several leading academic and professional institutions from across the country, thus providing a rounded and well-informed view of sport development in a new era.

This book is an essential read for those actively interested in, or just intrigued by, sport and its development. However, it is also an invaluable baseline reference for those policy makers and practitioners in other areas where sport may have a contribution to make in improving the quality of life and in developing best practice.

Derrick Anderson, CBE, is Chief Executive of Lambeth Council and started in the post on 1 March 2006. He was previously Chief Executive of the City of Wolverhampton Council for ten years.

xviii

Derrick, who was born in London, has twenty-five years' senior management experience in local government and more than thirty years in the public sector.

Derrick is a member of the University of Birmingham Council, Committee Member of The Princes' Trust London Council, a member of the Skills Funding Agency Advisory Board, a Board Member on the Department for Communities and Local Government's Voluntary and Community Sector Partnership Board, a member of the Arts Council England Organisation Review: External Reference Group and Vice President of UK Youth.

Derrick's other past engagements include: Non-Executive Director on the Home Office Board; Board Member of Sport England – London; Non-Executive Director of the 2012 Olympic Bid Company; and Chair of Sports England West Midlands 2004–2006.

ACKNOWLEDGEMENTS

I would like to thank colleagues in the Carnegie Faculty of Leeds Metropolitan University for their ongoing contribution to this work and to the development of sport development nationally. Included in this note of recognition are colleagues based at Brunel University, the University of Sheffield, Sheffield Hallam University and Southampton Solent University for their support in the writing of this book.

It has been an interesting journey over three editions to get to this point. In that time colleagues, students, practitioners, policy makers and even governments have come and gone. However, I would like to mark the contribution of colleagues who were involved in the early days of this book whose efforts helped to shape this book into an essential sports studies text. These are the initial editors, Dr Mark Nesti, Dr David Jackson (first edition), Peter Bramham (first and second edition) and contributor Dr Hazel Hartley (first edition).

I would also like to thank Rachel Thornton for her administrative efforts over three editions of *Sport(s) Development: Policy, Process and Practice*.

The editor and publishers are grateful to the copyright owners for permission to reproduce material acknowledged in the captions to figures and at the foot of tables.

Whilst every effort has been made to ensure the accuracy and acknowledgement of the information contained within figures and in tables, Sport England and Mintel cannot be held responsible for any errors, omissions and/or the completeness of such information. Sport England and Mintel accept no liability for the consequences of error and/or omissions or for any loss or damage suffered as a result. Where the information contains third party intellectual property, Leeds Metropolitan University and/or the publishers have sought all necessary consent, permission and/or clearance in such third party intellectual property.

Every effort has been made to contact copyright holders for their permission to reprint material in this book. The publishers would be grateful to hear from any copyright holder who is not acknowledged here and will undertake to rectify any errors or omissions in future editions.

Professor Kevin Hylton

CHAPTER 1

INTRODUCTION

KEVIN HYLTON

This third edition of *Sport Development: Policy, Process and Practice* has a distinctive philosophy and structure. This book covers a wide range of material and, although a systematic reading of the content is advisable, it could be just as fruitful to enjoy each chapter in its own right. Each chapter now includes learning activity questions for teachers and students at the end of each chapter. The learning activities are further supplemented by a separate web companion that includes PowerPoint slides for teachers, and web resources to assist the gathering of further exemplary materials. Case studies are also set at the end of most chapters as opportunities to showcase some of the main ideas where they facilitate further discussion in vocational and academic terms.

This book again advocates that sport development should be thought of more broadly as comprehensive inclusive processes that engage an extensive array of policy makers, agencies, organisations, practitioners and participants. It is still argued that sport development must be 'used to describe processes, policies and practices that form an integral feature of the work involved in providing sporting opportunities' (Hylton and Bramham, 2008: 1). For sport developers to be effective they must continue to pay attention to new policy frameworks that demand strategic partnerships and interprofessional cooperation, all within a performance-driven culture. The chapters in this third edition exemplify how sport development has been drawn into a raft of debates that include Olympic Games development, lottery funding, mass participation, social inclusion, talent development and elite performance as well as into justifying its distinctive contribution to wider educational, social and economic policies and practices.

The structure of this book reflects upon the expanding remit for sport development. Original chapters have been updated and in addition there are newly commissioned chapters on volunteering, sport for development, disability, and the Olympic and Paralympic Games. Most of the chapters in this edition have been written by staff working in the Carnegie Faculty of Leeds Metropolitan University, though they have been joined by colleagues in Sheffield, Brunel and Southampton Solent. Consequently the book as a whole offers a distinctive account of sport development, which has been enriched by researching and teaching undergraduate and postgraduate courses in Leeds. It also reflects the breadth of experience, commitment and professional engagement in the field of sport development.

Sport development has changed a lot since the first edition in 2001, yet experience would suggest that most core issues remain. Equality is still a key concern for sport providers and participants; partnerships and joint working are prominent in policy discourses; sport must continue to justify itself even more forcefully to funding agents; policies on elite and community sport are regular discussion issues at all levels; and, as always, events continue to remind us that sport and politics are inextricably linked. Because of these and related issues this third edition provides interesting and compelling perspectives and debates on sport development policy, process and practice.

It is quite common to hear the argument that sport development is the traditional responsibility of sport development officers (SDOs), but this view is not the approach taken here. It is reiterated that sport development is more accurately a term used to describe policies, processes and practices that form an integral feature of work involved in providing sporting opportunities and positive sporting experiences. Such a process-orientated perspective leads to the challenging conclusion that physical education (PE) staff, teachers, coaches, facility managers, community outreach workers, youth workers, health specialists, policy makers and many others, including SDOs, are all engaged in sport development work. However, other key stakeholders include volunteers, paid professionals, coaches and related support staff, academics and related practitioners. These sectional interests have created a 'crowded policy space' (Houlihan, 2000), a perplexingly dynamic environment, within which this work takes place. There are good times when sport policy and funding have been robustly promoted and bad times when they have been collectively defended against the retrenchment typified by the global austerity measures in 2012, an Olympic year. However, considerable tensions exist between different actors and institutions. Such conflict and dissonance arise from competing discourses, policies and practices. Indeed, substantial academic research has highlighted a history of political tensions between advocates of elite sport development and wider mass participation (see Collins, 2008; Houlihan and White, 2002). These tensions are clearly present in the history of sport in the UK as well as in other nation states, such as Australia and Canada (see Green and Houlihan, 2005).

Dissonance further emerges in developments to establish a coherent organisation to articulate the views of those involved in sport development in the UK. The paradox occurs that the new Chartered Institute for the Management of Sport and Physical Activity (CIMSPA) has the job of defining policy and standards for its members

2

in sport development whereas there are many more professionals in other sectors who could legitimately lay claim to sport development activity. A task such as this is not without risk, for, although time can be spent fine-tuning the semantics of what is and who is involved in sport development, to define it is always to exclude something. However, there are practical implications for this necessary exercise because to professionalise a sector a professional association must know who its members are, especially if it intends to advocate for them and to meet the needs of the members and the sector.

During the past three decades there have been periods of substantial growth in full-time paid employment within sport development. Those working in the public sector have diverse roles to play in developing sporting opportunities. Within local authority settings, staff have experienced important changes, with a strong emphasis on accountability, planning and cost-effectiveness. Different elements of everyday operation, dictated by the culture of performance indicators, are a continual squeeze on both capital and revenue budgets. Effective sport development workers have had to develop skills and competences to work in partnership with a range of others, both inside and outside sport. This has led to growing concern with training, education and qualifications. National governing bodies of sport, local authorities, public non-government agencies and higher education institutions all offer a plethora of courses and training opportunities, ranging from one-day seminars to postgraduate qualifications.

Those engaging in sport development must be in the business of devising better and more effective ways of promoting interest, participation or performance in sport. This apparently neat account of sport development nevertheless obscures the arguably more important issues of who has the responsibility for this activity, and questions around where, how, why and ultimately what should be done. In simple terms, there are some who believe that sport development should be used to meet broader social, political, economic and cultural aims: the contemporary cross-cutting, joint working agendas which stress sport's externalities. Meanwhile, others contend that 'sport for sport's sake' is the only legitimate philosophy, therein emphasising the intrinsic benefits of sport participation, and naturally another group would argue that sport is equally capable of defending itself on both fronts. There are clearly different intrinsic and extrinsic rationales for sport policies and provision. Sport development is an arena where passions can run high and, as one should expect with enthusiasts, parochial and self-interested views are frequently found. Again, contrary to the general view, politics at both macro (central government) and more micro (local authorities, governing bodies) levels have played a major part in policy formulation in sport development.

Although not everyone would agree, the drive towards professional status in sport development is set to raise standards of operation and improve service delivery. For an industry that has been increasingly accused of being piecemeal and ad hoc as well as uncoordinated and fragmented [reflected in a massive range of entities involved in the structure of sport in the UK, and CIMSPA's merger of the Institute of Leisure and Amenities Management (ILAM), the National Association for Sports Development (NASD), the Institute for Sport, Parks and Leisure (ISPAL) and the Institute of Sport and Recreation Management (ISRM)], sport has an opportunity to secure a coordinated shift in its governance and overall funding. At this time it is apparent that sport is high on the agenda for government for a whole host of reasons that range from the frantic emphasis on healthy lifestyles and obesity issues to the increasing focus on world-class sports events such as the 2012 Olympics in London.

SPORT DEVELOPMENT: 'SPORT DEVELOPMENT'; 'SPORT DEVELOPMENT'?

Sport development is an ambiguous and contested term, especially as the exact meaning and use of 'sport development' cannot be presumed, as different policy and professional contexts have incrementally acquired salience and meanings that cannot be ignored. Similarly, Houlihan (2011: 1) argues that this process of defining a policy area 'starts as an apparently straightforward process [. . . and] soon becomes mired in ambiguity'.

Sport development incorporates the practices and related processes of a broad and diverse group of sport workers (including self-identified 'sport development' officers/workers). The use – and, some would argue, misuse – of the term 'sport(s) development' can be appreciated by a closer examination of what each word is describing. Sport has at times been narrowly defined in terms of competitive, rule-governed games, involving some degree of physical activity and exercise. Development conjures up ideas of maturation, of education: the gradual consolidation of knowledge; the teaching of competences and practical skills (see also Girginov, 2008: 6). Consequently, to develop someone or something suggests a transition through progressive stages where new and improved outcomes are both possible and desirable. But put two strange words together, each drawing on different vocabularies, such as sport and development, and what do you get? A new hierarchy or range of meanings emerges. This has parallels in the debates around sport for development and peace (SDP), which uses recognised approaches to sport development but with a historical and policy context that challenge some common notions of sport development (see Levermore and Beacom, 2009). What if there is an unequal intonation on each half, as in 'sport development' or conversely 'sport development'? Does a change in emphasis signify different fields of policy and practice, where professional actors have different scripts or roles to interpret? What if we are dealing with a hybrid word, a compound noun, made up of equal halves, as in 'sport development'? Philosophers, linguists and others have warned against the mistaken belief that we can define a word so precisely and accurately

4

as to distil the essence of the meaning of the word itself. The definition acts as a sieve to include or catch all essential characteristics, whilst excluding all non-essential elements or meanings. In a dynamic process the meaning of a particular word becomes a 'form of life'; it depends on how people use the word in their everyday lives. So the influence of academic discourses, the naming of key concepts, policy prescriptions recommending intrinsic and extrinsic benefits of sport, changing organisation structures and leadership styles, new coaching regimes and so on must not be taken lightly.

An important and contentious area facing sport development has been the need to work at both grassroots and elite levels. Disagreements over where the focus should be and disputes about the importance of each have bedevilled the policy area. Sports councils and others have attempted to provide a means of identifying the different roles and responsibilities for those involved in sport development from the lowest to the highest levels of achievement. The first, and some would say clearest, sport development continuum locates development on a hierarchical basis from foundation through participation to performance and excellence (see Figure 1.1). The sport development continuum model has been used by diverse organisations to provide a logical coherence to their plans, policies and strategies for sport. As with all models it offers an idea of how things 'ought to be' in a perfect world rather than how things necessarily operate in each situation. (See also Figures 1.2 and 1.3.)

This simple and powerful model of sport development has been further modified and refined by sports agencies to articulate new policy agendas and initiatives.

These issues and themes are explored throughout the chapters that follow. *Chapter 2* provides a general introduction to the policy process and then focuses

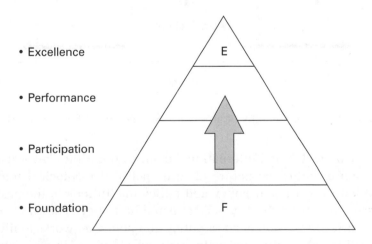

- Excellence

- Performance

- Participation

- Foundation

Figure 1.1 The traditional sport development continuum.

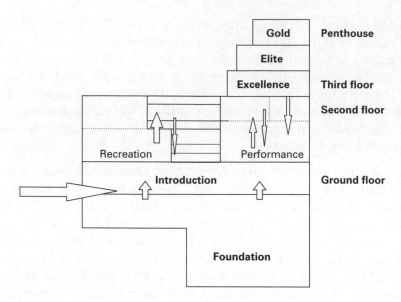

Figure 1.2 The house of sport. Source: Cooke (1996).

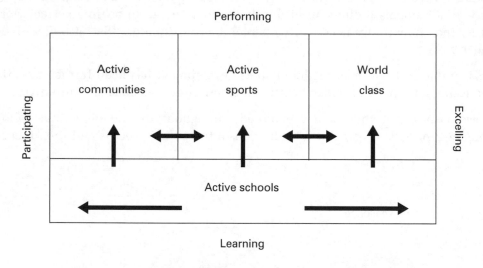

Figure 1.3 Sport England: the active framework. Source: Sport England (2000: 3).

on sport policy in the UK and international context. It outlines key stages in public policy and then explains the nature of three political ideological traditions that have shaped both government policy and policy institutions in the post-war years and progresses to outline the key stages in public policy. The final section concludes with a brief discussion of sport policy and policy networks to illustrate how political traditions place different values on sport's intrinsic and extrinsic costs and benefits.

6

Chapter 3 focuses on Sport for All and in particular equality in sport. This chapter outlines how the leadership and management of equalities can strengthen or challenge the cause of Sport for All. It conducts a critical consideration of debates and issues that have been invigorated by the new equalities landscape brought into sharp relief by recent equalities legislation and frameworks. The relevance and implications of state equalities legislation are explored after key terms are defined and critiqued. The sociological imagination is centred in this chapter as readers are encouraged to become 'active sociologists' in how they view sport and its development. Thompson's (2006) PCS model (personal, cultural, structural) is used to identify and challenge conceptual and practical issues of discrimination, inclusion and exclusion. The sociological interpretations of sport development that have proved popular in previous editions are further employed and developed.

Chapter 4 illustrates the wider current and historical context that makes up the work of community sport development. It engages in debates that examine community sport development as community development or as sport development. It does this by systematically introducing the philosophical and political values that underpin provision, unpacking them in an accessible but critical way. A number of original ideas from the second edition are reintroduced in this chapter, such as the community sport development (CSD) continuum, partnership domains, structural dimensions of provision matrix and models of CSD policy. Such models facilitate the analysis of key aspects of the social, political and practical settings where community sport initiatives are undertaken.

Chapter 5, as with previous editions, provides an overview of contemporary thinking in terms of the underpinning concepts of partnership working. The existing discussion on the benefits and problems of partnership working, which has been extensively utilised by academics and practitioners across the UK, is updated and lent a more critical edge through the use of experienced practitioner views. In particular the inbuilt assumption within many funding regimes, that partnership working is the only means of achieving success in sport development settings, is subject to close scrutiny.

Chapter 6 considers how the last decade has seen significant changes in the infrastructures and policies around young people's PE and sporting opportunities. This chapter considers some of the key policy initiatives as they have evolved, and evaluates their impact on practice, including the national curriculum in PE, now in its fourth iteration, school sport partnerships and specialist sports colleges, all key aspects of the national strategy for PE and Sport for Young People. The chapter explores key questions and issues for those working with young people. The recent change of government, and subsequent financial and political shifts are also explored.

Chapter 7 contests the notion that sport, as currently conceived, can be a major contributor to improved public health. Updated case studies illustrate both the changing nature of sport development work and the tensions between competitive sport-specific development and wider mass physical activity participation initiatives. Mass physical activity initiatives are often strategically planned and delivered at local level through C-SPANs (community sport and physical activity networks), which serve as a nexus for the work of sport development and health/ physical activity professionals. The planned abolition of Primary Care Trusts and its potential impact upon the work of C-SPANs is addressed in a discussion of whose responsibility mass physical activity should be in more austere times.

Chapter 8 assesses the approach that sport development has adopted previously when dealing with challenges that have arisen around resourcing issues and whether delivery mechanisms need to be adapted in the future. It investigates whether the development of sport is best served by focusing on current public sector and third sector (which covers social enterprises and voluntary organisations) delivery of programmes designed to make sport more accessible through the concept of Sport for All, or whether there may be the potential to employ a more commercial approach to sport development to ensure access.

Chapter 9 begins by defining volunteering in sport development, applying theoretical and practical lenses. The significance of volunteering to sports clubs is examined drawing on the Central Council of Physical Recreation survey of sports clubs (Taylor *et al.*, 2009) and secondary analysis of the Scottish Opinion Survey. The implications for sport development of sports clubs as a government policy tool are debated with a focus on the tensions between independence and conditional support. The place of sports clubs and active citizenship are reviewed in light of the new coalition government's 'Big Society': a third sector alternative. Hence this chapter considers what this means in terms of the tensions of sports clubs run by their members as a valuable resource, but one which will need to adapt to changes in society, and its relationship to the private and public sector.

Chapter 10 examines the boundaries of sport development and sport coaching and illustrates the symbiosis between them. This is followed by a critical appraisal of a number of potential issues that challenge the skills of the coach: the emergence of domain-specific initiatives such as multi-skills clubs, long term athlete development, talent development and instructor-led provision. The chapter also highlights the UK strategy for ensuring that high-performance sport is adequately served by coaches from the UK. The chapter focuses on the government's renewed emphasis on competitive (particularly team) sport, and the omnipresent quest for an Olympic legacy. The vehicle of participant development models and coach development models is used to question if there is an over-arching strategy for the development of sport coaching in the light of the demands made by participants in each sector.

Chapter 11 considers issues concerning disability and sport development and explores the extent to which contemporary society has been able to 'keep in step' with sport for disabled people. Consideration is given to the notion of disability, which is a contested concept, and two key models used to explain disability are outlined. Three illustrative examples of how organisations are attempting to work towards policy developments in disability sport are later explored. This chapter then considers the key challenges and barriers that disabled people experience when participating in sport.

Chapter 12 is founded on the observation that professionals working in sport development will encounter research in one form or another: all will have to read and interpret its findings, some will be charged with commissioning research projects and others will be responsible for conducting research themselves. The starting point involves a consideration of the necessity of research and an appraisal of the right sort of research to meet professional needs. Practitioners and students in sport studies are encouraged to familiarise themselves with techniques to gather data and related information about what they do and how they do it to ensure the efficacy of practice.

Chapter 13 examines the contested relationship between sport development and the Olympics by engaging with the Games' capacity to shape the domain of sport development and vice versa. The chapter first interrogates the Olympics as a developmental project promoting universalised visions of the ideal human being and conceptualises sport development. It then analyses the constitutive ideological, economic and organisational elements of the relationship between the Games and sport development. Finally, this relationship is located within six core sport development processes and there is discussion of the need to leverage the social, economic and legitimising powers of the Olympics, as well as to affect the developmental design of the Games.

Chapter 14 introduces Sport for Development, which involves organisations and individuals using sport (and other forms of physical recreation) to facilitate social improvement in communities and nations targeted for development. Over the last decade, and especially since the UN passed resolution 58/5 of the General Assembly entitled 'Sport as a means to promote education, health, development and peace' in November 2003 and then declared 2005 to be its International Year of Sport and Physical Education, there has been a global intensification of Sport for Development activities. It is worth noting that, as a social phenomenon, the notion of Sport for Development is not new, though as an academic one it is only just emerging. Sport has historically been viewed by governments, other social institutions and actors as an important contributor to the maintaining of social order and promoting a wide range of development agendas. These are explored in this new chapter. Furthermore, Sport for Development is considered a contested concept with a wide range of interpretations.

- Examine Figure 1.1, 'The traditional sport development continuum', and discuss how useful it is as a way to conceptualise development pathways in sport.
- Examine Figures 1.1 and 1.2 and articulate which model you find the more realistic.
- Write your own simple definition of sport development and see if you can capture its essence in relation to sport policy and practice.

REFERENCES

Collins, M. (2008) 'Public policies on sports development', in Girginov, V. (ed.), *Management of Sports Development*, London: Butterworth-Heinemann.

Cooke, G. (1996) 'A strategic approach to performance and excellence', in *Supercoach, National Coaching Foundation*, 8 (1): 10.

Girginov, V. (2008) 'Management of sports development as a field and profession', in Girginov, V. (ed.), *Management of Sports Development*, London: Butterworth-Heinemann.

Green, M. and Houlihan, B. (2005) *Elite Sport Development, Policy Learning and Political Priorities*, London: Routledge.

Houlihan, B. (2000) 'Sporting excellence, shools and sports development: the politics of crowded policy spaces', *European Physical Education Review*, 6 (2): 171–193.

Houlihan, B. (2011) 'Defining sports development', Sportdevelopment.info, www. sportdevelopment.info/index.php?option=com_content&view=article&id=265: definition&catid=54:introsv

Houlihan, B. and White, A. (2002) *The Politics of Sport Development: Development of Sport or through Sport?*, London: Routledge.

Hylton, K. and Bramham, P. (eds.) (2008) *Sport Development: Policy, Press and Practice*, London: Routledge.

Levermore, R. and Beacom, A. (2009) *Sport and International Development*, London: Routledge.

Sport England (2000) *Active Communities: An Introduction*, London: Sport England.

Taylor, P., Barrett, D. and Nichols, G. (2009) *Survey of Sports Clubs 2009*, London: CCPR.

Thompson, N. (2006) *Antidiscriminatory Social Work*, Basingstoke: Palgrave Macmillan.

CHAPTER 2

SPORT POLICY

CHRIS WOLSEY AND JEFFREY ABRAMS

This chapter provides a general introduction to understanding the policy process and then focuses on sport policy in the UK and international contexts. It outlines key stages in public policy and then explains the nature of three political ideological traditions that have shaped both government policy and policy institutions in the post-war years and progresses to outline the key stages in public policy. The final section concludes with a brief discussion of sport policy and policy networks to illustrate how political traditions place different values on sport's intrinsic and extrinsic costs and benefits.

PUBLIC GOODS, PUBLIC POLICY AND SPORT

Sport may be valued intrinsically for its own sake because it develops personal skills, competition, individual self-esteem and fun for participants. Sport can also produce wider externalities, by making a valuable contribution to other government policy with respect to national prestige, to foreign policy and international diplomacy, to tourism and city regeneration, to local community development and to health, as well as helping to redress social divisions around class, race, gender and disability. In other words, sports exhibit the qualities of a 'public good', which has positive benefits beyond the pure economic value of the activity itself. In theory, at least, subsidies plug the gap between the economic and societal value by increasing the level of investment beyond that provided purely through commercial criteria alone. Hence, sport as a 'public good' becomes a legitimate activity within the public policy domain. However, this is rarely a straightforward process and reflects the diversity of political ideologies across nation states and, indeed, regions. By way of example, Green and Collins (2008: 227) observe:

Lavelle (2005, p. 753) notes, 'Neo-liberalism has dominated public-policy making [in Australia] since at least the 1980s'. By contrast, Finland's political system is firmly rooted in the social democratic tradition (Collins, 2008). Elite sport development has been a key policy priority for Australian federal governments for at least the past 25 to 30 years (Green & Houlihan, 2005), whereas the emphasis in Finland has been clearly on sport development priorities at the mass participation level (Vuori, Lankenau, & Pratt, 2004).

Furthermore, Lee and Funk (2011) investigate the power of sports participation to have a positive impact on the assimilation of immigrants from Asia into mainstream Australian culture. Paradoxically, they find that there is an inversely proportional relationship between the desire to maintain existing cultural links and the propensity of immigrants to use sports as a method of social integration into Australian life. In the UK, the galvanising effect of the London 2012 Olympic Games provides further evidence of macro influences upon sport policy. Phillpots and colleagues (2011: 270) describe how the sport policy agenda has shifted in order to better accommodate the potential opportunities afforded by the Games.

> Sport England and the National Governing Bodies of sport now had to concentrate on policy outcomes that focused upon London 2012 and a shared commitment to maximizing British sporting success.

This demonstrates the dynamic and sometimes fickle nature of public policy and how power dynamics can influence policy and strategic direction within sporting organisations. Powerful stakeholders, such as central government, have the power to influence both policy and practice in order to justify investment decisions (inputs) and differentially prioritise the intrinsic and extrinsic benefits (outputs) of sport.

Sport policy occupies a contested space on the margins of mainstream government policy discourse relating to areas such as education, health and social services. Ideology is, therefore, crucial to understanding sport policy inputs, processes and subsequent outputs at macro (societal), meso (institutional) and micro (individual and small subgroup) levels. These are not mutually exclusive, but operate in a dynamic system that attempts to rationalise frequently competing priorities and multiple stakeholders. Despite its interrelationships with other areas, the importance of sport is increasingly recognised by a number of different bodies and institutions. The European Union, for example, through the Lisbon Treaty (December 2007) has, for the first time, provided a mandate to develop a European approach to sport based around three broad areas: namely the societal, the economic and the organisational dimensions of sport. However, this presents issues of ongoing public transparency and accountability for related sport organisations.

Coalter (2007) argues that the evidence base required to justify sports expenditures is not strong and is constrained by the inherent methodological difficulties of trying to separate sport from other areas of investment input and public policy outputs.[1] Moreover, public policy and sport policy should also be considered within the wider political and managerial domain. In this context, sport organisations can be considered policy-attaining systems, as often the political and ideological agendas set the parameters within which sport organisations operate. For example, Tan and Bairner (2011) review the pervasive influence of the Chinese government on the professionalisation of basketball within that country, whilst Chung and Won (2011) lament the inability of South Korean sport to break free from authoritarian government control, despite a general liberalisation and democratisation of society as a whole. It is often within this macro context that sport organisations set their long-term mission, ongoing goals and related measures of performance. However, it is at the meso and micro levels of analysis that there is a more pragmatic link between policy, management, practice and subsequent performance.

UNDERSTANDING THE POLICY PROCESS

One starting point for most policy analysts is a descriptive model of discrete stages in the overall policy process. Jones and colleagues (1994) traced three main stages in the policy journey: initiation, formulation and implementation. Others further subdivide this threefold division to provide a more precise account.[2] One detailed model that has dominated policy literature has been provided by Hogwood and Gunn:

Stages in the policy process:

- deciding to decide (issue search or agenda-setting);
- deciding how to decide (or issue filtration);
- issue definition;
- forecasting;
- setting objectives and priorities;
- options analysis;
- policy implementation, monitoring and control;
- evaluation and review;
- policy maintenance, succession or termination.

(Hogwood and Gunn, 1984: 24)

Yet even this more sophisticated model of stages in the policy process has problems. The authors openly acknowledge some themselves:

Viewing the policy process in terms of stages may seem to suggest that any policy episode is more or less self-contained and comprises a neat cycle of initial, inter-mediate and culminating events. In practice, of course policy is often a seamless web involving a bewildering mesh of interactions and ramifications.

(Hogwood and Gunn, 1984: 24)

The above model therefore provides an explanatory heuristic device or ideal type for rational decision making: policy makers define policy problems, plan policy strategies, implement best policies and evaluate policy outcomes. This can be illustrated through the ongoing work of Grant Thornton, who has been commissioned by the UK's Department for Culture, Media and Sport to provide a meta-analysis of the legacy and impact of the London 2012 Olympic Games. This represents a five-stage research process, the first of which entails defining the relative outcomes of the games in the context of a range of different stakeholders and policy initiatives. This covers all four aspects of Hogwood and Gunn's model and characterises the baseline policy issues and intrinsic/extrinsic benefits (outputs) as follows:

- Sport: harnessing the UK's passion for sport to increase school-based and grass roots participation in competitive sport and to encourage the whole population to be more physically active;
- Economy: exploiting to the full the opportunities for economic growth offered by hosting the Games, particularly with reference to inward investment and tourism;
- Community Engagement: promoting community engagement and participation in voluntary work across all groups in society through the Games;
- East London regeneration: ensuring that the Olympic Park can be developed after the Games as one of the principal drivers of regeneration in East London, with a particular focus on the high-tech and creative industries.

(Thornton, 2012: 1)

The relative and ongoing success of the Games can then be monitored, evaluated and reviewed in the light of outcomes measured against policy intentions. Policy makers often appeal to this systemic model in order to justify choices among alternatives and to legitimise outcomes. Policy development can then be presented as a rational process, and articulated simply as a neutral and technical discourse. All policy 'tick boxes' are systematically covered and audited. There are clear stages in decision making: objective professional advice is taken, plans are agreed and policy outcomes are evaluated. Policy is defensively grounded in good practice and 'common sense'.

This model, however, does not fully account for the wider organisational and political realities experienced within the theatre of policy formulation and implementation. Often external pressure generates the need to take action with little consideration of rational approaches to decision making. In practice, policy can be irrational, pragmatic and incremental, driven forward or subverted by powerful vested interests. Policies can slip the grasp of policy makers and create unintended consequences, stubbornly 'working behind the backs' of people and their good intentions. For example, when cities compete to host international sporting mega-events, conventional rationality, realistic time scales, forecasting, accurate budgets and data analyses may disappear. Decisions to locate summer or winter Olympic Games have been clearly shaped by global politics of international sports federations, internal tensions within transnational agencies, media sponsorship, scheduling and advertising, as well as by legitimate lobbying, and by serendipity (see Horne, 2006); in the post-mortem after the Olympic Committee's decision to award the 2012 Games to London in 2005 there were media stories about one delegate voting for London by mistake![3]

Definitions of public policy are rooted in the political ideology that underpins the actions that follow. For example, Houlihan and Green (2008: 680) state that in the UK:

> the genealogy of modernization can be traced most strongly through Thatcherism and in the promotion of managerialism in the 1990s with the concern of the Labour government being to retain the neo-liberal economic gains of Thatcherism and build upon the Conservatives' managerialist legacy.

Their conclusion suggests that the modernisation process that followed led to the adoption of business-orientated approaches and a 'command and control' regime within both Sport England and UK Sport designed to focus specifically on the political imperative of overall Olympic games success.

Maurice Roche's (1994) detailed case study of Sheffield City Council's decision to host the World Student Games in the 1990s has documented that policy decisions were taken with limited economic forecasting, crucial financial information suppressed from public debate and democratic processes bypassed. Short- and long-term costs and benefits, as well as the legacy or heritage of sporting venues, have been the focus of much debate and research. The 2002 Commonwealth Games in Manchester told a similar story, with shortfalls in funding alongside fierce political and economic controversy over the decision to pass the City of Manchester Stadium over to Manchester City Football Club; likewise, the controversy surrounding the competition between West Ham United and Tottenham Hotspur football clubs to occupy the Olympic stadium after the 2012 London Games and the alleged willingness of local councils to boost one of the bids through further public subsidy. Indeed, many community groups in Barcelona, Athens and London have run anti-Olympic bid protests on account of each bid's social, cultural, economic and environmental impact on disadvantaged neighbourhoods, but they have tended to gain little media coverage or political influence. Sometimes, however, bidding for mega sporting events is recognised as an expensive distraction from more pressing social, economic and political concerns; the Italian government's decision not to back Rome's bid for the 2020 Olympics, whilst the country struggles to cope with the impending realities of worldwide economic difficulties, is a case in point.

Indeed, it is generally accepted that major sporting events, such as the Olympics and the World Student Games, may not generate a financial benefit. For example Tien and colleagues (2011) found that the economic impact of the Olympic Games on the host countries is significant only in terms of certain short-term parameters (e.g. gross domestic product performance and unemployment). Chung and Won (2011) found that hosting the Olympic Games significantly improved the image of China but did not affect the image of its products in a positive way. Furthermore, Porter and Fletcher (2008: 470) suggest that the economic models used to justify mega events, such as the Olympics, 'greatly overstate the true impact'. There is often a justification that goes beyond the financial benefit and includes social, cultural and legacy benefits and justifications. This often means that there needs to be a political imperative, in terms of national status, or other less tangible benefits in order to justify decisions that do not always appear to be wholly rational measured purely against commercial rather than 'public good' criteria.

Such marked deviations from the rational model of decision making have led writers such as Simon (1960) and Lindblom (1959) to describe policy makers as exhibiting 'bounded rationality', informed by partial knowledge, hamstrung with limited room for manoeuvre by powerful structural forces and offering pragmatic rather than optimal solutions. Given the number of stakeholders, time pressures and resultant policy complexity that are often involved, it is not surprising that decision makers tend to 'satisfice', rather than pursue the best possible solutions. This confounds the ability of policy makers to solve long-term policy problems. Instead it is much more typical for politicians to move on quickly to other problems as they appear on the political and media agenda. They seldom wait to judge and evaluate earlier decisions. Success and failure, in policy terms, may have little to do with rational decision making to solve long-term problems but rather more to do with short-term gain to appease interested parties, to secure re-election and to maintain control over the policy process. What remains is a series of compromises limiting the optimal outcome of the policy decision-making process. This has to become frustrating for the professionals who operate in such areas, as they are often held accountable for longer-term targets, but are buffeted by changing political whims and circumstances, which necessitates constantly re-evaluating the means and sometimes the ends, in other words the central mission.

If we look at recent examples of policy statements in the United Kingdom we can see clear links to the rational planning framework outlined above. For example, in its National Planning Policy Framework Consultation document, Sport England (2011) outlined four key policy drivers:

Key Policy 1 Positively plan for sport
Ensure that local policies should plan for a good quality network of locally accessible sports and recreational facilities in order to maximize the opportunities for communities and neighbourhoods to play and take part in sport and physical activity.

Key Policy 2 Flexible and viable approach
Take a positive and flexible approach to the future development of sport and recreation facilities, so as to ensure long term sustainability and viability of facilities.

Key Policy 3 Local policies and planning decisions must be based on robust assessments of needs and a clear evidence base
Ensure robust assessments of the current and future needs of all communities are undertaken and used for devising local planning policies for sport and recreational facilities, and for determining planning applications.

Key Policy 4 Maintain, enhance and protect
Maintain, enhance and protect sports and recreational facilities that are needed and/or valued, both at national and local level, by individual sports and local communities, in particular playing fields.

These policy statements are clear indicators of intent and no doubt will drive the policy agenda to a certain extent. This approach is rational, systematic and clear but does not take into account wider political and contextual issues. For example, what is the degree of freedom that Sport England has to drive through such policy frameworks? To what extent is Sport England responsible to the government in relation to funding and what impact may this have on strategy and policy decision making?

In this context, according to Jennie Price, the Chief Executive of Sport England:

What's very clear as we go forward is that the national governing bodies of sport, or NGBs as they tend to be called, really are going to be at the heart of delivery for us. So it is very much going with what they know about their sports, the priorities they're setting in their sports and us supporting that, but supporting it in terms of what it's right to use government funding for – so it is about things like growing the sport, it's about talent identification, it's about giving a really good service to their members as well, so we want them to be very player and participant-centric and I think there are going to be some really interesting dialogues between Sport England and those NGBs as they put together their plans for the next four years.

(www.youtube.com/watch?v=p4R7CaOcrkY)

The above position needs to be set against research suggesting that such policy approaches, although ambitious, are not without considerable challenges. For example Green and Houlihan (2005: 189) state:

> it is hard to avoid the conclusion that elite sport development and achievement on the one hand and mass participation and club development on the other are deeply incompatible functions within the policy frameworks current in Australia, Canada and the UK.

In addition, Grix and Phillpots (2011: 1) argue:

> Further, we put forward the notion of 'asymmetrical network governance' to highlight the modified forms of governance which still rest on asymmetrical power relations and largely unchanged patterns of resource dependency operating in the sports policy sector at both elite and mass participation levels.

When the real power lies with those able to control resources and funding, it is not surprising that NGBs have to respond, in a very flexible way, to the needs of their paymasters. Being seen to be responsive, however, is not always the same as being accountable for delivery against the expressed requirements of such important stakeholders. Under such circumstances, there may be a lack of willingness to engage in the final component of Hogwood and Gunn's (1984) model advocating the need to evaluate policy outcomes; providers are afraid of what this may uncover! For example, in the UK, the 'Active People Survey' provides a comprehensive assessment of how participation levels have been affected in the period up to the London 2012 Olympics. Perhaps surprisingly, given the degree of public investment and claims made in relation to the benefits of sport, it does not always make happy reading for professionals and politicians in this area. In the run-up to the Olympics, far from providing a participation springboard, there was actually a reduction in the active participation levels of young adults. This is particularly apparent amongst girls, leading to a re-evaluation of the 'participation' criteria within the survey. Benjamin Disraeli is famously reported to have said, 'there are lies, damn lies and statistics'. We have already commented upon the inherent difficulties of researching impacts in this area. However, if you do not like the answers, you can always avoid asking the questions or change them to provide a better fit in relation to previously expressed targets. In this instance, the 'Active People Survey'

18

benchmark for participation was revised down from three times per week to once per week for the targeted 14–25 age group. Similarly, in New Zealand, following a disappointing medal-based drive at the 2006 Melbourne Commonwealth Games, the body overseeing such preparations decided not to release any targets for the Beijing 2008 Olympic Games (Piggin *et al.*, 2009).

It is clear that the practice of policy development and implementation is complex, driven as much by political ideology and opportunism as it is by rational decision making and the achievement of short-term goals leading to a central mission. In each case, described above, there will be multiple stakeholders and constituencies, competing objectives, political imperatives, power dynamics and resource dependencies. Quinn (1978) would describe this approach to policy implementation as logical incrementalism; in other words, taking a pragmatic approach to strategic policy implementation based on a step-by-step approach rather than a rational and traditionally strategic approach.

INSIDERS AND OUTSIDERS

A distinction can be drawn between 'insiders' and 'outsiders' in the policy arena. 'Insiders' usually carry discrete professional, commercial or departmental interests and are committed advocates of policy, and 'outsiders' are those experts who lay claim to offer a more detached, analytical and holistic approach. The 'outsiders', often social science academics interested in politics, society and organisational behaviour, gather contextual knowledge of policies and processes at work, whereas 'insiders' have careers in consultancy, public relations and marketing, in partnerships, projects and research networks. The sport policy universe becomes an increasingly crowded place, with politicians, political advisers, civil servants, local government officers, non-departmental public bodies (NDPBs), think tanks, consultancy firms, journalists and academics all seeking to make an impact (see Figure 2.1).

Ibsen and Jorgensen (2002: 294) provide another framework to analyse sport policy from structural and societal perspectives (see Figure 2.2). They categorise the various sectors public, voluntary, commercial and informal. These are then set against the market, the state and wider society. The key focus is on the intersection between these key variables. In theory such a model could be used to evaluate sport policy in any national context. A mix of the two models would provide a useful tool in assessing macro (societal), meso (institutional) and micro (individual and small subgroup) perspectives on the development of sport policy accounting for key stakeholders at different levels of process, analysis, advocacy and subsequent policy operationalisation.

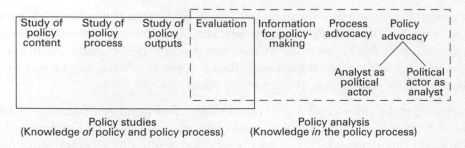

Figure 2.1 Types of study of public policy making. Source: Hogwood and Gunn (1984), cited in Ham and Hill (1993: 8).

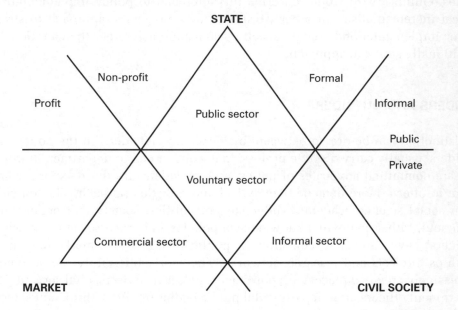

Figure 2.2 The organisation of society between state, market and civil society. Source: Ibsen and Jorgensen (2002: 294).

IDEOLOGIES

If one wants to understand how public policy works, it is helpful to start at the policy studies end of the continuum by examining broad ideological assumptions that not only direct policy but also underpin the very institutions that shape and deliver policy. Consequently, before spelling out the three ideologies or major traditions of conservatism, liberalism and social reformism, it is worth clarifying how ideologies work in general.

20

Political ideologies are best described as reflections of the world and reflections on the world. They prescribe how the world ought to be and offer a guide or mandate for policies and action. One function of political ideology is to provide a particular perspective on the world and to highlight key issues, debates and problems that need to be tackled. Ideologies not only provide an understanding of how the world works but also map out mission statements about how the world needs to change and to be managed.

In the 'restricted' view, ideology refers to different political ideas debated and contested between and within political leaders, parties and party activists. It is the narrow politics of Westminster, the Reichstag or Capitol Hill, of national and local news broadcasts, of local government debates and plans. In the more 'relaxed' or broader view, ideologies permeate and mediate economic, social and cultural life. Coherent frameworks of attitudes and interpretation shape practices in families, at work, in mass media, in education and in local communities. Commonsense ideas or discourses about what is 'natural', about men, about women, social class, sexuality, 'race', age, ethnicity and so on are all powerfully embedded in institutions, in relationships and in language. One useful concept here is interpellation, as ideologies literally speak to concerns of people by addressing them as individual subjects and articulating their unique problems and their personal resolution. Take the case of racism against minority ethnic groups and asylum seekers, when tight immigration rules and repatriation offer instant 'solutions' to problems of unemployment, poor housing, poor education and so on. Racist political parties can target white working-class communities as those most neglected by existing political parties and policies. In various distorted ways racist messages tackle silences in mainstream policy discourses, as demands for equity and natural justice, with respect to policy outcomes, are sometimes dismissed and labelled as exhibiting excessive levels of 'political correctness'.

In conventional accounts of policy analysis and rational decision making, political ideologies provide values, ideals and mandates for action, whereas policy sciences provide technical knowledge and advice to administer policies effectively and efficiently, that is on target, on time and on budget. Politics provides the chosen value-laden ends, with policy and administration securing appropriate means to achieve political ends. This separation between political values and facts of policy administration is one cornerstone in Weber's view of social science. Politics and political debates are inevitably grounded in different values and beliefs about how the world ought to be; differences of opinion are inevitable and irreconcilable. Politics is a battlefield, fought by warring tribes with different values. By way of sharp contrast, Weber argues that social science must be value-free. It must produce knowledge about the world as it is. Social research must be objective, neutral and unbiased and not subjective, partisan or committed to some form of politics. As individual citizens we can voice and act upon personal beliefs and idiosyncratic prejudices, but as social scientists and researchers we must exercise value freedom and remain neutral.

This boundary between facts and values, between science and ideology has been fiercely contested throughout the history of social sciences. More recent developments in postmodern analysis argue that many claims of scientific method to secure objective detached knowledge are bogus. Like any other stock of knowledge, science does have its own coherent ontology (categorisations), epistemology (knowledge base) and distinctive logical techniques for generating and testing data. Scientific method celebrates technique by collecting reliable data by means of experimentation, causal analysis and accurate measurement. However, it can no longer claim to provide a single universal objective truth about the world, as there are other discourses to listen to: non-Western, non-scientific and so on. Science does have its own coherent discourse but this is just one approach among many. Other voices can provide distinctive and different narratives about the world, how it works and who and what is important. One needs only to think of the criticisms of mainstream science and technology from the radical politics of Marxism and feminism, black critical studies and 'green' politics of environmentalism. Within these counter-traditions there are many internal debates. Processes of globalisation, the information age (Castells, 1996) and scientific knowledge itself are all directly challenged by religion, most powerfully by fundamentalists who reassert Christian, Islamic or Buddhist traditions and teachings.

Postmodern times offer a variety of such discourses. In the past, in modernity, it was felt that science alone could provide universal laws to explain natural and social worlds. Politicians and policy makers would be knowledgeable and could legislate to impose order. It was as if the natural and social worlds were gardens that could be carefully cultivated and improved by knowledgeable policy makers. With postmodern thinking, the ideal of an orderly garden gives way to diversity and disorder. Neat horticulture is no longer an option as individually constructed meanings and perceptions dominate (relativism). We all live in what Giddens (2002) calls a 'runaway world', where all nation states are permeated by transnational processes of migration, global communications, environmental pollution and global warming. Moreover, life is a babble of competing voices of different sorts of gardeners, different experts, each providing conflicting advice. It is hard to choose or know whom to trust. In postmodern times, risk and uncertainty seem inherent features of decision making.[4] Public policies lag behind new science and technologies, as people now must face what Giddens (1991: 132) terms manufactured risk in ordinary everyday life. Public policies may even seem to make things worse with nuclear power, global warming and genome research.

POLITICAL IDEOLOGIES

Conservatism

One strategy of dealing with uncertainty and accelerated change is to turn to the past and rely upon tradition. Conservatism has deep historical roots and emerged as a coherent political ideology of the aristocracy to resist the 1789 political revolution in France that demanded democracy, political representation and citizenship. Conservative ideas sought to legitimise the status quo and protect it from democratic demands for equality. For conservatism, existing inequalities were natural, pre-ordained and inevitable, even God-given; people should accept their position in the world and perform their defined roles within tried and tested institutions. The status quo was a moral order, ordained by religion and monarchy, and ingrained in custom and practice.

The three core values of the French revolution, liberty, equality and fraternity, still divide modern political ideologies. For conservative thinkers, fraternity (like-minded grouping) is not possible under the conditions of equality and liberty; they simply produce chaos and anarchy. Conservatism as a political tradition is clearly anti-individualistic, as individuals are not citizens with political rights but are subjects who must be loyal and obedient to the state or monarchy. In conservative ideology, the state is seen as a powerful organism that has the will to strongly destroy external and internal enemies that threaten its lifeblood. All people therefore intuitively belong to the nation state; they are born into it, they constitute its tribe, with a common language, communal institutions, shared heritage, history and landscape. For an updated exposition of conservative ideas, Scruton (2001) maps out the key values of tradition, allegiance and authority. Linked with its fear of democracy, such values carry shades of totalitarianism. However, these tendencies are tempered by the conservative affinity with pragmatism and intuition that permit conservative political ideologies to absorb incremental changes rather than to remain blindly committed to defending the past. Modern conservatism aims to be a living museum rather than a mausoleum. However, if we are truly living in postmodern times, it could be argued that conservative thinking will, at best, always be fighting against the stronger forces of uncertainty and change.

Liberalism

If the origins of conservatism lay with the French aristocracy straining to protect privilege in turbulent revolutionary times, liberalism was the political creed of the emerging commercial middle classes, the bourgeoisie, made up of industrialists, financiers and intellectuals. Liberalism throughout the Age of Enlightenment demanded individual freedom in thought and deed from control by tradition and privilege, embedded in the institutions of church and monarchy. Liberalism as a political ideology stresses both individualism and democracy: individuals should be free from governance, free to exercise rights to property, free speech and political suffrage. A contract is struck between the individual and the state: the individual is free to maximise his/her self-interest but s/he must abide by legislation to guarantee order. Individual citizen rights can be written down as constitutional guarantees protected by the courts against state encroachment and any misuse of authority and power. Some liberal writers fear democratic utilitarian institutions pursuing 'the greatest happiness of the greatest number', as the tyranny of the majority may generate legislation that impinges on individual self-interest.

The main function of the liberal or minimalist state is to provide law and order, a secure context within which individuals are free to maximise their own self-interests, in an open market environment. It is a nightwatchman state. Unlike conservative ideology, liberalism demands a clear divide between private and public spheres, as the state has no justification for penetrating the boundary between its own public domain and civil society. Institutions of family, education, work and mass media are private concerns; they must be free from state intervention. Market forces, equations of supply and demand through delicate price mechanisms, are the lifeblood of liberalism and of consumer choice. Adam Smith's 'invisible hand of the market' is seen as the most efficient and, more important, most just means to maximise individual self-interest and to distribute scarce resources. Governmental bureaucracy and state regulation serve only to distort market forces, to weaken work discipline and to discourage profit maximisation and capital accumulation. Whereas Keynes would advocate state intervention, to correct for perceived market failures, both Hayek and Friedman were strong advocates of monetarism, which demands a minimal state whose major function is to control the money supply and check destabilising inflation.

In the world of politics, democracy enables individuals to choose their own rulers through representation, and even more direct forms of democracy may be possible at a local or community level. In a similar democratic vein, individuals are free to organise themselves into pressure groups to protect their collective interests and to influence political parties in both shaping and implementing policies. Such pluralism denies the concentration of power into a strong state and encourages governments to seek public consent to legitimise and secure their policies among citizens.

Social reformism

If the political ideology of conservatism developed in the pre-industrial eighteenth century, and liberalism blossomed in the industrial capitalism of the nineteenth

century, social reformism is very much the product of the twentieth century. It grew out of a range of working-class movements that sought government intervention to mitigate the intended and unintended consequences of market forces. Confronted with capitalist economics that spawned gross inequalities of income, capital and property, social reformists stressed the need for equality, for the state to redistribute resources in order to protect wage labourers and the poor, particularly those groups who were unable to sell their labour power through force of circumstance: the sick, the mentally ill, children, the unemployed, the elderly.

In the early part of the twentieth century, radical sections of the working class looked to Marxist ideologies and revolutionary struggle to destroy class inequalities as well as political dominance of the state by the ruling class. In sharp contrast, social reformists were disenchanted with socialism and Marxism, feeling that gradual change or reform was both possible and desirable. Rather than overthrowing capitalism by civil war and establishing a communist state, social reformism argued, equality in capitalism could be achieved by political intervention in the form of a welfare state. Governments had a major role to play: they should own and plan sectors of the economy, guarantee minimum wages and income support for all by redistributing wealth from the rich to the poor through direct taxation. The welfare state should abolish poverty and deprivation by providing health care, social services, education and adequate housing. It would be funded out of taxation, social insurance paid by the working population and by a growing economy. It would also witness the growth of a powerful public sector bureaucracy, staffed by professionals and semi-professionals who would set standards of care and define appropriate levels of social need and provision.

For social reformism, individual freedom could not be realised under the conditions and constraints of inequality, so substantial central and local government intervention would have to be targeted at disadvantaged groups. For example, children could not be expected to develop their full potential if they were trapped in poverty, living in inadequate, overcrowded housing, learning at under-achieving schools and playing outside in damaged communities. Consumer choice was no real option for the working classes unless the state intervened to manage capitalism and its social consequences. In social reformist ideology, government had to deal with market failure, with negative consequences or externalities in markets, and had to control monopolistic and oligopolistic practices that generated surplus super-profits for business and commerce. Many of the key ideas of social reformism have been articulated by Titmuss (1958). He argued that one of the key values that should inform welfare is altruism, which is closely linked to fraternity. Citizens should seek to generate collective welfare for the greater good rather than pursuing their own self-interest, often at the expense of others. To illustrate his position he contrasts the gift relationship of blood donorship in the UK with the market relationship of blood sales in the United States. In the UK healthy donors provide

25

good blood for nothing whereas in the United States many disadvantaged groups sell their own blood, possibly contaminated by drugs and problems of ill health, to supplement their meagre income.

After considering the three traditional ideologies that have dominated UK political institutions in the post-war period, namely conservatism, liberalism and social reformism, we are now better placed to make sense of two ideological hybrids which have shaped governance during the past thirty years. Stated boldly, 1980s New Right ideas mix conservatism and liberalism whereas commentators see New Labour, from the late 1990s and on into the new millennium, as a mix of liberalism and social reformism.

The New Right

New Right ideas were developed in the UK from the 1970s on through a variety of think tanks and pressure groups, including notably the Institute of Economic Affairs, the Adam Smith Institute and many others. They were dissatisfied with the institutional legacy of the post-war welfare state, underpinned by social reformism, arguing that state intervention was inefficient and ineffective and led to dependence on the state rather than encouraging responsibility and self-reliance. No part of the institutional structure of welfarism was exempt from criticism; politicians promised to increase public expenditure and services to secure re-election; bureaucrats maximised their own budgets and departmental power, whilst professionals denied choice to the individual. These criticisms, in academic circles, led to the elucidation of public choice theory, which demanded restructuring of the state and the introduction of market forces. Voters must be made to pay more directly for public services received, which must be shaped by the tested disciplines of the private sector: profitability, entrepreneurship, income generation, customer care, quality audits and performance-related pay.

Although New Right ideas were a clear restatement of liberalism in the face of an established social reformist welfare state, it was more than that. The startling contradiction or paradox in the heart of New Right thinking was its fusion of market liberalism with elements of its ideological arch-enemy, conservatism. The New Right was a mixture of the two: a strong nation state and a strong deregulated market. In the person of Margaret Thatcher, the Conservative Party in the 1980s was driven forward to restructure the welfare state and change its relationship with local government. Throughout two decades, central government introduced a series of fiscal and legislative measures to control local government expenditure as well as open up local professionals to New Right thinking, enshrined in such initiatives as the Community Charge, standardised spending assessments, rate capping, local management of schools and compulsory competitive tendering (see I. Henry, 2001).

Non-departmental public bodies and agencies were created to implement policy and the Audit Commission could assess the performance of central and local government departments against market ideals measured in performance indicators of cost, efficiency and customer care.

New Labour

It has been suggested that UK elections are lost by governments rather than won by the opposition. Indeed, it was the failure of Conservative supporters to turn out on election day, tactical voting in marginal seats and general disenchantment with Tory sleaze that resulted in a landslide majority for the Labour Party in 1997. Having modernised the party by distancing itself from its trade union and socialist roots, the Blair government accepted continuing New Right economic policies as parameters to guide the first two years of new government. There were substantial continuities in policies such as best value, public–private business partnerships (PPBPs) and private finance initiatives (PFIs) as well as privatisation. Indeed, some writers felt that New Labour was nothing but Blair's presidential style and his pragmatism to choose 'whatever works' in policies. Others saw New Labour as a progressive discourse in postmodern politics because traditional ideologies had lost popular support and their traditional class alignment. Governments could no longer deal with growing individual aspirations, globalisation, new technologies and transnational migration (Kelly, 2003). If New Right ideology drew on liberalism and conservatism, New Labour was another hybrid, finding its direction from mixing neo-liberalism and social reformism. Guided by think tanks such as Demos and the Institute for Public Policy Research (IPPR) as well as by the prolific writings of Anthony Giddens (see Giddens, 1998, 2000, 2002), Labour presented itself as offering a 'Third Way' to deal with these 'new times' of globalisation. New Labour argued that neither the 'first way' of liberal capitalism nor the 'second way' of state socialism was viable. A free unregulated market and the planned collective socialist state were anachronisms. Indeed, Blair targeted the 'forces of conservatism' (of both left and right) in his millennium speech as major opponents to progressive politics. Since re-election in 2001 and 2005 the language of New Labour has stressed monotonously and remorselessly modernisation and reform of public services. Marxist academics (see Hall, 2003) and Old Labour see current reforms and finance strategies in health, education and workfare as covert privatisation and marketisation. There is a 'hollowing out' of governance. Nation states must open themselves up to competition from global market forces, to new technologies and to flexible patterns of work whilst trying to fill a growing democratic deficit of declining voter interest by devolving power to the local state and community organisations.

New coalition (2010–)

In the UK, the necessity to create a Conservative-led coalition government, following the 2010 General Election, represents a continuation of such trends, merely under a different banner. The New Right and neo-liberal tendencies of the Conservatives, under David Cameron, are balanced by the social reformist inclinations of Nick Clegg's Liberal Democrats. The danger is that uneasy compromise, initially fashioned in order to attain power, leads to stalemate and the antithesis of the 'strong and stable' leadership promised by both parties at the outset of the relationship. This is likely to have real consequences for the many sports organisations that are directly or indirectly reliant upon government patronage and subsidy for their continued development. There are early signs that this will leave some areas of sports provision exposed. As Curtis and Tran (2010) explain:

> The government has cancelled or frozen £10.5bn worth of projects announced in the dying days of the Labour government . . .
> The government said it was forced into difficult cuts by the 'irresponsible planning' of its predecessors, but Labour accused the coalition of being ideologically driven to reduce the size of government and its involvement in stimulating the economy.

This has led to the cancellation of flagship projects such as free swimming for children and the elderly and a £6 million reduction in funding for County Sports Partnerships, which gives strategic sports leadership on a local/community-based level. Clearly, in times of financial stringency, expressions of 'public good' are counteracted by the opportunity costs involved. Whereas the continuing world financial and economic context may not bode well for future levels of investments (inputs) in such areas, it is clear that future sport policy must continue to anticipate, or at least be in a position to quickly adapt to, the opportunities that are presented. In the UK, for example, the government have announced a five-year strategy to build upon the legacy of the Olympic Games, with up to £1 billion of public funding available in 2013–2017 (Li, 2012).

POLITICAL TRADITIONS, NON-DEPARTMENTAL PUBLIC BODIES (NDPBs) AND SPORT POLICY

The major political ideologies of conservatism, liberalism and social reformism clearly offer different prescriptions for public policy; they define the preferred relationship between nation state, civil society and markets. Several writers have spelt out what sports policies would look like if driven directly by political ideology (see Bramham and Henry, 1985, 1991; Henry, 2001; Whannel, 1983; Wilson,

1988).[5] There is also a wealth of cross-national literature on how socialist ideas have shaped sports policies in communist nation states (see Riordan, 1978; Tan and Bairner, 2011).

Political traditions direct public policy as well as mapping out contours of key institutions that define and empower stakeholders in the policy process. In the post-war UK, policy has been shaped by social reformism in the domain of culture, leisure and sport. Conservative and Labour governments gradually set up NDPBs such as the Arts Council, the Sports Council and the Countryside Commission to plan and develop facilities and opportunities. In 1994 the Department of National Heritage empowered agencies to distribute National Lottery funds. Despite changes in governments, this 'arm's length' approach to policy has been both politically and ideologically expedient in providing institutional continuity. Governments provide subsidy and appoint NDPB personnel but are not directly accountable in Parliament for policy decisions and outcomes. This is in no way to suggest that sport policy is an ideologically battle-free zone. Sport policy cannot avoid moral panics in the media about national elite sports performance, alcohol and drug abuse, football hooliganism, racism and sexism, childhood obesity and so on. The sport policy universe is inevitably drawn into each government's political ideology and policy agenda. For example, a major focus of the current UK coalition government is to reduce public spending. As a consequence there has been a significant reduction in the number of NDPBs during the tenure of the incumbent government, including organisations such as the Film Council and Audit Commission, despite arguments concerning the level of actual savings, combined with ongoing issues of coordination, transparency and accountability.

Detailed histories of the development of UK sport policy are already well established. Accounts have been provided by Sports Council personnel (Coughlan, 1990; Pickup, 1996) and by academics writing policy textbooks (Haywood *et al.*, 1995; L. P. Henry, 1993; Houlihan, 1991; Houlihan and White, 2002), as well as a range of detailed studies evaluating various policy initiatives, for example for the unemployed (Glyptis, 1989), for community sport (Haywood, 1994; Lentell, 1994; McDonald, 1995) and for women (Hargreaves, 1994; Talbot, 1979).

The establishment of the Sports Council in 1972 was a response to successful lobbying by voluntary governing bodies organising sport (NGBs), orchestrated by the Central Council for Physical Recreation (CCPR), but was also a clear expression of conservative beliefs in the intrinsic value of sport. Sport and recreation were also seen as means to deal with disaffected youths. National culture had to be preserved within the next generation as the 1960s witnessed growing moral panic about the corrosive impact of American media and consumer culture. The 'expressive' revolution of sex, drugs and rock-'n'-roll diluted the traditional authority of the family, school and community. Equally, black youths were scapegoated as the cause of inner-city problems rather than victims, as news media amplified 'mugging' into a symptom of a violent, racially divided society (Hall *et al.*, 1978). Youth work and sport were therefore seen as crucial ingredients to divert youths, particularly those who were unemployed and living in inner-city working-class neighbourhoods, away from crime and delinquency and into sport and active lifestyles.

Youth sport, whether organised by physical education (PE) teachers, youth development workers, coaches and sports animateurs or the police, was and still is defined as a crucial site to re-establish moral values and healthy lifestyles and so rebuild fragmenting communities and avoid social exclusion. For example, Sport Leaders UK is a charitable organisation delivering sports awards to community leaders across the UK. Its Chief Executive, Linda Plowright, sees her role as providing

> a vision for sport and physical recreation to enrich whole communities through the involvement and achievement of individuals. At Sports Leaders UK I believe I have the unique opportunity to bring together the threads of education, delivery and commercial involvement that have informed my career and now define the new social agenda for sport.
>
> (http://sportmk.wordpress.com/links/committee/
> linda-plowright-sports-leaders-uk/)

These themes have been popularised by Robert Putnam's (2000) idea of 'social capital': US bowling leagues had acted as social glue, binding together healthy community networks. High-achieving schools, excellent health and care services, high rates of employment and sporting opportunities all served to build local relations of trust; good neighbourliness helped to suppress high rates of family breakdown, of crime, delinquency and social disorder. Conservatism defined the performance of national teams in international sport as an important indicator of successful sport policy. Conservatism valued the voluntary sector in sports organisations (see Roberts, 2004), particularly traditional male 'English' team games, such as cricket, rugby and football. Failures in World and Olympic Games were read as significant historical indicators of decline in UK culture and competitiveness. Consequently, tension between national elite performance and local community participation, albeit often focused in targeted populations, has been the hallmark of post-war UK sport policy. Shifting priorities in sports policies have been conflated in the Sports Council's sporting pyramid, a continuum from foundation, through participation and performance, to elite excellence. A broad base of mass participation and talent identification of young athletes was perceived as essential for excellence in elite performance. Sport development should increase sport participation, whilst simultaneously providing sporting and coaching pathways to elite performance.

If the Conservative government was attracted to sport mainly because of its intrinsic benefits, during the 1970s a social reformist Labour government was keen to

30

promote sporting opportunities as an integrated part of a comprehensive welfare state. Such an inclusive approach was heralded in the 'Sport for All?' campaign. One important physical expression of this policy appeared in the planning, management and development of sports facilities. Local authorities, encouraged by Regional Sports Councils, invested heavily in both large-scale and community-based facilities. As with other aspects of state welfare provision, there developed a growing professionalism within the public sector around the marketing and delivery of leisure services. At the same time, there was growing dissatisfaction with social reformism, typified by New Right ideas around public choice. Sport policy was now felt to be dominated by local government. The nature of sports provision was seen to be inefficient, ineffective and unnecessary.

New Right ideology argued that government subsidy in sport was inappropriate. Individuals should be free to meet their sporting wants through the commercial or voluntary sectors rather than having their sporting needs defined by distant NDPBs or central or local government. Olympic elites and national governing bodies should look to business sponsorship for support rather than rely on welfare subsidies from a 'nanny state'. However, faced by inner-city riots, the New Right Thatcherite government was not completely deaf to the extrinsic benefits of sports provision for troublesome young people. During the 1980s, unemployed and black minorities were drawn into a variety of community-based sports leadership schemes, financed by urban aid programmes. This was the emergence of what came to be seen as the new profession of sport development through the 'Action Sport' programme (see Hylton and Totten, Chapter 4 below).

Another paradox of New Right policies at this time was the growth of diverse government NDPBs to bypass the power of local authorities and to weaken the collective professional base and trade union rights of public sector producers. The Thatcher hegemonic New Right project vaunted a minimalist state yet simultaneously presided over the expansion of a wide range of government agencies and NDPBs. Traditional government bureaucracies and civil servants were viewed by the New Right as self-serving inefficient bureaucrats and the Sports Council itself was subjected to numerous reviews which raised severe doubts about its future policy direction and possible continuation.

During the mid-1990s the Major government pragmatically breathed new life into the Sports Council through National Lottery funding and with its commitment to the UK Sports Institute to secure excellence. The government reasserted the intrinsic benefits of team sports and introduced a raft of policy initiatives in *Sport: Raising the Game* (Department of National Heritage, 1995) to strengthen sporting opportunities within the PE curriculum and within extra-curricular activities. Emergence of the Youth Sports Trust provided new pathways for youth sport through TOP Sport programmes in combination with the National Coaching Foundation's 'Champion Coaching' scheme. Some commentators argued that media panic about the loss of school playing fields and sports opportunities has overstated the crisis in youth sport (Roberts, 1996).

From the 1990s New Labour pursued similar sports objectives to those of New Right administrations,[6] but it is a complicated narrative. During the first years of this century government departments such as the Department for Culture, Media and Sport and the Social Exclusion Unit in the Cabinet Office have put increasing pressure on Sport England, NGBs and local authorities to demonstrate how sporting outcomes contribute to its broader policy agenda related to social exclusion (Collins and Kay, 2003). With its PE, School Sport and Club Links (PESSCL) initiatives, the Labour government also funded education and sporting partnerships between specialist sports colleges and NGBs, both to increase mass participation and to identify talent and gifted young athletes. Deep-seated contradictions between intrinsic and extrinsic rationales for sport abound and are glossed over in sport policy discourse. For example, the presentation bid, strongly supported by New Labour, to host the 2012 Olympics in London illustrated sport's complex position in relation to broader government agendas of social, economic and cultural policies. A multi-racial group of inner-city school children were taken along to help Lord Coe justify the British bid, as if they were to be the main beneficiaries of the Olympic sporting facilities. It is this capacity of sport to offer governments help in achieving wider policy goals which explains continuity in support for sports policies, albeit from governments working from different ideological scripts.

The pattern of sport policy development over the last fifty years in the UK and many parts of Europe has shifted from one with an emphasis on direct government intervention to one of more competition for service delivery, a focus on increased efficiency, and need to do more with less without reducing service quality. In the UK this has been driven by wider economic problems leading to stringent spending reviews in the public sector followed by cuts to public spending and almost a zero-based budgeting approach to service delivery in order to reduce the public deficit. The coalition government's flagship 'Big Society' idea is an attempt to give power back to local communities and shift power away from politicians. The policy is contested, as some consider this to be a way of reducing the public sector purse without reducing the service provision by having local volunteers fill the void left by the spending cuts while others think differently (see Hylton and Totten, Chapter 4 below).

In a globalised world in which transnational economic, environmental, security and cultural forces reign supreme, even transcending nation state boundaries, sports policies continue to offer national governments the tempting illusion that ideologically based interventions can make a difference. Whether in bidding for mega events, changing mass participation rates in sport or using activities to regulate disorderly youths, sport policy remains politically salient, and has even grown more so, in the twenty-first century.

32

In January 2012, the UK government announced a £1 billion investment in a five-year Youth and Community Sport Strategy, with around £450 million being earmarked by Sport England for NGBs. Using the issues highlighted during the chapter, research and answer the following questions:

1 How does this fit into the overall strategy for Sport England?
2 What opportunities does this present for NGBs?
3 In what ways can County Sport Partnerships influence the policy/resource inputs and outputs in this area?
4 Choose one of the following: (a) an NGB, (b) a local government sports department, (c) a local sports club, (d) a sporting-based charitable organisation, (e) a commercial-based sports organisation or (f) a university/college sports department. Investigate ways in which it may be able to benefit from the additional investment highlighted above, in relation to one or more of the Sport England talent and participation outcomes, shown below:
   a   a growth in participation in the 14–25 age range;
   b   a growth in participation across the adult population;
   c   high-quality talent development that creates a strong England talent pathway to link with UK Sport World Class and English elite programmes;
   d   a growth in participation by people who have disabilities, including those with talent.
5 Who are the stakeholders that would be involved in moving things forward for your named sporting organisation?
6 What barriers can be foreseen?
7 How might such barriers be mitigated?

NOTES

1.   See also Thornton (2012: 3) for a review of the methodological difficulties of evaluating the legacy of the London 2012 Olympic Games.

2.   See, for example, a fivefold division by Forman (1991): policy germination, policy formulation, decision making, policy execution and policy fulfilment.

3.   This alleged mistake occurred in one of the early elimination rounds, which would have meant that Paris or Madrid was awarded the 2012 Olympic Games.

4.   See Beck (1992) for a full discussion of how the development of scientific knowledge and technological intervention seems to mean that no one knows and, worse still, no one is in control.

5.   See Yule (1990) for a discussion on how a political counter-ideology such as feminism would shape sport and leisure policy.

6.   Towards the end of its first term of office New Labour produced a prescriptive national sports strategy (see Department for Culture, Media and Sport, 2001; Department for Culture, Media and Sport and Cabinet Office Strategy Unit, 2002).

REFERENCES

Beck, U. (1992) *The Risk Society: Towards a New Modernity*, London: Sage.

Bramham, P. and Henry, I. (1985) 'Political ideology and leisure policy', *Leisure Studies*, 4 (1): 1–19.

Bramham, P. and Henry, I. (1991) 'Explanations of the organisation of sport in British society', *International Review for the Sociology of Sport*, 26: 139–150.

Castells, M. (1996) *The Rise of the Network Society*, Oxford: Blackwell.

Chung, J. and Won, D. (2011) 'The authoritarian policy in South Korean sport: a critical perspective', *European Journal of Social Sciences*, 20 (1): 146–157.

Coalter, F. (2007) *A Wider Social Role for Sport: Who's Keeping the Score*, Abingdon (Oxon): Routledge.

Collins, S. (2008) *An Analysis of Public Policy toward Adult Lifelong Participation in Sport in Australia, New Zealand and Finland*, unpublished doctoral dissertation, Loughborough University, UK.

Collins, M. and Kay, T. (2003) *Sport and Social Exclusion*, London: Routledge.

Coughlan, J. (1990) *Sport and British Politics since 1960*, London: Falmer Press.

Curtis, P. and Tran, M. (2010) 'Government shelves Labour projects worth £10.5bn', www.guardian.co.uk/business/2010/jun/17/government-scraps-labour-projects

Department for Culture, Media and Sport (2001) *The Government's Plan for Sport: A Sporting Future for All*, London: DCMS.

Department for Culture, Media and Sport and Cabinet Office Strategy Unit (2002) *Game Plan: A Strategy for Delivering Government's Sport and Physical Activity Objectives*, London: HMSO.

Department of National Heritage (1995) *Sport: Raising the Game*, London: HMSO.

Forman, F. (1991) *Mastering British Politics*, London: Macmillan.

Giddens, A. (1991) *Modernity and Self-Identity*, Cambridge: Polity Press.

Giddens, A. (1998) *The Third Way: The Renewal of Democracy*, Cambridge: Polity Press.

Giddens, A. (2000) *The Third Way and Its Critics*, Cambridge: Polity Press.

Giddens, A. (2001) *The Global Third Way Debate*, Cambridge: Polity Press.

Giddens, A. (2002) *Runaway World: How Globalisation Is Reshaping Our Lives*, London: Profile Books.

Glyptis, S. (1989) *Leisure and Unemployment*, Milton Keynes: Open University Press.

Green, M. and Collins, S. (2008) 'Policy, politics and path dependency: sport development in Australia and Finland', *Sport Management Review*, 11: 225–251.

Green, M. and Houlihan, B. (2005) *Elite Sport Development: Policy Learning and Political Priorities*, London: Routledge.

Grix, J. and Phillpots, L. (2011) 'Revisiting the "governance narrative": "asymmetrical network governance" and the deviant case of the sport policy sector', *Public Policy and Administration*, 26 (1): 3–19.

Hall, S. (2003) 'New Labour has picked up where Thatcherism has left off', *The Guardian*, 6 August.

Hall, S., Critcher, C., Jefferson, T., Clarke, J. and Roberts, B. (1978) *Policing the Crisis*, London: Macmillan.

Ham, C. and Hill, M. (1993) *The Policy Process in the Modern Capitalist State*, London: Harvester Wheatsheaf.

Hargreaves, J. (1994) *Sporting Females: Critical Issues in the History and Sociology of Women's Sports*, London: Routledge.

Haywood, L. (ed.) (1994) *Community Leisure and Recreation: Theory and Practice*, Oxford: Butterworth-Heinemann.

Haywood, L., Kew, F., Spink, J., Capenerhurst, J. and Henry, I. (1995) *Understanding Leisure*, Cheltenham: Stanley Thornes.

Henry, I. (2001) *The Politics of Leisure Policy*, Basingstoke: Palgrave.

Henry, L. P. (1993) *The Politics of Leisure Policy*, Basingstoke: Macmillan.

Hogwood, B. and Gunn, L. (1984) *Policy Analysis for the Real World*, Oxford: Oxford University Press.

Horne, J. (2006) *Sport in Consumer Culture*, Basingstoke: Palgrave Macmillan.

Houlihan, B. (1991) *Government and the Politics of Sport*, London: Routledge.

Houlihan, B. and Green, M. (2008) *Comparative Elite Sport Development: Systems, Structures and Public Policy*, Oxford: Elsevier/Butterworth-Heinemann.

Houlihan, B. and White, A. (2002) *The Politics of Sport Development*, London: Routledge.

Ibsen, B. and Jorgensen, P. (2002) 'Denmark: the cultural and voluntary development of sport for all', in DaCosta, L. and Miragaya, A. (eds.), *Worldwide Experiences and Trends in Sport for All*, Oxford: Meyer and Meyer.

Jones, B., Gray, A., Kavanagh, D., Moran, M., Norton, P. and Seldon, A. (1994) *Politics UK*, 2nd edn, London: Prentice Hall.

Kelly, P. (2003) 'Ideas and agendas in contemporary politics', in Dunleavy, P., Gamble, A., Hefferman, R. and Peele, G. (eds.), *Developments in British Politics*, Basingstoke: Palgrave Macmillan.

Lavelle, A. (2005) 'Social democrats and neo-liberalism: a case study of the Australian Labor Party', *Political Studies*, 53 (4): 753–771.

Lee, Y.-S. and Funk, D. C. (2011) 'Recreational sport participation and migrants' acculturation', *Managing Leisure*, 16: 1–16.

Lentell, B. (1994) 'Sports development: goodbye to community recreation?', in Brackenridge, C. (ed.), *Body Matters: Leisure Images and Lifestyles*, Brighton: LSA Publications.

Li, N. (2012) 'Sporting chance', *S&PA Professional*, 1 (April): 22–26.

Lindblom, C. (1959) 'The science of muddling through', *Public Administration Review*, 19: 79–88.

McDonald, I. (1995) 'Sport for All: RIP? A political critique of the relationship between national sport policy and local authority sports development in London', in Fleming, S., Talbot, M. and Tomlinson, A. (eds.), *Policy and Politics in Sport, Physical Education and Leisure*, Eastbourne: Leisure Studies Association.

Phillpots, L., Grix, J. and Quarmby, T. (2011) 'Centralized grassroots sport policy and "new governance": a case study of County Sports Partnerships in the UK – unpacking the paradox', *International Review for the Sociology of Sport*, 46 (3): 265–281.

Pickup, D. (1996) *Not Another Messiah: An Account of the Sports Council, 1988–1993*, Edinburgh: Pentland Press.

Piggin, J., Jackson, S.J. and Lewis, M. (2009) 'Telling the truth in public policy: an analysis of New Zealand sport policy discourse', *Sociology of Sport Journal*, 26: 462–482.

Porter, P. K. and Fletcher, D. (2008) 'The economic impact of the Olympic Games: ex ante predictions and ex post reality', *Journal of Sport Management*, 22 (4): 470–486.

Putnam, R. (2000) *Bowling Alone: The Collapse and Revival of American Community*, New York: Simon & Schuster.

Quinn, J. B. (1978) 'Strategic change: "logical incrementalism"', *Sloan Management Review*, 20 (1): 7–19.

Riordan, J. (ed.) (1978) *Sport under Communism*, London: Hurst.

Roberts, K. (1996) 'Young people, schools, sport and government policies', *Sport, Education and Society*, 1 (1): 47–58.

Roberts, K. (2004) *The Leisure Industries*, London: Palgrave Macmillan.

Roche, M. (1994) 'Mega-events and urban policy', *Annals of Tourism Research*, 21 (1): 1–19.

Scruton, R. (2001) *The Meaning of Conservatism*, Basingstoke: Macmillan.

Simon, H. (1960) *Administrative Behaviour*, London: Macmillan.

Sport England (2011) *National Planning Policy Framework: Consultation Response*, www.sportengland.org/facilities_planning/developing_policies_for_sport.aspx

Talbot, M. (1979) *Women and Leisure*, London: SSRC/SC.

Tan, T.-C. and Bairner, A. (2011) 'Managing globalization: the case of elite basketball policy in the People's Republic of China', *Journal of Sport Management*, 25: 408–422.

Thornton, G. (2012) *Report 3: Baseline and Counterfactual: Meta-Evaluation of the Impacts and Legacy of the London 2012 Olympic Games and Paralympic Games*, London: DCMS.

Tien, C., Lo, H.-C. and Lin, H.W. (2011) 'The economic benefits of mega events: a myth or a reality? A longitudinal study on the Olympic Games', *Journal of Sport Management*, 25 (1): 11–23.

Titmuss, R. (1958) *Essays on the Welfare State*, London: Allen & Unwin.

Vuori, L., Lankenau, B. and Pratt, M. (2004). 'Physical activity policy and programme development: the experience in Finland', *Public Health Reports*, 119: 331–345.

Whannel, G. (1983) *Blowing the Whistle*, London: Comedia.

Wilson, J. (1988) *Politics and Leisure*, London: Allen & Unwin.

Yule, J. (1990) 'Gender and leisure policy', *Leisure Studies*, 11 (2): 157–173.

CHAPTER 3

DEVELOPING 'SPORT FOR ALL': ADDRESSING INEQUALITY IN SPORT

KEVIN HYLTON AND MICK TOTTEN

Sport has been consistent in its claims to be an arena where we can play unfettered by the inequities of a wider society. The power of sport to transform individuals and communities is a popular argument evident in sport policy and practice at all levels (Houlihan and White, 2002; Polley, 1998). Even though this position is the source of some contention, due to the lack of robust evidence and the sporting arena's potential to generate hostilities and exclusion, many remain undeterred. Sport remains a positive symbol of a social good and as a result many social goals are reliant upon it working; hence the universal acceptance of sport for all. The original 'Sport for All?' campaign in the UK was a creation of the early 1970s and has long since been succeeded by a multitude of campaigns and causes. However, the ideals of 'Sport for All' internationally still have resonance today as a clarion call for all involved in sport development. Sports ministers from across Europe have thrown their collective support behind a 'sport for all principle' and conclude that:

> The Council [of the European Union] adopted conclusions on the role of sport as a source of and a driver for active social inclusion. The conclusions identify three common priorities for promoting social inclusion through sport: the accessibility of sport activity for all citizens ('sport for all' principle), better use of the potential of sport as a contribution to community building, social cohesion and growth, and transnational exchanges of strategies and methodologies.
>
> (EU, C.o.t., 2010: 12)

Despite its attractions, the reality of 'Sport for All' has never been fully achieved, and successes remain incomplete and partial. Gains have been made, but massive disparities and inequalities still remain. However, tackling inequality and widening participation must continue as a central premise and aim of sport development. In order to tackle inequality, inequality itself must be better understood. If the aim is to foster 'inclusion', then 'exclusion' and its social context must be better identified and understood.

CONTENT AND PROCESS

This chapter examines the nature and extent of inequality in sport, and outlines strategies to tackle inequality through sport development policy and practice. The first section draws out some of the challenges and issues that sport development workers have been engaged in when trying to provide sport for all. It commences with an analysis of how inequality is exhibited and can be identified within sport. It then explains how that inequality is linked with broader social processes in society. Sport and society are in symbiosis. Sport is directly influenced by society, which in turn is influenced by sport, and as a consequence many of the wider processes of society express themselves in the realm of sport. Loosely translated, where there are prejudice, discrimination, power differentials and social exclusion in wider society they will also be manifest in sport.

The chapter considers how inequality can be understood in sport and society. The use of sociology is viewed as an essential and important weapon in the armoury of an effective sport professional. The authors draw on sociological theory and analysis to gain a deeper understanding of the issues. Four differing interpretations (or perspectives) offer the sport development worker and policy maker alternative views of issues surrounding equality and inequality in sport. These are applied to sport, sport development and Sport for All. These views enable the sport professional to understand that competing views or arguments are grounded in the way that other people see the world *and* sport development. Having established the social context of inequality in sport, the authors then analyse significant strategic policy responses and specific examples of practice in the light of previous theory and argument. Political and policy implications are explored in a case study of good practice, alongside other related examples, of the way in which different organisations have attempted to develop Sport for All.

SPORT FOR ALL?

The revised European Sport Charter (CoE, 2001: 3) builds upon the 1975 European Sport for All Charter, which acted as the major catalyst in disseminating the ideals of Sport for All. The two key aims of the Charter are:

Article 1. to enable every individual to participate in sport and notably, and more specifically; to ensure that all young people should have the opportunity to receive physical education; to ensure that everyone should have the opportunity to take part in sport and physical recreation in a safe and healthy environment; to ensure that everyone with the interest and ability should have the opportunity to improve their standard of performance in sport and reach levels of personal achievement and/or publicly recognised levels of excellence.

Article 2 of the Charter states that:

1. For the purpose of this Charter:
    a. 'Sport' means all forms of physical activity which, through casual or organised participation, aim at expressing or improving physical fitness and mental well-being, forming social relationships or obtaining results in competition at all levels.

Sport for All is a European phenomenon marked by cultural differences and tensions. The 'sport' in 'Sport for All' has always been contentious because it is so broad and is often interpreted differently according to the many policy makers and practitioners that work with it. Though Article 2 of the European Charter (CoE, 2001) defines what 'sport' is, it is done in such a way for it to be interpreted in diverse ways that include competitive and non-competitive sport from the grassroots to the highest levels of excellence. This complicates the politics of Sport for All and reveals much about its complex and multi-dimensional interpretations. These dynamics are illustrated by the relationships between the state, market and civil society as they interact with structures of governance in sport across Europe (Eichberg, 2009). As a result, the top-down implementation of Sport for All in public sector sport across Europe led to policies and practices underpinned by a philosophy based on equality 'in' and 'through' sport.

For many in competitive sport, the inclusion into these structures brought with it some tensions, especially where excellence was sovereign and therefore seemingly compromised. Houlihan and White (2002) described this friction in the UK by illustrating the differences underpinning sport development's community welfare views (development through sport) and the talent development emphasis of elite sport development (development of sport). However, Eichberg (2009) suggests that the conception and implementation of Sport for All is further complicated by its consistent cross-national adaptations at the level of participation and practice, as Sport for All became embedded in the customs and traditions of sporting participation. Eichberg (2009: 444) goes on to describe how Sport for All resonated with civil ideologies (community welfare views) in play across countries in Europe when he states that:

Movements and organizations could now recognize their traditional striving in the new concept of sport for all. Whether coming from a National Romantic tradition as the German Turner gymnastics . . . the Slavic Socol . . . from Laicist republican roots as the French UFOLEP, . . . former workers' sports movements could recognize sport for all as an extension of their original socialist dreams of solidarity, as was the case in Finnish (TUL) and in Italian sports (UISP) . . . And Christian sports movements such as in the Netherlands could join sport for all according to their own religious preferences . . . the different sports organizations could integrate the new approach into their historical self-understanding.

Though not the focus of this chapter, Eichberg's perspective on Sport for All here suggests that to understand what Sport for All is, and how it developed, a recognition of national settings has a varied story to tell in terms of its philosophies, policies and practices.

INEQUALITY AND SPORT

Sport development has been at the cutting edge of what are seen as innovative and refreshing approaches to traditional sport provision. Despite constraints within their organisations, sport workers today are attempting to offer more opportunities to the public. The house of sport development was built on the foundations of Sport for All, which has always been an ideal rather than a coherent realisable object. This ideal can be viewed from differing perspectives which open up interesting views on sport and recreation and their development. Sport development professionals are challenged to plan, implement and monitor equality work in sport. Furthermore, cultural shifts that have to take place in organisations for long-term change need to go hand in hand with political and social change. Sustainable strategic planning becomes a realistic proposition only when both resources and commitment are in close attendance. Recent years have seen significant investment in sport though the global economic downturn has forced a major reconsideration of priorities at all levels.

Social exclusion and inclusion

Persistent barriers to participation can be understood as 'social exclusion'. Social exclusion is more than exclusion from sport. Fifteen years after social exclusion became one of the major foci of the UN world summit on social development, the UN Under Secretary, Sha Zukang, stated that though progress has been made there are still many daunting challenges ahead (UNCSD, 2010). Social exclusion is typified by social and economic inequalities and by continual aggravation of differences and divisions in the life chances of members of the same society. For example, divisions can be expressed socially in terms of gender differences in sport; economically in terms of differences in income; or culturally through ethnic differences. 'Exclusion' and 'inclusion' affect individuals in different ways, but ultimately have a decisive impact on overall quality of life. The establishment of a Social Exclusion Unit (SEU) in the UK, superseded by a new task force in 2006, and then abolished by the coalition government, aimed to centre issues of social exclusion in public provision. The SEU states that social exclusion happens:

> When people or places suffer from a series of problems such as unemployment, discrimination, poor skills, low incomes, poor housing, high crime, ill health and family breakdown. When such problems combine they can create a vicious cycle.
>
> (Social Exclusion Unit Taskforce, 2012)

Sport development workers need to be conscious of the evident common ground that sport shares with other 'social' services working towards social inclusion. Shared professional knowledge and integrated resources across departmental areas can improve services. These shared areas of interest become fields for integrated coherent policies and are often referred to as 'cross-cutters'. Cross-cutters enable professionals to work together to reduce social exclusion and include:

- community development;
- lifelong learning;
- social cohesion;
- community safety;
- active healthy lifestyles;
- social and economic regeneration;
- job creation;
- equal opportunities;
- crime prevention;
- environmental protection.

All the above emphasise that sport must not be considered in isolation from other aspects of society.

Social exclusion and 'Sport for All'

Research undertaken by the Fundamental Rights Agency (FRA, 2010) into racism, ethnic discrimination and exclusion of migrants and minorities in sport found that different forms of racism, ethnic discrimination and exclusionary practices occurred across different sports and at different levels in the EU. Though there were specific national differences, the report announced that:

> Despite significant progress made in past years, sport continues to face a number of challenges related to racism and ethnic discrimination. Incidences of racism and ethnic discrimination affect sport at professional as well as at amateur level. . . . Moreover, few Member States have established effective monitoring systems to record racism and racial discrimination in sport.
>
> (FRA, 2010: 3)

The systematic nature of the intentional and unintentional exclusions in each Member State poses a number of complex problems for the key stakeholders of sport. In the UK the demand for 'joined-up thinking' confirmed that sport should be used as one instrument within a broad diet of activity influenced by government and related stakeholders. An agenda to combat social exclusion subsumes sport equity/equality and other institutionalised equality work. Inclusion through sport and inclusion in sport are positive steps on a much broader agenda for those defined as socially excluded (Collins and Kay, 2003; Levitas, 1998; Room, 1995). In effect, these considerations give some insight into the potential and limits of sport and sport development in the twenty-first century. Where inequality remains an issue for social groups, even the contested benefits of sport will remain hard to reach.

In the UK, activities relating to equality in sport have become more prominent since the Equality and Human Rights Commission (EHRC) was established in 2007. This forced, at the very least, a minimal change in the way sport was managed and developed. In the UK, a sport professional's requirement to comply with the law has never been more acute as it is now under the Equality Act 2010. Though sport for all is a commonly held philosophy in sport development, some groups in society have been subject to unfair and discriminatory practices in policy and in the day-to-day delivery of facilities and services. The Equality Act 2010 ensures that it is unlawful to discriminate against those with the protected characteristics of age, disability, gender reassignment, marriage and civil partnership, pregnancy and maternity, 'race', religion or belief, sex and sexual orientation. The dissolution of the Commission for Racial Equality, the Equal Opportunities Commission and the Disability Rights Commission has forced public organisations to reconsider how they structure their specific equality policies and practices in relation to a generic equality and diversity focus. This remains an ongoing problematic for organisations in sport, though there are examples of progress. For example the UK Sport Equality Strategy (2010–2013) states specifically that:

Kevin Hylton and Mick Totten

UK Sport will take necessary action to eliminate individual and institutional discrimination; to comply with its statutory and legislative obligations; to meet the needs of its staff and partners and to make equality and equal treatment a core issue in the development, delivery and refinement of its policies, initiatives and services and the way it manages its staff.

(UK Sport, 2010: 3)

The authors advocate a commitment to more equality development work within sport as a primary responsibility for sport's providers. So the proviso to implement equality strategies as a mandatory condition of the national funded agreements between Sports Councils, governing bodies, and regional sports organisations and their partners is a small but significant and welcome step forward. Subsequent analysis will consider the nature of inequality and how it can be tackled.

Equity and equality

The idea of equity (or fairness) is often used interchangeably with equality. However, equality is different and more wide-ranging, as it has both descriptive and specific components. Equity is a more arbitrary and vague concept than equality, as an individual or organisational view of 'fairness' can be conspicuous but superficial whereas a more action-orientated collective view of equality would be more effective and specific. Clarity in this area must be reached if sport intends to work towards equality and inclusion as positive outcomes.

On this note, it is important to recognise that equality does not necessarily mean equity, as equality may be advocated for reasons other than sharing resources evenly (equity), as we will see later in this chapter. Edwards (1990) suggests that equal opportunities are in effect equal opportunities to compete for rewards, and hence to be unequal. He suggests that previous historical differences between groups must be taken into account in terms of who has, and who has not, got access to opportunities in sport. Given the historical inequalities that have emerged across most sporting domains, the notion of fairness rather than purposeful actions to address them will only lead to the continuance of these disparities. This is a principle of the Equality Act 2010 and many proactive sporting organisations.

Significantly, the Sport Equality Standard (2004) at the very least stimulates a shared equality discourse that makes institutional equality frameworks more transparent, accountable and relevant to good practice across sport development. Regulated equality or equal opportunities (as it is otherwise known) attributes something more credible to the rhetoric of equity. In the Sport England Equality Standard (Sport England, 2004: 20) equality is defined as:

The state of being equal – treating individuals equally, which is not necessarily the same as treating them the same. In some cases the need for equality may require unequal effort to ensure that the principle of equality is achieved.

Equity is defined as:

In its simplest sense, 'fairness'; the process of allocating (or reallocating) resources and entitlements, including power, fairly and without discrimination. It includes fairness in opportunity and the upholding of individual human rights through social justice.

Understanding equality and inequality

A number of authors have tried to articulate the elusive concept of equality, which consistently provides thinkers with a kaleidoscope of choices about its constituency and subsequent eventual achievement (Desai, 1995; Mithaug, 1996; Rawls, 1971). Like academics, professionals in sport have competing views on equality, which is one reason why there are inconsistencies in approach. Bagilhole (1997: 7) prefers to deploy 'equal opportunities' only in inverted commas, as she defines it as a contested notion. Similarly, the rhetoric in sport development, concerning Sport for All, is another indicator of a philosophy of provision which has been interpreted inconsistently. The notion of equality itself is ambiguous as it implies that it constitutes an achievable end point. Clearly true equality is impossible, even in the most equitable of societies. Here the saying 'some are more equal than others' makes sense as it hints at the relative nature of equality and inequality. In a modern, globalised, capitalist society it is an inevitable part of the human condition to experience some level of inequality (Blakemore and Drake, 1996). Therefore, Blakemore and Drake's (1996) view that we cannot have equality but must always be working towards it encapsulates the challenge of equality in sport. However, the necessity of underpinning sport development policies and practices with equality principles is crystal clear.

In everyday life there will be social groups who experience direct or indirect discrimination because of any combination of age, social class, gender, religion, sexuality, disability, 'race' and/or ethnicity. Both individuals and organisations in sport are affected by and implicated in this discriminatory behaviour and therefore it is incumbent upon those entities within sport to make sport as equitable as possible. However, whereas working towards equality might be a priority for some within sport development, practice has shown it not to be as high on the agenda for others. There are some whose philosophy is such that they would argue for the state to leave providers to compete for custom. This would allow the open market

44

to provide for a range of public needs, without subsidising public facilities and services, and take the burden away from the public sector (Coalter, 1998). The irony of this position is that the profit-orientated, competitive nature of the unregulated market creates inequality, exclusion and community breakdown in the first place (Ledwith, 2005). So involvement of the public sector is imperative to provide a safety net for those who are most vulnerable and traditionally excluded (Clarke, 1994).

As a result of differing personal, political and institutional views on the nature of equality, different approaches are taken to sport policy and practice that range from radical to minimal. There is a growing body of research around inequality in the development of sport that highlights patterns and trends that act as drivers of counter-initiatives. There are different approaches to identifying inequality in sport. Inequality can be considered 'macroscopically' where it can be observed or tracked across sections of society or comparatively between different societies. It can also be analysed 'microscopically' in relation to more specific contexts. Inequality can be considered 'quantitatively' in terms of the numbers or percentages participating. It can also be considered 'qualitatively' in terms of distinctive reasons behind how and why people participate and their experiences of participation or spectating in sport (Gratton and Jones, 2004; Long, 2007; Veal, 1992; see also Chapter 12).

Trends in participation patterns: the quantitative analysis of sport

Quantitative analysis of participation relies mostly on surveys of participation: in particular, who does or does not participate, frequency, costs and other measurable factors. Analysis can focus on sport as a whole, on types of sports or on specific activities. Participation rates are sometimes monitored in isolation, but more usefully when set against other variables. Most commonly variables will include socio-economic factors which characterise the demographic composition of a population. These factors might include the age of participants, gender, social class, occupation, level of educational attainment, wealth, ethnicity, access to car use and others. These variables when set against levels of participation reveal patterns of participation. Such patterns can be compared with average, or expected, levels of participation. When specific variables reveal levels of participation which are significantly above or below average, one can conclude that that variable has an influence in predicting likelihood of participation. For example, women, those with physical impairment and the unwaged are significantly less likely to participate in snowboarding than men, the able-bodied and the highly paid. Collectively, patterns of participation highlight trends which reveal disparities in participation. The Evidence for Policy and Practice Information and Co-ordinatng Centre (EPPI) study on culture and sport engagement for the Department for Culture, Media and Sport (EPPI/Matrix, 2010) established some interesting patterns to this effect.

According to EPPI/Matrix (2010: 42–48) indicators of higher participation are likely if someone is male, with a higher income and higher education and not in social housing. These findings can then be used to identify specific groups or populations in society less likely to participate, such as the elderly, the disabled, many women, certain ethnic groups, the unwaged and others. These can then be considered priority groups in terms of focusing initiatives to promote and increase participation. This common strategy of targeting provision can concentrate efforts to include the previously excluded. Initiatives might take the form of policies, specific projects or innovation around established or new structures. Doing so increases the likelihood that participation will increase in that group, so changing patterns of participation, and decreasing inequalities in sport participation (see Tables 3.1 and 3.2).

By analysing Table 3.1 one can deduce that participation in sport, games and physical activities varies by socio-economic group: the 'higher' the group, the more likely participation becomes. This table presents some of the key indicators of class difference, demonstrating that overall socio-economic status appears to bear a direct relationship to ability to participate in physical activities, thus reflecting social inequalities. Increasingly austere times are likely to exacerbate class differences, sport and recreation participation and 'choices'.

By analysing Table 3.2 a few aspects can be surmised: overall, men participate more frequently than women; younger people participate more commonly than older people; again, socio-economic status betrays a direct relationship to participation; finally, those who are married are less likely to participate than others. So sex, age, class and marital status all appear to have a strong influence on the likelihood of participation. Other socio-economic factors can be expected to exert similar variations in participation. This reveals that ability to participate manifests itself in many different ways. All these inequalities pose challenges for sport development to resolve.

Table 3.3 identifies a range of concerns for sport development. One issue in particular relates to how ethnicity indicates a lower or higher level of participation. The statistics become even more marked as gender, disability and age affect levels of participation. As a starting point for a discussion on issues of ethnicity and sport participation this table becomes useful, though none of the statistics offer insight into the processes that contribute to the manifestation of these figures (see also Long *et al.*, 2009).

Table 3.4 shows not only that there are overall variations in sport participation, but also that there are differences in the 'types' of activities chosen by people. This table illustrates that different social groups participate more and less frequently in different types of sport, games and physical activities. This would appear to reflect elements of diversity and inequality in both opportunities as well as tastes. Quantitative methods of analysis are useful in identifying such broad patterns in

Table 3.1 Participation in sport in England, 2002

| *Active sports, games and physical activities* | *National Statistics socio-economic classification* | | | | | | | | | |
	1.1 *Large employers and higher managerial*	*1.2* *Higher professional*	*2* *Lower managerial and professional*	*3* *Intermediate*	*4* *Small employers and own account workers*	*5* *Lower supervisory and technical*	*6* *Semi-routine*	*7* *Routine*	*8* *Never worked and long-term unemployed*	*England*
At least one activity (exc. walking)	82.5	80.6	75.5	63.1	65.1	62.6	53.4	48.8	45.3	65.6
At least one activity	89.1	88.9	84.2	72.7	74.0	72.0	64.6	59.9	53.5	74.9
Base (all adults)	858	1131	3068	1051	1266	1607	1646	1628	317	12841

Source: Sport England (2002a: 15).

Notes
Participation rates in the 12 months before interview by National Statistics socio-economic classification (% of respondents). Adults aged 16+.

Table 3.2 Sports-related activities, by gender, age, socio-economic group and marital status, September 2005 (%)

	Doing any sport or exercise		Going to live sporting event	
	Weekday	Weekend	Weekday	Weekend
All	32	29	11	15
Men	39	38	17	23
Women	26	21	5	8
18–24	47	41	14	20
25–34	42	36	11	18
35–44	34	32	12	17
45–54	29	30	9	15
55–64	30	28	13	13
65+	19	15	7	9
AB	45	42	13	19
C1	41	37	12	17
C2	34	29	14	18
D	17	16	6	8
E	12	10	6	8
Married	31	28	11	14
Not married	35	31	11	15

Source: Mintel Leisure Intelligence (2006).

Note
Base: 2,102 adults aged 18+.

participation, but do not really uncover their full meaning (see Sport England, 2012, the Active People Survey).

Participatory experiences: the qualitative analysis of sport

Qualitative analysis of participation is much less common in sport than quantitative analysis, even though it is increasing in popularity in many sport disciplines (Gratton and Jones, 2004; Chapter 12 below). Thus it is a type of research which could, or should, be developed more fully. It is more likely to be used by academics than by policy makers or practitioners. This is not only because it is costly in terms of both time and resources, but also because it reveals more complex information which is open to differing interpretations. Such complexity is often perceived by policy makers as too resource-intensive or imprecise to be worthwhile. Additionally,

Table 3.3 Adult participation: Sports Equity Index

Rank	Age	Group	Index
1	16–19	Male	231
2	20–24	Male	208
3=	16–19	Without a disability	191
3=	16–19	White	191
5	16–19	Black and ethnic minority communities	190
6	16–19	With a disability	187
7	20–24	AB*	178
8	25–29	Male	176
9	16–19	DE	173
10	20–24	White	166
11	25–29	AB	165
12	20–24	Without a disability	164
13	16–19	AB*	154
14	16–19	Female	152
15	20–24	With a disability	148
16	30–44	Male	146
17	20–24	DE	145
18	25–29	Without a disability	143
19	25–29	White	142
20	30–44	AB	136
21	30–44	Without a disability	126
22	20–24	Female	125
23	25–29	With a disability	122
24	30–44	White	121
25	25–29	Black and ethnic minority communities	120
26	45–59	AB	116
27	25–29	DE	115
28	25–29	Female	111
29	20–24	Black and ethnic minority communities	109
30	30–44	Black and ethnic minority communities	102
Norm	All Adults		100
31	45–59	Male	98
32	30–44	Female	97
33	45–59	Without a disability	96
34	30–44	DE	94

Table 3.3 Continued

Rank	Age	Group	Index
35	30–44	With a disability	93
36	60–69	AB	90
37	45–59	White	87
38=	60–69	Male	77
38=	60–69	Without a disability	77
40	45–59	Female	76
41	60–69	White	69
42=	45–59	With a disability	62
42=	45–59	Black and ethnic minority communities	62
44=	45–59	DE	58
44=	60–69	Female	58
46	60–69	With a disability	52
47	60–69	DE	49
48	70+	AB	48
49	70+	Male	39
50	70+	Without a disability	38
51	70+	White	29
52	60–69	Black and ethnic minority communities	24
53	70+	Female	21
54	70+	With a disability	19
55	70+	DE	13
56	70+	Ethnic minority communities*	12

*Small sample size therefore findings not necessarily valid
Source: Sport England (2001: 10).

the findings are often perceived as too challenging to be implemented and translated into practice.

Qualitative research veers away from a preoccupation with numbers and concentrates on the meaning and significance of participation. It offers deeper insights into the motivations of participants and the social significance of their participation. It often employs methods such as semi-structured interviews, focus group discussions or observations of practice to gain insights. It concentrates on the 'social relations of participation', how people behave and what that behaviour means to them and to others. Understanding how and why people behave and relate to each other in particular ways, and what that signifies, is at the root of sport participation and choice. Behaviour can be seen to be structured in particular ways and linked to broader social influences.

Table 3.4 Sports, games and physical activities

Active sports, games and physical activities	National Statistics socio-economic classification									England
	1.1 Large employers and higher managerial	1.2 Higher professional	2 Lower managerial and professional	3 Intermediate	4 Small employers and own account workers	5 Lower supervisory and technical	6 Semi-routine	7 Routine	8 Never worked and long-term unemployed	
Walking	47.1	46.2	41.7	32.7	30.0	29.4	28.5	23.5	19.5	34.1
Any swimming	24.0	19.9	17.7	13.7	11.9	11.2	8.8	7.8	7.4	13.9
Swimming: indoor	20.6	17.2	15.8	11.5	10.5	9.2	7.8	6.8	6.4	12.1
Swimming: outdoor	5.3	4.7	3.4	2.7	2.8	2.7	1.4	1.3	1.0	2.9
Keep fit/yoga	20.8	18.3	15.3	14.8	11.1	9.4	7.1	6.3	4.6	12.2
Cycling	13.0	12.0	11.5	6.5	8.1	7.2	6.3	6.8	7.5	9.0
Snooker/pool/billiards	9.9	9.2	9.6	10.2	9.4	9.1	8.5	7.0	5.5	9.2
Weight training	11.4	8.5	7.3	6.9	5.1	4.0	4.0	2.5	2.0	5.9
Running (jogging etc.)	10.3	8.1	6.6	5.2	3.3	3.4	2.2	2.3	3.2	5.0
Golf	9.5	8.4	6.1	4.2	4.9	3.6	1.8	1.7	0.0	4.5
Any soccer	6.1	5.4	5.5	4.2	4.8	4.7	3.3	3.8	4.2	4.8
Soccer: outdoor	5.0	4.2	4.4	3.1	4.3	4.0	2.7	3.1	4.2	3.9
Soccer: indoor	2.7	2.3	2.6	1.5	1.2	1.7	1.2	1.3	1.0	1.8
Tenpin bowling/skittles	4.8	4.0	3.9	4.2	3.2	3.1	2.9	2.0	0.3	3.3

Table 3.4 Continued

Active sports, games and physical activities	National Statistics socio-economic classification									
	1.1 Large employers and higher managerial	1.2 Higher professional	2 Lower managerial and professional	3 Intermediate	4 Small employers and own account workers	5 Lower supervisory and technical	6 Semi-routine	7 Routine	8 Never worked and long-term unemployed	England
Tennis	3.1	4.0	2.7	1.8	1.7	0.5	0.8	0.5	1.0	1.9
Badminton	2.8	3.6	2.4	1.5	1.4	1.6	1.3	0.7	0.9	1.8
Fishing	1.1	1.1	1.2	1.5	2.5	2.3	1.6	1.5	0.8	1.6
Any bowls	1.8	1.0	1.1	1.1	1.3	1.6	1.1	1.4	0.0	1.2
Carpet bowls	1.1	1.0	0.6	1.0	1.0	1.3	0.5	0.9	0.0	0.8
Lawn bowls	0.9	0.1	0.5	0.2	0.4	0.5	0.7	0.6	0.0	0.5
Weight-lifting	2.0	0.9	1.9	1.7	1.2	1.0	1.1	1.1	0.5	1.3
Table tennis	1.8	1.8	2.0	1.2	1.1	0.9	1.5	0.2	1.1	1.2
Squash	2.1	3.5	1.5	1.1	0.8	1.0	0.2	0.4	0.3	1.2
Horse riding	1.7	0.9	1.2	1.0	1.8	0.8	0.7	0.5	0.9	1.1
Martial arts (inc. self-defence)	1.3	1.0	1.3	1.2	1.7	0.5	0.5	0.9	0.9	0.9
Shooting	0.9	0.6	0.9	0.9	0.9	1.1	0.7	0.6	0.0	0.8
Basketball	0.9	1.0	0.7	0.5	0.8	0.4	0.3	0.1	1.6	0.7
Sailing	1.2	1.5	0.7	0.2	0.8	0.3	0.1	0.3	0.4	0.5
Cricket	0.7	1.7	0.9	0.3	0.2	0.5	0.4	0.2	0.0	0.6
Climbing	0.6	1.2	0.6	0.7	0.4	0.3	0.3	0.1	0.0	0.5
Motor sports	1.0	1.3	0.7	0.3	0.7	0.5	0.4	0.3	0.2	0.6
Ice skating	0.9	0.2	0.4	0.5	0.7	0.5	0.6	0.3	0.6	0.5

Skiing	1.5	0.9	0.5	0.5	0.0	0.2	0.0	0.1	0.0	0.4
Rugby	0.8	0.7	0.5	0.2	0.1	0.3	0.2	0.3	0.3	0.4
Netball	0.4	0.3	0.4	0.2	0.5	0.4	0.1	0.2	0.0	0.3
Hockey	0.5	0.8	0.3	0.5	0.1	0.2	0.1	0.3	0.0	0.3
Canoeing	0.4	0.5	0.4	0.3	0.2	0.1	0.1	0.2	0.0	0.3
Volleyball	0.3	0.2	0.4	0.5	0.1	0.3	0.1	0.0	0.0	0.2
Athletics: track and field	0.2	0.4	0.1	0.2	0.3	0.0	0.1	0.1	0.0	0.2
Windsurfing, boardsailing	0.1	0.2	0.2	0.1	0.3	0.1	0.1	0.1	0.0	0.2
Gymnastics	0.4	0.3	0.2	0.5	0.2	0.4	0.0	0.2	0.0	0.3
At least one activity (exc. walking)	60.5	58.4	51.2	42.9	43.1	38.8	31.0	29.4	26.1	43.4
At least one activity	76.1	73.9	67.3	57.3	56.6	54.0	46.6	42.7	36.7	58.3
Base (all adults)	858	1131	3068	1051	1266	1607	1646	1628	317	12841

Source: Sport England (2002a: 16).

Notes

Participation rates in the four weeks before interview by National Statistics socio-economic classification (% of respondents). Adults aged 16+.

The interrelation of sport and society is manifest as social influences are brought to sport, and as influences are exported from it to wider society. The analysis of sport must also encompass other more informal manifestations such as recreation and play. Sport is a social activity, partly composed of elements which might involve some form of competitive activity. Analysis must extend beyond the playing field, into the locker room, and for some even into the bar afterwards as well. These are all part of sport and sports cultures. If you were to observe behaviour in a multi-sport and social club bar you could focus on the influence of gender, class, ethnicity, disability or age. Sticking with gender, it is most likely, though not always the case, that women and men would behave differently and adopt different behavioural roles in the same setting. Different views of masculinity and femininity can be detected to result in different 'gendered' role behaviours. The setting or social space might be seen to be dominated by a specific gender, or a particular type of masculinity or femininity. This might differ in some way from another context, such as a rugby club bar: however, the resulting atmosphere might make some groups or individuals feel more or less welcome. That in turn might lead to the partial exclusion of certain groups through perceptions of discomfort or simply feelings of alienation or disengagement. Those groups are unlikely to be attracted to that setting or organisation while these gender norms prevail, despite best official efforts to countenance an open-door policy. Fully including those excluded groups is unlikely to occur without first challenging, and then changing, that prevailing 'gender order' or culture. The same observation but focused on class, ethnicity or disability would be as likely to generate similar results and conclusions. A prevailing class or ethnicity or a prevailing cultural perspective or attitude towards disability could all be identified. As with other forms of hegemony, dominant views and actions can be seen to include or exclude.

Dominant cultures are often revealed as similar in patterns across many sport settings. Consequently these specific cultures can become the norm and appear to shape and create expectations across sport as a whole. To be more inclusive those dominant cultures need to be challenged or resisted in some way. Evidence of such resistance could be exemplified by the likes of women's rugby teams, which could be seen as invading and culturally challenging what was once exclusively male territory. This can be understood as individual social 'agents' acting against the prevailing cultural norms of social 'structures'. The complexities of beginning to address cultural change in practice deter many attempts from the outset. So in relation to gender, class or ethnicity, the prevailing order or culture persists, and with them so too does exclusion. The inherent difficulty in addressing participation in a qualitative way signals why it is less common. However, until participation is addressed in a qualitative way, exclusion will continue to manifest itself and therein lies a challenge for sport development!

Barriers to participation

Promoting inclusion and tackling exclusion involve identifying inequalities. Ultimately inequality is shaped by different social, cultural, political and economic processes. Using previously identified quantitative and qualitative methods of analysing participation, the same influences crop up regularly. Key influences include disposable income, levels of educational attainment, occupational status, social class, culture, ethnicity, gender, sexuality, age, ability and disability.

These social influences can either empower or discourage sports participation. In terms of exclusion, influences can also act as potential barriers to participation. These can be further categorised as physical, economic, motivational, cultural and political. Physical barriers to participation include the location of facilities, activities and services, and physical access into and within those facilities, activities and services. Economic barriers relate to affordability, cost and perceived value at that cost. Motivational barriers to participation relate to the perceived absence of value in activity, or towards a conflict with self-image when viewed in the light of the perceived image of an activity. Cultural barriers to participation include direct conflicts with codes, customs and conventions or values inherent in an activity, or perhaps, less directly, with a discomfort associated with the perceived cultural image of an activity. Political barriers to participation relate to feelings of alienation from, or lack of ownership over, the existing choice of provision. This may stem from a lack of representation, consultation or involvement in decision making about provision and design, which may generate feelings of being disenfranchised from provision. These barriers are all issues which sport development must grapple with in order to promote inclusion. Cultural and political barriers provide particularly complex challenges for the development of sport.

Alienation can occur at a local level in relation to a particular facility. One anecdotal example would be an aerobics group within an area of multiple deprivation in Leeds who preferred to participate in the local community centre rather than in the local sports centre. (The community centre was a blighted Portakabin in the car park of the sports centre.) For these local participants there was an invisible cultural barrier preventing entrance to the sport and leisure centre. This perceptual barrier conveyed class values and tastes which were alien to the locals, whereas those participating were mainly 'outsiders'. The community had little sense of 'ownership' of the local authority facility on their doorstep. A further example, but at a civic level, was the feelings of many of the people of Sheffield towards the provision for the World Student Games. Again perceptions of loss rather than gain clouded community views of this new sports provision. Concerns were raised about local access to international facilities. Why were local community centres not built? Why were local sports centres closed in the shadow of this massive spend on prestige capital investments? Similar risks attach themselves to the London

2012 Olympic and Paralympic Games, where local businesses have been driven out by compulsory purchase orders on their land. Those excluded in the East End of London may need many things but it is debatable that elite sports stadia are top priorities on their long list of needs. Promises of jobs and investment are beholden to the practices of large corporations who may be as likely to drain money away to outside interests (Hargreaves, 2002; Poynter and MacRury, 2009; Rigauer, 2000; Schirato and Webb, 2003).

All the previously highlighted barriers can exclude and lead to feelings of 'this isn't for me'. Remedying inequalities and overcoming barriers involve development strategies. These must challenge the inequitable nature of existing provision. There are limitations to what can be achieved solely within sport. Many barriers are founded on broader processes and institutions in society. However, if the barriers are physical, economic, motivational, cultural and political, then so too are the solutions. If sport development strategies can address structural issues, then they are on the way to establishing facilities and services valued and supported by the majority of the community rather than a privileged few.

INEQUALITY AND SOCIETY

The social context of inequality

Sport is more than just an activity. It has far more meaning for the individual and significance to society. It does not exist in a vacuum and there is a plethora of evidence to demonstrate its place as a vital social tool and cultural product:

> Nelson Mandela understands the powerful role that sport can play in changing people's lives – both on and off the sporting field. The London 2012 Olympic Games shares the same vision. The Games in London will help to build new bridges of understanding between cultures and nations and leave a legacy of much needed new sporting venues and facilities that will continue to change people's lives for generations to come.
>
> (Coe, 2006)

Inequitable processes and practices in society are contributory reasons why sport development workers have a difficult job in developing Sport for All. Inequality exists on the field of play and it exists also in the rest of society. Analysis must embrace a more comprehensive social enquiry beyond the unique institutional framework which constitutes 'sport' itself: it must also consider society.

56

Inequality and discrimination

Sport institutions are constituted by members of society whose actions influence inclusion and exclusion. To varying degrees they may work towards, or indeed against, equality in society. Among groups who are traditionally excluded in society, some have regularly been the focus for sport development. Gender, disability, 'race' and ethnicity have preoccupied the attention of many policy makers, practitioners and social commentators who recognise inequalities in the location of women, disabled people and black people to positions of power and control in sport. Class, age and sexuality have been considered less systematically, but their influence on life chances should not be underestimated. There are few people from these excluded groups in managerial and administrative positions in sport and this has a clear qualitative impact on the opportunities for individuals from these groups to access sport and recreation (Sport England, 2002a).

Inequality in sport and society can be caused through discriminatory practices and processes which can occur intentionally or unintentionally at three different levels:

- individual (micro);
- institutional (meso);
- societal (macro).

Thompson's (2003) PCS model (personal, cultural and structural; see Figure 3.1) is a useful way for those in sport to conceive of how discrimination and oppression work in their daily settings. The use of the PCS model to illustrate how discrimination and oppression function demonstrates that not only does discrimination operate at personal, cultural and structural levels but they also work with, across and against each other. Sport is often described as an institution yet it is made up of a multitude of social groups that could be described as cultures in themselves. Thompson's use of the term 'cultural' rather than 'institutional' emphasises that, though it is important to consider formal organisations as significant social entities, we should not forget that most people experience sport and recreation in less formal spaces too. These spaces may be after-school clubs, recreational work settings, local gyms, on the street or with friends and family. These spaces extend into networks that develop cultures of their own in which practices and forms of behaviour become dominant and commonplace. These behaviours become custom and practice among coaches, student teams and just about any regular social gathering. Though there are groups that can be described as having a 'culture' within organisations or institutions we also find them in less formal settings where there are social networks.

The PCS levels, sometimes referred to elsewhere as individual, institutional and societal levels, are interrelated in that everyone is influenced by and influencing each aspect of them. Each individual (personal level) in sport is influenced by groups or cultural contexts. The personal is entrenched in the cultural or institutional levels just as individual (P) players are affected by a team (cultural level) or an individual sport development worker (P) by an organisation (C). The industry of sport development is a reflection of larger processes and practices which continue in wider society (structural level). The societal (macro) issues which impact on us all in our day-to-day lives are carried with us back into our teams and organisations (C) and affect us in varying ways as individuals (P) in sport. The relationships across all three levels of the PCS are dynamic, as each level can affect the other. So where there are power and structural advantages that accrue for or against particular groups in society they are likely to be replicated in sport in diverse ways. For example, discrimination against disability in sport can be viewed as follows.

(Personal) individual-level discrimination (micro)

Disabled people are regularly the focus of personal-level thoughts and actions affecting the quality and way that sport is resourced (see Chapter 11 below). Prejudice through discrimination disadvantages many, as stereotypes and unfounded

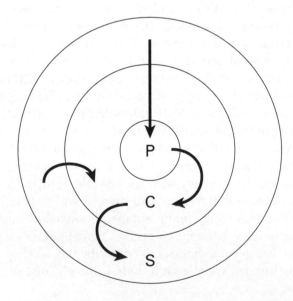

Figure 3.1 The PCS model (Thompson, 2003: 17). P, personal; C, cultural; S, structural. Reproduced with permission of Palgrave Macmillan.

Kevin Hylton and Mick Totten

assumptions take hold. Stereotypes in relation to physicality such as frailty and ability have often limited the participation of disabled individuals. These constraints may have the effect of filtering disabled athletes away from some sports and channelling them into others. It is very similar to the concept of 'channelling' or 'stacking' in other areas of sport. Emphasis on the needs of the individual rather than on collective needs and rights means that isolated piecemeal change and good practice occur but remain elusive and unsustainable for all. The effects of stereotyping and stigmatising disabled people rather than challenging sport and society remain an obstacle to equality and diversity for those disabled by society.

Further, this behaviour might also be a combination of overt and/or covert discrimination and a further complication could be that it might be conscious or unconscious. Overt behaviour is the easiest to identify, although responses to any type of discriminatory action are never simple, and often inadequate. Thompson (2003) urges us not to put too much emphasis on individual- or personal-level prejudicial behaviours because it then suggests that discrimination and related behaviours are not problems within sporting cultures, and for that matter, organisations and wider society. Similarly, sexist behaviour in football is not solely the problem of the one or two people who manifest it in one incident. The need to situate the personal-level behaviours in the cultural enables sport developers to understand that as individuals we are informed by a range of norms and attitudes from other settings, many of which we find in sport and leisure.

Table 3.5 Views on equality in sport and society

Swinney and Horne (2005)	• *Gestural:* organisations described as 'gestural' are generally confident that they are able to be 'fair' without producing any specific Equal Opportunities policies • *Reactive:* 'reactive' organisations are likely to have equality policies in place. They are likely to sometimes be complacent or confident that they do not have a problem with inequality • *Proactive:* 'proactive' organisations are likely to be active in systematically challenging racism. These organisations are generally in the minority
Bagilhole (1997)	• *Equality of opportunity:* there is recognition here that all social groups need equal access to facilities and services • *Equality of condition:* here it is acknowledged that even where access is open there may be material and cultural disparities that need to be considered. These may revolve around travel, cost, religion, physical access, timing and environment • *Equality of outcome:* here the impact of historical disadvantages is considered. Action is taken to privilege marginalised groups; this is sometimes referred to as positive or affirmative action

Table 3.5 Continued

Forbes (1991)	• *Liberal:* traditional liberals believe that the state should not interfere in the life chances of individuals. It is the market that will provide where there are needs. Competition should be left unfettered • *Neo-liberal:* traditional liberal values around the market are adapted with a social agenda. The market is central to a strong community, although inequality is recognised as needing to be checked by social welfare, hence the New Right • *Radical:* a radical perspective criticises the conservative nature of traditional liberals and the liberal nature of advocates of New Right politics. Equal opportunities will reconstitute inequality only if it does not take a radical 'alternative' approach
Cunningham (1992)	• *Minimalist:* holders of a minimalist ideology base equality on merit and the removal of barriers to achievement. Here the market offers individuals the chance to compete to be unequal, procedure-led policies are adopted which are 'race' and gender blind, and rewards are awarded on merit alone • *Maximalist:* this view refers to more radical activism. Practical outcomes that transform the status quo (social change) are the main focus of this activity in opposition to a minimalist incrementalism or procedural approach
Jewson and Mason (1992)	• *Liberal:* the authors refer to this as the bureaucratisation of action. The formality of rules and regulations causes good ideas to atrophy and slows the process of change • *Radical:* the politicisation of implementation frames institutional change. Power, resistance and empowerment are used to champion the cause of marginal or disenfranchised social groups. Procedure and regulation are overtaken by critical consciousness, action and outcomes
Young (1989)	• *Regulative:* regulative discourses are concerned with the conformity of systems and behaviour to an acceptable level. Thus, challenging institutional discrimination, discrimination in the workplace and the training of staff to increase their capacity to ensure awareness are three modes of regulatory behaviour • *Distributive:* distributive discourses tend to view equality in terms of increases in resources such as jobs, low inflation, increased pay or new sports coordinators in schools, which have a trickle-down effect on everyone and therefore everyone benefits. It does not discriminate in any way and there are no obvious 'losers' where these resources are being distributed • *Redistributive:* redistributive discourses are often seen as ways to target marginalised populations in communities and are often measured in quantitative terms, unlike regulatory policies. For example, employment is often a way to redistribute key resources in a bid to ensure diverse sensitive provision

(Cultural) institutional-level discrimination (meso)

Disabled people are underrepresented among major institutions and policy makers of sport and this again is typical of society. DePauw and Gavron (2005: 13) summarised institutional barriers to disabled people in sport as:

- lack of organised sport programmes;
- lack of informative early experiences;
- lack of access to coaches and training programmes;
- lack of accessible sport facilities;
- limiting psychological and sociological factors.

For example, where a manager encourages discrimination or where the centre or local authority simply does not have policies and systems (remedies and/or sanctions) to ensure staff awareness of these discriminatory actions (or non-actions) it could be said to be perpetuating institutional discrimination. Ironically, organisational behaviour through systematised activities, policies and language can inadvertently exclude many from sport while actively trying to encourage participation (see Swinney and Horne, 2005, in Table 3.5). Again this activity (or inactivity) by organisations might be overt or covert, intentional or unintentional.

(Structural) societal-level discrimination (macro)

On an even more fundamental level a responsible society would remove any obstructions in public arenas, buildings and services such as transport, education, health and housing (Rheker, 2000). A disabling society favours a medical model of disability whereby the individual is seen as a patient, rather than a social model which accepts that economic, social and political processes militate against people with disabilities; these processes are reproduced in sport. Saraga (1998) outlines how 'able-bodiedness' is seen as the norm and that disability becomes a euphemism for people who are somehow defective or impaired. This process has been described as 'disablement' but has some utility in initiating a more constructive critical dialogue on the way disabled people are structurally oppressed. Writers on sport are beginning to focus on these under-theorised norms that are sometimes seen as 'invisible' because of the lack of analysis on them (Collins and Kay, 2003; Fitzgerald, 2005; Gillborn, 2005; Hylton, 2005, 2009; Long and Hylton, 2002; Messner, 1992; Scraton and Flintoff, 2002; see also Chapter 11 in this edition). For example, society has practices and processes which are (to varying degrees) knowingly or unknowingly discriminatory. Sport developers such as the one imagined under the previous heading draw their staff from members of society who (to varying degrees) inherit and reflect these broader prejudices.

Equality in practice

Working towards equality in different contexts can take interesting turns depending on the strategy/ies employed by practitioners and policy makers. As institutions operate in differing contexts it is clear that some will adopt policies to suit their own philosophies or politics (see Table 3.5). Equality of opportunity implies that all persons, regardless of their background, should be given equal access to the same facilities, services, employment and other conditions. Statutes have made it unlawful to discriminate in the provision of goods, facilities and services. Equality of opportunity, equality of condition and equality of outcome are three significant policy foci for understanding equality processes in sport development. For example, if a sports worker were to adhere to the minimum conditions of the Equality Act 2010, yet members of the community were still excluded, then 'Equal Opportunities' could still be seen to exist, even though it would be ineffective in this instance. However, if the excluded groups were filtered away from the sports worker's sessions because of a lack of transport or technical equipment, or for cultural reasons, but these gaps were then addressed, the sports worker would have moved beyond just providing equality of opportunity. As illustrated in Table 3.5, the sports worker would also be providing equality of condition in that considerations other than physical access would have been identified as reasons for a lack of participation by groups in this community. The worker would be moving towards what Cockburn (1989) terms a long agenda rather than a short one. Jewson and Mason (1986) would argue also that the worker is moving from a liberal to a more radical agenda. The long-term implementation and monitoring of equality strategies is complex and involves more than policy statements and rhetoric.

A more radical view of equality in operation might come through the use of equality of outcome principles. Here more positive and explicitly differential provision takes into account some of the larger structural inequalities in society. Practitioners and policy makers taking structural differences into account will challenge inequality in sport through new initiatives and strategies. Sport professionals occasionally find it necessary to focus on equality outputs (CRE, 1995) or positive action initiatives to refocus work towards providing more equal and sensitive provision. The Adults with a Disability and Sport survey by Sport England (2002b) suggests one type of positive action through the implementation of leisure credits. It suggested that leisure credits be used as a way to reduce multiple inequalities that affect people with a disability. Therefore this recommendation takes into account inequalities that accrue as a result of low income and disability, thus bringing a direct sporting benefit to disabled people. Women-only sessions, or work with young people from minority ethnic communities, could be viewed as examples of positive action strategies. Positive action, because of the statutes mentioned earlier, can also be applied to recruiting people to work in those areas of provision where they are underrepresented. This basic regulation and distribution of resources is something that has been recognised as one essential aspect of progressive equality policies.

Sport, then, is not isolated from inequalities in society. Sport developers have an endless task if they take on the responsibility for reducing social exclusion. Sport's role as part of a broader social policy strategy might go some way towards contributing to reducing social inequality, increasing community cohesion and acting as a catalyst for social regeneration. The creation of the Social Exclusion Unit in the UK and its use of sport as part of its strategy to increase social inclusion is an indication of, at the very least, the ideological and material significance of sport in society.

EQUALITY AND SPORT DEVELOPMENT

Certain managerial and political perspectives have informed the practice of equality work since the late 1970s. Taylor's (1994) work encapsulates some of the thinking in this area. Two major competing views in this period have revolved around a New Right ideology which has focused on the primacy of the market as the guardian of individual rights and natural justice. More recently a New Right view has been modified with elements of a social reformist agenda and this has taken a more inclusive stance in public sector interventions. The social reformist perspective encourages a more 'active society' through proactive support mechanisms which encourage community development, capacity building, social cohesion and the reduction of social exclusion. More conservative influences encourage a further rolling back of the state, self-determination and competition for scarce resources. 'Big Society' ideals rely heavily upon public enthusiasms and community ownership of the potential for self-reliance. The major downfall of such an approach involves perceptions of under-resourcing and a lack of leadership in such a massive undertaking.

Ellis (1994) and Escott (1996) have examined positive aspects of working towards equality within 'bottom line' pressures of the commercial sector. In the past, one of the major drawbacks in the UK of the contracting process as a result of the Local Government Act 1988 was that social objectives or equality targets were not necessarily written into contracts. Equality targets in the political climate of 1988 were seen as non-commercial considerations. The then Sports Council's National Information Survey on the first round of Compulsory Competitive Tendering (Sports Council, 1993) bore testimony to this. It was established that out of many local authorities only a few incorporated social objectives into clauses for contracts that went out to tender. However, more enlightened organisations have tied equality targets into contractor activities by linking them inextricably with quality targets and principles of best value. For example the Rugby Football League has incorporated equality and diversity targets in the host city bidding process for the 2013 Rugby World Cup.

In support of this view Taylor (1994) advocates the use of Equal Opportunities policies in any industry, not just from a moral perspective (although there is an element of that) but from a business perspective as well (see Coalter, 1998; Commission for Racial Equality, 1995; Equal Opportunities Commission, 1996; Etzioni, 1961). Taylor outlines the major skills a manager needs to be successful in business. Five major considerations to develop management skills in this area are:

- human rights and social justice;
- business efficiency;
- quality management;
- the labour market;
- legal considerations.

So equal opportunities is not just defined as the exclusive preserve of the social reformist agenda in the public and voluntary sectors, but can be a desirable aspect of the economics of the commercial private sector as well.

Sociological approaches to understanding inequality

An understanding of the social context of sport necessitates some understanding of society itself (Eckstein *et al.*, 2010; Jarvie, 2006). In terms of sport development, enlightened practitioners must embrace this social perspective and its analysis, in other words sociology. Only then can they hope to have any significant understanding and impact on the social context of sport. This prospect can seem daunting, as society is all-encompassing and the individual practitioner often feels isolated in relation to the scale of it all. However, sociology is not just about thinking. Sociology is alive and breathing. Sociology also involves doing, and the enlightened sport development worker (whether aware of it or not) can be an active sociologist. Social processes which create inequality, and solutions (albeit with limitations), must be investigated not just in sport but in society as a whole. Let's face it, either you're part of the cure or you're part of the disease.

Introducing sociology

Sociology is the study of society and is committed to developing a greater understanding of it. The 'sociological imagination' enables a deeper, more significant insight into society and how it works (Giddens, 2006; Mills, 1970). Sociology attempts to explain, and sometimes predict, social behaviour. A grasp of sociology

64

will enable the enlightened practitioner to more accurately understand the profound and complex influences which affect sport participation. The following analysis deploys sociological theory and applies sociological perspectives to the study of inequality in sport. For the uninitiated it may initially be challenging or cause mild befuddlement, but persevere, as it may prove quite illuminating. It begins with an analysis of how significant social influences are in determining participation in sport. It will then work towards offering different perspectives to understand Sport for All. It will establish what sociological perspectives are, what they explain and how they interpret society, sport, sport development and then Sport for All. So hang on to your hat!

Influencing participation

Social influences such as gender, ethnicity and class, which can act as barriers or gateways to participation in sport, can be considered as structures which permeate society. However, individuals make choices and exercise free will in leisure and sport, and this is known as 'agency'. Social structures influence individuals as they make these choices. Structures inhibit total freedom from constraint. As much as individuals perceive themselves to be exercising free choice, they are either consciously or subconsciously constrained by these structures. Social structures can make certain choices more or less likely. They influence individual choices whether we are aware of it or not. So individuals attempt to make free choices in sport grounded in their own unique opportunities and tastes. However, these very opportunities and tastes are informed by social structures. So total free choice is illusory. Still, we are free to choose, even if we have less control than we think over what our choices are. So choice is constrained by structures outside the immediate influence of the individual. In short, once again, society influences sport, and sport influences society. The combined influence of structure and agency on choice can be described as a dichotomy. Dichotomies, or real contradictions and tensions in policy and practice, are discussed in Chapter 4, below, on community sport development.

Understanding society

Within sociology, different perspectives have emerged from which to view and understand institutions and social contexts such as sport. These perspectives put more or less emphasis on the role of structure and/or agency in determining choice. Furthermore, they offer different interpretations of the entire social world. They may overlap, but some find more strengths in one interpretation than the others; therefore disagreement and argument ensue, and are inevitable. Sociology as an academic discipline is contested territory.

Four dominant perspectives are outlined below as tools that academics and practitioners may use to better understand sport and society. Ideally the four views should be utilised strategically by sport development professionals to interpret processes and practices in sport. Understanding the way people make sense of society, sport, sport development and Sport for All enables reflective practitioners to evaluate the relative merits of competing or alternative views more effectively. If an individual were to imagine their day-to-day relationships at work, or at leisure, then just that small group of acquaintances could offer up (from their diverse backgrounds) different, very challenging views on developing Sport for All.

Table 3.6 Interpretations of society

Functionalist	Society is based on broad agreement (consensus). This consensus reflects a balance between different interests. The 'social system' regulates the smooth flow of these plural interests (see Loy and Booth, 2000)
Neo-Marxist	Society is based on coercion and consensus. 'Social relations' are dominated by power struggles. The economically and politically powerful attempt to lead, and protect their dominance. People either consent to these arrangements or offer resistance to them (see Carrington and McDonald, 2009; Coakley and Dunning, 2000)
Feminist	Society is unfairly based on male dominance or patriarchy. Social relations exist within a gender order. Masculine values dominate society. Traditional femininity prescribes a subservient role for women (see Scraton and Flintoff, 2002)
Postmodernist	Society is fragmented and diverse. There is no universal truth, only individuality and different interpretations of reality. The only certainty is uncertainty! Society is in a perpetual state of change and flux. Traditional structure and order are things of the past (see Rail, 1998)

Table 3.7 Interpretations of sport

Functionalist	Sport is greatly valued, as it has many positive benefits. It contributes to the smooth running of the social system. It acts as a form of 'cultural glue' which helps to hold society together
Neo-Marxist	Sport can liberate or constrain. It largely serves the interests of dominant groups and institutions, but it can also act as a site for resistance or change by subordinate groups or individuals
Feminist	Sport reinforces patriarchy and traditional masculine and feminine values. It promotes masculine values over feminine but it can also act as a site for women, or men, to challenge these traditional values
Postmodernist	Sport is a paradox. It can be highly significant to individual self-image and lifestyle, but it is ultimately superficial. It can be highly symbolic of society, but it is ultimately unreal. It is in this sense 'hyper-real'

As sociological perspectives consider much more than just sport, the four perspectives will be introduced from a bigger picture, before working progressively towards a more specific consideration of Sport for All. Table 3.6 highlights four key perspectives: functionalist, neo-Marxist, feminist and postmodernist (see Coakley and Dunning, 2000). Tables 3.6 and 3.7 offer simplified versions of society and sport from the four perspectives. You can attempt to judge which perspective you find the most convincing. Ideally, you may find that one perspective seems to emerge as more compelling, or you may choose to apply different perspectives at different times. Whichever you choose, the adoption of a sociological imagination and analysis offers a critical insight into how society works (or does not).

Comparing perspectives of society

Historical relationships help to clarify differences. Functionalism reflects the most traditional view of Western society and sport. It is perhaps the most popular perspective among the political establishment and the wider population. Its ideals tend to be dominant in current sport and social policy. However, it is savagely criticised by more critical perspectives for being at best too 'rose-tinted', unconditionally positive and unrealistic, and at worst ideologically divisive, conning the general public into believing in a society which ultimately works against collective interests. Neo-Marxists draw attention to power inequalities and conflicts which functionalists overlook, particularly in the economics of society and of sport. Feminism arose as a critique of the failure of the two previous perspectives to take sufficient account of gender divisions and power relations. Feminists promote the influence of gender as the primary determinant of social relations and sport. Postmodernism is the most recent perspective. It criticises all three perspectives for clinging to any form of clear determination in an increasingly unpredictable world.

Neo-Marxism could be seen as adaptable enough to account for the massive changes in current society. Functionalism, on the other hand, could be viewed as oversimplifying the world, as unrealistic and naive. It is the world we would like to live in but do not. Some might say it is blinkered by its naive faith. Neo-Marxism considers the power processes overlooked and ignored by functionalism. Neo-Marxism can also be argued to encompass and account for the concerns of both feminists and postmodernists. Neo-Marxist analyses then take account of cultural power as inclusive of concerns about gender division, as well as other dynamics such as ethnicity, class and disability. Neo-Marxism interprets postmodernism as a context, not a perspective. It is the times we live in, not the way they should be understood, as everyday structural inequalities are ignored for more abstract critiques.

Comparing perspectives of sport

Functionalists clearly place an enormous value on sport, but there are other important issues that have been considered in this chapter yet carry less significance for functionalists; they are considerations of power. A neo-Marxist perspective on sport recognises that sport, like society, can liberate, for example by offering opportunities, and at the same time constrain, by reducing choice through processes of discrimination. Feminist writers and practitioners in the field have also acknowledged power differentials in society. However, in this case the differences are due to a male-dominated or patriarchal system that results in a more oppressive society for girls and women than for boys and men. So gender relations are a primary source of focus here. Other related areas and issues build upon many of the arguments by neo-Marxist and feminist thinkers. 'Race' and ethnicity, class, disability and age among others are crucial concerns for the enlightened practitioner. These issues are not mutually exclusive in that individuals are identified by, and identify with, combinations of these socio-economic variables.

Comparing perspectives of sport development

Table 3.8 indicates that functionalism is one view which takes as its basic premise that broad agreement typifies the way that sport and sport development is structured and functions in society. The ability of individuals and groups to access opportunities in society and sport is based upon combined interest groups. Simply, if something has not been set up or established in society then individuals in society do not see a need for it. If this point is applied to Lottery funding, then, if particular groups in society are accessing funding and others are not, the funding should still be going to the right places because some groups are showing interest in terms of organisation and application.

A neo-Marxist viewpoint accepts that there are constraints at the same time as there is a level of agency in sport and society. Even a local authority which is proactive in its sport equality work may be working against a backdrop of historically inadequate resourcing which still causes the limitation of choice and opportunities. This is the context for many practitioners and policy makers in sport. This is also a challenge for the development of Sport for All.

Postmodernists base their views on the development of sport and society on an analysis and description of the speed of change and the fragmentation of society. They reflect upon how technology, structures, processes and practices today no longer resemble the form they had yesterday, for example the difference between the 1980s and the 2000s. In sport development the multi-agency, cross-departmental work, common in the achievement of best value for the customer, is one example

68

Table 3.8 Interpretations of sport development

Functionalist	Sport development polices gaps in provision and participation. It distributes social justice in the face of market trends. It circumvents barriers to participation. It spreads the benefits of sport. It presides over competing plural interests. It advocates on behalf of marginalised interests. It applies the glue to bind diverse strands into an integrated whole
Neo-Marxist	Sport development reflects conflict between the interests of dominant groups and institutions, and the needs and wants of subordinate groups and individuals. It illustrates social tensions between structures and free agency. It perpetuates the dominant agenda, and can act as a site of resistance to that agenda
Feminist	Overall, sport development perpetuates sport as a patriarchal institution. Token attempts are made to incorporate more women into sport without challenging the fundamentally patriarchal nature of its institutions and culture. However, it does also offer some limited opportunities for women to infiltrate and reclaim previously masculine territory
Postmodernist	Sport development reflects an institutional anxiety to exercise control and impose order in an increasingly disorganised world. It attempts to navigate a complex map of diverse sources of provision and motivations for participation. It is prone to a layering of disparate influences at local, regional, national and transnational levels. It is insecure. The only constant is change

of a significant shift in the industry. Another example of the shift in practices is the way that proof of sport's worth is part of the move towards more accountability. This was not part of its dominant discourse in the 1970s and 1980s.

Comparing perspectives of 'Sport for All' and inclusion

Having taken a theoretical detour to set the scene, let us return specifically to Sport for All. The different ways of interpreting Sport for All in Table 3.9 are starting points to understand why Sport for All's objectives and equality in sport development are rarely acclaimed uniformly across the profession. You can analyse the following perspectives of Sport for All and, as before, critically evaluate the worth of each. Subsequent sections of this chapter will turn more directly to consider policy and practice, but it is hoped that you will continue to exercise your sociological imagination throughout.

SPORT POLICY ADDRESSING INEQUALITY

So inequality is a significant cause of social exclusion whereby individuals or communities are unable, for a variety of reasons, to participate with others. In sport development, unless there is recognition of the needs and aspirations of diverse people in society and among client groups, providers will continue to maintain

Table 3.9 Interpretations of 'Sport for All' and inclusion

Functionalist	In a maturing society, equity and inclusion are ultimately and inevitably achievable. Historical inequities in sport are gradually eroded. Social consensus necessitates inclusion. The social system is committed to a project of inclusion. Exclusion is 'dysfunctional' and undesirable
Neo-Marxist	Sport for All is unlikely to happen against the backdrop of a capitalist society, which is based on competition and inequality. Sport reflects and reinforces this. Power struggles in sport mirror those in society. Sport is a site of cultural struggle. This struggle includes the vested political and commercial interests of the dominant culture, the diverse self-interests of communities, and the emancipatory interests of the oppressed. The need to redistribute opportunity is paramount to create a fairer society
Feminist	In recent years, there has been partial success in terms of addressing numerical inequalities in participation, but women are still institutionally excluded from the governance of sport. Ultimately the quality of women's and men's experiences in sport is still vastly unequal. The culture of sport is still male-dominated. Gender equity in sport is impossible in the context of a broader patriarchal society
Postmodernist	Concepts such as sports equality and inclusion are outmoded. There is nothing objectively fixed to determine inclusion or exclusion. Society is increasingly influenced by global processes which lead to the redundancy of traditional boundaries, social structures and inequalities. Class, gender and ethnic boundaries are collapsing. Lifestyle and identity are increasingly individualised and self-determined through consumption, like sport

inequalities in society. An example of a sport equality policy initiative is the Brighton Declaration (International Working Group on Women and Sport 1994), which was written by national and international policy makers to develop a sporting culture that would enable and value the full involvement of women in every aspect of sport. The major areas of the declaration revolve around the following guiding themes.

- equity and equality in society and sport;
- facilities;
- school and junior sport;
- developing participation;
- high-performance sport;
- leadership in sport;
- education, training and development;
- sports information and research resources;
- domestic and international cooperation.

Similarly, at the conclusion of the UK presidency of the European Commission in 2005 a meeting of European sports ministers supported the recommendation to promote equal opportunities and diversity in and through sport at both the national and European levels (European Union, 2005).

70

Research, equality and sport development

The case study at the end of this chapter focuses on the London borough of Greenwich and considers how economic and social objectives can be successfully balanced in a robust and transparent way. Documented experiences of sport and recreation's inability to work consistently towards equality have led writers and practitioners to look in detail at the reasons for this lack of success. Carrol (1993), Horne (1995), Swinney and Horne (2005) and Spracklen *et al.* (2006) have all concluded that a policy implementation gap exists or emerges between formulation and implementation of equal opportunities strategies. This in itself carries implications for prospects of success in any organisation.

Horne (1995), and Swinney and Horne (2005) have identified three types of local authority provider and labelled them gestural, reactive and proactive (see Table 3.5). Gestural authorities included those that had a policy or policy statement but did not feel it necessary to go beyond that step, whereas the reactive authorities would have a policy but would not have a rigorous and actively monitored plan to work towards equality. In fact they would react to demand from their local communities, which might have the effect of 'the louder you shout the more you get'. Proactive authorities had policy statements and plans and were actively working towards achieving their goals. Unfortunately, only a few organisations were placed in the proactive category; most tended to react to local community and staff needs rather than plan ahead. When Swinney and Horne (2005) revisited Horne's (1995) work, they came to similar conclusions about uneven practices among sport providers, between their rhetoric and what they implement. Spracklen and colleagues (2006) also revisited a study that considered the impact of racial equality in sport organisations, Sporting Equals Equality Standards (Long *et al.*, 2003, 2005). This study arrived at similar conclusions about the symbolic but superficial use of racial equality standards, as nearly all the governing bodies consulted reported little or no change in their organisation's equity policies in the preceding twelve months.

In *Anyone for Cricket?* (McDonald 1998), research commissioned by the Essex Cricket Association and the London Cricket Association, the task was to find out why black and Asian teams tended not to affiliate to the county association. The research recognised that institutional systems were not enough to effect lasting change, but a critical mass of people was needed to be motivated to change the culture of the sport. In fact the research gave an indication of where to begin but, owing to the size of the task, was vague on how it was to be achieved. The English Cricket Board followed this work up in 1999 with further research, *Clean Bowl Racism*, where it reinforced the notion that the majority of those researched (58 per cent) believe that there is racism in the sport (ECB Racism Study Group: 8).

All organisations vary in their ability to implement all-embracing equality initiatives. Hylton (2003) examined three local authorities in England and compared

Table 3.10 Interpretations of sport policy

Functionalist	There is broad satisfaction with the current organisation of sport, and the value of the role that sport plays in society. There is conservative support for the status quo and milder liberal reforms. Minor reform acknowledges 'dysfunctional' exceptions in need of remedy but their extent does not threaten the overall institutionalised arrangements
Neo-Marxist	Attention is drawn to the institutionalised and unequal distribution of power within sport, how that supports the interests of dominant groups and how other groups' interests are marginalised or even oppressed. Given the all-pervasiveness of injustice, radical reforms are imperative
Feminist	There are differences of opinion about the extent to which patriarchy is institutionalised. So, whereas there are some arguments for stronger liberal reform to advance 'a level playing field of opportunity', there are also some arguments for a much more radical approach, even separatism
Postmodernist	The collapse in influence of the traditional institutions is envisaged, and the growth, and importance, of individualised cultural choice is predicted and championed. Accordingly, less paternalistic reforms are favoured which empower individuals rather than specified groups

their operational environments. The three authorities varied in size, location, history, industry, wealth, demography, politics and policies, although they were similar in their diversity of local people, especially where 'race' and ethnicity were concerned. Each authority was publicly committed to 'Equal Opportunities'. After further analysis it was found, through comparing each authority, that their political and professional commitment to equal opportunities work was not the same as the rhetoric. Differences in perception and focus on equality of opportunity, local politics and policies and related variables all impacted upon the quality of equal opportunities work in each organisation.

Analysing the impact of strategies in sport can often reveal some of the glitches in what many would see as a rational decision-making process (see Chapter 2 above). Young and Connolly (1984) categorised over 100 local authorities in order to understand the work that they had conducted towards policy development and implementation in equal opportunities. They stated that there were those who:

- as a matter of political preference set their minds against change and were prepared to ignore the requirements of their (statutory) duties;
- were reviewing their policies but were moving cautiously forward in a fairly conventional manner albeit with a willingness to accept the need for change;
- were aware of a changed social, moral and legal climate presenting a challenge to traditional practices but were not sure of the appropriate response;
- were testing out the political and legal possibilities and developing approaches aimed at giving a fair deal to people.

72

If policy approaches were to be considered from the previous sociological perspectives the conclusions in Table 3.10 could be drawn.

Addressing inequality in practice

A sport organisation in context

The Rugby Football League (RFL) has been at the forefront of national governing bodies of sport proactively engaged in work on equality and diversity. Though 'sport for all' is a common mantra inside and outside the industry, sport can be accused of offering piecemeal and ad hoc approaches to these important issues (Hylton, 2010; Long *et al.*, 2009; Spracklen *et al.*, 2006). The RFL commitment to equality and diversity is based on three core beliefs: that *it is the right thing to do*, *it makes good business sense* and *there is an obligation to comply with legislation*. The RFL states that its moral and social responsibility to ensure rugby league is inclusive and welcoming is reflected in the core values of the national governing body's (NGB) core values (care, share, fair and dare) and the wider values of the game (passionate, inclusive, uncompromising and a family sport). These can be set within Bagilhole's (2009: 29) framework on equality and diversity, which described equality and diversity work as (1) aiming for equality for all, (2) social justice, (3) saying no to discrimination, (4) making the best use of human resources, (5) making services accessible, (6) offering a fair chance for jobs and (7) meeting legal obligations. By pursuing this agenda the RFL argues that rugby league is continuing its strategy of being a welcoming and inclusive sport.

Each sector and organisation has its own unique context, economies of scale and organisational culture which will impact upon the implementation of equality initiatives. The Badminton Association of England (Badminton England) is another national NGB that saw a need to implement an equality strategy that would assist the sport in becoming more representative of society (Badminton Association of England, 2006). The organisation's staff decided that there was a problem and that the problem itself needed some form of definition. What brought the Association to this point was a series of acknowledgements by the staff. These acknowledgements recognised the following catalysts for action:

- image/profile: predominantly white male middle-class, stuffy, all-white kit;
- administration/coaching: very few black and ethnic minority coaches, women and disabled people;
- executive members: not close to reflecting the population mix;
- no equal opportunities strategy or monitoring: unable to get an accurate profile of coaches and players.

In today's economic climate there is increasing pressure to justify all expenditure and to cut back on services that are not essential to the core business. This has affected equality and diversity initiatives in many sport governing bodies. By contrast the RFL believes that, when there is an increasingly competitive market and reduced resources, inclusive policies and practices can lead to growth and have significant benefits to rugby league, such as:

1 opening up new markets;
2 being more responsive to diverse communities;
3 increasing the talent pool;
4 improving retention and customer loyalty;
5 securing funding and sponsorship; and
6 becoming the employer and sport of choice.

This is supported by Collier's analysis of equality in organisations when he states that: 'By incorporating equality and diversity principles an organisation should be able to reach a wider public, respond to varied needs and offer satisfaction to a more diverse group of customers' (Collier, 1998: 14). Equality strategies that attempt to rebalance historical inequalities are sometimes criticised for their denial of resources to those whose status in the past has rendered them privileged. However, contrary to popular opinion, this work by the RFL is not purely focused on groups commonly described as minorities but also counters the exclusion of, discrimination against and disadvantage of women, who make up more than half of the population. This is no lame liberal wish list but one that has been recognised for some time and now has the support of law, forcing many organisations to actively pursue an agenda that embraces equality and diversity. It must also be recognised that these social groups are not homogeneous and do intersect in ways that force governing bodies to become smarter in engaging marginalised communities.

Case study 3.1 shows how the London Olympic Borough of Greenwich has successfully attempted to balance the social and economic demands of a diverse resident community. In its quest to achieve equality in sport through best value, Greenwich has managed to satisfy the demands of the external inspectors in this respect, while still leaving itself an ongoing challenge of continual improvement.

SUMMARY

This chapter has raised and debated the contemporary relevance of the quest for Sport for All. It has identified continuing inequalities which permeate sport and society, and therefore the failure to realise Sport for All. In drawing attention to the social nature of inequality in sport, the chapter has advocated the importance

The London Olympic Borough of Greenwich has a population of over 200,000 with a significant black and minority ethnic population. The borough's strategy has as its central focus its role in planning and hosting the London 2012 Olympic and Paralympic Games and implementing its legacy promises beyond 2015.

The London Research Centre suggests that 10,000 people in the borough between sixteen and twenty-four years old are registered disabled. As in many multi-cultural settings, there are over 100 different languages in the borough. The Department of Transport, Local Government and the Regions ranked Greenwich forty-fourth in the Indices of Deprivation in 2000.

Greenwich has three key principles:

- *Inclusion and Cohesion:* We will continue to provide access to opportunities and services, allowing all our residents to take advantage of the benefits of living, working, learning in and visiting our borough.
- *Sustainability:* Our actions will meet the needs of the present without compromising the ability of future generations to meet their own needs.
- *Prosperity:* We will actively seek to make Greenwich competitive in economic terms, attracting investment and providing an environment that enables wealth to be created.

The 'vision' for the authority – the council's Community Plan – states that it is 'The place to live, work, learn, visit and play'. The four themes, Live, Work, Learn and Visit/Culture, are continued from the first Greenwich Strategy. The introduction of the two new themes, Greener Greenwich and Olympic and Paralympic Host Borough, represent the borough's commitment to changing agendas since the first Greenwich Strategy.

The authority's sport strategy for 2006–2015 built upon its 2001–2006 promises to harness the transformational power of sport, in all its forms, as an instrument for promoting social and economic change in a way that secures lasting improvements to the quality of life of all borough residents, irrespective of their racial or ethnic origin, gender, age, class, disability or sexuality. Greenwich was awarded a three-star rating from the Audit Commission (2008: 1), who stated that it is 'improving well'.

of 'active sociology' to practical sport development. It has considered policy approaches to addressing inequality and, finally, aspects of good practice.

Practitioners still occupy distinctive and different roles and responsibilities in the delivery and development of sport. This can cause strategic tensions in the provision of sport, and perennial competition for resources. Sport development can be viewed in a number of different ways by practitioners, policy makers and academics. The significance of sport in society is beyond question. The future of sport and its consequent development in society are also beyond question. Its exact role, however, is in dispute when it comes to developing Sport for All. Concepts such as Sport for All, 'equality', 'social exclusion' and 'equity' are problematic because they are complex and require critical sport developers to engage with them intellectually as well as in a practical sense. This exacerbates the complexity of policy decisions and the practices that sport development workers aim to implement. Sport development workers and policy makers have a variety of challenges facing them in the twenty-first century. The continued development of opportunities for people in sport is consistently questioned when key stakeholders have differing aims, objectives and basic philosophies about their role and place in developing sport.

It was previously stated that 'sport affects society and society affects sport'. This relationship can be described as dialectical, or symbiotic. Thompson's (2003) PCS model illustrates how empowering and disempowering processes and practices essentially cut both ways. Individuals in sport and society reproduce inequality, but it can be challenged at each of the three levels as outlined by Thompson. A fairer arrangement cannot be achieved in one and not the others. So the marriage of sport and policy is more than just one of convenience. According to the UK Social Exclusion Unit Taskforce, social exclusion is constraining the opportunities of members of society, and therefore those in sport should respond accordingly. Sport can play a part in reducing the constraints which exclude social groups. Sport developers can help to reduce social exclusion by enhancing community development opportunities, social cohesion, equal opportunities, crime prevention and community safety, lifelong learning, active healthy lifestyles, social and economic regeneration, job creation and environmental protection. The following chapter, on community sport development, develops these ideas further.

Significantly, there is no clear consensus on the importance of unconditionally increasing access for disenfranchised groups in sport. This is a result of competing viewpoints and causes. Sociological perspectives should begin to stimulate the sociological imagination to illustrate different ways of seeing sport development and inclusive sport. Effective sport development workers (active sociologists) should be able to use the appropriate analytical tools and research available to them to ensure that they 'work smart' in trying to address inequality.

LEARNING ACTIVITIES

Have a look at the Equality Standard (www.equalitystandard.org/).

1 Identify the four levels of evidence that national governing organisations must achieve.
2 Identify how your favourite sport is doing and state why you think it is at that point.
3 State what you think it needs to do to get to the next level.

Kevin Hylton and Mick Totten

REFERENCES

Audit Commission (2008) *London Borough of Greenwich Sport and Leisure Provision, Best Value Inspection*, London: Audit Commission.

Badminton Association of England (2006) 'Badminton Association of England Targets', www. badmintonengland.co.uk/text.asp?section=0001000100110001

Bagilhole, B. (1997) *Equal Opportunities and Social Policy*, London: Longman.

Bagilhole, B. (2009) *Understanding Equal Opportunities and Diversity: The Social Differentiations and Intersections of Inequality*, Bristol: The Policy Press.

Blakemore, K. and Drake, R. (1996) *Understanding Equal Opportunity Policies*, London: Prentice Hall.

Carrington, B. and McDonald, I. (eds.) (2009) *Marxism, Cultural Studies and Sport*, London: Routledge.

Carrol, B. (1993) 'Sporting bodies, sporting opportunities', in Brackenridge, C. (ed.), *Body Matters: Leisure Images and Lifestyles*, Eastbourne: Leisure Studies Association.

Clarke, A. (1994) 'Leisure and the new managerialism', in Clarke, J., Cochrane, A. and McLaughlin, E. (eds.), *Managing Social Policy*, London: Sage.

Coakley, J. and Dunning, E. (2000) *Handbook of Sports Studies*, London: Sage.

Coalter, F. (1998) 'Leisure studies, leisure policy and social citizenship: the failure of welfare or the limits of welfare?', *Leisure Studies*, 17: 21–36.

Cockburn, C. (1989) 'Equal opportunities', *Industrial Relations Journal*, 20 (3): 213–225.

CoE (Council of Europe) (2001) Recommendation No. R (92) 13 Rev of the Committee of Ministers to Member States on the Revised European Sports Charter.

Coe, S. (2006) 'Mandela backs London's Olympic Bid', *Mail Online*, www.dailymail.co.uk/sport/othersports/article-343953/Mandela-backs-London-Olympic-Bid.html

Collier, R. (1998) *Equality in Managing Delivery*, Buckingham: Open University Press.

Collins, M. and Kay, T. (2003) *Sport and Social Exclusion*, London: Routledge.

Commission for Racial Equality (1995) *Racial Equality Means Equality*, London: CRE.

Cunningham, S. (1992) 'The development of Equal Opportunities theory and practice in the European Community', *Policy and Politics*, 20 (3): 177–189.

DePauw, K. and Gavron, P. (2005) *Disability Sport*, Leeds: Human Kinetics.

Desai, M. (1995) *Equality*, London: LSE.

ECB Racism Study Group (1999) *Clean Bowl Racism – Going Forward Together: A Report on Racial Equality in Cricket*, London: England and Wales Cricket Baord.

Eckstein, R., Moss, D. and Delaney, K. (2010) 'Sports sociology's still untapped potential', *Sociological Forum*, 25 (3): 500–518.

Edwards, J. (1990) 'What purpose does equality of opportunity serve?', *New Community*, 7 (1): 19–35.

Eichberg, H. (2009) 'Bodily democracy: towards a philosophy of sport for all', *Sport, Ethics and Philosophy*, 3 (3): 441–461.

Ellis, J. (1994) 'Developing sport through CCT', *Recreation*, 53 (9): 31–33.

EPPI/Matrix (2010) *Culture and Sport Evidence: Understanding the Drivers of Engagement in Culture and Sport*, London: DCMS.

Equal Opportunities Commission (1996) *Mainstreaming Gender Equality in Local Government*, London: EOC.

Escott, K. (1996) *Equal Opportunities Strategy for CCT*, London: Centre for Public Services Organisations.

Etzioni, A. (1961) *A Comparative Analysis of Complex Organizations*, New York: Free Press.

EU, C. o. t. (2010) *Education Youth Culture and Sport*, Brussels: European Union.

European Union (2005) 'UK Presidency of the EU 2005', www.eu2005.gov.uk

Fitzgerald, H. (2005) 'Still feeling like a spare piece of luggage? Embodied experiences of (dis) ability in physical education and school sport', *Physical Education and Sport Pedagogy*, 10 (1): 41–59.

Forbes, I. (1991) 'Equal opportunity: radical, liberal and conservative critiques', in Meehan, E. and Sevenhuijsen, S. (eds.), *Equality Politics and Gender*, London: Sage.

FRA (2010) *Racism, Ethnic Discrimination and Exclusion of Migrants and Minorities in Sport: A Comparative Overview of the Situation in the European Union*, Vienna: European Union Agency for Fundamental Rights.

Giddens, A. (2006) *Sociology*, Cambridge: Polity Press.

Gillborn, D. (2005) 'It takes a nation of millions . . .', in Richardson, B. (ed.), *Tell It Like It Is: How Our Schools Fail Black Kids*, Stoke on Trent: Trentham Books.

Gratton, C. and Jones, I. (2004) *Research Methods for Sports Studies*, London: Routledge.

Hargreaves, J. (2002) 'Globalisation theory, global sport, and nations and nationalism', in Sugden, J. and Tomlinson, A. (eds.), *Power Games: A Critical Sociology of Sport*, London: Routledge.

Horne, J. (1995) 'Local authority black and ethnic minority provision in Scotland', in Talbot, M., Fleming, S. and Tomlinson, A. (eds.), *Policy and Politics in Sport, Physical Education and Leisure*, Brighton: Leisure Studies Association.

Houlihan, B. and White, A. (2002) *The Politics of Sport Development*, London: Routledge.

Hylton, K. (2003) *Local Government 'Race' and Sports Policy Implementation*, unpublished PhD thesis, Leeds Metropolitan University.

Hylton, K. (2005) '"Race", sport and leisure: lessons from critical race theory', *Leisure Studies*, 24 (1): 81–98.

Hylton, K. (2009) *'Race' and Sport: Critical Race Theory*, London: Routledge.

Hylton, K. (2010) 'How a turn to critical race theory can contribute to our understanding of "race", racism and anti-racism in sport: interrogating boundaries of "race" and ethnicity in sport', *International Review for the Sociology of Sport*, 45 (3): 335–354.

International Working Group on Women and Sport (1994) *Brighton Declaration on Women and Sport*, Brighton: IWG.

Jarvie, G. (2006) *Sport, Culture and Society*, Abingdon: Routledge.

Jewson, N. and Mason, D. (1986) '"Race" employment and Equal Opportunities: towards a political economy and an agenda for the 1990s', *Sociological Review*, 42 (4): 591–617.

Jewson, N. and Mason, D. (1992) 'The theory and practice of Equal Opportunities policies: liberal and radical approaches', in Braham P., Rattansi, A. and Skellington, R. (eds.), *Racism and Anti-racism: Inequalities, Opportunities and Policies*, London: Sage.

Ledwith, M. (2005) *Community Development: A Critical Approach*, Bristol: Policy Press.

Levitas, R. (1998) *The Inclusive Society? Social Exclusion and New Labour*, London: Macmillan.

Long, J. (2007) *Researching Leisure, Sport and Tourism: The Essential Guide*, London: Sage.

Long, J. and Hylton, K. (2002) 'Shades of white: an examination of whiteness in sport', *Leisure Studies*, 21 (2): 87–103.

Long, J., Robinson, P. and Welch, M. (2003) *Raising the Standard: An Evaluation of Progress*, Leeds: Leeds Metropolitan University.

Long, J., Robinson, P. and Spracklen, K. (2005) 'Promoting racial equality within sports organizations', *Journal of Sport and Social Issues*, 29: 41–59.

Long, J., Hylton, K., Ratna, A., Spracklen, K. and Bailey, S. (2009) 'A systematic review of the literature on black and ethnic minority communities in sport and physical recreation', conducted for Sporting Equals and the Sports Councils by the Carnegie Research Institute, Leeds Metropolitan University, www.sportingequals.org.uk/resources.php?resources_ID=1#anchor

Loy, J. and Booth, D. (2000) 'Functionalism, sport and society', in Coakley, J. and Dunning, E. (eds.), *Handbook of Sports Studies*, London: Sage.

78

McDonald, I. (1998) *Anyone for Cricket?*, London: University of East London.

Messner, M. (1992) *Power at Play: Sport and the Problem of Masculinity*, Boston, MA: Beacon Press.

Mills, C. W. (1970) *The Sociological Imagination*, Harmondsworth: Penguin.

Mintel Leisure Intelligence (2006) *Leisure Time UK*, London: Mintel Intelligence Group.

Mithaug, D. (1996) *Equal Opportunity Theory*, London: Sage.

Polley, M. (1998) *Moving the Goalposts: The History of Sport and Society from 1945*, London: Routledge.

Poynter, G. and MacRury, I. (eds.) (2009) *Olympic Cities: 2012 and the Remaking of London*, Farnham: Ashgate.

Rail, G. (ed.) (1998) *Sport and Postmodern Times*, New York: State University of New York Press.

Rawls, J. (1971) *A Theory of Justice*, London: Oxford University Press.

Rheker, U. (2000) *Integration through Games and Sports*, Oxford: Meyer & Meyer.

Rigauer, B. (2000) 'Marxist theories', in Coakley, J. and Dunning, E. (eds.), *Handbook of Sports Studies*, London: Sage.

Room, G. (ed.) (1995) *Beyond the Threshold: The Measurement and Analysis of Social Exclusion*, Bristol: Policy Press.

Saraga, S. (ed.) (1998) *Embodying the Social Construction of Difference*, London: Routledge.

Schirato, T. and Webb, J. (2003) *Understanding Globalisation*, London: Sage.

Scraton, S. and Flintoff, A. (2002) 'Sport feminism: the contribution of feminist thought to our understanding of gender and sport', in Scraton, S. and Flintoff, A. (eds.), *Gender and Sport: A Reader*, London: Routledge.

Social Exclusion Unit Taskforce (2012) 'Facts', http://webarchive.nationalarchives.gov.uk/+/http://www.cabinetoffice.gov.uk/facts/socialexclusion.aspx

Sport England (2001) *Sports Equity Index*, London: Sport England.

Sport England (2002a) *Participation in Sport in England*, London: Sport England.

Sport England (2002b) *Adults with a Disability and Sport Survey*, London: Sport England.

Sport England (2012) 'Active People Survey', www.sportengland.org/research/active_people_survey_6.aspx/

Sports Council (1993) *Compulsory Competitive Tendering Sport and Leisure Management*, National Information Survey report, London: Sports Council.

Spracklen, K., Hylton, K. and Long, J. (2006) 'Managing and monitoring equality and diversity in UK sport', *Journal of Sport and Social Issues*, 30 (3): 289–305.

Swinney, A. and Horne, J. (2005) 'Race equality and leisure policy: discourses in Scottish local authorities', *Leisure Studies*, 24 (3): 271–289.

Taylor, G. (1994) *Equal Opportunities*, London: Industrial Society.

Thompson, N. (2003) *Promoting Equality: Challenging Discrimination and Oppression*, Houndmills: Palgrave Macmillan.

UK Sport (2010) 'UK Sport Equality and Diversity Strategy 2010–2013', www.uksport.gov.uk/pages/policies-and-strategies/

UNCSD (2010) 'Since 1995 Progress Made Promoting Inclusion of Marginalized Groups, but Challenges to Social Development Remain 'Daunting', Under-Secretary-General Tells Commission', www.un.org/News/Press/docs/2010/soc4758.doc.htm

Veal, A. J. (1992) *Research Methods for Leisure and Tourism*, London: Longman.

Young, K. (1989) 'The space between words: local authorities and the concept of Equal Opportunities', in Jenkins, R. and Solomos, J. (eds.), *Racism and Equal Opportunities in the 1980s*, Cambridge: Cambridge University Press.

Young, K. and Connolly, N. (1984) 'After the Act: local authorities' policy reviews under the Race Relations Act, 1976', *Local Government Studies*, 10 (1): 13–25.

CHAPTER 4

COMMUNITY SPORT DEVELOPMENT

KEVIN HYLTON AND MICK TOTTEN

This chapter examines some of the structural changes in community sport development as policies and sports organisations have adapted over time. It also considers how the inevitability of change over the years has not significantly reduced the necessity for alternatives to mainstream provision. The previous chapter, on Sport for All, emphasised how sport development has struggled to engage some social groups and communities, and it is often towards community sport practitioners that policy makers turn for answers to this failure. For many involved in community sport development, the experience of cyclical change in policy and practice reinforces the view from experienced practitioners on how effectively others have learned (or not) from past successes and failures. This chapter aims to uncover the essence of these changes and so explore the fundamental ideals of community sport development. Further, the dynamics of the situated practice of community sport development are considered in relation to divergent forms of community sport development.

Community sport development is a form of practice that conveys a philosophy and spirit which address many themes raised in the previous chapter on Sport for All. It arose as a response to enduring concerns about inequality and issues around equal opportunities and participation in sport. An understanding of the precise meaning of community sport development (hereafter most often referred to as CSD) will be developed in this chapter, but a cursory glance would reveal that CSD is more than sport in the community. It is also a form of provision which addresses social and political concerns about the nature and extent of inequality, significantly demonstrated by its genesis being concurrent with 'Sport for All?' in the 1970s.

This chapter analyses significant tensions and issues in the theory, policy and practice of CSD. It considers delivery models ranging from 'top-down' to 'bottom-up' and explores CSD from social, cultural and political perspectives. Theoretical concerns about policy, process and practice are grounded throughout by specific examples

80

of practice. We start with an exploration of three key concepts and issues: sport development, community development and 'community' itself. We then examine the complex sectors, levels and partnerships in CSD provision. Next, CSD policy is considered, with a historical overview of the development of community sport policy leading to its contemporary context. Our analysis then shifts to a macroscopic view of different policy models and their rationales. These will be contextualised throughout by a case study of Action Sport located in inner-city areas in the north of England. CSD practice is then critically analysed against a policy backdrop of two further case studies in Leeds and Rochdale. In conclusion, CSD will then be reconsidered and re-evaluated by drawing on the concept of hegemony.

CONCEPTUALISING COMMUNITY SPORT DEVELOPMENT

Community sport is often subsumed under the title of community recreation. This is in recognition that practice often reflects inclusive informal activities which blur the boundary between sport and recreation; some activities at first glance seem hardly to constitute sport at all. Community sport is provided through many different types of organisation. It is not solely the preserve of local authority leisure services or of sport development officers. It is mostly located in the public sector, often also in the voluntary sector, but seldom in the commercial sector. It is practised in youth and community work, social services, probation services, education and many other realms as well. Community sport originally arose out of the realisation that traditional participation patterns were dominated by advantaged sections of the population and that an alternative approach was needed. In conceptualising community sport, it must be understood as a contested concept (Coalter and Allison, 1996; Haywood, 1994; Houlihan and White, 2002; Lentell, 1994; McDonald, 1995). With shifting politics and changes in terminology over time, 'community sport' has been interpreted by different bodies, organisations and individuals in substantially different ways.

Community Sport Networks (CSNs) were established under New Labour in an attempt to rationalise the fragmented structure of sport into a new 'delivery system for sport' (Sport England Delivery Plan, 2005a: 1). CSNs were essentially alliances of local providers hosted by a lead organisation, such as a local authority, which worked with partners from a mix of sectors. The new coalition government established in 2010 has since led to a change in emphasis and a move towards a more voluntary sector focus under the auspices of 'Big Society'. This has led to the establishment of community sports hubs (CSHs) whose 'primary objective is to create new industry best practice and sustainable community sports provision, which can be replicated across the country' (Sport England, 2012). Sport England (2011) sees this as the 'growth and maturing of the third sector' in response to cuts in public provision amid a downturn in the economy. This growth envisages asset transfers to community ownership, social enterprise and public–private hybrids, and the integration of services contributing to wider social policy areas such as health, childcare provision and lifelong learning, all with the aim of enhancing sustainability. Sportscotland envisages its contribution to the Scottish Government's 2014 legacy plan as 'an exciting and innovative approach to increase the number of people of all ages participating in sport in communities across Scotland' by 'providing information, support and advice on a wide range of sports and physical activities to make it easier for local people to get involved and engage in a more active and healthier lifestyle' (Sportscotland, 2011). A generic notion of 'community' is being applied here which includes joint working in mainstream provision and the more alternative forms of provision that have more recently been considered under the umbrella of CSD.

To complicate matters further, there are many instances where it is claimed that community sport is practised when in fact it is not. Certain agencies have 'hijacked' the word 'community' as a flag of convenience because of its perceived 'feel-good' value and currency with policy makers (Butcher *et al.*, 1993: 3). This has variously been described as deploying community as 'a fashionable label with virtually no recognition that a particular set of practices and values is implied' (Haywood, 1994: 27; see also Standing Conference on Community Development, 2001) and as often 'sprayed on' purely to lend legitimacy and positive feelings, credence and acceptability (Plant *et al.*, 1980). Many very senior providers at both national and local levels are prone to such accusations, as are smaller-scale organisations. Not everything which claims to be CSD really is. There are frauds and imposters out there who may be involved in community sport for other reasons than to develop or significantly benefit the community. There are at least four possible reasons why this might take place: income generation, talent identification, public relations and marketing. Organisations whose primary purpose is mainstream sports participation, which include some local authorities, national governing bodies (NGBs) and professional sports clubs, know that they may be more likely to receive funding or other support if they portray a 'community' or social focus. Terry Smith, a councillor in the north-west of England, describes one example thus:

> In America storm chasers charge around the country taking pictures of storms and then sell them on. Over here we have SRB [Single Regeneration Bid] chasers who come from outside the community to take what they can from the projects [financially], denying those on the streets any opportunity.
>
> (cited in Morgan, 2000: 30)

Another more cynical use of the term 'community sport' was revealed in research by the Centre for Leisure and Sport Research (2003) about a sports club which received an 'Awards for All' grant on the premise that it would develop opportunities for black and minority ethnic young people. However, there were no black young people in the group or in the surrounding catchment area. Like many other projects it received funding because it understood the salience of social goals in sport policy and the attractiveness of community sport in sport-funding mechanisms (Jackson *et al.*, 2003).

Talent identification, public relations and marketing are major motivations behind many projects (though not all) such as 'Football in the Community'. Some professional clubs may well go into schools to provide short-term coaching sessions which bring some community benefit, but this operation acts as an opportunity for talent spotters who later may invite only the most talented young people for further coaching. This provision is primarily focused on ability, not need. The Football in the Community schemes are generally aimed at encouraging more people (especially children) to play and watch football; promoting closer links between professional football clubs and the local community; encouraging more people to become interested in and support their local club; and maximising community facilities and their community use at football clubs. Some football (and also similar rugby) clubs in the community schemes offer free tickets for young people to attend games but only on condition that their parents then buy tickets to 'accompany their child'. The professional clubs also know that, peculiar to sport, potential 'customers' define themselves as 'fans' and an affiliation initiated most likely creates a customer for life, so early recruitment is most profitable.

Other examples of marketing ploys would include corporate sponsorship such as that of Cadbury Schweppes's (2006) 'Get Active' programme designed to support the training of teachers and to supply schools with equipment, but only if they could generate enough tokens in wrappers bought from sweet packets, in another seemingly controversial step into 'community sport'. Cadbury also extended its profile in sport at an elite level with its 'spots versus stripes' campaign that highlighted its London 2012 Olympic Partner status. *The Guardian* (2011) claims that schemes such as these are really about retailers boosting their profiles and profits and do not provide value for money. It calculates that for Sainsbury's supermarket's Active Kids vouchers scheme a skipping rope equates to a £280 spend, and assorted-colour bean bags to a £2,490 spend.

Local factors dictate the emphasis of each project, as some may have more of a football focus than others, which have a closer connection with communities (FA Premier League, 2006). The Football Foundation (2006) has been involved with some Football in the Community schemes that have worked with disabled, anti-racist, anti-crime, healthy lifestyles and tenants-based groups that have built capacity, new skills, empowered and motivated different communities through the game of football.

So in addition to all this good work there are those involved in community sport whose emphasis is the development of sport, which may lead to other externalities, rather than the development of community. However, in order to progress, CSD will be referred to as a form of intervention in sport and recreation provision which in some way addresses inequalities inherent in more established, mainstream sport provision.

SPORT, DEVELOPMENT AND COMMUNITY

The term 'sport development' (also taken to include more informal aspects such as recreation) dictates that something or someone is indeed developed. This suggests either some form of professional intervention or local voluntary action. Various models have been developed by NGBs of sport, local authorities and other key stakeholders in sport to characterise the nature and intent of these interventions. Chapter 1 illustrated various sport development continua. What each of these continua share is a distinction in type or level of development within sport. They imply a hierarchical meritocratic progression through levels from participation towards performance and excellence, so the primary focus of development is very much on traditional established sports, and community sport is subsumed therein. In short, they are elitist. However, community sport development is not solely concerned with the development of sport. It is not simply 'sport in the community'. It also encompasses the realm of 'community development'. Such models do not necessarily value community sport as an entity in its own right; they conceive of it primarily as a staging post, creating a wider participatory base, from which to identify talent and improve performance, so an alternative continuum can and should be developed which values the primacy of the social role played by CSD (Figure 4.1).

As this CSD continuum implies, different aspects of practice can be located with different degrees of emphasis at different points on the continuum. At one extreme is pure 'sport' development, or 'sport in the community', in which the practice of sport is an end in itself. Here practice does not stray beyond the primary focus of participation in sport, as sport development beyond participation is best catered for by other mainstream agencies. At the other extreme is sport as 'community development', in which sport is simply a means to human development. Accusations of the use of the term 'community' as a flag of convenience are mainly aimed at initiatives and organisations that fall into the left-hand side of the spectrum (sport development). Coalter (2002) restricts himself to exploring community sport as sport development practised in areas of social and economic deprivation. Haywood

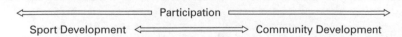

Figure 4.1 The community sport development continuum.

and Kew (1989) are critical of sport in the community; they describe it as 'old wine in new bottles'. It is the same sport as practised in the mainstream but simply repackaged. Community sport implies a much more fundamental adaptation or change of approach and practice. So what does it mean when sport engages in elements of community development?

Community

The term 'community', like 'community sport development', is contested and can be interpreted to have multiple meanings. Community implies some notion of collectivity, commonality, a sense of belonging or of something shared. A community can be self-determined by its members or it can be a label externally constructed and defined by some statutory agency. Either way, community can be imagined as much as it can be realised. It can be inhabited, as 'place', a specific locality or a geographical area. It can be an 'experience', through a gathering, an interest or affiliation to a social, leisure or sports activity. It can also be experienced as a shared identity, history or nostalgia, or as an action when engaged in some form of interactive process. It can be 'protective' of a way of being, or 'expansive' in terms of some aspiration (Brent, 2004; Butcher *et al.*, 1993; Chaskin, 1997; Fremeaux, 2005; Popple, 1995; Popple and Shaw, 1997). These dimensions of community can be illustrated in relation to the community activity of Sankt Pauli football fans (Totten, 2011). Sankt Pauli is a professional German football club from Hamburg whose fans enjoy an extraordinary reputation for left-wing political activism and an atmosphere like no other. Sankt Pauli exudes a strong sense of community, which can be understood as more than just about place. 'Place' certainly features as community for Sankt Pauli; the unique district of Hamburg, the Reeperbahn red-light drag, the Millerntor stadium, the Jolly Roger supporters bar, the Rota Flora nightclub squat and others. But community is also an 'interest' in the blend of football and far-left politics, an 'experience' on match day and nights and tours further afield, an 'action', supporting, campaigning and protesting, as well as 'imagined' as an ideal for a worldwide support network of hundreds of thousands with supporter bases across Germany and in many other countries, and through the symbolism of the Toten Kopf (the rebel skull and crossbones motif which identifies the club).

Analysis of community by place or locality is diminishing in the eyes of many academics, as social relations and society transcend locality as a result of increased personal mobility. However, this narrow model traditionally courts more favour from policy makers and is in greater evidence in working practice. In this approach the state has traditionally taken a leading role in identifying disadvantaged communities and in targeting groups of disenfranchised people. This approach also links with notions of community as shared identity. This deterministic concept of community has connotations of working-class status, shared experiences and living in the inner city. The inner city itself is further characterised by special social needs, high unemployment, high-density poor-quality housing, social disadvantage and concentrations of marginalised powerless groups. It would appear that the Olympic Delivery Authority (ODA) 'sold' London 2012 to the International Olympic Committee on the basis of the uniqueness of place, multiculturalism, community and history. Its use of a 'world in one city', an idealised, diverse but settled East End, was a successful combination of hope and hubris. 'Sold' on the promise of a sporting, cultural and community legacy, the wishful but prescriptive cloak of local and national community, cohesion and the additionality of community urban regeneration met many of the strategic legacy wishes of the IOC. Community and community development are of course neither exclusively urban nor exclusively working-class but these remain dominant images (Hylton and Morpeth, 2012: 7).

Community development

Community development challenges passive consumer culture. It is about community consultation, empowerment and involvement in sustainable transformative change. Community development actively promotes a participatory democracy (Ledwith, 2011). Work with communities ranges between external agencies imposing their deterministic approaches in a manipulative 'top-down' way and more 'bottom-up' interactive models of intervention through community self-help (Haywood *et al.*, 1994; Torkildsen, 2005). Figure 4.2 shows how Arnstein's 'Ladder of Citizen Participation' (Arnstein, 1969, reproduced by Gates and Stout, 1996) outlines a wide spectrum of approaches between those two extremes. The bottom rungs identify all too common forms of public non-participation experienced with mainstream sport, namely manipulation (social control through sport) and therapy (for example physiotherapy or anger management) whereby those with power retain absolute control over provision and dictate the nature of provision. The middle rungs identify informing, consultation and placation as forms of tokenism, which applies to much CSD provision and characterises a reluctance by many professionals to relinquish their control and engender deeper public involvement. The higher rungs on the ladder are what sustainable best practice in CSD aspires to, whereby citizen power is exercised from the bottom up in genuine partnerships between providers and communities, beyond that to degrees of delegated community power and ultimately to citizen control. Unfortunately this is seldom realised in practice, perhaps because most CSD workers are insufficiently trained in community development, but it does clearly signpost where CSD needs to aim in order to genuinely embrace community development goals. Any individual initiative can be located at a given point on that spectrum.

Rochdale community sports (Partington and Totten, 2012; see also Case study 4.2 below) is an example of a relatively 'bottom-up' approach jointly plotted by

86

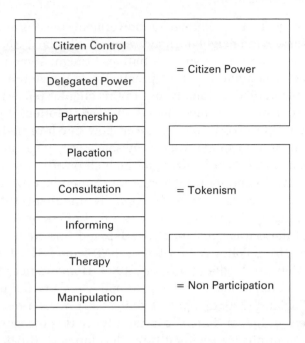

Figure 4.2 'A Ladder of Citizen Participation' (adapted from Arnstein, 1969, reproduced by Gates and Stout, 1996).

enabling professionals and the community, whereas the nationally driven Action Sport initiative (Rigg, 1986) is an example of a more 'top-down' policy that engendered both participatory as well as more conventional approaches to CSD. Booth (1997: 156) informs us that the community development approach is 'to facilitate the involvement of people in the participative structures. Community development is oiling the wheels of participation. It is "bottom-up".'

> Community development is a set of values and practices which plays a special role in overcoming poverty and disadvantage, knitting society together at the grass roots and deepening democracy. There are active citizens who use CD [community development] techniques on a voluntary basis, and there are also other professions and agencies which use a CD approach or some aspects of it . . . It is about strengthening the ability of people to act on joint interests and in the common interest, including having equal concern for other communities.
>
>   (Department for Communities and Local Government, 2006: 13–14)

Instances of attempts at community development practice in sport included the Active Communities Projects (Active Communities, 2002; Sport England, 2000), whose underpinning ideals resonated with the Association of Metropolitan

Authorities' (1989) goals: to encourage empowerment, devolution, self-determination, active citizenship and neighbourhood renewal. Similarly Sports Action Zones (Sport England, 2001) and other such initiatives brought something new to CSD. A classic example of community sport practice was the Action Sport project. It was originally implemented nationally, but in this chapter reference will be largely confined to research on the project based in Leeds (Totten, 1993). During this study, when Action Sport workers were asked how much of their work was community work as opposed to sports work, they saw a very large and significant part of their work as community work, owing to the high priority placed on community development activity (Standing Conference on Community Development, 2001). On balance, they saw sports work as fractionally dominant, though one worker described community sport (conceptually) as a part of community work. All concerned concluded there was substantial overlap and this was clearly reflected in policy and practice, from Policy Action Teams' PAT 9 and PAT 10 recommendations (Department for Culture, Media and Sport, 1999; Home Office, 1999) through to the joint government department guidance to policy makers and practitioners published by Sport England (2005b), *Sport: Playing Its Part*. As a result of recognition from policy makers and practitioners, community sport is recognised as a valuable tool to pursue community or socio-cultural development (Coalter, 2002; Coalter and Allison, 1996; Department for Culture, Media and Sport, 1999; Sport England, 2005b). The Community Development Exchange offers the following definition:

> Community Development is a long-term value based process which aims to address imbalances in power and bring about change founded on social justice, equality and inclusion.
>
> (CDX, 2013)

In the interests of transparency and ensuring that community development was indeed taking place, the PAT 10 report on Sport and the Arts (Department for Culture, Media and Sport, 1999: 41) devised a test for sports organisations that purported to be involved in community development. Many mainstream providers, governing bodies and voluntary groups perpetuate sporting inequalities because they are insensitive to some or all of the key principles that underpin working with marginalised or excluded communities. The PAT 10 test included ascertaining if the following are taking place: valuing diversity; embedding local control; supporting local commitment; promoting equitable partnerships; working with change; securing sustainability; pursuing quality; connecting with the mainstream. However, none of these ensures any form of challenge to power structures, and community development necessitates social transformation and anti-discriminatory action against broader social inequality.

Helping people find common cause on issues that affect them, helping people work together on such issues under their own control, building the strengths and independence of community groups, organisations and networks, building equity, inclusiveness, participation and cohesion amongst people and their groups and organisations, empowering people and their organisations where appropriate to influence and help transform public policies and services and other factors affecting the conditions of their lives, advising and informing public authorities on community needs, viewpoints and processes and assisting them to strengthen communities and work in genuine partnership with them.

(Department for Communities and Local Government, 2006: 39–40)

CSD does not exist in a 'sport bubble', as it requires an engagement with social justice. One consequence of practitioners and policy makers not considering community development principles is outlined by Ledwith (2011), who describes the pitfalls of 'thoughtless action' and 'actionless thought'. 'Thoughtless action' would include attempts at CSD which failed to engage with underlying social issues. 'Actionless thought' would be recognition of social issues but no plan for change. Clearly, when it comes to community development, CSD must represent a form of 'thoughtful action'. Thoughtful action is clearly energised when CSD is planned in a holistic way that incorporates the needs of all parties without recourse to short-term gains.

The identification of a critical praxis which challenges embedded inequalities and injustices with a view to creating social transformation through 'thoughtful action' is aspirational for best practice in CSD.

(Partington and Totten, 2012: 33)

Historically, sport has groped towards community development in a way which often perpetuates thoughtless action. Coalter (2002) produced a comprehensive attempt to apply sport to community development. It was written for professionals working with communities and offers some very good practical advice especially in its summary of best practice (Coalter, 2002: 32), where he is bolder in his assertions, which encapsulate issues to consider on CSD's journey to thoughtful action (see Table 4.1). However, the strength and weakness of this text is that it is a 'manual' for professionals. It does not consider more community-led practice, and community development is implicit but not remotely defined or distinguished from other forms of community practice. CSD must also engender critical consciousness and engage on a more philosophical or socio-political level from which to challenge existing power structures where a more critical theoretical perspective is desirable. Research on Rochdale community sports (Partington and Totten, 2012: 44) revealed that 'CSD practitioners need to be critically conscious, reflexive, and constantly

Table 4.1 Good practice in community sport development planning

Partnerships and agreed aims	It is not enough for partners and stakeholders to have shared agendas but they must also have jointly agreed ones too. There needs to be empathy between partners and clear commitment to, and understanding of, what they are setting out to achieve
Aims and objectives	Transparency is important here. Do those setting the aims have a clear idea of community needs? What are the aims, objectives, inputs and outputs for the project? Where is the proof?
Staffing	Whenever staff join a project they should be fully involved and conversant with strategy development and its underpinning philosophies
Identity and status	For CSD work to be taken seriously it needs to establish a professional identity and be recognised as a significant contributor to mainstream sport development (Skills Active, 2006)
Long-term commitment	Community development is a long-term process, so partners should be aware of this ongoing commitment to development processes taking priority over short-term gains (Sport England, 2001)
Innovation	Innovation is the cornerstone of CSD, as it often offers unconventional approaches to what should be mainstream issues. A plethora of good practice has emerged in sport development from new approaches adopted in CSD (Hylton, 2003)
Empowerment and ownership	Most commentators on CSD and community work support the notion of empowerment and capacity building whereby responsibilities are devolved to the community so that control and confidence are substantive, not tokenistic (Home Office, 1999)

Source: Adapted from Coalter (2002: 32).

evaluating their work; whilst engaged in praxis'. Partington and Totten outline how an emancipatory action research approach within the organisation allowed critical consciousness to be fostered, a more transformative approach to provision cultivated, and how critical consciousness was extended to include the community itself in recognising the structural constraints that resulted in social exclusion.

THE STRUCTURE AND ORGANISATION OF COMMUNITY SPORT DEVELOPMENT PROVISION

Most CSD does not take place in isolation. Any understanding of why specific activity takes place (or does not) at a local level necessitates an understanding of what influences have been brought to bear from a wider policy context. Understanding how CSD works and why it does what it does at the point of delivery to clients is part of a more complex picture of how policy makers and funders influence the scope of activity. This in turn is mediated by factors at a community-engaged level. Overwhelmingly, CSD is framed within policy and funding contexts which are

90

determined by larger organisations remote from the participants themselves. Their influence and motivations can be tracked, analysed and understood through the use of certain models. Subsequent sections will introduce and explain these models, building towards a more holistic and crucial analysis of who and what determines practice and why. By selecting organisations and initiatives and evaluating them systematically through these models, the reader can uncover some of the reasons why practice occurs as it does and who influences it and to what degree.

Levels of provision

CSD provision operates at different levels: local, regional, national and even trans-national. The lens that is taken to view CSD must also take into account different economies of scale, tensions and organisational and personal demands that the different levels must impose on any CSD organisation. Different levels of provision and different organisations involved in CSD can be plotted as a simple continuum, as shown in Figure 4.3. However, the continuum indicates that organisations can be located or positioned beyond and in between the four levels based on their scale of operations. Readers might consider where other organisations that they are familiar with could be plotted, or how an individual initiative and its constituent partners, funders and policy makers could be plotted.

■ *Transnational.* This refers to organisations and processes which occur across or beyond national boundaries. The clearest example of this for CSD is the increasing influence of the European Commission (EC) on policy and practice. This is especially true in relation to the setting of policy and the funding of pro-jects and initiatives. In its White Paper on sport (European Union, 2012: section 1.2.5) it outlines its role in social inclusion:

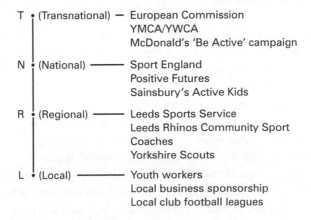

Figure 4.3 Levels of provision continuum.

to develop, for the benefit of people at risk of exclusion, services and accompanying measures which will allow them effective access to education, justice and other public and private services, such as culture, sport and leisure [. . .] sporting activity should be accessible to every man and woman.

- *National.* Nationally, the Department for Culture, Media and Sport (DCMS), the Department for Education (DfE), the Department for Communities and Local Government (DCLG) and the Home Office are four leading government departments involved in setting influential policy direction for CSD.

  National governing bodies (NGBs) and non-departmental public bodies also have a major influence on sport in the UK. There are approximately 112 sports recognised by Sport England and nearly 400 NGBs, ranging from the All England Netball Association to the Yachting Association (RYA).

- *Regional.* Governing bodies and non-departmental public bodies tend to set policy at a national level. However, specific policy implementation strategies occur regionally, as can be seen with the county sports partnerships and CSNs. Sports coach UK serves coaches and recreation consortia which coordinate work at a regional level but also work at other levels.

- *Local.* Ultimately CSD is most often delivered at a local level and often in a specific geographical area. At this point there are greater differences in delivery as CSD focuses and sets priorities to support specific local needs. Policy may have trickled down from organisations working at wider levels, but practice and micro-policy are generally adapted to suit those specific needs. There are also organisations and individuals who work at a purely local level such as the Langley Youth Project (Morgan, 2000) or a local youth worker or CSD officer. Community Sport Networks are likely to take a more significant role at this level.

The mixed economy of provision

Another important aspect of CSD policy is that it occurs in all three sectors of the economy: commercial, public and voluntary. The overwhelming majority of community sport initiatives have been funded by the state. This has been directly from central government, indirectly through non-governmental public bodies, and most often by local government. The Sports Council plays a lead role in developing policies and influencing provision. Community sport has operated as a manifestation of the aim of 'Sport for All', but community sports provision has seldom been funded in its own right and has been legitimised for more instrumental reasons (Collins and Kay, 2003; Houlihan and White, 2002). Sport has been viewed largely from the standpoint of the social function it fulfils, and is as much a part of social policy as it is of sports policy. Nationally, Action Sport has been a demonstrative project which has legitimised the role sport can play in urban regeneration by 'super-concentration' on a few streets (Glyptis, 1989; McIntosh and Charlton, 1985). This social agenda for community sport has been particularly well documented (Collins and Kay, 2003; Department of the Environment, 1989; Haywood and Kew, 1989; Houlihan and White, 2002; McIntosh and Charlton, 1985; Sports Council, 1982; Yorkshire and Humberside Council for Sport and Recreation, 1989). More recently Sport Action Zones, Active Communities projects and potentially the community sports hubs have progressed more unconventional but innovative and successful techniques further.

The public, commercial and voluntary sectors have influenced the paths CSD has taken. Voluntary groups, clubs and societies are often the independent face of CSD. The scale of voluntary sector organisations is such that they range from small local organisations, such as Rochdale Community Sports (Partington and Totten, 2012), to national/internationally linked organisations, such as the YMCA and YWCA. The Sports Volunteering in England survey (Sport England, 2002) clearly outlined how voluntary clubs provide a safety net for people who engage in activities which tend to be niche-orientated. This means that the private sector does not see a profitable market there, nor can the public sector provide a coherent rationale for supporting those specialist activities. Even in the area of volunteering, the Institute for Volunteering Research (2004) is adamant that those responsible for sport have a challenging task to reduce inequalities.

Commercial sector CSD is often a more extrinsically driven affair in which organisations such as professional football and rugby clubs work with schools and other breeding grounds to identify and develop talent and generate income, as well as for marketing and public relations. Some clubs have, in addition, established community units as charities which then allow them to draw on the tax concessions and economies that this mode of operating affords to its owners. For example, the West Ham United Football Club Community Sports Trust, a not-for-profit arm of the club, has added its support to the West Ham Asians in Football project, which should generate a number of positive outcomes for the club through reinforcing community links and widening its search for local talent in under-represented communities (Active Communities, 2002). Leicester City Football Club has also used its community links to promote an anti-racist message through its support of the Foxes Against Racism (FAR) group. Such links with minority ethnic communities for professional clubs have been successful in forging close relationships but can also be seen as effective comprehensive marketing or public relations opportunities.

The public sector, where most CSD work occurs, is often actively implemented at a regional and at local level. Still, the range of interested parties is diverse. The Office of the Deputy Prime Minister (ODPM)'s (2004) report into the joint working of sports organisations and those working in neighbourhood renewal gives some indication of the possible range of parties interested in CSD. The ODPM's agenda identified what people in sport have known for some time, that there is a problem regarding sport participation in deprived areas and that there needs to be a more creative or radical approach. Recreation from a sport-specific view, but with a complementary social policy focus, may emanate from youth work, community work, housing, policing, sport, lifelong learning and recreation departments, arts workers, education, health services and related organisations.

Some organisations operate exclusively in one single sector, but specific projects are more often linked with organisations from more than one sector. Public sector links are more likely to create national and local public policy influences. Commercial sector links are more likely to create some form of marketing opportunity for the indirect generation of profits. Voluntary sector links are perhaps more likely to operate more flexibly and freely, as they are subject to less political scrutiny, accountability and interference. Figure 4.4 incorporates the three sectors of provision as well as levels of provision. Organisations from specific sectors have been shown on the diagram. Once again the reader might consider where other organisations would be plotted, or how an individual initiative and its constituent partners, funders and policy makers could be plotted.

Partnerships

Specific initiatives involve partnerships and incorporate involvement from organisations from different sectors. A hypothetical initiative, X, with equal involvement from all three sectors is shown in Figure 4.5. The hypothetical initiative is placed at the centre of the diagram. An initiative with more emphasis from one sector would be placed closer to that particular axis. Another hypothetical initiative, Y, is placed to demonstrate stronger involvement from the public and voluntary sectors, with only partial involvement implied from the commercial sector. Y could be a 'football in the community' project. Analysis would have to consider that the project may be an arm of a private sector professional football club whose marketing department, as well as coaches, has an influence on talent identification. There may also be equipment funded by a private corporate sponsor. There may be public sector involvement as well, including schools which host the project and local council interest in the form of sport development or community workers. Not least, there may be voluntary sector involvement from the community itself including the children who participate, as well as their parents. The overall influence of these parties conspires to create a complex web of tensions and demands of those involved that ultimately determines how the project works and where it would be located on the framework.

The diagram can be used to reveal how, ultimately, any initiative's operations are the product of complex interrelationships with a variety of partners. Most initiatives

94

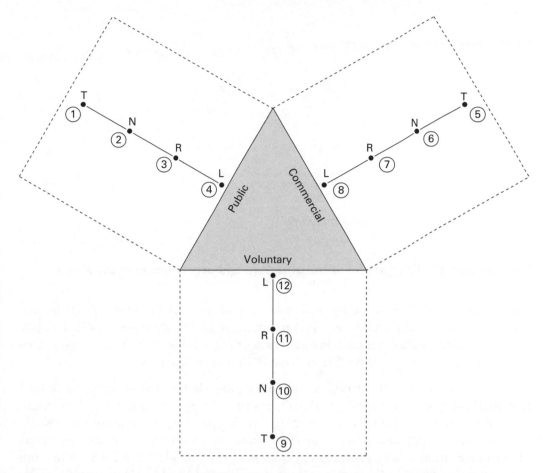

Figure 4.4 The sectors and levels of provision framework. 1, European Commission (transnational, T); 2, Sport England (national, N); 3, Leeds Sports Services (regional, R); 4, youth workers (local, L); 5, McDonald's 'Be Active' campaign (T); 6, Sainsbury's 'Active Kids' vouchers (N); 7, Leeds Rhinos community coaches (R); 8, local business sponsorship (L); 9, YMCA, YWCA (T); 10, Positive Futures (N); 11, Yorkshire Scouts (R); 12, local club football leagues (L).

owe their mode of operation to the outcome of complex networks of influence. The reader may choose to consider an initiative they are familiar with or wish to understand a little better. First identifying partners and then using the diagram, the reader can weigh and assess contributory influences upon the project overall and locate where the balance of power falls.

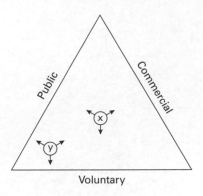

Figure 4.5 Partnership domain framework.

CSD matrix: a holistic model of the structure and organisation of provision

Any ideal model should incorporate elements of each of the previous diagrams. Such a model would enable a vigorous analysis of the structure of CSD policy provision, and enable comparative analyses of organisations, initiatives and partnerships. Such a model, the 'CSD matrix', is shown in Figure 4.6.

To follow the matrix the reader should recognise that a 'Toblerone'-type hybrid has been assembled from the previous diagrams. An appropriate metaphor would be origami. Imagine the base of the matrix is the 'partnership domain framework' diagram, which can also be seen as the central triangle in the 'sectors and levels of provision framework'. Next, three squares of the models are folded up to form external walls. Thus in three dimensions the partnerships domain permeates every point, top to bottom along the continua, like the message in a stick of seaside rock.

As digital technology and communications develop the reader may have access to this book and this model through virtual reality. One could explore the matrix as though excavating one of the ancient pyramids. Different CSD organisations and initiatives could be understood, or located, at different points and levels in three dimensions. The matrix offers a holistic way of understanding each of the previously discussed elements of structure, provision and policy. So, despite the limitations of a text in one dimension, it is perhaps worth considering where further analysis would locate other initiatives on this matrix.

Any consideration of the complexities of CSD will emphasise ambiguities. Utilising the models enables sensitivity to generic issues that must be considered if CSD is to be critically examined across diverse sport settings. Applying models necessitates a rigorous analysis, which in turn develops a deeper understanding of practice.

Kevin Hylton and Mick Totten

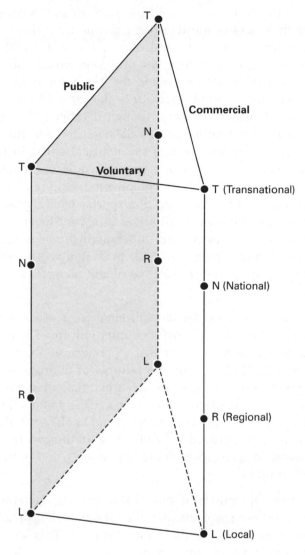

Figure 4.6 CSD matrix.

COMMUNITY SPORT DEVELOPMENT POLICY

Historical overview

Community sport development is a practice, a policy direction and in particular a philosophy of provision which has developed since the late 1970s. The first decade of the twenty-first century witnessed a massive expansion of CSD provision led by government, but the next decade started with the largest cuts in public sector history, precipitated in the UK by a coalition government, against a backdrop of global financial crisis. CSD has hardly been immune from these cuts. Direct cuts to local authority provision and more indirect cuts to grants and other aspects of community provision conspired to decimate provision whilst rising unemployment and poverty were increasing the very need for it. Contemporary contractions in CSD provision echo earlier news of its death in the early 1990s (see Lentell, 1994; McDonald, 1995) which was premature, though it reflects the cyclical nature of policy and resourcing in the public sector. CSD persisted and thrived in a number of diverse settings and contexts. Despite the political shifts in the 1990s which made CSD policy seem less fashionable in some quarters, continuity persisted elsewhere in the use of community development techniques. In difficult times the CSD torch was often carried by other non-sports-specific practitioners such as youth workers or by specific sports initiatives at a very local level. So, although the long-term impact of such devastating cuts remains to be seen, it is not beyond plausibility that the obvious benefits of CSD provision will re-emerge, especially where mainstream provision is failing or government plans for social policy require a populist vehicle.

CSD was initially seen as a challenge to traditional ways of approaching provision for disadvantaged groups; it was almost a counter-culture. The emphasis on community practice in public services is almost a paradox, as the turn to community approaches is often a tactic to ameliorate failures of mainstream provision. It is apparent that in policy systems that are dysfunctional in some way it becomes necessary to offer remedial treatment. In a way CSD is a side effect or by-product of sport development. The change in emphasis from facility-based sport to community sport and recreation has proved to be effective. In the past this shift persuaded many to 'take on board' ideas by mainstreaming projects, and/or project philosophy into more established units.

Community sport development grew out of the roots of anxieties fuelled by the massive sport centre building projects that did not return the participation expected by local authorities and driven by the Sports Council. This was felt to be to the detriment of more personal community provision.

'People, not bricks' was an ideal which came through quite clearly in London, where it transpired that the major users of facilities such as the Brixton Sport Centre were mainly white middle-class males from outside the area. Many of the local community felt the centre to be unwelcoming and not a facility they could identify with (Murray, 1988).

Lessons like those learnt in Brixton were occurring all over the UK. However, it took a dramatic series of events culminating in severe social disturbances and a reaction from the government before massive resources were poured into what many practitioners saw as the first recognisable community sport projects. It was no coincidence that young people were targeted in the rush to reduce actual and perceived threats of crime and anti-social behaviour. Ironically, a closer look at the areas affected by the urban unrest showed that they were, in reality, deprived of most social welfare services. The Midlands and London were chosen as areas for the pilot projects of Action Sport to see if there was a way for sport to defuse tensions in inner-city areas which had been scenes of civil unrest in the early 1980s. At that time, the use of focusing on target groups achieved prominence, although, for practitioners involved in good practice, this came as no surprise. Young people, the unemployed, women, black and other minority ethnic groups, disabled people and the elderly were targeted in a combination of partnerships between local government and central government.

The success of the pilots was such that they became national projects wherever partnerships, such as those with Action Sport, could be formed. Indeed, evaluations of Action Sport nationally and regionally were very positive (McIntosh and Charlton, 1985; Rigg, 1986). Overall, researchers were unanimous in commenting that leadership skills, outreach and active consultation resulted in successful ways of identifying minimal participants and non-participants and ensuring regular sports participation. National demonstration projects built on the success of the Action Sport and Community Recreation initiatives. Target groups were strategically mapped on to each initiative in an effort to reproduce the success of these projects in different contexts. The Coventry Active Lifestyles project, the Solent Sports Counselling initiative and the Scunthorpe Black and Ethnic Minority project are three examples of the evolution of CSD policy, process and practice (Sports Council Research Unit, 1991).

Community sport development, or community recreation, as it has been known, went through a period of enlightenment in the 1980s, when new forms of knowledge and ideas about community recreation and CSD were tried and the results disseminated. As Lentell (1994) and McDonald (1995) attest, the 1990s were not a constructive time for mass participation and Sport for All as the Conservative government became more focused on school sport and excellence. The devolution of mass participation goals to local authorities meant a lack of leadership nationally on inclusive sport, which was clearly successful, if resource-intensive, but politically not a vote winner for the struggling Conservatives (Houlihan and White, 2002). Further, the pressure on local authorities to be more competitive and more accountable for their sport and leisure provision meant a withdrawal from more traditional areas of provision that had been the safety net for infrequent participants and those in a pre-contemplation stage of participation (McDonald, 1995).

With the election of the New Labour government in 1997, and through to 2010, community sport development became higher profile and better supported. There had been a sharpening of ideas around core issues that have challenged many in community sport development. Social exclusion, community cohesion, social networking and sustainable community development, the development of communities through sport and the development of sport through communities became policy slogans that made prominent appearances in substantive sections of national-level policies (Cabinet Office, 2002; Department for Culture, Media and Sport, 1999, 2001; Sport England, 2004). More significantly, many of these dimensions of sport and social policy have been supported by resources and political will. Developments around neighbourhood renewal, social exclusion and Policy Action Teams led to a closer melding of government department agendas. This meant that community sport development became but one tool to be used in tackling a range of social issues (Department for Culture, Media and Sport, 1999; Home Office, 1999). Demarcations between established and what were emergent ways of providing sport and recreation opportunities for most priority groups in society became much less obvious. In reality the use of the term 'community sport' became almost as ubiquitous as the term 'community' in other areas of social provision. It invoked positive images of considerate client-orientated practice. For example, when Sportscotland considered sport it considered both community recreation, which it saw as the 'informal world of sport', and sport development, as part of the 'more formal world of sport' (Scottish Sports Council, 1998: 2). The mainstream validity of both forms of provision became unquestioned and they were characterised as 'co-dependent'. Community sport development was now on the agenda in a more comprehensive way than ever before and although CSD had 'never had it so good' there was sufficient evidence to demonstrate that this was just the start that practitioners and policy makers needed to capitalise on.

Such certainties evaporated in the second decade of the new century when the election of a new Conservative and Liberal Democrat coalition government in 2010 coincided with a series of catastrophic and often unforeseen downturns in the buoyancy of the economy. Global financial markets crashed, confidence was lost in national financial institutions, and investments in sport and leisure previously predicted on economic growth became precarious. The coalition government responded with a series of historic austerity measures never before seen, including massive cuts in public expenditure. Political theorists will argue about the extent to which these cuts reflected economic prudence or an ideological discomfort with the state as a public provider of services, but the consequences for CSD provision were savage. CSD provision nationally and locally were slashed as part of a wider effort to restrain public spending. (In the UK this was accentuated by a preference to maintain spending levels on the 2012 Olympic and Paralympic Games.)

The government envisaged a 'Big Society' led by the voluntary sector that would supplant the primary role of the state as a community provider. Although many of those ideals about community-led provision share similarities with aspects of CSD's community development orientation, there were significant concerns that the means of facilitating this transformation were being disabled. At a time of soaring unemployment, particularly amongst younger people, and increasing poverty, especially including children, it could be argued that CSD's role as a link to impoverished communities and as a facilitator for inclusion had never been more important. For 'Big Society' to work, communities needed to be empowered, capacity for social capital needed to be built and cultural capital was necessary to navigate the maze of bureaucracies and funding streams. Against a backdrop of increasing social inequality, CSD offered the potential to enable this amongst those most excluded but its erosion made this less likely.

The next era for CSD is likely to reflect all those before in that its buoyancy ebbs and flows on political tides. It may curry more favour as an instrument to address increasing inequalities or it may fade from mainstream view as it did for much of the 1990s. Whatever transpires, those who advocate its social purpose and benefits face a struggle to resurrect its prominence in public provision.

MODELS OF COMMUNITY SPORT DEVELOPMENT POLICY

Community sport development can be understood as a form of 'socio-cultural' intervention. Different policy models have characterised this mode of intervention. Subsequently five models will be explored: two 'social' models which illustrate the 'instrumental' use of sport, social control and social welfare; and two 'cultural' models which illustrate attempts to extend the participatory franchise, democratisation of sport and sport democracy. A fifth political model which characterises the counter-hegemonic political motivations of some practitioners will also be explored, sport activism. It is the intention not for these models to be contrasted against one another exclusively but for them to be seen as operating simultaneously, and exhibiting varying degrees of influence. Individual projects are subject to different policy rationales and power struggles. Often they will feel pulled in different directions as they juggle different policy aims of partners, funders and policy makers. In this respect they reinforce the notion of CSD as a 'site of cultural and hegemonic struggle' (Hargreaves and McDonald, 2002) rather than one of static consensus. (The processes of hegemony and ideological consensus will be discussed later.) Dominant institutions, such as the state, are able to form a coalition of support for its policies and unite diverse interests behind a dominant project. This approach offers an 'economy of remedies', a single solution to a variety of issues, all within one policy, with a broad base of support (Coalter *et al.*, 1986: 92).

Social control

Social control is performed by the state directly and indirectly, through organisations and institutions. The state intervenes directly to legislate for and against particular leisure forms. Sport is used explicitly as a form of social control. The Sports Council (1982: 3) openly believed 'Young people in sport don't throw bricks', and still does. Although this appears to be a crass simplification, overestimating the power of sport and underestimating the associated necessary conditions for positive change to occur, such ideas continue to be propagated. An example is Positive Futures, which was established as a vehicle to use sport to reduce anti-social behaviour, crime and drug use among ten- to sixteen-year-olds in local neighbourhoods (Sport England, 2002). There are many local examples such as the Bradford Sports Web project (Hylton, 2003), Hackney's Midnight Basketball (Sport England, 2002) and Wolverhampton's Midnight Soccer Leagues (Football Task Force, 1999) in which sport is used to combat crime. Research reveals that the sports player tends to be conformist in nature (Coalter, 1991). The police have taken an open interest in involvement in community sport (Morgan, 2000); so much so that Carrington and Leaman (1983: 10) state, 'Community policing and community sport would appear to share an identical logic and perform an identical ideological function.' Sport is used as surrogate violence, channelling aggression into a socially acceptable activity. Hargreaves (1986) describes how community sport targets various categories of potential user, but it is clear that the main concern is the 'potentially troublesome'. Hargreaves goes on to argue how a cadre of sports leaders are developed, who are 'co-cultural' with users, to enable infiltration and the exercise of influence by the dominant culture.

In 2011, riots returned to the UK's cities, and significant aspects of sport provision have long been seen as a response to urban community unrest. The final Cantle Report (Cantle and Institute of Community Cohesion, 2006) on the civil disturbances in Oldham made recommendations to develop sport and leisure services further in order to ease tensions and enhance community cohesion. Similarly, the salient impetus for Action Sport nationally had been a response to the urban riots of the 1980s (Totten, 1993). The Action Sport workers from inner-city Leeds were overwhelmingly in agreement that they owed their existence to the riots there. One worker commented ironically that if there was another riot their budget would be doubled, and applied the following comparison: 'We act a little like community policemen . . . We walk the beat. We go back to our station house and fill in our forms' (ibid.: 51). Another worker said he felt responsible for motivating people to get a job. Despite a clear awareness of their use as potential instruments of social control, Action Sport workers were uncomfortable with this role and recognised their own ability for resistance and to pursue and realise their own objectives: 'We're not just a bunch of "jolly non-whites" doing the bidding of faceless bureaucrats!' (ibid.). One worker pessimistically pointed out that drug pushers went back to their trade after doing their sport (a rather poignant failure of control over individual agency). Despite the fact that Action Sport workers were insistent that they promoted sport purely for fun, one worker observed, 'we may have far less freedom than we think' (ibid.). Conscious of the controlling role of the state, and the role of

Action Sport in that process, he commented that, for community sport in the social context of the community as a whole, 'There are certain ways of behaving and attitudes towards people that have to be fostered, that are of paramount importance to the survival of the community, survival of the people' (ibid.).

Social welfare

Sport England and other government agencies have often sought to integrate sport and social policy, with much attention drawn to the importance of community sport as a form of social welfare (Collins and Kay, 2003; Lentell, 1994) which links directly to notions of development through sport (Coalter, 2002). Bernard Atha, when Vice-Chairman of the Sports Council (1978: 14), stated:

> Deprivation takes place in many forms – social, educational, cultural, housing, emotional, and recreational to mention just a few. This deprivation exists at great cost to our society, a cost most easily seen in terms of crime and vandalism, but more serious in terms of loneliness and alienation.

In similar mood, Glyptis (1989) pointed out that the 1975 White Paper on Sport and Recreation (HMSO, 1975) heralded a shift from policies of 'recreational welfare' to the use of 'recreation as welfare'. Dennis Howell (cited in Coalter *et al.*, 1986, when Minister of Sport) declared that without a social purpose sport would be irrelevant. The Association of Metropolitan Authorities (1989) viewed community sports as vital to community development. As the new millennium dawned, nothing much had changed. As Chris Smith (1998: 9), Secretary of State for Culture, Media and Sport, stated:

> Sport offers direct economic benefits. It contributes to the regeneration of towns and cities, improving health, productivity and quality of life. It contributes to savings in the cost of health care and leads to a reduction in crime and vandalism. It offers local environmental benefits that can change the image of a city or community and lead to increased inward investment.

Echoing this point in 2005 was the Chief Executive of Sport England, Roger Draper, who added the contribution that sport could make to quality of life, stronger, safer communities and the economy (Sport England, 2005b). The value of sport is often trumpeted (Coalter, 2001), and often too optimistically and uncritically (Collins and Kay, 2003; Long and Sanderson, 2003), once again without fully considering what the associated necessary conditions may be, but nevertheless it continues to prompt considerable swathes of policy. Action Sport workers have paid great attention to the value of their work in terms of social welfare and the contribution it could make to the quality of life of their users (Totten, 1993). Workers described how people gained a sense of achievement and self-determination which they could apply to other areas of their lives. People were able to enjoy themselves, to self-actualise and increase their feeling of self-worth. Action Sport workers agreed that they were facilitating people's right to the opportunity to participate. Community sports initiatives certainly have the potential to bring about change in people's lives, but individual projects are more likely to stimulate personal change than effect any structural change.

Democratisation of sport

This model is directly derived from the democratisation of culture model most commonly talked of in relation to community arts but can equally be applied to CSD. The concept of the democratisation of sport presumes a single national sport culture. This sport culture, though not fully appreciated, understood or participated in by large sections of the population, can be spread from the top downwards. This process can be described as the demystification, or clarification, of the value of participation (Totten, 1993). Sport is promoted by evangelists as a source of national pride. CSD can act as a tool to overcome social and perceptual barriers, and in some cases to demystify negative perceptions or limited knowledge of sport and recreation, through participation. Some community sports initiatives are premised on the idea that communities are a homogeneous entity and aim to integrate those unattached into participation (Fremeaux, 2005; Hargreaves, 1986). If they extend the franchise to participation through CSD and its 'soft' integration into sport, the then enlightened participant can cultivate the sports habit. Continued participation might then lead participants towards mainstream provision. Examples of this would include the Cities Tennis Programme in Liverpool (Morgan, 2000) and many Football in the Community projects whereby mainstream organisations venture into the community attempting to improve 'sporting literacy'. The Olympic Legacy is another example of a top-down attempt to extend participation by sports missionaries preaching to the natives. They present established forms of sports that are largely the same as practised elsewhere. Freedom to choose is presented here with an implicit constraint. Thus they propagate the dominant culture of institutionalised sport. This resonates with the 'old wine in new bottles' argument (Haywood and Kew, 1989) referred to earlier.

Two Action Sport workers in Leeds felt that it could be a 'stepping stone' or 'foundation' towards integration into mainstream sport (Totten, 1993). Another example would be the way Sport England gives preferential treatment to approving certain sports for funding, such as the Outdoor Basketball Initiative. In macro-policy terms, this has the overall effect of lending greater legitimacy to some forms of sporting activity than others.

Sport democracy

Like the previous model, sport democracy is directly derived from a model used in the arts – cultural democracy – but can equally be applied to CSD. The model of cultural democracy is in part a critique of the democratisation of culture, which is seen as a paternalistic and elitist idea (Parry, 1986; Simpson, 1976a). Likewise, the democratisation of sport can thus become 'a foredoomed and wasteful effort to graft an alien culture on to tissue where it cannot thrive' (Simpson, 1976b: 50). Sport democracy describes a more fundamental challenge to the means of provision. It interprets provision as going beyond the consumption of traditional institutionalised forms of sport. Sports such as rugby league have been adapted for wheelchair users and judo for blind participants. Judo was also adapted by Armley Disabled Judo Group, in Leeds, when young people with differing disabilities adapted the sport so that techniques with a lowest common denominator were incorporated into their own tailor-made more inclusive grading system. Sport democracy also advocates devolution of power away from centralised agencies and back to the people. It argues for a plurality of access to means of provision and against passive consumption. The Armley group were not affiliated to any mainstream judo body and functioned quite happily on their own. There are 'gay football' networks which operate semi-autonomously from the Football Association (Stonewall, 2006) and similarly organised 'Asian cricket leagues' (Carrington and McDonald, 2001).

Sport democracy supports the finding of the 'Leisure and the quality of life experiments' (Department of the Environment, 1977: 161) that:

> The lessons of the experiments may be that a true community applies its development opportunities across the whole spectrum of interest groups rather than in trying to provide a homogenised mass leisure.

It is in recognition of the special needs of subcultures and subgroups that a sport democracy is proposed. It calls for a decentralised and more democratic and representative structure of sport and leisure management, allowing effective participation in decision making by the community (Department of the Environment, 1989). Devolved strategies promote ownership by, and co-authorship with, the community.

Action Sport workers described how they have provided an organisational framework for the community and have employed animation techniques to give people 'the drive to get up and go', a 'sort of injection' (Totten, 1993). One worker described Action Sport as a 'local sports council' (ibid.: 56). Workers were critical of the notion of a homogeneous national culture and of policy which was over-prescriptive. A worker pointed out that integration could be oppressive for some Asian women who could see it as infringing their right to their beliefs. 'People should be aware of others' cultural needs. If people were aware of those differences it helps, not just sport, but many other things as well' (ibid.). Workers described how the work had become much more community-led. Representation had been valued, particularly in relation to ethnicity and gender, and had been promoted in appointments, decision making, programme planning and activity leading. In this way the project strived to remain co-cultural with its community. Sport democracy allied closely to community development principles and the concept of participatory democracy (Ledwith, 2011).

Sport activism

In contrast to the four previously state-sanctioned models of community leisure (though perhaps less so sport democracy), sport activism represents a radical intervention in the community which is politicised against, rather than on behalf of, the status quo. Whereas sport democracy emphasises a challenge to cultural values, radicalism emphasises a challenge to social and political values. Ledwith (2011: 2) describes radicals as 'critical educators' with a transformative agenda to bring about social change. One sustained attempt to implement a radical cultural agenda by the state was that of the Greater London Council between 1981 and 1986 (Bianchinni, 1989). This was extraordinary cultural action by the local state in defiance of the national state, although smaller conflicts of interest between national and local government are still widespread in an era of excruciating and centralised accountability. Radical cultural agendas in Britain have often been carried out by small groups or individuals within larger organisations. Frustrated by conventional approaches with their enslaved accountability to political masters and an inherent bureaucracy, some CSD workers will act outside the view of those authorities. The 'Street Sport' project, Stoke on Trent (Morgan, 2000), employed innovative and unconventional methods to bypass conventional restrictions. Also an Action Sport worker saw himself as infiltrating with an agenda to change (Totten, 1993). He was conscious of his ability to resist and interpret 'top-down' policy and carry out his own mission, saying, 'the bosses don't visit the coal face'. Basically he would 'do his own thing' beyond surveillance. At a later interview, he corrected, 'It's not radical at all. It's very liberal', but went on to say that there was a potential for radicalism but it cannot be made public. He described using 'dual language' as 'one for bureaucrats and one for practitioners' (ibid.: 59). Action Sport illustrated a potential for sport activism and opposition to the dominant hegemonic order, but also highlighted the difficulties of resisting assimilation as well as risks of marginalisation or expulsion.

There is a history of radicalism in community arts which is not equalled in the history of community sports (Kelly, 1984). This does not mean that there is no potential for radical action in community sports. Such activists exist in CSD, but their profiles are often predominantly covert (perhaps necessarily so). Sport does not share the historical tradition of protest that the arts have. Many still believe sport and politics do not mix. So activists in CSD may jeopardise their longevity if they raise their heads too high above the parapet. For many it is about infiltration and subversion rather than revealing their true colours. So, for a theoretical framework from which to view sport activism, it is more profitable to consider community arts.

Kelly (1984) maintains that the role of community arts is to topple capitalism. Kelly advises that community artists should explore alternative modes of cultural production, distribution and reception, and have a clear analysis of their work as part of a revolutionary programme committed to cultural democracy:

> Storm the citadels, and tear them down brick by brick; to demolish the oppressive and imperialist structures and to build in their place a series of smaller haciendas where activity and participation are encouraged and welcomed, and the only activity which is prohibited is the building of citadels.
>
> (Kelly, 1984: 138)

Kelly's analogy applied to sport implies a programme of infiltration by practitioners with political motivations, and subversion by those workers and participants against the dominant institutional culture within sport; namely they might seek to undermine conservative practices and values inherent in organisations governing sport. Ledwith (2011) advocates radical community action as necessary to redress inequalities inherent in current society. She cites Chomsky (2003: 236) to convey the need to be 'challenging the reigning ideological system and seeking to create constructive alternatives of thought, action and institutions'.

Although all CSD workers are involved to varying degrees with disadvantaged groups, radicals embrace a more overwhelming ideological commitment to social change than others. Sport activists seek more than merely reform. They seek transformation:

> collective action for change has to follow through from local to structural levels in order to make a sustainable difference. Anything less is ameliorative.
>
> (Ledwith, 2011: 14)

Examples would include Marxists committed to the redistribution of sporting resources towards the working class, feminists committed to working with women towards challenging the prevailing gender order in sport, and also black activists committed to the advancement of black culture, representation and countering racism in sport.

There are also examples of 'radical networks' which operate outside the sight and control of mainstream provision, such as 'Freedom through Football' (Totten, 2011). It consists of multi-sports clubs such as the Easton Cowboys (2012) in Bristol and Republica Internationale (2012) in Leeds, which are anti-capitalist organisations, 'a breeding ground for the political left through the plethora of opportunities to engage in radical community development, enhancement of social cohesion and development of social inclusion' (Tucker, 2011: 152). They have international political links and stronger allegiances with other like-minded European organisations than they do with the English Football Association or more commercialised non-political events. Close links include Sankt Pauli Football Club (2012; *The Guardian*, 2012) in Hamburg – whose matches are regularly accompanied by political protests by their fans resisting football commerce and commodification, capitalism, bigotry, fascism, patriarchy, racism, homophobia, state control and mass media influence (Totten, 2011) – and with hundreds of other teams through such events as the Anti-racist World Cup (2012). The network engages in sports activism, engenders critical consciousness, and acts as a form of critical praxis and resistance to dominant hegemony, ideologically, economically, politically, socially and culturally. This can be understood as utilising the emancipatory potential of subcultural activity (and through football) to challenge dominant norms and structures, and to promote radical and sometimes revolutionary action (Totten, 2011). The network has international political links. Radicalism may be well hidden or even obscure but it is out there.

COMMUNITY SPORT PRACTICE

Community sport development is characterised by its approach to service planning, delivery and practice. CSD is a movement away from mainstream or dominant sport provision, with their focus on performance and excellence and their historical failure to reach all. CSD focuses on the initial threshold to sports participation. CSD is a reaction against elitism and inequality; it is person- or community-centred. There is recognition of the structural barriers to participation discussed in the previous chapter on Sport for All, and access and inclusion are promoted. Disadvantaged groups are identified and prioritised or targeted. Haywood and Kew (1989) emphasise the flexible, proactive style and process of community sport. Community sport is more empathetic and focuses more on the participant and participatory processes. Thus, sport is often merely a means towards these developmental aims. Consultation is valued to determine and be responsive to expressed needs and wants, and so to extend the participatory franchise. In that sense community sport development tends to adopt a distinct, less formal, more flexible management style. It is a movement away from 'top-down' deterministic models of provision towards 'bottom-up' community-led provision. Decision making is more devolved to enable community participation. In that sense the community and provider may become co-authors of destiny or partners in policy and practice. In the main, community sport workers attempt to empower through advocacy, facilitation and enablement.

From the early 1980s into the 1990s Action Sport conformed fairly comfortably with this common understanding of community sport (Totten, 1993). It promoted a sense of informality and a feeling of ownership among participants. A worker explained 'We try to cater for people on their own terms' (ibid.: 33). Action Sport started offering established mainstream activities, but left space and has successfully provided for other activities such as chairobics and kabbadi. These principles are still identified as characteristics of best practice in CSD and have been identified by Coalter (2002) in his summary of good practice in planning, delivery and participants in CSD. Action Sport was about enjoyment. Fun was stressed repeatedly as the bottom line. Workers were critical of serious participation. Using their own conceptions of 'community' they described how community sport brings people together, contributing, in a general sense, to community spirit. Workers saw Action Sport as promoting socialising and interaction, and making people happier. Action Sport was concerned with the development process from start to finish, although participation was most important because ultimately that determined if people came back again. The basis of Action Sport was social and the consultation process was important in developing the sense of ownership. Action Sport provided an organisational framework sometimes lacking in a local community. It emphasised an initial pitch of low ability requirements as the threshold to participation. Any ability focused on excellence was channelled towards other forms of provision. Through their unconventional, proactive outreach work Action Sport and other such initiatives bridge the gap in participation between people and facilities. The challenge for CSD is to promote a philosophy that participation in sport and recreation is positive, and to extend the participatory franchise within the local community.

Case studies of CSD practice

The following two case studies (Case studies 4.1 and 4.2) represent two very different but not atypical examples of CSD. They illustrate both individually and comparatively many aspects of practice. The reader might evaluate them considering the conceptual and theoretical issues discussed previously in this chapter.

CASE STUDY 4.1: LEEDS ACTIVE SPORT AND ACTIVE LIFESTYLES TEAMS

Leeds Active Sport and Active Lifestyles Teams are the primary agencies engaged in community sport development as part of the Leeds City Council Sport Service, which also includes business development and extensive facilities management. In addition to a number of other services such as Parks and Countryside, Libraries, Arts and Heritage, and Highways, the Sport Service is part of the City Development directorate.

The Active Sport Team consists of three Club Development Officers, three Active Schools Officers, a Disability Sport Officer and a Positive Futures Officer. The Active Lifestyles Team consists of the Active Lifestyles Officers, an Older People's Officer, a Women and Girls Officer, and officers who oversee health-related programmes known as 'Heartwatch' and 'Cardiac Phase 3'. They operate citywide in three geographical wedges, and the Active Sport and Active Lifestyles Officers work within these. Each of the three wedges has one Club Development Officer, one Active Schools Officer and one Active Lifestyles Officer who work as a team to develop provision across the respective geographic wedge.

Social context

Leeds has a large, diverse population of 798,000, the second highest local authority population in the UK (after Birmingham). The demographic picture of the city is diverse and includes inner-city urban areas and relatively rural ex-mining villages. Areas of Leeds rank in the highest and lowest ranges of the national indices of deprivation. This wide-ranging demographic means that each Officer must be very sensitive to local demands and needs.

Main aims

The main aim of the Sport Service is to contribute to improved health and wellbeing in the city by increasing participation in sport and physical activity, and the Active Sport and Active Lifestyles Teams are an important part of the overall city sports strategy.

The Active Sport Team's primary aim is to increase participation in structured sport by working with local communities, schools, voluntary sports clubs, national governing bodies and public sector agencies to improve and increase the range and quality of opportunities available, in particular for young people. The specialist work of the Positive Futures Officer aims to work with hard-to-reach groups using sport as a vehicle to engage young people into education, training and volunteering. This position aims to expand the successful national Positive Futures programme funded by the Home Office.

The Active Lifestyles Team is responsible for developing opportunities for informal sport and physical activity provision, predominantly for those who are 16 or over. This team works with local communities, leisure centres and the health sector to develop opportunities to engage people in activity who, perhaps, traditionally have not participated in sport.

Working practice

The teams support the development of clubs by providing direct support for achieving Club Mark (the national sports club kite mark scheme) and assist clubs in gaining funding through funding workshops. They develop and increase numbers of active volunteers and provision for young people including holiday activity programmes, out-of-school activities and school competitions. In addition they develop informal sport and physical activity opportunities for those who choose

110

not to engage in traditional sports provision.

The teams work with young people at risk of crime and anti-social behaviour through the Positive Futures diversionary sport and educational programmes. This included introducing a 'Boxing Academy' to the city, which develops the non-contact version of the sport in a safe environment focusing on the skills of the sport, and operated in four leisure centres, nine schools and one community centre. The academy aimed to use boxing as a tool to develop young people in a range of ways including health, fitness, lifestyle, self-esteem, anger management and self-discipline. The Amateur Boxing Association's boxing awards are incorporated into the academy to accredit the work of the participants.

All members of the teams also seek to improve equality of opportunity in sport but particularly the Disability Sport, Women and Girls and Older People's Sport Development Officers do so. For example a Leeds Disability Sport Youth Panel was established with the aim of engaging disabled young people in decision making and development of sport in the city. The panel agreed a key aim of its work would be to promote disability sport to a wider audience and play a key role in delivering Paralympic legacy events and competitions in Leeds in the run up to London 2012. The group has already delivered several events including a 'Paralympic Sport Taster Day' which offered young people from across the city the opportunity to try many of the disability sports that are available in the area.

Another example is how the Women and Girls' Sports Development Officer manages the Sport England-funded Active Women project. It offers women the opportunity to take part in 10 weeks of sport and physical activity provision (including netball, badminton, racketball and tennis) and, at minimal cost, an off-peak gym card for council leisure centre facilities. Outcomes from the project have included Indian women who had never accessed a leisure centre before setting up their own group to meet and play badminton on a weekly basis at the leisure centre. Other women allied their activity to weight loss and increasing self-esteem through regular sports activity.

(We acknowledge the support of Katy Elliott, Senior Sports Development Officer, in compiling this summary.)

CASE STUDY 4.2: ROCHDALE COMMUNITY SPORTS

The Rochdale Community Sports Project (hereafter referred to as RCS) was an arm of the Rochdale Federation of Tenants and Residents Associations (hereafter referred to as RoFTRA). RoFTRA's main focus was traditionally around supporting its members (individual tenants' and residents' associations on social housing estates), by lobbying and campaigning on their behalf to mainstream agencies, predominantly around housing issues (RoFTRA, 2004). Established in 2001, RCS represented an organisational shift away from dealing with just housing issues, towards a broader remit of social regeneration.

RCS was funded through a series of grants, originally from Sport England and later from the Neighbourhood Renewal Fund. RCS worked in partnership with tenants' and residents' associations to engage children and young people in and through sport, and to plan and deliver sport and recreation services in the heart of their own council housing estates. It had very few externally driven targets and objectives; this results in a degree of freedom to respond to community needs. This gave RCS the autonomy, and RoFTRA's members and their communities a 'voice', to challenge the balance of power held by the local authority and Rochdale Cultural Trust (which houses the sport and leisure functions for the borough), and to influence the planning and delivery of service provision.

Social context

RCS operated in a variety of social housing estates across Rochdale typified by high levels of anti-social behaviour and crime, health inequalities, low educational attainment and above-average levels of unemployment. This is illustrated by Rochdale's ranking as the tenth worst borough in England and Wales (out of 354) in terms of 'hot spots' ('rank of local concentration') in the 2007 Index of Multiple Deprivation (Department of Communities and Local Government, 2008).

Main aims

RCS aimed to balance delivery of sports activities with the development of skills and capacity (RoFTRA, 2001). RCS also represented the interests of social housing communities on borough-wide partnerships and attempted to ensure that the needs of these communities were considered when making decisions at this strategic level. The project provides an example of the 'development of communities through sport' rationale, and was underpinned conceptually from its inception by five key principles (RoFTRA, 2001):

- participation catalyst
- community engagement
- capacity building
- community empowerment
- sustainability.

The methods employed by RCS enabled staff members to develop critical consciousness about their own working practices, and to understand how the project could tackle larger social issues and oppressive power structures in order to empower local communities.

Working practice

RCS combined direct delivery with longer-term capacity building. RCS acted as a medium for community empowerment, to develop community involvement in activities, build capacity within tenants' and residents' associations and develop social capital in communities.

RCS strived to actively consult with and involve local residents (through the mechanism of tenants' and residents' associations) in decision making, planning and, where possible, the delivery of activities. Regular meetings were held with tenants' and residents' associations to identify and discuss local issues and needs, and activities developed to meet those needs. This bottom-up approach created a sense of community ownership of the project, and was crucial to its success. It resulted in the project being endorsed by community leaders, which helped gain the trust of other tenants and residents; in particular, 'hard to reach' young people. This is a service that tenants and residents associations wanted, felt was beneficial to their communities, and were able to choose their level of involvement in. In the terms of Butcher (Haywood *et al.*, 1994), RCS was seen as a resource that is 'on tap' rather than 'on top'.

Activities were delivered in the heart of local communities utilising whatever facilities were available. These ranged from purpose built multi-use games areas and community centres to small patches of land. Decisions were based around what the young people felt comfortable

112

with as opposed to the quality of the facility. Sport was used as the tool to engage young people, and sports sessions were frequently used as a medium through which practitioners from other agencies could reach these young people to provide support and advice on a range of issues from education and employment to healthy lifestyles.

[We acknowledge the support of Janine Partington, former manager of Rochdale Community Sports, in compiling this summary. A fuller analysis also been conducted by Partington and Totten (2012).]

When comparing the two case studies there are some very obvious similarities and differences. Although both will draw upon partners in other sectors and at other levels, the Leeds Active Sport and Active Lifestyles Teams (hereafter to be thought of as Leeds Community Sport and referred to as LCS) are very much a product of the local authority in the public sector whereas RCS is rooted in the voluntary sector. Whereas LCS has a citywide and perhaps regional remit, RCS is focused more locally around social housing estates in a much smaller town, but both have aims to work with more specific target groups, especially young people, within smaller geographical communities. The work of both is linked to more strategic efforts at social regeneration and development, but whereas RCS is part of a relatively small organisation and tightly conceived LCS is more diffuse and part of a larger and much more complex web of sport services within one of the largest local authorities in the UK. LCS policy is also part of a much broader council strategy whereas RCS is more locally driven.

Both the case study organisations share some aims based around inclusion, promoting health and well-being, and tackling anti-social behaviour, but Leeds puts more emphasis on sport development and Rochdale on community development. Both appear examples of successful practice, and above all espouse a 'bottom-up' way of working or client-led delivery and facilitation. The imperative on both organisations to consult and work in tandem with local people is paramount. In each case active citizenship means people in Leeds and Rochdale claiming or reclaiming access to resources for sport and recreation. It also means taking ownership of their own and other people's sport and recreation opportunities and working towards addressing quality-of-life and lifestyle issues in a bid to enhance social inclusion and cohesion. Although they both reflect a measure of both, LCS appears to be more of a top-down approach whereas RCS appears to have more emphasis on being bottom-up. Accordingly Leeds may reflect more of the democratisation of sport and Rochdale sport democracy. This may mean there is more potential for community involvement in decision making in Rochdale; indeed one of the strengths of its community engagement is perceived to be that it is not the council (Partington and Totten, 2012).

Both aim to improve social welfare but for both this is also conflated with social control. They both take a wider emancipatory view of purposive leisure activity, and diversion where young people are concerned. This generates another accusatory chorus against CSD workers as acting as 'soft police' – indeed, policing on behalf of concerned citizens and controlling the way young people behave and act. In the past, providers have argued that giving people the opportunity to play sport as a diversion from their daily activity allows them to do something constructive and yet different with their time. However, doubts are expressed that this will alleviate crime, or act as a palliative for negative social and economic conditions. Indeed, Glyptis (1989) suggested that this view has been prominent in sport for a number of years:

> The promotion of opportunities for enjoyment has long been paralleled by a belief that recreation opportunities can help to contain urban problems, to build a sense of community, and to overcome class and other social conflicts.
>
> (Glyptis, 1989: 42)

What has been missing from similar claims is evidence of causal relationships between project aims and activities, and any significant change (see Chapters 3 and 12). The previous chapter on Sport for All discussed the merits of qualitative information gathering as a means of understanding the collective experience of individuals and community members. Here information can be gathered to test ideals such as active citizenship, social regeneration, social cohesion and capacity building. CSD practitioners and policy makers who move beyond sport's reliance on quantitative measurements will have a more rounded view of the success of projects which carry such ambitious objectives. These points were endorsed by the recommendations on sport and social exclusion in 1999 (PAT 10): qualitative measures were advocated as ways to understand the impact of projects from the experience of participants. They were seen as an essential part of the monitoring of active community initiatives. Finally, Rochdale appears to be more overtly engaged in sport activism through emancipatory practice but such evidence is less transparent in Leeds, although that in itself is no reason to suggest that there are not practitioners who do so.

In summary, both case studies have different pressures on them. What is clear from the 'CSD matrix', however, is that when professionals discuss community sport development there is now a clear need to clarify whether it is policy, process or practice which is the precise focus of discussion. In addition, the scale, context and levels are all important factors in the way organisations and individuals operate in CSD.

114

RECONCEPTUALISING COMMUNITY SPORT DEVELOPMENT

This chapter has discussed key concepts and considered key dimensions to provision, policy and practice. In so doing it has revealed a complexity in pinpointing exactly what CSD is, how it works, what it does and who does it. Having already explored some of these issues, the remaining section will endeavour to pull these often divergent strands together into a coherent whole. To do so it will employ the concept of 'hegemony' as central to the analysis of CSD.

As highlighted earlier, there are various key themes which must be accounted for:

- CSD is a 'contested concept' which has sometimes been used solely as a 'flag of convenience'.
- The CSD policy community ranges from local to regional to national and even transnational.
- Provision is often founded on a partnership between organisations with different motivations.
- There is a capacity for different individuals engaged in the same work to have politically diverse and opposing motives.
- Policy and provision can be orchestrated either as 'top-down' or 'bottom-up'.
- There are tensions between social welfare and social control, community empowerment and soft policing.
- There are tensions in social and cultural policy between community development and sport development.

Hegemony

Hegemony is a socio-cultural process which also takes account of political and economic processes (Hargreaves, 1982). It is central to theorising around CSD and community development (Ledwith, 2011). Hegemony encompasses cultural relations and implies some form of dynamic or dialogue of power relations between and across people and organisations. Hegemony can occur 'vertically', between the powerful and the weak, or the dominant and the subordinate; for example, between the service provider and the community, between sport councils and the national governing bodies or between the local authority sport development unit and individual CSD workers. However, it can also occur horizontally, across governing bodies, between departments in the same organization, between partners working on the same project or, indeed, between workers within the same initiative. Hegemony is a

> lived system of meanings and values . . . It thus constitutes a sense of reality for most people in society, a sense of absolute 'because experienced'

reality. It is, that is to say, in the strongest sense a 'culture' which has also to be seen as the lived dominance and subordination of particular groups.

(Williams, 1977: 110)

So, as much as most organisations and workers may not be familiar with the term 'hegemony', they nevertheless participate in it and it is a fundamental influence on their daily lives. As a socio-cultural process, hegemony permeates all aspects of the theory, policy and practice of CSD.

Hegemonic groups

There are different types of hegemonic groups that represent different interests in CSD and have varying degrees of influence. McDonald (2002) is clear that it is not a simplistic struggle of powerful elites shaping sport into something only they wish to see. In recognition of these complexities, Raymond Williams (1977) categorises hegemonic groups as dominant, residual and emergent, and all parties involved in CSD provision can be so categorised according to their hegemonic position and influence. These groups in turn can be evidenced as traditions, institutions or formations, and all parties involved in CSD provision can be so categorised according to their hegemonic size and position. These provide a useful starting point for the analysis of the dynamics of CSD policy and practice. The notion of hegemonic groups or influences could be expanded to incorporate other aspects such as policy formation and agenda setting.

The reader might use the previous 'Sectors and Levels of Provision Framework' to identify hegemonic players. It is important to consider the following questions. Who works at what levels? What partners are organisations involved with? What is the precise role of the local community (even when it is historically marginalised, a notable absentee from much of the policy-making process)? What different priorities and agendas do organisations and individuals have? Who wields power and influence? The answers to these questions will allow you to begin your hegemonic analysis; to consider how power and hegemony can be experienced between organisations, within organisations and by community members.

Power, freedom and control

CSD works against inequality and discrimination. Any such work necessitates an analysis of who influences hegemonic power and how it can be challenged (Ledwith, 2011). Change will be sustainable only if communities are close to networks of power. This entails empowerment: 'power to the people'! Giving power to the community means taking it away from somewhere else, normally the providers (Taylor, 2000).

CSD is a paradoxical combination of control and planning through state intervention, and freedom, as expressed by the individual in sport or 'at leisure'. Sport is one discrete aspect of life over which people are believed to exercise considerable autonomy and freedom. If not, is it sport at all? This interpretation of sport as freedom is usually at odds with notions of state planning and control. There is an ambiguity of rights to participate in sport in coexistence with more prescriptive concerns to use sport more instrumentally. Long (1981), Gamble (1981) and Coalter (1989) have all described how all leisure, including sport, operates as a dichotomy riddled with conceptual couples such as liberation and control, freedom and constraint, the public and private spheres. Long (1981) was satisfied that a coherent theory should be able to encompass dichotomies; so sport can be both a tool for community development, and an opiate (which ameliorates deprivations). The sophisticated hegemonic power player, such as the state, national governing organisation or local authority, is quite aware of this dichotomy and does not hesitate to take cunning advantage of its utility. So it aims to exercise control over sport, and to promote freedom to participate in sport at the same time!

Community sport development must be understood in the context of both structure and agency as described in Chapter 3. Social structures influence the social context of sport even where individual human agents appear to 'choose' their own sports. Structure and agency work with and against one another to influence outcomes. CSD is sensitised to the needs of the community as perceived by the providers and as expressed from within the community. CSD is influenced structurally by provider organisations such as Sport England or a local authority recreation department, and also by wider social reality, but it is flexible to adapt and respond to human agency determined by communities.

Hegemony accounts for those inherent contradictions, or dichotomies, apparent in the policy and practice of CSD. It acknowledges the role of both structure and agency (McDonald, 2002) implicit in the 'sphere of exchange' (Bennett, 1981a: 5) between the provider and the community. It reconciles the situated practice between planning and participant autonomy in practice. It also describes a dialogue between 'top-down' and 'bottom-up' dimensions of provision. CSD is complex; it simultaneously spans different intervention policies, and so achieves an 'economy of remedies' (Coalter et al., 1986: 92). This combination of rationales demonstrates the hegemonic power of dominant groups such as Sport England, County Sport Partnerships and Community Sport Networks.

The previously cited models of CSD policy – three of which are most often forms of state-driven intervention (social control, social welfare and democratisation of sport) – describe attempts by dominant cultures, manifested in institutions such as sports' governing bodies and local authorities, to influence the sport culture of communities, whereas sport democracy and sport activism are more likely to be attempts to influence state provision by communities. Historically, the Sports Council(s) has rarely legitimised sport as carefree enjoyment as experienced by most people. It has been preoccupied with externalities such as social order and health rather than the cultural meaning of participation. Hegemony describes sport as a site of cultural struggle. This struggle takes place with each of the previous intervention rationales, whereby there are attempts to implement or impose each and respond either to consent or to resist that imposition. However, there is also a struggle between the rationales, whereby they may be vying with each other for superior prominence amidst a more complex web of acceptance and resistance. Dominant culture is contested locally by workers in the field, and by the community itself. For that reason the sport activism model of CSD was also introduced, as it can be understood as a hegemonic subculture, oppositional to the dominant order.

This perpetual conflict is acted out in CSD between dominant, residual and emergent cultural traditions, institutions and formations. Community sport can be a concession of power by the dominant hegemonic order. This can be seen as a means towards the incorporation of other more marginalised groups that may welcome the provision and thereby accept the dominant culture and order. In this sense CSD may provide aspects of surrogate satisfaction without addressing structural oppression and whilst incorporating the oppressed themselves into the dominant hegemonic culture (Hargreaves, 1986).

Dominance, resistance and incorporation

Hegemony describes incomplete attempts by dominant cultural groups to incorporate opposition as well as resistance (Williams, 1977). CSD is sited directly in the midst of cultural struggles whereby the dominant order, such as Sport England and Leeds City Council, through projects and initiatives, such as Active Communities and the Community Sport Team, attempts to enfranchise dissociated sections of the population. Practitioners are conscious, at times, of being the broker between policy makers and the community. They are conscious of carrying out aims set by policy makers and yet are responsive to and supportive of leadership and self-determination from within the community. There is often conflict between what a policy instructs and what the community needs.

However, dominant groups do not rule society; they merely lead it. Dominant groups attempt to engage the support of others fostered around the dominant values. So Sport England sells 'Active Communities' as a framework for all major providers to work within. Leeds City Council 'buys' into that, and 'sells' the Community Sport

118

Team to its own local co-providers. Thus, dominant groups lead mainly by consensus rather than by coercion. However, they can resort to more overtly directive forms of coercion or social control by exercising their power. To support, or not to support? To fund, or not to fund? That is the question. The state shapes and directs national sports culture and so enables the construction of a specific dominant culture. Popular cultural forms, alternative to the dominant culture, are incorporated through market forces such as commercialisation, or directly by the state itself (McDonald, 1995).

> Hegemony works through ideology but it does not consist of false ideas, perceptual definitions. It works primarily by inserting the subordinate class into the key institutions and structures which support the power and the social order of the dominant order. It is above all in these structures and relations that a subordinate class 'lives its subordination'.
>
> (Gramsci, 1971: 164)

The tendency of dominant groups to structure or frame the conditions for CSD practice does not enable them to dictate results. So 'we operate, within constraints, which we are free to change, but we are not free to abolish the principle of living within constraints' (Kelly, 1984: 4). Individual agents still ultimately make their own sport by responding to their own situations. Resistance is as much a part of hegemony as are conformity and control. Capacity for interpretation and reaction, agency itself, is dependent upon the situation. Individuals and groups find alternative, sometimes radical, cultural expression such as 'Freedom through Football' (Totten, 2011) in opposition to the status quo, despite the centralising tendencies of sports policy and provision. Sport (as leisure) has provided an increasingly more malleable arena for agency than other spheres of life (Hall and Jefferson, 1976). Sport has emancipatory potential, the 'extent to which the politics of the popular provides a point of resistance to bourgeois hegemony' (Hargreaves, 1986: 220).

The state preserves its position as the dominant culture in CSD by pursuing its own hegemonic project and responding to hegemonic opposition. The government has been vigorously involved in CSD, but it still regulates the mainstream market in which inequalities in choice occur. It may intervene using a social justice agenda (Roberts, 1978) but without fundamentally changing the mainstream infrastructure. A more transformative notion of CSD may be necessary to challenge those inherent vested interests and inequalities as well as the structures which maintain them. However, the responsive state is the hegemonic state which incorporates resistance and preserves mainstream order. In relation to community arts, Kelly concedes that a radical programme, lacking coordination, has been diluted by assimilation into the arts establishment in a legitimised form, in which radicals have become foot soldiers in their own movement: 'we came as invaders, but without a language of our own we were soon acting and talking like the natives of the citadel' (Kelly, 1984:

29). The same fate has no doubt been met by many of those radical idealists working within CSD. This polemical analysis demonstrates the hegemonic power of the dominant culture to incorporate and disarm even the most radical of opposition. It also illustrates the potential for alternative and oppositional hegemonic cultures to emerge in a subcultural form. Any transformative ambitions for CSD need to consider the extent to which they can resist and overcome dominant hegemonic interests.

Partington and Totten (2012) have outlined how hegemonic processes permeated Rochdale Community Sports and how a very locally embedded credibility meant sports activities were viewed as strengthening and empowering existing community groups, and providing a link into a wider social movement that could challenge power relations externally. A sense of local democracy helped to build capacity for self-help, which strengthened community empowerment. The organisation acted as a conveyer for 'participatory democracy' (Ledwith, 2005), as a vehicle for raising social and political concerns, and as a means through which communities could organise to gain representation, to campaign and to engage in resistance against the injustices they faced. This enabled communities to move from passive resistance to taking action to transform structures that previously constrained them and offered the potential for sports activities to contribute towards wider transformative action.

Hegemony: a dynamic process

So hegemony accommodates elements of both resistance and control, and must therefore be seen as a dynamic process. The dominant actors within CSD policy and provision seek to impose control, and subordinate groups either consent to that or offer resistance. CSD is an arena in which this cultural struggle can be acted out (McDonald, 2002). Hegemony is a continual process. It is continually assembled and reassembled, reproduced and secured (and set back) (Bennett, 1981b). Hegemony is never completed; 'it has continually to be renewed, recreated, defended and modified. It is also continually resisted, limited, altered and challenged by pressures not all its own' (Williams, 1977: 112). In hegemonic terms, that position, in limbo, will never be resolved. The struggle is ongoing: top-down control and bottom-up resistance, but also between and across organisations and individuals operating at similar levels. Individual CSD workers are able to discriminate, within certain confines, on the balance they wish to achieve between these contradictory aims, but hegemony itself is perpetual and all-encompassing.

CONCLUSION

This chapter opened with an examination of key concepts and tensions in CSD. It then offered a vigorous analysis of the complex nature of CSD provision, policy and practice. It has raised many issues and debates about that very nature. It concludes with a theoretical reconceptualisation of CSD which accounts for ambiguities in practice.

The conceptual complexity of CSD is compounded by a diverse range of provision. Its true nature and meaning are therefore contested in theory, policy and practice. For some, the content is very much conventional institutionalised sport. For others, it is a more informal manifestation of sport or recreation and much else that may not be sport at all. For some, the central focus is sport. For others, who may not bear any particular allegiance to sport, the key focus is very much people or community. So CSD practice reflects these tensions between both sport development and community development.

The diverse range of CSD practices, and therefore its policy community, are reflected in the 'CSD matrix'. This model accounts for policy formulated and driven at different levels: transnational, national, regional and local. It draws attention to different styles of the management of provision, ranging from 'top-down' to 'bottom-up'. It plots the involvement of all three sectors of the mixed economy engaged in provision: mostly public or voluntary, and occasionally commercial. It brings attention to the fact that many individual initiatives are often partnerships between organisations from different sectors, perhaps at different levels, which, in turn, are in partnership with local communities. It further alluded to the different types of practitioners who may all share some interest in CSD: SDOs, facility managers, youth workers, education workers, health workers, social workers, probation officers and others.

This broad range of practitioners is reflected in the range of policy interests which rationalise or legitimise provision. CSD is orientated around different and overlapping social, cultural, political and economic concerns (Totten, 1995). It can be analysed from any combination of those perspectives. CSD accommodates a range of different philosophies, policy rationales and practices. They all share similar concerns about inequality, access and inclusion, marginalised groups and exclusion, democracy and participation. So CSD is a form of socio-cultural intervention in mainstream provision, and in the everyday lives of communities. Five overlapping models of policy rationale were introduced: social control, social welfare, the democratisation of sport, sport democracy and sport activism. Each can have some bearing on CSD, and their compound effect is to sustain the broad appeal of CSD to policy makers. CSD is dichotomous; it is about liberation and control. Its agenda ranges from tokenism to manipulation, and radically to emancipation.

All the above complexities underline the crucial fact that CSD is conceptually dynamic, a hegemonic 'cultural struggle' between varied institutions, organisations and interest groups who all share some commitment to this unconventional approach to provision. Best practice in CSD is varied, but what makes it so valuable and unique is its philosophy of approach or process. Community sport development is a flexible, adaptable, informal, consultative, people-centred approach, aimed at the initial threshold to participation in order to address the deficiencies of mainstream provision.

LEARNING ACTIVITY

Using Figure 4.5 (Partnership domain framework) choose an initiative with partners from different sectors that you are familiar with or wish to understand a little better. First identify its partners and then, using the diagram, assess the balance of influences/resources from each partner and place the initiative in the diagram.

REFERENCES

Active Communities (2002) *Active Communities: Initial Findings from the 2001 Home Office Citizenship Survey*, London: Home Office.

Anti-racist World Cup (2012) 'Homepage', www.mondialiantirazzisti.org

Arnstein, S. (1969) 'A ladder of citizen participation', *Journal of the American Institute of Planning*, 35 (4): 216–224.

Association of Metropolitan Authorities (1989) *Community Development: The Local Authority Role*, London: AMA.

Bennett, T. (1981a) 'Popular culture and hegemony in post-war Britain', *Politics, Ideology and Popular Culture*, 1: 5–30.

Bennett, T. (1981b) 'Popular culture: themes and issues 2', *Popular Culture: History and Theory*, unit 3, Milton Keynes: Open University Press.

Bianchinni, F. (1989) *Urban Renaissance? The Arts and the Urban Regeneration Process*, Liverpool: Centre for Urban Studies, University of Liverpool.

Booth, M. (1997) 'Community development: oiling the wheels of participation', *Community Development Journal*, 32 (2): 151–158.

Brent, J. (2004) 'The desire for community: illusion, confusion and paradox', *Community Development Journal*, 39 (3): 213–223.

Butcher, H., Glen, A., Henderson, P. and Smith, J. (1993) *Community and Public Policy*, London: Pluto Press.

Cabinet Office (2002) *Game Plan: A Strategy for Delivering Government's Sport and Physical Activity Objectives*, London: Cabinet Office.

Cadbury Schweppes (2006) 'Get active', www.bitc.org.uk/resources/viewpoint/cadburygetactive.html

Cantle, T. and Institute of Community Cohesion (2006) *Challenging Local Communities to Change Oldham*, Coventry: ICC.

Kevin Hylton and Mick Totten

Carrington, B. and Leaman, O. (1983) 'Sport as community politics', in Haywood, L. (ed.), *Sport in the Community – the Next Ten Years: Problems and Issues*, Ilkley: Leisure Studies Association.

Carrington, B. and McDonald, I. (2001) 'Whose game is it anyway? Racism in local league cricket', in Carrington, B. and McDonald, I. (eds.), *Race, Sport and British Society*, London: Routledge.

CDX (Community Development Exchange) (2013) 'Defining community development', www.cdx.org.uk/community-development/defining-community-development

Centre for Leisure and Sport Research (2003) 'Awards for All: an impact study evaluating sports projects in the Awards for All programme', unpublished report to Sport England.

Chaskin, R. (1997) 'Perspectives on neighbourhoods and communities', *Social Service Review*, 71 (4): 521–547.

Chomsky, N. (2003) *Hegemony or Survival*, New York: Metropolitan.

Coalter, F. (1989) *Freedom and Constraint*, London: Routledge.

Coalter, F. (1991) 'Sports participation: price or priorities?', *Leisure Studies*, 12: 171–182.

Coalter, F. (2001) *Realising the Potential of Cultural Services: The Case for Sport*, London: Local Government Association.

Coalter, F. (2002) *Sport and Community Development: A Manual*, Edinburgh: Sportscotland.

Coalter, F. and Allison, M. (1996) *Sport and Community Development*, Edinburgh: Scottish Sports Council.

Coalter, F., Long, J. and Duffield, B. (1986) *Rationale for Public Sector Investment in Leisure*, London: ESRC.

Collins, M. and Kay, T. (2003) *Sport and Social Exclusion*, London: Routledge.

Department for Communities and Local Government (2006) 'The community development challenge', www.cdf.org.uk/c/document_library/get_file?uuid=483850bf-ba92-46d0-9bc4-a35c635c5ae3&groupId=10128

Department for Culture, Media and Sport (2001) *The Government's Plan for Sport: A Sporting Future for All*, London: DCMS.

Department for Culture, Media and Sport Policy Action Team (10) (1999) *PAT 10: A Report to the Social Exclusion Unit*, London: DCMS.

Department of Communities and Local Government (2008) 'Index of Multiple Deprivation', www.communities.gov.uk/documents/communities/xls/576504.xls

Department of the Environment (1977) *Recreation and Deprivation in Inner Urban Areas*, London: HMSO.

Department of the Environment (1989) *Sport and Active Recreation Provision in Inner Cities*, London: Crown Publications.

Easton Cowboys (2012) 'Homepage', www.eastoncowboys.org.uk

European Union (2012) 'White Paper on sport', http://ec.europa.eu/sport/white-paper/the-2007-white-paper-on-sport_en.htm

FA Premier League (2006) 'Homepage', www.premierleague.com

Football Foundation (2006) 'Case studies', www.footballfoundation.org.uk/about-the-football-foundation/case-studies

Football Task Force (1999) *Investing in the Community*, London: Ministry of Sport.

Fremeaux, I. (2005) 'New Labour's appropriation of the concept of community: a critique', *Community Development Journal*, 40 (3): 265–274.

Gamble, A. (1981) *An Introduction to Modern Social and Political Thought*, London: Macmillan.

Gates, R. and Stout, F. (eds.) (1996) *The City Reader*, 2nd edn, London: Routledge Press.

Glyptis, S. (1989) *Leisure and Unemployment*, Milton Keynes: Open University.

Gramsci, A. (1971) *Selections from the Prison Notebooks*, New York: Lawrence & Wishart.

The Guardian (2011) 'Should we collect vouchers to fund equipment for schools?', www.guardian.co.uk/education/mortarboard/2011/feb/16/should-we-collect-school-vouchers

The Guardian (2012) 'St Pauli: a socialist football club in Hamburg's red light district – video', www.guardian.co.uk/travel/series/marcel-theroux-new-europe+football/stpauli

Hall, S. and Jefferson, T. (1976) *Resistance through Rituals*, London: Hutchinson.

Hargreaves, J. (1982) *Sport, Culture, and Ideology*, London: Routledge.

Hargreaves, J. (1986) *Sport, Power and Culture*, Cambridge: Polity Press.

Hargreaves, J. and McDonald, I. (2002) 'Cultural studies and the sociology of sport', in Coakley, J. and Dunning, E. (eds.), *Handbook of Sports Studies*, London: Sage.

Haywood, L. (1994) *Community Leisure and Recreation*, London: Heinemann.

Haywood, L. and Kew, F. (1989) 'Community sports programmes: old wine in new bottles', in Bramham P., Henry, I., Mommaas, H. and van der Poel, H. (eds.), *Leisure and Urban Processes*, London: Routledge.

HMSO (1975) *White Paper on Sport and Recreation*, Cmnd 6200, London: HMSO.

Home Office (1999) *Report of the Policy Action Team 9 on Community Self-Help*, London: Home Office.

Houlihan, B. and White, A. (2002) *The Politics of Sport Development*, London: Routledge.

Hylton, K. (2003) *Sportsweb: An Evaluation*, Leeds: Centre for Leisure and Sport Research.

Hylton, K. and Morpeth, N.D. (2012) 'London 2012: "race" matters, and the East End', *International Journal of Sport Policy and Politics*, 4 (2): 1–18.

Hylton, K. and Totten, M. (2001) 'Community sports development', in Hylton, K. Bramham, P., Jackson, D. and Nesti, M. (eds.), *Sports Development: Policy, Process and Practice*, 1st edn, London: Routledge.

Institute for Volunteering Research (2001) *Volunteering for All? Exploring the Link between Volunteering and Social Exclusion*, London: IVR.

Jackson, D., Totten, M. and Robinson, P. (2003) 'Evaluating sports projects in the Awards for All programme', *Yorkshire and Humber Regional Review*, 13 (3): 27–28.

Kelly, O. (1984) *Community, Art and the State*, London: Comedia.

Ledwith, M. (2005) *Community Development: A Critical Approach*, Bristol: Policy Press.

Ledwith, M. (2011) *Community Development: A Critical Approach*, 2nd edn, Bristol: Policy Press.

Lentell, B. (1994) 'Sports development: goodbye to community recreation', in Brackenridge, C. (ed.), *Body Matters: Leisure Images and Lifestyles*, Eastbourne: Leisure Studies Association.

Long, J. (1981) 'Leisure as a tool for community development and the opiate of the masses', in Tomlinson, A. (ed.), *Leisure and Social Control*, Brighton: Leisure Studies Association.

Long, J. and Sanderson, I. (2003) 'The social benefits of sport: where's the proof?', in Gratton, C. and Henry, I. (eds.), *Sport in the City*, London: Routledge.

McDonald, I. (1995) 'Sport for All: RIP? A political critique of the relationship between national sport policy and local authority sports development in London', in Fleming, S., Talbot, M. and Tomlinson, A. (eds.), *Policy and Politics in Sport, Physical Education and Leisure*, Eastbourne: Leisure Studies Association.

McDonald, I. (2002) 'Critical social research and political interventions: moralistic versus radical approaches', in Sugden, J. and Tomlinson, A. (eds.), *Power Games: A Critical Sociology of Sport*, London: Routledge.

McIntosh, P. and Charlton, V. (1985) *Action Sport (MSC): An Evaluation of Phase One*, London: Sports Council.

McIntosh, P. and Charlton, V. (1985) *The Impact of the Sport for All Policy*, London: Sports Council.

Morgan, D. (2000) *Sport versus Youth Crime*, Bolton: Centre for Sport and Leisure Management, Bolton Institute.

Murray, K. (1988) 'The Brixton Recreation Centre: an analysis of a political institution', *International Review for the Sociology of Sport*, 23 (2): 125–138.

Office of the Deputy Prime Minister (2004) *Teaming Up: How Joint Working between Sport and Neighbourhood Renewal Practitioners Can Help in Deprived Areas*, Wetherby: ODPM.

Parry, J. (1986) 'The Community Arts: an arts revolution incorporated', in Parry, J. and Parry, N. (eds.), *Leisure, the Arts and Community*, Brighton: Leisure Studies Association.

Partington, J. and Totten, M. (2012) 'Community sports projects and effective community empowerment: a case study in Rochdale', *Managing Leisure Journal*, 17 (1): 49–66.

Plant, R., Lessen, H. and Taylor-Gooby, P. (1980) *Political Philosophy and Social Welfare*, London: Routledge.

Popple, K. (1995) *Analysing Community Work*, Buckingham: Open University Press.

Popple, K. and Shaw, M. (1997) 'Editorial introduction: social movements: reasserting "community"', *Community Development Journal*, 323 (3): 191–198.

Republica Internationale (2012) 'Homepage', www.republica-i.co.uk

Rigg, M. (1986) *Action Sport: An Evaluation*, London: Sports Council.

Roberts, K. (1978) *Contemporary Society and the Growth of Leisure*, London: Longman.

RoFTRA (2001) *Community Sports Project Strategic Plan 2001–06*, Rochdale: RoFTRA.

RoFTRA (2004) *RoFTRA Strategic Plan 2004–07*, Rochdale: RoFTRA.

Sankt Pauli Football Club (2012) 'Homepage', www.fcstpauli.de

Scottish Sports Council (1998) *Sport 21: Nothing Left to Chance*, Edinburgh: Scottish Sports Council.

Simpson, J. (1976a) *Towards Cultural Democracy*, Strasbourg: Council of Europe.

Simpson, J. (1976b) 'Notes and reflections on animation', in Haworth, J. and Veal, A. (eds.), *Leisure and the Community*, Birmingham: CURS.

Skills Active (2006) *A Summary of the Community Sport Development Research Report*, London: Skills Active.

Smith, C. (1998) *The Comprehensive Spending Review: New Approach to Investment in Culture*, London: DCMS.

Sport England (2000) *Active Communities: An Introduction*, London: Sport England.

Sport England (2001) *Sport Action Zones: A Summary Report on the Establishment of the First 12 Zones – Issues, Successes, and Lessons for the Future*, London: Sport England.

Sport England (2002) *Positive Futures: A Review of Impact and Good Practice*, London: Sport England.

Sport England (2004) *The Framework for Sport in England: Making England an Active and Successful Sporting Nation – a Vision for 2020*, London: Sport England.

Sport England (2005a) *Delivery Plan, 2005–2008*, London: Sport England.

Sport England (2005b) *Sport: Playing Its Part*, London: Sport England.

Sport England (2011) 'Background to community sports hubs', www.sportengland.org/funding/iconic_facilities/background_to_the_fund.aspx

Sport England (2012) 'Background to community sports hubs', www.sportengland.org/funding/sustainable_facilities/background_to_the_fund.aspx

Sportscotland (2011) 'Community sport hubs', www.sportscotland.org.uk/ChannelNavigation/Topics/TopicNavigation/Community+sport/Community+sport+hubs

Sports Council (1978) *Sport and Recreation in the Inner Cities*, London: Sports Council.

Sports Council (1982) *Sport in the Community: The Next Ten Years*, London: Ashdown Press.

Sports Council Research Unit (1991) *National Demonstration Projects: Major Lessons and Issues for Development*, London: Sports Council.

Standing Conference on Community Development (2001) *Strategic Framework for Community Development*, Sheffield: SCCD.

Stonewall (2006) 'Homepage', www.stonewallfc.com

Taylor, M. (2000) *Top Down meets Bottom Up: Neighbourhood Management*, York: Joseph Rowntree Foundation.

Torkildsen, G. (2005) *Leisure and Recreation Management*, London: Routledge.

Totten, M. (1993) *Birds of a Feather: A Comparative Analysis of Community Sports and Community Arts*, unpublished MA dissertation, Leeds Metropolitan University.

Totten, M. (1995) 'Conceptualising community leisure: unravelling the rationale', in Long, J. (ed.), *Nightmares and Successes: Doing Small Scale Research in Leisure*, Leeds: Leeds Metropolitan University.

Totten, M. (2011) 'Freedom through Football; A tale of football, community, activism and resistance', in Ratna, A. and Lashua, B. (eds.), *Community and Inclusion in Leisure Research and Sport Development*, Eastbourne: LSA.

Tucker, L. (2011) 'Forza, Forza Republica: a case study of politics and socialist culture in a Sunday league football club', in Ratna, A. and Lashua, B. (eds.), *Community and Inclusion in Leisure Research and Sport Development*, Eastbourne: LSA.

Williams, R. (1977) *Marxism and Literature*, Oxford: Oxford University Press.

Yorkshire and Humberside Council for Sport and Recreation (1989) *A Sporting Chance*, Leeds: Yorkshire and Humberside Council for Sport and Recreation.

Kevin Hylton and Mick Totten

CHAPTER 5

PARTNERSHIPS IN SPORT

STEPHEN ROBSON AND JANINE PARTINGTON

> Work in partnership like never before – we are in this together.
> (Sport England, 2010: unnumbered)

These thoughts from Sport England, in the wake of the announcement of the most far-reaching public sector cuts in a generation, spell out what sport and recreation development professionals have known for many years, namely that working in isolation is not an option. Since the onset of County Sports Partnerships, a more formal recognition has existed that it is unrealistic to expect resource-strapped sport development organisations to achieve all of their goals without a considerable amount of their work being undertaken collaboratively. This compulsion to pool resources is confirmed by Slack and Parent (2006: 164):

> No sport organization exists in isolation from the other organizations in its environment, the source of the material and financial resources a sport organization needs to survive.

The range of alliances now in existence in sport and recreation is immense. They span the entire spectrum from major transnational consortia, delivering the Glasgow 2014 Commonwealth Games, to local authority sport development professionals, assisting the local netball team in its attempts to attract new players. A specific skill set is required of any professional seeking to initiate, maintain or join successful partnerships. This is recognised in the curricula of undergraduate degree courses in sport development as well as in the Level 3 National Occupational Standards for Sports Development (SkillsActive, 2010).

Partnership working centres on the idea that individuals or representatives make a commitment in terms of what they are able to *input* into the relationship, on the basis that some or all of the *outputs* will help them to achieve their overall goals.

Recently theorists have become interested in *throughputs*, the sustained benefits of staff development when working with other partners. Strategic alliances, relationships with still greater forms of interdependence, are differentiated by their capacity to enhance or foster organisational learning. According to Johnson and colleagues (2011) organisations engaged in strategic alliances should grow in competencies as they learn from one another. This issue of mutual benefit permeates the present chapter, but it is to be acknowledged that in some instances the rewards are not always clear or shared.

The purpose of this chapter is to explore both benefits and problems experienced by organisations working together. It provides practitioners and students with the means to analyse and optimise alliances by drawing on relevant organisation and management theories. A brief historical perspective details the recent growth in strategic partnerships. It is useful, initially, to reflect conceptually upon the term 'partnership', and to consider its relevance to the world of sport and recreation development.

KEY TERMS

Throughout this chapter a number of terms are used interchangeably. Expressions such as 'alliance', 'collaboration', 'joint working' and 'working together' carry the same emphasis as the key concept 'partnership'. A satisfactory definition is offered by Service de police de la Ville de Montréal (2012):

> A formal agreement between two or more parties that have agreed to work together in the pursuit of common goals.

In the context of sport and recreation development professions, this definition accommodates the gamut of alliances to be considered, although perhaps the *formal agreement* aspect is not always present. However, the definition emphasises that any coming together of organisations (through 'qualified' representatives) or interested individuals to further sport experiences can be considered to constitute a partnership. Yoshino and Rangan (1995: 5) assert that 'strategic alliances' involve two or more organisations uniting in the pursuit of common goals, to share both the benefits and the assignment of tasks. Importantly, as reinforced by Dussauge and Garrette (1999: 2), there is no loss of 'strategic autonomy'; in other words, organisations retain their independence. They offer a 'representation' of an alliance for further clarification:

Figure 5.1 clearly illustrates that a partnership or alliance is distinct from a merger, in which two organisations are replaced by a single new entity. The alliance is

Stephen Robson and Janine Partington

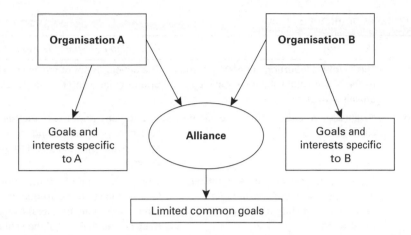

Figure 5.1 Representation of an alliance (adapted from Dussauge and Garrette, 1999: 3).

constituted to deal with issues relevant to goals that the organisations have in common; meanwhile each organisation will be engaged in its core work elsewhere.

THE NATURE OF PARTNERSHIPS

Partnerships in sport and recreation take on a myriad of forms, each one as unique as a fingerprint. This section considers the main factors involved in characterising any given partnership.

The first of these factors is *timescale*. Partnerships may be temporary or permanent, and thus operate over vastly different time periods. Johnson and colleagues (2011) describe the evolution and lifespan of a partnership or alliance as moving through a number of phases. Table 5.1 illustrates this in relation to Sport England's Sport Makers initiative (see Sport England, 2012a).

The second factor to consider is the *type* of partners. These may be drawn from any combination of public, voluntary and commercial sectors. There is also an increasing emphasis on *stakeholder* involvement in public policies and their implementation, with a requirement to provide evidence of consultation within strategic plans and funding applications. In this sense, stakeholders such as residents or sports clubs have the potential to enjoy a dual role as customer and partner (see later section on stakeholder salience). Partnerships involving commercial bodies as a sponsor of services delivered by public and voluntary sector organisations are becoming more commonplace in sport development, such as the sponsorship of the English Cricket Board's Kwik Cricket initiative by Asda (English Cricket Board, 2012).

Table 5.1 Stages of alliance evolution

Stage	Description	Applied to the Sport Makers initiative
Courtship	This involves 'courting' different potential partners and establishing strategic and organisational 'fit'	The development of the alliance between Sport England and the National Lottery
Negotiation	Negotiation of each partner's role in the alliance	The agreement between the National Lottery to provide funding for the scheme and Sport England to oversee delivery
Start-up	This stage typically involves significant investment of resources, and often involves introducing further partners to the alliance	The involvement of County Sports Partnerships (who subsequently recruited other community partners) as regional hubs for the delivery of the scheme, and subsequent launch of the scheme nationwide
Maintenance	Ongoing operation of the alliance	Regular progress meetings between all partners and reporting on progress against targets. Continued delivery of Sport Makers training courses and recruitment of volunteers
Termination	Completion of the alliance once aims have been fulfilled. There is the potential to extend the alliance if successful	Funding for the Sport Makers programme scheduled to finish in September 2013

It is also important to recognise that partnerships effectively occur *within*, as well as *between*, organisations. For instance, a sport development team, the parks department and youth services from within the same local authority might work together to run a summer sports activity programme for young people.

Power distribution is the next factor to consider in characterising a partnership. Although many alliances are entered into with all partners on an equal footing, others may have a dominant or lead agency. Slack and Parent (2006) introduce the term 'alliance control', the degree to which partners are able to influence and control the behaviour and outputs of other partners. In addition, partners may have control over different elements of the partnership (as shown in Table 5.1). Ideally, an alliance should exercise 'selective control' whereby organisations are given the power to undertake those tasks to which they are best suited. In the Sport Makers programme, for example, the coordinating role is taken by Sport England whereas the delivery role is adopted by partners such as County Sports Partnerships.

The *scale* or size of partnerships can vary greatly. There is scope for joint working at every level, from a joint venture between a table tennis club and a local school to the aforementioned transnational venture to deliver the 2014 Commonwealth Games in Glasgow, involving multiple types of organisations from different sectors.

Stephen Robson and Janine Partington

The scale is often determined by the *aims* of the partnership. Once again, there are as many possible motivations for entering into collaboration with others as there are projects. Johnson and colleagues (2011) identify a number of rationales or aims for the establishment of alliances. 'Scale alliances' exist when organisations work together to gain a competitive advantage they would be unable to achieve alone, for example a number of sports clubs working together to submit a funding application for a multi-sports facility. 'Access alliances' involve using the capabilities (such as resources or knowledge) of another organisation to achieve a specific goal, exemplified by the establishment of Community Badminton Networks that operate at a local level involving Badminton England and local authorities. Finally, 'complementary alliances' exist where the alliance serves to bolster each partner's weaknesses. An example of this is the sponsorship by McDonald's of the Football Association's 'Your Game' programme (Football Association, 2012). Although this may be morally troubling for some, it undoubtedly allows McDonald's to be seen to fulfil its corporate social responsibility obligations, and the Football Association is able to provide additional resources and support to administrators, coaches and volunteers working at grassroots level.

THE DEVELOPMENT OF PARTNERSHIP WORKING

This section offers a further update to the historical overview of sport and recreation partnerships offered in the first two editions of this book. The focus here is on developments in the late and post-New Labour eras; readers should therefore consult the previous editions for a more detailed breakdown of the development of partnership working from the 1970s to the early 2000s.

Central government's explicit role as a *partner* in major national sport and recreation initiatives is a relatively recent development, which took hold during the Blair and Brown New Labour governments (1997–2010). Governmental interest has developed as the sector has gradually become more definable and organised. The extent to which one has been determined by the other is a subject of ongoing debate.

While sport development has become firmly embedded in local government structures and countless formal and informal partnerships have resulted, all levels of sport have continued to wrestle with a bewildering and illogical structure that seems to confound all parties rather than offering support. In 2005 Carter bemoaned that there was

> no clear alignment between local and national sports delivery, nor is there a systematic, joined up approach towards community sport.
>
> (Carter, 2005: 20)

With its leadership status assured by its function as distributor of National Lottery money, Sport England attempted to minimise confusion in England by instigating a Delivery System for Sport (Sport England, 2006). This focused on subregional strategic bodies (County Sports Partnerships) and local delivery mechanisms (Community Sport Networks). In theory, all key stakeholders should be represented in one or both of these structures. Perspicaciously the previous edition of this book advised cautious optimism at best regarding the likelihood that the Delivery System would finally clarify roles and relationships for partners across sport in England. Sport England's priorities shifted yet again when it was decided that a greater proportion of National Lottery funding was to be channelled directly through selected national governing bodies and their Whole Sport Plans (Sport England, 2008). Accompanying this was a diminution of core funding to county sports partnerships, which in response had to diversify and seek new income streams, leading to a far less standardised approach to the facilitation of strategic partnership working across subregional structures. Active People Survey figures (Sport England, 2012b) suggest that this new funding regime did not have the desired impact upon mass participation. Consequently Sport England's (2011a) decision to refresh the four-year Whole Sport Plan funding cycle was greeted in some circles with derision and elsewhere with ironic surprise that for once the landscape was not to shift dramatically.

Partnership working in sport had become part of the political landscape of New Labour governance. The investment in School Sport Partnerships and the *de facto* sport development role of many Partnership Development Managers signalled a previously unseen level of political appreciation for the power of partnership working. The Conservative–Liberal Democrat coalition's choice to cut public services as a response to the global financial crisis had a major impact upon this programme (Conn, 2010; see also Chapter 6 below) but galvanised support in many quarters for a continuation of its work. As with County Sports Partnerships, the survival of many of these sporting alliances, albeit fundamentally altered in scope and mission, shows that the role of partnership working has forever been upgraded from a desirable sport and recreation development tactic to its present status as a *necessity* for prosperity and survival. Thus, having hinted at the benefits and accompanying issues experienced in sport development partnerships, the chapter turns its attention to itemising these characteristics.

BENEFITS OF PARTNERSHIP WORKING

Political pressure for sporting organisations to work in partnership has resulted in partnerships being viewed as the accepted way of delivering services, and there is widespread acknowledgement of the benefits of collaboration. This section provides an overview of these benefits.

Stephen Robson and Janine Partington

Pooling of resources

The previous edition of this book made reference to the relatively healthy state of resources for sport development, describing it as a 'golden age of increased funding'. The same is certainly not true at the time of writing this chapter. The above-mentioned public sector cuts initiated by the coalition government threatened the very existence of sport development services in local authorities and impacted significantly on the infrastructure of sport, particularly in relation to school sport. As a result, it is even more necessary for a culture of cooperation rather than competition to exist in order for meagre resources for sport to stretch further and be utilised effectively. Given this, the benefits of pooling resources are even more relevant than before to professionals working within this challenging climate.

- An important benefit of pooling resources is the potential to identify and eliminate *duplication* of services between partner organisations. This reduces the financial burden on both organisations, enabling desired outcomes to be realised. The need to develop a more coordinated approach to sport and physical activity provision is identified by Plymouth City Council in its Sports Development Strategy for 2010–2013, stating that the department will

  actively seek to work with appropriate public, private and voluntary bodies at local, regional and national level to develop shared objectives and to deliver an integrated approach to sport and physical activity provision in the city.

  (Plymouth City Council, 2010: 17)

  In addition, Sport England, perhaps sensing competition rather than collaboration between NGBs, has indicated that, in order to receive funding for Whole Sport Plans for 2013–2017, there must be a greater emphasis on 'joint working between NGBs to achieve critical mass and grow demand' (Sport England, 2011b). Clearly, if NGBs are to achieve the challenging targets set within Whole Sport Plans it will be essential for them to work collaboratively and develop integrated programmes.

- *Human resources* can be maximised. This can involve developing partnerships to *access* human resources, for example a sport development team working with a further education college to source volunteers for school holiday programmes, or to *create* a new human resource, for example jointly funded staff posts. An example of this is the Rugby League Development Officer post for Rochdale, Bury and Bolton, funded jointly by a combination of the local authorities/cultural trusts and the Rugby Football League. It is unlikely that any partner would have been able to fund the post single-handedly. Elsewhere there is evidence of sharing human resources to deliver large events such as the West Yorkshire Area Youth Games. This entails the County Sports Partnership coordinating staff and volunteers from NGBs, the five West Yorkshire local authorities, schools and Leeds Metropolitan University, all of which collaborate to deliver the regional event (West Yorkshire Sport, 2011). Events such as these also provide opportunities for *workforce development*, with many young volunteers gaining valuable personal development opportunities.

■ *Expertise* and *knowledge* are other aspects of human resources that can be pooled. This may involve traditional alliances, such as those between local authorities and NGBs, or more unique partnerships which involve the pooling of expertise in innovative ways. Link4Life's Youth Sport Volunteer Engagement Officer has a remit for developing volunteering across Rochdale with a particular focus on young people from hard-to-reach backgrounds and deprived communities. The officer's sport development knowledge and expertise is coupled with the expertise of key local figures, not only to identify and act upon opportunities to develop volunteering but also to use that opportunity to facilitate community development outcomes. An innovative partnership with Petrus, a homelessness charity, was particularly successful in training a number of homeless young people (some of whom were also dealing with issues relating to drug and alcohol abuse) as sport leaders and then integrating them into more mainstream programmes as volunteers. Whereas the sport officer was able to provide support and guidance relating to sport leadership, staff from Petrus assisted with health and housing issues and offered encouragement.

Pooling influence

Partnership working often facilitates realisation of otherwise unattainable goals. This is important in terms of getting favourable decisions made, such as approval for projects to go ahead, particularly in the context of sharing vital resources. From pooling influence at a national level for investment to support a specific policy agenda, to campaigning at a grassroots level to secure the continued use of facilities or provision of services, it is clear that doing so in partnership with other agencies is far more powerful than working alone. Influence can be exerted in a number of different settings and ways:

■ *Personal links* between individuals at similar levels in partner organisations often 'open doors'. Productive personal relationships lead to a shared commitment to pooling resources, sharing information or acting as a gatekeeper to enable and support access to a new community setting. Barriers of technical language and professional jargon can be overcome by the presence of an advocate within an organisation and can enhance the credibility of the intended activity. Many of the host of sport-health alliances now in operation across the UK (see Chapter 7 for detailed examples) owe their success to sport development and health professionals setting aside suspicion and doubt in interagency working.

Once convinced of the benefits of partnership arrangements, key players are in a position to argue the case for the project within their organisations and so take the work forward collaboratively.

- *Political power* can be exercised in ways which have productive or destructive effects upon sport and recreation development. Politics and politicians are intrinsically linked to the management and provision of sport at all levels. It is always desirable, and often essential, to have capacity to influence politicians, whether they are local authority elected members, executive members in an NGB or Members of Parliament. The decision to award England the Rugby World Cup in 2015 is an excellent example of the pooling of political power. The Rugby Football Union gained support for the bid from the UK government, national sports organisations such as Sport England and UK Sport, and professional clubs. Without this political backing it is unlikely that it would have been able to develop as strong a bid to put forward to the International Rugby Board (IRB).

- *Lobbying* involves interest groups making representations to politicians in order to secure support on issues of consequence. At a local level, for example, Sport Action Zones (SAZs) such as those in Liverpool (see King, 2009) and Braunstone in Leicester (see Walpole and Collins, 2010) were particularly successful at lobbying for sport as a tool to tackle social issues. Funded by Sport England, SAZs were typically based in areas of socio-economic deprivation and were often established as a result of partnership working between regeneration agencies and local authority leisure departments. They often had high levels of political power and were able to use this to lobby for additional resources to support their work, resulting in the delivery of sport and community development programmes and large-scale facility development.

- *Key contacts and gatekeepers:* Having access to important people is crucial at an interpersonal as well as an organisational level. Effective working together means sharing contacts, whereby tactical use is made of each partner's professional relationships. This is another example of the ability of alliances to open avenues to resources. Contacts range from community leaders to senior politicians. Utilising existing contacts, personnel can act as gatekeepers, giving colleagues in partner organisations access to key individuals which might otherwise be denied. Vail (2007: 575) discovered that Canadian grassroots tennis programmes had a far higher chance of success if professional staff worked collaboratively with community representatives to plan, manage and deliver activities; Vail describes this approach as 'collaborative leadership'.

- *Internal lobbying:* Partnerships can also enable those in less senior, but strategically vital, positions in organisations to elicit support for their extended work amongst their own senior managers and politicians – a kind of internal lobbying which embraces the notion that politics takes place in a non-governmental sense within organisations (Kingdom, 2003). In the current climate of public sector cuts, sport development officers within local authorities are under increasing pressure to demonstrate that they are offering value for public money. Frequently this is done by linking their work to social objectives such as education and regeneration.

■ Collaborations with other departments or local agencies can be a successful way of creating alliances and *minimising or sharing risk*. The Bury Sport and Physical Activity Alliance, developed by the local authority's Sport and Physical Activity Service, provides strategic coordination of sport and physical activity across Bury (Bury Sport and Physical Activity Alliance, 2008). Its members include the Primary Care Trust alongside the children's services and adult care departments from within the council. Mutual dependencies have been created between partners around shared objectives and programmes of activity. As a result the alliance enables the Sport and Physical Activity Service to lobby for support within the council and establish its position as an important service which contributes to a range of corporate targets. This position offers the service some protection (albeit not immunity) from cost-cutting measures.

Accessing resources

In an era of financial restrictions, partners with a joint mission can use their combined strength and influence to attract finance for programmes. Indeed, the current financial and political climate dictates that, when it comes to obtaining major funding support, partnership working is a necessity rather than merely an advantage. Sport England's criteria for prospective applicants to its 'Themed Round' programme expressly require engagement with partners in terms of the development and delivery of a project (Sport England, 2012c). This applies uniformly at all levels of sport, from participation initiatives at local level to support mechanisms aimed at developing and nurturing elite performers.

In conclusion, thousands of prosperous ventures are not simply improved by partnership working; they are predicated upon it. There is a powerful case that the vast majority of sport development objectives can be attained more readily, and to a higher standard, through partnership working. It would be foolhardy, though, to assume that joining forces with another organisation cannot also generate problems. By acknowledging what can go wrong, the professional with vision can anticipate potential difficulties and take steps to overcome them.

PARTNERSHIP PROBLEMS

Ideally organisations would collaborate voluntarily as a result of a combination of those benefits outlined in the previous section. However, in reality not all partnerships are entered into this way. Political and/or public pressure for organisations

136

to work together can result in *enforced* partnerships, which are often inherently troublesome.

Enforced partnerships

As two distinct organisations will undoubtedly possess different structures, cultures and methods of operation, so it follows that individuals within and between partner agencies will be inherently different. The experience of countless practitioners tasked with aligning significant aspects of their work to that of 'outsiders' bears this out. First consider how these issues are manifested at an organisational level:

- *Organisational priorities* may vary greatly between the players in the partnership. These conflicts can centre on such factors as financial imperatives, social objectives and political direction. Discord between organisations may be so great that, rather than overcoming the issue, at best, an accommodation may be achieved which enables the initiative to move forward, albeit not always satisfactorily for all partners. Sport England's funding of NGBs through Whole Sport Plans offers an example of this issue. Under the terms of their Whole Sport Plan agreements, NGBs were tasked with leading the charge to increase participation in sport and physical activity at grassroots level, a challenge that required them to move away from their traditional delivery mechanisms and forge new alliances with community-based sport organisations. Early indications suggest that this was a problem for NGBs as they struggled to adapt to these somewhat 'forced' organisational priorities (Gibson, 2011). It also offers an indication of the limited freedom available to partners when adhering to prescribed agendas (Lindsey, 2009).
- *Political obstacles* may also be encountered in so-called enforced relationships. Elected officials may have personal or partisan agendas at the forefront of their thoughts and actions. Governmental interest in sport varies with the political cycle, and the potential resulting change in political ideology of the ruling party (or parties) will impact on policy decisions. A prime example of this is the approach of successive governments to the School Sport Partnerships. Delivery of the Physical Education and Sport Strategy for Young People (PESSYP) required schools, under the guidance of Partnership Development Managers, to form hubs around a Specialist Sports College and work collaboratively to increase the quantity as well as quality of sport and physical activity available to their pupils. Despite widespread recognition of the success of the PESSYP strategy, the change in government to the Conservative–Liberal Democrat coalition resulted in funding being withdrawn from the programme. This decision was widely criticised as being driven by political ideology and not sporting need.

- *Initiative overload* is a real issue for sport development professionals, worsened by frequent changes to national policy and programmes requiring the professional to adapt, often necessitating new alliances to deliver new initiatives. This can create *partnership overload* whereby the sport development professional spends time on servicing a wide range of partnerships while undertaking only limited action as a result of them. There is a real danger of partnerships becoming nothing more than 'talking shops', especially if they have been enforced in a top-down manner (I&DeA, 2009).
- *Culture* is another organisational factor that may differ greatly between partner organisations. Organisational culture can be considered to be the 'personality' of an organisation (Hoye *et al.*, 2012) or a pattern of shared assumptions that outline how an organisation behaves and how its members interact (Schein, 2010). Colyer (2000) discovered that a lack of cultural compatibility between volunteer-led organisations (such as sports clubs) and staff-led governing bodies in Western Australia had a significant impact on the organisations' ability to achieve their shared objectives. This lack of 'cultural fit' (Slack and Parent, 2006) can undermine the strength and durability of an alliance.

Further obstacles may be encountered even in operations between willing collaborators. Historical difficulties between organisations may still have resonance; individual hostility between senior managers and/or politicians could have an impact on support offered to the partnership; and key personnel changes can also have negative consequences. In many cases, mechanisms for resolving such issues have not been agreed in advance and this can be a further source of difficulties.

Planning and relationship problems

Management texts exhort managers to plan rationally and effectively. For a variety of reasons this does not always occur. *Bounded rationality* (see, for instance, Cairney, 2012) dictates that individuals take decisions under a number of external and psychological constraints. All relevant information is not available and, even if it were, decision makers would be unable to process it all, nor would they necessarily choose to do so. Thus, individuals involved in a sport development partnership cannot be expected to plan effectively for every contingency. Despite the threat of emergent difficulties, in some partnership settings potential problems are rarely raised or discussed at the outset, resulting in situations all too familiar to experienced practitioners:

- A *lack of strategic direction* both nationally and locally can result in knee-jerk partnerships being established that lack a clear vision and do not have fit-for-purpose systems and structures. Charlton's (2010) research on Lancashire Sport identifies the importance of a clear strategic vision for a partnership and the need to monitor the *external environment*, which changes constantly and may result in partners being unable to fulfil their obligations to the partnership, thereby affecting its ability to meet its aims.

■ Closely related to the issue of strategic direction is that of 'routinization inertia' (Slack and Parent, 2006: 138), whereby organisations get into the habit of working with the same partners irrespective of their appropriateness to achieving the aims of the alliance. This can result in poorly structured partnerships and possible under-representation of key stakeholders. Houlihan and Lindsey (2008) are wary of dominant partners that push through their agenda at the expense of others, when community involvement can become purely tokenistic.

Leadership is therefore crucial to the success of a partnership. Whilst it is often necessary for there to be a lead partner (or practitioner) that takes responsibility for driving the partnership, it is crucial that they operate inclusively. Partnerships without a 'leader' often suffer from a lack of *management intensity* and drift haphazardly towards achievement of their goals (Shaw and Allen, 2006). To work in partnership requires organisations, and more importantly the staff responsible for managing relations with partners, to possess what Lindsey (2009: 85) describes as 'collaborative capacity', namely the skills needed to forge relationships and negotiate agreements with potential partners. An accountable partnership is likely to have carefully considered and conducted *delegation* of the workload. In multi-agency undertakings the nature and scope of tasks that need to be performed can be large and complex. Delegation is not merely about 'dumping' work on people but should be more to do with empowerment and development of skills and experience, whilst contributing to the overall effort (Green, 1999). This is as true in multi-agency partnerships as it is in single organisations, the crucial distinction being that leaders may not have direct authority over other key individuals, who may have to surrender elements of internal organisational status to benefit the alliance.

■ In the event of problems, individual and organisational *responsibility* must be negotiated, and each partner should share *accountability* for the issues within the alliance. Crucially, this accountability should not be placed solely at the feet of the lead agency (or practitioner) in the partnership. In any event, when problems are experienced it is vital to have agreed in advance who will 'carry the can' and troubleshoot those situations on behalf of the partnership. If a positive approach is taken to difficulties, the likelihood of a *blame culture* will be diminished. This avoids expending energy assigning liability for issues which could be better spent rectifying problems.

Within large-scale, strategic partnerships it is necessary to *operationalise* wider goals into tangible action plans that can be implemented by different combinations of organisations. This is an intense and demanding, but essential process in order that every individual at every level knows what is expected of her/him. Cultural differences and personal animosities need to be set aside for the greater good. To conclude, it is as well to restate that it would be unusual for any sport and recreation partnership not to experience some form of obstacle at some stage. Consequently, partners can plan for contingencies and tackle them maturely and productively as and when they arise. Relationships built on trust are far more likely to thrive than those in which a hidden agenda or a mood of suspicion is allowed to prevail. The next section considers how academic theory can inform partnership processes in sport development and enable collaborators to access a greater proportion of the benefits of collective working.

PARTNERSHIPS AND ORGANISATION THEORY

Numerous disciplines offer themselves for academic scrutiny of sport and recreation partnerships, for example psychology, sociology, economics and political science as well as fields of study including management, business studies and policy studies. As Cousens and colleagues (2006: 33) suggest, discourses about partnerships are often vague:

> It appears that the term partnership is used by leaders and managers of local governments to describe virtually all interactions with organisations with which they are involved, regardless of the strength or pattern of the relationships.

This section therefore illustrates how key components of one field of study can help develop a sharper understanding. *Organisation theory* encapsulates key debates underpinning strategic partnerships and joint working. Theories of organisation offer 'abstract images of what an organization is, how it functions, and how its members and other interested parties interact with and within it' (Hatch and Cunliffe, 2006: 7). This notion of organisation theory provides for the study of partnerships, particularly at the level of examining interactions between people. Owing to restrictions of space, the focus of this section will be on one central issue: the management of stakeholder interactions. Although this topic will be dealt with discretely, as with most aspects of organisational life, it is interconnected with a host of other factors. Prior to considering this in detail, by way of setting the scene brief consideration should be given to the sport development organisation's interactions with the external environment (for a fuller discussion see earlier editions of this book).

140

The organisation and its environment

Every organisation is located within an environment in which are situated all 'other organisations and people with whom transactions have to take place' (Pugh and Hickson, 1996: 52). The organisational environment for a sporting body incorporates national and regional governing bodies, government and other political institutions, the public, commercial and voluntary sectors, current and potential sports participants, suppliers and so on. The environment is subject to changes to which the organisation needs to be able to respond. Relationships with the environment are complex and include ways in which the organisation copes with uncertainty and turbulence; how it seeks to influence the environment; and the extent to which it behaves proactively or reactively (Pettinger, 2000). From this it can be inferred that all inhabitants of the external environment are potential partners.

Hatch and Cunliffe (2006) place the organisation at the centre of an inter-organisational network which includes suppliers, competitors, partners and others with whom daily interactions take place. Wider forces also impact upon the organisation or partnership, categorised by Hatch and Cunliffe (2006) as the *general environment*, incorporating demographic, economic, cultural, technological, political and related factors. The sport development practitioner can conduct an *environmental analysis* (see, for instance, Rapid BI, 2012) to assess forces outside the partnership which cannot be directly controlled but need to be accounted for. Such an appraisal helps managers to locate the place of the partnership within the environment and to identify issues to be addressed.

Partners as stakeholders

Everyone within the inter-organisational network, as well as bodies and individuals within the general environment with an interest in a sport development organisation's work, can be thought of as *stakeholders*. In a general sense, stakeholders may have a commonality of purpose. For example, the vast majority of organisations with an interest in swimming would subscribe to the view that it is desirable to increase mass participation, but there are likely to be many, diverse opinions about how this might be achieved. It follows that the members of a partnership can be thought of as stakeholders who, whilst entering the alliance in order to play a collaborative role in achieving its mission and aims, are carrying individual viewpoints and organisational 'baggage' that will have a significant impact upon their behaviours in the partnership setting. Understanding the politics of stakeholder interactions is therefore vital to the successful management of strategic partnerships in sport development. A keener appreciation of the motivations of potential partners, allied to an understanding of the likely value of their contribution to partnership working, can aid practitioners in pursuit of the benefits of collective working. This section therefore considers the relevance or *salience* of potential partners to the organisation's work and shows how the insightful mapping of all stakeholders within a partnership can enable it to move forwards.

Stakeholder salience

Mitchell and colleagues (1997) were among the first to propose the notion of *stakeholder salience*: simply put, the relevance to the organisation of individual or institutional actors. Summarising earlier literature they identify that those engaged with the organisation in joint value creation and those with the ability to influence or be influenced by the organisation have a legitimate claim to be considered stakeholders. Unlike many commercial relationships, organisations and individuals in sport development are brought together by shared social objectives. This can lead to a blurring of the boundaries between relevant stakeholder-partners and those whose contribution may be marginal. Equally, the previously discussed threat of hidden, political agendas is ever present and can lead to a strain on scant resources, so it is vital to reliably identify the salience of potential partners.

Mitchell and colleagues (1997) categorise stakeholder salience as a combination of three factors: power (A has the ability to get B to do something which B which would not otherwise have done), legitimacy (a relationship already exists or the stakeholder is affected in some way by the organisation's actions) and urgency (the extent to which the organisation has pressing business with the stakeholder). The authors therefore propose that:

> Stakeholder salience will be positively related to the cumulative number of stakeholder attributes – power, legitimacy, and urgency – perceived by managers to be present.
>
> (Mitchell et al., 1997: 873)

Stakeholder types can be categorised as in Table 5.2. With limited resources available to address organisational objectives, practitioners can use this model to identify and prioritise the key relationships without which they will be unable to move forwards in the desired fashion. Categories 1–3 identify 'latent' stakeholders who, although they possess one of the three specified attributes and thus a certain measure of importance and relevance to the sport development organisation, might not be given priority, particularly in lean times. For example, from the point of view of a local authority sport development professional, a local football club which is already at or near to capacity in terms of membership and is succeeding in providing opportunities to diverse audiences may be viewed as a discretionary stakeholder, as there will be similar clubs in greater need of support. These other

142

Table 5.2 Stakeholder typology

Type of stakeholder	Power	Legitimacy	Urgency
Dormant stakeholder	✓	✗	✗
Discretionary stakeholder	✗	✓	✗
Demanding stakeholder	✗	✗	✓
Dominant stakeholder	✓	✓	✗
Dangerous stakeholder	✓	✗	✓
Dependent stakeholder	✗	✓	✓
Definitive stakeholder	✓	✓	✓
Non-stakeholder	✗	✗	✗

Source: adapted from Mitchell *et al.* (1997: 874).

clubs would be categorised, therefore, as dependent stakeholders. This emphasises the greater salience of the group of 'expectant' stakeholders: those with two of the three attributes. Mitchell and colleagues (1997) suggest that these are of moderate salience, but in the politically charged arena of sport development it may be neither desirable nor possible to afford them lower priority. Dangerous stakeholders, for instance, may include predatory property developers seeking to build on land currently used recreationally (e.g. green belt land used for orienteering or playing fields). Creating partnerships with such stakeholders may lead to the immediate threat being staved off and new opportunities created as a consequence.

Self-evidently the most useful application of the stakeholder salience model is the identification of definitive stakeholders. Dominant stakeholders will already be 'on the radar' of the sport development manager because of their power and legitimacy, so when a new development lends urgency to the situation they command immediate and detailed attention. Clearly it would be highly undesirable for an antagonistic relationship to exist with a definitive stakeholder, so once again partnership working is the key to success. For example, from the point of view of a Whole Sport Plan-funded NGB, Sport England's role is that of a dominant stakeholder in terms of the day-to-day operations of the NGB, but at key times, when outcomes are reviewed and funding cycles determined, Sport England becomes a definitive stakeholder to be kept satisfied with the NGB's performance. (There are a variety of useful stakeholder analysis tools to enable practitioners and scholars to gain deep insights into actual and potential stakeholder relationships; see Simpson and Partington, forthcoming, for example.)

Contingency theory

Organising in response to the demands of the environment is clearly a crucial part of the sport development professional's work; much of this activity relates to stakeholder interactions and partnerships. Ackermann and Eden (2011: 234) confirm that 'stakeholder management is invariably more complex, problematic and uncertain in the public sector'. *Contingency theory*, a body of academic work which prescribes options for *how* to deal with the uncertainties of the environment, is dealt with more fully in previous editions of the book, but it is useful in the space available to consider its applicability to stakeholder relationships.

Sport development professionals will identify with the notion of *resource dependence*, which assumes that organisations are controlled by their environments because of the need for resources such as knowledge, labour, equipment, customers and political support. Pfeffer and Salancik (cited in Pugh and Hickson, 1996), who developed this theory, determined that an organisation should attempt to create a 'counter-dependency'; in other words, it should endeavour to render elements of the environment dependent on it. From a sport and recreation perspective, the power of definitive stakeholders is often connected to *resources*, in the tangible form of funding and the less concrete guise of political influence. Modern sport development professionals have become adept at identifying ways to match their own strategic agendas to those of definitive stakeholders, creating counter-dependencies which temper the effects of their organisations' vulnerability to the environment.

Environmental theory also provides for managers to defend the organisation against the uncertainty inherent in most environments. One response to uncertainty is *isomorphism*, when the organisation attempts to match the complexity of the environment. Scott (cited in Hatch, 1997: 91) suggests *buffering* and *boundary spanning* as two essential techniques in achieving this. Both emphasise the skills and characteristics necessary for successful partnership working. Buffering entails an individual acting as a 'shock absorber' to ensure that abrupt external changes do not destabilise the sport development organisation (Slack and Parent, 2006). The Partnership Development Manager of a surviving School Sports Partnership may provide a buffer between the operational staff, who deliver coaching, and subtle or sweeping changes in the priorities prescribed by central government, which would otherwise serve to distract coaches from their objectives. The boundary-spanning role, meanwhile, is at the heart of partnership working. Individuals working in partnership settings provide decision makers within their 'home' organisations with information relating to the environment whilst also representing the organisation in the partnership setting. The human aspect of managing partnership relations is highlighted in National Occupational Standard 'A324 Develop productive relationships with colleagues', which exhorts colleagues to 'clearly agree what is expected of others and hold them to account', 'seek to understand people's needs and motivations' and 'consider the impact of your own actions on others' (SkillsActive, 2010: 3). The behaviours apply equally to intra- and inter-organisational dealings, and remind us that, even in a resource-starved era, partnership working is about negotiation rather than submission, and collaboration rather than coercion.

CONCLUSION

The foregoing discussion has shown that partnership working continues to occupy a critical role in the strategic development of sporting opportunities. Partnership working is predicated upon intelligent, respectful but challenging interactions between professionals from a range of disciplines. Sport development professionals often demonstrate an extraordinary flair for shifting seamlessly between the parochial setting of the organisation and the vibrant and diverse partnership environment. This commitment to the spirit of collective effort characterises modern sport development professionals as outward-looking and orientated towards wider goals that benefit a broader cross-section of society than just those they are paid to serve directly.

CASE STUDY 5.1: STREETGAMES

The national charity StreetGames is an example of an organisation that has benefited from adopting a proactive approach to collaboration and partnership. Established in 2007, the charity has developed from a small organisation, championing a 'doorstep' approach to delivering sport and physical activity in deprived and disadvantaged communities, to the lead national organisation for this type of work. By lobbying at a political level for 'doorstep sport' and utilising the personal influence of staff and trustees, the organisation has secured significant investment from Sport England, the Co-operative and Coca-Cola. This investment has been directed to local communities through the creation of regional StreetGames networks (or alliances) which utilise the key contacts and links possessed by other organisations working at a local level, such as local authorities and voluntary organisations, to deliver StreetGames initiatives and activities. This approach has enabled a coordinated programme of support to be provided to those running grassroots sports programmes, including volunteer schemes, regional festivals and events, and perhaps most importantly the sharing of expertise, knowledge and good practice between partners. The success of this work has resulted in further high-profile political support from MPs and from elite sportspeople, coaches and managers, which further enables the charity to extend its influence nationally, culminating with the development of 'doorstep clubs' being included as a priority within the coalition government's sports strategy for young people (DCMS, 2012).

These achievements would not have been realised without a positive approach to managing relations with the external environment. The growth of StreetGames has been attributable in part to the creation of counter-dependencies with key partners. For example, StreetGames receives financial resources and political endorsement from Sport England, whilst Sport England utilises the StreetGames network to help deliver its strategic community sport goals. StreetGames

---

can therefore be characterised as a definitive stakeholder for Sport England, thereby firmly establishing itself as a key agency in the strategic sport development arena. The delivery of these jointly agreed objectives is dependent upon a network of StreetGames Regional Managers. These professionals play a vital boundary-spanning role, creating and servicing regional, subregional and local alliances for the delivery of 'doorstep sport'. The complex skill set necessary for success in this endeavour should not be underestimated and is part of a wider appreciation of the subtleties of partnership working, from which others can learn.

LEARNING ACTIVITIES

1 Conduct an analysis of the benefits and limitations of a sport development partnership with which you are familiar. Suggest ways in which the benefits can be maximised and the limitations minimised.

2 With reference to the 'courtship' aspect of Johnson and colleagues' (2011) 'Stages of Alliance Evolution' model, identify a prospective new partner for a sport development alliance with which you are familiar. Outline the ways in which you would 'court' the prospective partner (e.g. identify mutual benefits).

3 From the point of view of a sport development organisation with which you are familiar, conduct an analysis of 'stakeholder salience' in respect of one of its key partnerships. In particular you should seek to identity any definitive stakeholders and suggest actions the organisation might undertake in order to strengthen relationships with them.

REFERENCES

Ackermann, F. and Eden, C. (2011) *Making Strategy: Mapping Out Strategic Choices*, London: Sage.

Bury Sport and Physical Activity Alliance (2008) *Bury Sport & Physical Activity Alliance 2008–2010: Visioning Document*, Bury: Bury Metropolitan Borough Council.

Cairney, P. (2012) *Understanding Public Policy: Theories and Issues*, London: Palgrave Macmillan.

Carter, P. (2005) *Review of National Sport Effort and Resources*, London: Sport England.

Charlton, T. (2010) 'A new active sports partnership: Lancashire Sport', in Collins, M. (ed.), *Examining Sports Development*, Abingdon: Routledge.

Colyer, S. (2000) 'Organizational culture in selected Western Australian sport organizations', *Journal of Sport Management*, 14 (4): 321–341.

Conn, D. (2010) 'Spending review: where the axe will fall on our sporting infrastructure', *The Guardian*, 20 October.

Cousens, L., Barnes, M., Stevens, J., Mallen, C. and Bradish, C. (2006) '"Who's your partner? Who's your ally?" Exploring the characteristics of public, private and voluntary recreation linkages', *Journal of Park and Recreation*, 24 (1): 32–55.

DCMS (2012) *Creating a Sporting Habit for Life*, London: DCMS.

Stephen Robson and Janine Partington

Dussauge, P. and Garrette, B. (1999) *Co-operative Strategy: Competing Successfully through Strategic Alliances*, Chichester: John Wiley & Sons.

English Cricket Board (2012*)* 'ASDA Kwik Cricket', www.ecb.co.uk/development/kids/kwik-cricket/

Football Association (2012) 'Your game', www.thefa.com/yourgame

Gibson, O. (2011) 'Funding boost for growing sports as fears grow over Olympic legacy', *The Guardian*, 4 October.

Green, P. (1999) *Managing Time*, London: Chartered Institute of Marketing.

Hatch, M.J. (1997) *Organization Theory: Modern, Symbolic-Interpretative and Postmodern Perspectives*, Oxford: Oxford University Press.

Hatch, M.J. and Cunliffe, A.L. (2006) *Organization Theory: Modern, Symbolic and Postmodern Perspective*, 2nd edn, Oxford: Oxford University Press.

Houlihan, B. and Lindsey, I. (2008) 'Networks & partnerships in sports development', in Girgonov, V. (ed.), *Management of Sports Development*, Oxford: Butterworth-Heinemann.

Hoye, R., Smith, A.C.T., Nicholson, M., Stewart, B. and Weesterbeek, H. (2012) *Sport Management: Principles & Applications*, 3rd edn, Abingdon: Routledge.

I&DeA (2009) *Making partnership work better in the Culture and Sport sector*, London: I&DeA.

Johnson, G., Whittingham, R. and Scholes, K. (2011) *Exploring Strategy: Texts and Cases*, 9th edn, Harlow: Prentice-Hall Europe.

King, N. (2009) *Sport, Policy and Governance: Local Perspectives*, Oxford, Butterworth-Heinemann.

Kingdom, J. (2003) *Government and Politics in Britain: An Introduction*, 3rd edn, London: Polity Press.

Lindsey, I. (2009) 'Collaboration in local sports service in England: issues emerging from case studies of two local authority areas', *International Journal of Sport Policy*, 1 (1): 71–88.

Mitchell, R., Agle, D. and Wood, B. (1997) 'Toward a theory of stakeholder identification and salience: defining the principle of who and what really counts', *Academy of Management Review*, 22 (4): 853–886.

Pettinger, R. (2000) *Mastering Organisational Behaviour*, Basingstoke: Palgrave.

Plymouth City Council (2010) *Sports Development Plan 2010–13*. Plymouth: Plymouth City Council.

Pugh, D. and Hickson, D. (1996) *Writers on Organizations*, 5th edn, London: Penguin.

Rapid BI (2012) 'PEST/PESTLE analysis tool: history and templates', http://rapidbi.com/the-pestle-analysis-tool/

Schein, E. (2010) *Organizational Culture and Leadership*, 4th edn, San Francisco: Jossey-Bass.

Service de police de la Ville de Montréal (2012) 'Definition of partnership', www.spvm.qc.ca/en/service/1_5_3_1_definition-partenariat.asp

Shaw, S. and Allen, J.B. (2006) '"It basically is a fairly loose arrangement . . . and that works out fine, really": analysing the dynamics of an interorganisational partnership', *Sport Management Review*, 9: 203–228.

Simpson, K. and Partington, J. (forthcoming) 'Strategic partnerships', in Leach, R., Robson, S., Simpson, K. and Tucker, L. (eds.), *Strategic Sport Development*, Abingdon: Routledge.

SkillsActive (2010) *A328: Develop Your Personal Networks*, London: SkillsActive.

Slack, T. and Parent, M. (2006) *Understanding Sport Organizations: The Application of Organization Theory*, 2nd edn, Champaign, IL: Human Kinetics.

Sport England (2006) *The Delivery System for Sport*, London: Sport England.

Sport England (2008) *Sport England Strategy 2008–2011*, London: Sport England.

Sport England (2010) *The Impact of Government's New Policies on Sport*, London: Sport England.

Sport England (2011a) *A Summary of Sport England's Strategy 2011–12 to 2014–15*, London: Sport England.

Sport England (2011b) 'Strategy consultation', www.sportengland.org/about_us/strategy_consultation.aspx

Sport England (2012a) 'Sport Makers', www.sportmakers.co.uk/terms_and_conditions

Sport England (2012b) 'Active People survey 5', www.sportengland.org/research/active_people_survey/aps5.aspx

Sport England (2012c) 'Assessment criteria', www.sportengland.org/funding/themed_funding_rounds/active_universities/assessment_criteria.aspx

Vail, S.E. (2007) 'Community development and sport participation', *Journal of Sport Management*, 21: 571–596.

Walpole, C. and Collins, M. (2010) 'Sports development in microcosm', in Collins, M. (ed.), *Examining Sports Development*, Abingdon: Routledge.

West Yorkshire Sport (2011) 'West Yorkshire Youth Games 2011', www.wysport.co.uk/play/wysg/about/

Yoshino, M. and Rangan, U. (1995) *Strategic Alliances: An Entrepreneurial Approach to Globalization*, Boston: Harvard Business School Press.

CHAPTER 6

PHYSICAL EDUCATION AND SCHOOL SPORT

ANNE FLINTOFF

This chapter was written a few months before the Olympic and Paralympic Games were held in London in the summer of 2012. An Olympic year usually results in a flurry of activity around sport, physical activity and physical education (PE), with governments justifying the costs of the games by stressing the benefits to the host nation, and by highlighting the 'legacy' that will be left behind once they are over. Young people are often cited as key beneficiaries of such legacies, and the London games were no exception (Department for Culture, Media and Sport (DCMS), 2010). For example, the launch of a youth sport strategy, *Creating a Sporting Habit for Life: A New Youth Sport Strategy* (DCMS, 2012) and plans for a revised national curriculum for PE (NCPE), were both aimed at harnessing the 'power of the games' to motivate more young people to take part in sport.

In announcing the new youth sport strategy for England, Jeremy Hunt, the Culture Secretary, argued that a more focused and tougher approach to funding new opportunities for youth sport is necessary:

> Despite huge investment of public funds since we won the right to host the Games, participation by young people in sport has been falling. We need a radical change in policy to address the deep-seated problem of people dropping out of sport when they leave school. Our bold approach will see money going to organisations that deliver on youth participation, but also withdrawn quickly from those which fail to meet agreed objectives.
>
> (Hunt, 2012)

The focus of the new strategy is particularly on the 14–25 years age group, and on ensuring that sport participation does not decrease when young people leave school. The focus is therefore on initiatives designed to link school PE with after-school sports participation, in particular, through the introduction of:

- the School Games, a national framework for competitive school sport in England at school, district, county and national level;
- improving the links between schools and community sports clubs (particularly in football, cricket, rugby union, rugby league and tennis).

Alongside these developments, the Department for Education has also announced a review of school PE, and the introduction of a new national curriculum from September 2013. Although its exact shape is yet to be decided (see Editorial, 2011), competitive sport is likely to play a central role. Unusually, PE even gets a specific mention in the government's recent White Paper, *The Importance of Teaching*:

> Children need access to high quality PE so we will ensure the requirement to provide PE in maintained schools is retained and we will provide new support to ensure a much wider take up of competitive team sports. With only 1 in 5 children regularly taking part in competitive activities against another school, we need a new approach to entrench the character building qualities of team sport.
>
> (Department for Education (DfE), 2010a: 46)

Policy changes such as these are characteristic of any new government coming to power. However, the introduction of the UK coalition government in 2010, coupled with new (and austere) financial times, has brought about significant changes in the arena of PE and school sport (PESS). One aspect of this change is to bring to an end a decade or more of unprecedented investment in PESS by the previous Labour government and, with it, a seven-year national strategy, the PE and Sport Strategy for Young People (PESSYP).[1] Although the coalition has been quick to introduce new policies, branding them as representing a better way forward, it is difficult not to see the current PESS landscape as significantly impoverished compared with that of the previous decade. In their historical analysis of the shifts in youth sport policy since the 1970s, Houlihan and Green (2006) argue that it was not until the 1990s that PESS became a government priority. Looking at the plethora of well-funded policies and initiatives of PESSYP in the years between 2003 and 2010, it is not difficult to suggest that PESS continued to be a priority throughout these years. Although Kirk (2005) laments the lack of a research base underpinning the development of the PESSYP programmes, they were carefully evaluated and monitored for their impact against clear performance targets. This means that there is considerable evidence, some of it longitudinal over several years, from which to draw to inform our understanding of the impact of recent policies, and of young people's PE and school sport participation.[2]

Drawing on this evidence, this chapter examines the changing nature of PE and youth sport policy, and the implications for youth sport participation. Specifically, the chapter is interested in exploring how government policy promotes *particular*

150

conceptions of PESS which may benefit some groups of young people and marginalise others. Will the coalition government's 'new' approach to youth sport participation really be 'radical' and different? Will it help prevent young people dropping out of sport once they leave school, as Jeremy Hunt suggests? Is the entrenching of the 'character building qualities of team sport' really what we need from a new NCPE? This chapter will address these and other questions that aim to shake up the taken-for-granted assumptions that PE and sport are a 'good thing', enjoyed by and accessible to all young people.

THE SOCIAL CONSTRUCTION OF PE

Any discussion about PE and school sport generates many questions of definition. What is PE? How does it differ from school sport? How different is school sport from youth sport, or sport in the community? One straightforward view of PE focuses on *where* physical activities take place and *who* is responsible for them. In this view, PE would refer to all activities that go on within school curriculum time, school sport relates to all those physical activities that take place outside curriculum time but are organised and run by the school, and community sport is that which is organised by clubs or organisations other than schools. Arguably, these are traditional and somewhat limited working definitions and tell us little about the aim of physical activities. The first National Curriculum in PE (NCPE) was clear that PE and sport were not synonymous:

> PE . . . is a process of learning, the context being mainly physical. The purpose of this process is to develop specific knowledge, skills and understanding and to promote physical competence. Different sporting activities can and do contribute to the learning process, and the learning enables participation in sport. The focus however, is on the child and his or her development of physical competence, rather than on the activity.
>
> (Department of Education and Science, 1991: 7)

Some authors have recently suggested that, although learning should remain central, it is not helpful to define PE as limited to formal and informal activities which happen in particular places such as schools or other educational institutions. Evans and Davies (2006) have suggested that PE needs to be conceived of as a complex social process that occurs in a wide variety of settings. This involves families, peer groups and the media and is not just limited to schools. As Macdonald (2002) maintains, whereas schools remain 'modernist' institutions, structured by timetables, subjects and so on, postmodern perspectives show us that young people learn about 'physical culture' (see Kirk, 1993, 1999) from a much wider range of sources and across a range of contexts. Young people's learning does not stop at the school door. So, although this chapter focuses on the particular context of curriculum PE and the formalised school sport opportunities, it is cognisant of these wider conceptions and the implications they raise for teachers and coaches.

Those who support PE as an important aspect of schooling argue its importance for introducing young people to different kinds of physical activity and for developing basic skills required to take part (QCA, 2007a,b). In addition, young people learn about the relationship between physical activity and health so that they are able to make informed choices and adopt an active lifestyle later in life. Others stress that school PE – in partnership with other agencies – plays an important role in the identification and development of future champions (Department for Children, Schools and Families (DCSF), 2008). At different times, these and other rationales for PE have gained recognition and acceptance. Struggles over what counts as PE have been reflected in contradictory and competing initiatives and policies (Kirk, 2010).

This chapter examines three key policies in relation to young people's opportunities to be physically active in school and beyond over the last decade: the NCPE, the School Sport Partnership Programme (SSPP, a central programme within PESSYP) and the new School Games. Drawing on the available national evaluations and other smaller-scale, qualitative case-study research on their impact, the chapter highlights key questions and issues for those involved in working with young people.

Although few might take issue with the aim of PE as stated in the NCPE above, what it should look like in practice – for example, which activities should be included, who should teach PE and how it should be taught – have all been subject to much scrutiny and debate. How PE is structured is not just a matter of academic debate for those of us working in universities or in sport development; it also matters for young people's everyday experiences in the gymnasium or on the playing field. Not all young people have a positive experience of PE. In 1986, Evans and Davies wrote:

> The most that many pupils may have learnt in . . . the Physical Education curriculum is that they have neither ability, status nor value and that the most judicious course of action to be taken in protection of their fragile educational and physical identities is to adopt a plague-like avoidance of its damaging activities.
>
> (Evans and Davies, 1986: 16)

After more than twenty-five years, one might seem justified in thinking that this scenario no longer exists. However, a recent book examining the future of PE suggests this may not be the case. Kirk (2010) argues that PE practice has remained largely unchanged from the 1950s, and continues to centre on the teaching of isolated sports techniques, a conception of PE that, he argues, serves many young people poorly. One of the arguments made in this chapter is that PE is *socially constructed* – that is, particular kinds of knowledge, pedagogies and assessment strategies are selected, others omitted or marginalised – and these constructions serve particular group interests better than others (Evans and Davies, 2006).

UNDERSTANDING YOUNG PEOPLE'S PARTICIPATION IN AND EXPERIENCES OF PE

What do we know about young people and PESS? The first point is that we know much more about *levels of participation* than young people's *experiences* of PESS (Dyson, 2006). This may be for two reasons. First, methodologically it is easier and cheaper to conduct large-scale surveys that measure rates of participation than to embark on qualitative time-consuming methodologies to understand and explore experiences. Evans and Davies (2010) note that participation rates have long been used to measure whether a programme or new curriculum in PESS is impacting on 'ability', largely because of the lack of an accepted alternative. Second, it is only recently that teachers and researchers have acknowledged that young people have something valuable and important to offer to our understandings of PE (O'Sullivan and MacPhail, 2010). Even so, it is still the case that we know little about particular groups of young people, such as minority ethnic or disabled young people (Fitzgerald, 2006; Kay, 2006).

By its very nature, 'participation levels' research is limited in what it can tell us about young people, PE and school sport. Although useful for mapping broad trends, it cannot, as Wright and colleagues (2003: 18) argue, tell us much about the significance or place of physical activities in young people's lives, how this might change over time or how young people might 'draw on discursive and material resources associated with broader aspects of physical culture to construct their identities in relation to physical activity' (see also Wright and Macdonald, 2010). Coakley and White (1992) highlighted this some time ago, when they argued that young people should be seen not as 'dropping out' of physical activity or sport but instead as actively negotiating when and where they will be active, depending upon changing circumstances in their lives. Another limitation of 'participation-levels' research is that particular groups of young people become highlighted as the 'problem' when compared with a 'norm' (usually the participation of young white middle-class males), so that the policy response to such 'deficit' is to provide more of the same opportunities. The participation rates of girls have been identified as lower than boys in several surveys, so one policy response has been to provide more opportunities for girls to participate, to target provision and to make a few changes to suit their differing needs. The Nike/Youth Sport Trust (YST)-sponsored project, Girls into Sport (Nike/Youth Sport Trust, 1999, 2000) and Scotland's Fit for Girls project (Inchley *et al.*, 2011) serve as a good examples. Although there were several worthwhile aspects of such projects, such as engaging teachers in reflection and discussion about their own practice, they do remain orientated towards making PE more 'girl-friendly' rather than challenging the nature and structure of dominant practices within PE (see also Penney, 2002a).

Despite their limitations, participation figures form the central basis for many government evaluations of policies and practices in PE. The impact of PESSYP was evaluated primarily through participation figures collected through an annual PE and School Sport Survey, against targets outlined in a Public Service Agreement (PSA) (Quick *et al.*, 2010). The PSA set ambitious targets in relation to young people's participation in PE and school sport, which were updated several times over the course of the seven years that the national strategy was in place. The last PSA target linked to PESSYP, called the 'Five Hour Offer', set the following target:

> By the end of the academic year 2010/11, 40% of young people to take part in five hours a week of PE and school sport (three hours for 16–19 yrs olds) . . . and by 2012/13, 60%.
>
> (Youth Sport Trust/Sport England, 2009: 6)

It was expected that schools would provide three of the five hours for children 5–16 years of age – two hours of high-quality PE within the curriculum, and at least one hour a week of sport for all young people beyond the school curriculum (out of curriculum hours but on the school site).[3] The remaining two hours were to be provided by community sports clubs.

The most recent survey of PESS shows that young people's participation levels have improved as a result of the seven-year PESSYP strategy (Quick *et al.*, 2010). According to the report, 55 per cent of pupils in partnership schools[4] participated in at least three hours of PE and sport in a typical week, an increase of 5 per cent on the previous year's levels. Participation levels did vary across age groups, between rural and urban partnerships, and between partnerships with different school intakes. Other notable successes included:

- the involvement of 78 per cent of pupils in partnership schools in some form of intra-school competition, with 49 per cent of pupils regularly involved in inter-school competition;
- each partnership school having school links with on average nine different sports clubs (although schools in areas of relatively high deprivation and those with higher percentages of youngsters from ethnic minorities had lower school–club links than others);
- an increase in the percentage of pupils actively involved in sports volunteering and leadership from 19 to 24 per cent since the 2008/9 survey.

154

PESSYP also does seem to have increased the time devoted to *curricular* PE for most children. On average, across years 1–11 (5- to 16-year-olds), 84 per cent of young people participate in at least two hours of curricular PE; this figure has increased from 44 per cent in 2003/4. However, the pattern does vary between year groups and between schools; for example, primary-aged pupils in Years 1 and 2 receive, on average, 126 minutes of curricular PE; Year 7 pupils, 131 minutes; Year 10 pupils, just 104 minutes. Averages do hide differences and, because data was collated and submitted by partnerships, the figures for individual schools are hidden within a combined partnership figure. Data show that the partnerships with lower participation rates (in terms of time spent on the curriculum *and* participation in school sport) are those with a higher percentage of children from minority ethnic backgrounds, disabled children, or those eligible for free school meals.[5] The 2009/10 report was the first to collect data on gender, revealing significant differences between girls' and boys' participation levels across a number of measures. Analysis of the school sport survey data shows, therefore, that class, disability, ethnicity and gender all impact on sports participation. The school sport survey enables useful mapping of national PESS participation trends over time. The demise of PESSYP means schools are no longer required to provide annual data, resulting in the loss of this valuable research information in the future.

Research that considers young people's *experiences* of PE is still a developing field, and there are significant gaps in our knowledge base. Such research highlights that the ethos and atmosphere in the PE classroom and the teacher's role are crucial. Young people view some of their PE teachers as unfair and elitist, as they spend more time with able pupils at the expense of the less able and with boys rather than the girls. Young people are critical of teachers who deploy pedagogical practices which centre on competition and winning for the elite minority at the expense of learning and enjoyment for all (see Dyson, 2006, for an overview). Innovative PE programmes such as Sport Education or Cooperative Learning, which shift the locus of power and control away from the teacher to young people, so that young people are given more responsibility for their own learning, through working in teams, adopting and learning different roles and working cooperatively, have been well received as alternative models (Penney *et al.*, 2005).

Other research has explored the way in which young people's PE lessons are structured by relations of gender, class, ability, sexuality and 'race'. There is now a large body of literature that has explored girls' experiences of PE and school sport (see Flintoff and Scraton, 2006, for an overview). Flintoff and Scraton (2001) show how young women are active decision makers about the intensity and extent of their involvement in PE, and that these decisions are often made within the wider context of economic and gender relations that have to be negotiated and managed. There is, however, little research that explores boys' experiences of PE (see Bramham, 2003; Carless, 2011; Gard, 2006; Hickey, 2008) and even less that centres on the experiences of minority ethnic or disabled young people (Fitzgerald, 2006; Fitzpatrick, 2011; Flintoff et al., 2008; Kay, 2006; Macdonald et al., 2009; Nelson, 2012; Nelson et al., 2010) or the important impacts of social class (Evans and Davies, 2006) or sexuality (Clarke, 2006). Although this work is slowly developing, too much of it has tended to be what Penney (2002a) has called 'single issue' research, focusing on gender or ethnicity or sexuality and so on, without a recognition of the complexities of young people's 'multiple identities' (Azzarito and Solomon, 2005; Flintoff et al., 2008). Understanding the place of PE and school sport in young people's lives needs to go beyond participation figures to appreciate the complex, changing ways in which young people make sense of physical cultures in and out of school as they actively construct their own physical identities. Research such as Wright and Macdonald's (2010) Life Activity Project, a longitudinal study conducted in Australia, provides one such example.

ANALYSING POLICY

The next section turns to a consideration of three aspects of contemporary PE policy and assesses their impact in meeting the needs of young people. In exploring the impact of any new policy initiative, the importance of *how* policy and practice are conceived is significant. In PE, Penney and Evans's research on the introduction and implementation of NCPE over the last decade and a half has been influential in contributing to this body of work (e.g. Penney and Evans, 1999, 2005). Penney and Evans (1999: 19) reject 'a traditional, hierarchical view of policy in which policy is reified as an artifact, commodity or "thing" made by certain individuals . . . to be implemented by others in levels or sites "below", thereby giving rise to "practice"'. Instead, they argue for a more sophisticated understanding of policy, whereby neither making nor implementing policy is restricted to one single site or individual or to a point in time. They argue that policy should be best seen as a *process*. This conception accommodates the different numbers of sites in which policy gets transformed or reinterpreted by different individuals, which is how 'slippage' occurs between the original and reinterpreted policy. The whole process of policy making and implementation is one in which there is the transmission of 'not one but rather a series of different policy texts', and so transforming policy into a 'new' or 'hybrid text' (Penney and Evans, 1999: 22). In arguing for a more 'fluid' conception of policy based on interactions between 'content and context', Penney and Evans stress inequities that exist in any policy process. They draw on the concept of *discourse* as a key tool to help explain how different values and interests are promoted and expressed through policy texts, and how others are marginalised or overlooked. Discourses are not simply sets of 'ideas' that can be accepted or dismissed but, as Penney and Evans note, are about language and meanings, about knowledge and power and their interrelationship, and about what can be said and by whom. They are about 'expressions of particular interests and values, they create and promote particular meanings and values' (Penney and Evans, 1999: 24). Policy texts are necessarily political, serving and promoting particular interests, while ignoring and subordinating other interests. Although their work has clearly shown the importance of attending to the capacity of individual actors, such as PE teachers, within specific contexts to *reinterpret* and implement the NCPE, it has also shown the *determining* influence of central government throughout the process, seeking to control the degree to which 'slippage' occurs.

THE NATIONAL CURRICULUM IN PHYSICAL EDUCATION

Drawing on such a conception of policy, it is clear that the NCPE should best be seen as a policy that is 'unfinished', 'always in the making'; 'in the process of (de- and re-)construction and contested and contestable' (Penney, 2006: 567). Teachers in England are now working with the fourth version of the NCPE, and a further revision is currently under way. Penney and Evans (1999) have detailed the complex ways in which the process of defining the first NCPE unfolded, showing the influence of dominant discourses and contexts outside education, most notably those of sport, on the finalised version implemented in schools from 1992 (Evans and Penney, 1995). The first three NCPE curriculum models (Department of Education and Science, 1992, 1995; Department for Education and Employment, 1999) were all constructed around discrete physical activity areas – games, gymnastics, dance and so on – with an emphasis on skill acquisition and performing, and with games privileged over other activity areas (Penney, 2001). Whereas, on one hand, the last two decades in PE could be described as one of extensive curricular change, on the other hand, it is clear that there are significant continuities between PE, prior to the NCPE, and current practice (Penney, 2006).

The fourth NCPE (Qualifications and Curriculum Authority (QCA), 2007a,b) is organised quite differently from the first three, and is structured around core concepts and processes rather than discrete activity areas. The Labour government argued that this revision to the curriculum was to 'Give schools greater flexibility to tailor learning to their learners' needs', by having less prescribed subject content. This would allow teachers more space to 'explore cross curricular links and dimensions such as healthy lifestyles and enterprise, globalization and sustainable development' (QCA, undated). Arguably this curriculum construction is a radical departure from the previous three versions, allowing for the introduction of significantly new practice. There is little or no research on which to draw to assess whether this curriculum model has actually changed teachers' everyday practice. However, analysing the impact of earlier NCPEs, Penney and Evans (1999) and Curtner-Smith (1999) argue that the flexibility inherent in the official texts means that there is plenty of room for teachers to accommodate new requirements in what is essentially unchanged pedagogical and curricular practice. Curtner-Smith (1999: 57) has described this as 'the more things change, the more things stay the same'. Historical research has shown how the multi-activity curriculum model, privileging and reproducing the dominance of discourses of sport performance, has remained *the* dominant model in PE (Penney, 2006).

The Office for Standards in Education (Ofsted) (2009) report confirms that PESSYP has had a positive impact on widening the range of activities provided, but suggests that the provision of non-traditional activities is still inconsistent across schools. Other research has confirmed that competitive team games still take up the lion's share of the curriculum (Ofsted, 2005; Smith *et al.*, 2007). Although standards and achievement in PE overall have improved, there is more inconsistency in primary schools; the subject knowledge of primary teachers is less secure than that of secondary teachers. Teachers' abilities to assess pupils' learning and achievement in PE appears to be inconsistent, with the result that individual needs are not always being met. So, whereas the NCPE may have provided a new discourse of PE, there remains more focus on *what* should be taught rather than on *how* it should be taught and the types of pedagogies that might bring about real change at the level of young people's everyday experiences (Evans *et al.*, 1996).

Another aspect that appears resistant to change is the gendered nature of the NCPE. Penney (2002b) argues that, through the privileging of games, the flexibility in the policy, and the silences and omissions around issues of equity, the NCPE is an implicitly gendered text. Although the NCPE does make mention of teachers paying due regard in their teaching to three principles of inclusion, they are given no guidance about how they might work to these principles and, to date, inclusion has tended to be interpreted in terms of ability, with a focus on the inclusion of children with special educational needs or with exceptional talent (Fitzgerald, 2011). In addition, male and female teachers continue to deliver different aspects of the curriculum (Waddington *et al.*, 1998); teachers use their gender as a key pedagogical resource (Brown and Rich, 2002; Flintoff, 2011), and even areas of the curriculum that have a less gendered history, such as health-related fitness, are delivered in very different ways to boys compared with girls (Harris and Penney, 2002).

So what will change with the introduction of yet another version of the NCPE? To date we have little information about the shape of the fifth version of the NCPE, as the development process is ongoing. The government has recently announced a delay in its introduction until September 2014 to allow for more 'radical reform' (DfE, 2012). This, however, may be more evident in other subject areas, rather than PE, since the review panel has recently recommended the 'downgrading' of PE from a core to a foundation subject (DfE, 2011), and there is a stronger expectation that all pupils should play competitive sport (Editorial, 2011). Hardly radical, given the history of the NCPE to date.

158

However, the NCPE has always been a flexible text, allowing for 'slippage' between the intentions of the policy makers and their implementation by teachers. The NCPE means different things in different schools; for some teachers, this means minimal change to their practice. However, although flexibilities in policy texts allow teachers to continue existing practice, it is also important to acknowledge that these are also spaces for others to develop new practice. As mentioned earlier, the introduction of Sport Education as a new pedagogical model is beginning to provide some young people with different experiences of sport (Dyson *et al.*, 2009; Hastie *et al.*, 2011; Kirk, 2006; Penney *et al.*, 2005). Sport Education is a pedagogical model in PE that aims to offer young people a more 'authentic' experience of sport through different kinds of learning and sport engagement in PE lessons (Seidentop, 1994, 2009). Typically, young people work in 'teams' over a significant period of time or 'season' of sport, and get to experience a number of different roles within that team (coach, scorer, referee, player). The focus is on a more holistic approach to learning – on sport *education*, rather than simply sport activity – and engages young people in taking responsibility for their own and others' learning. Another example is the Volunteering and Leadership programmes that have been a key strand of PESSYP, in which sport and physical activity are used as vehicles to develop leadership skills with young people.

In reviewing the impact of the NCPE, we need to ask what has actually changed as the result of its introduction and who has benefited from these changes. A curriculum dominated by games, with a sport-performance pedagogy, fosters *particular* conceptions of ability in PE. In so doing, some young people will succeed and enjoy PE but others will lose out, and be constructed as 'lacking in ability' (Evans, 2004; Fitzgerald, 2005; Wright and Burrows, 2006). Perhaps one final point to be made about the NCPE is that it is not a national curriculum at all, since private schools, and the newly introduced academies, are not required to adhere to it.

THE SCHOOL SPORT PARTNERSHIP PROGRAMME

The second policy initiative considered here is the School Sport Partnership Programme (SSPP). School sport partnerships (SSPs) were a key policy within PESSYP and, although they have now largely been disbanded, research evidence suggests they had a significant impact on improving the range and quality of PESS opportunities for young people (Office for Standards in Education, 2011; Loughborough Partnership, 2008a,b,c). When the coalition government announced within months of coming to power that it intended to no longer fund the scheme, the public outcry that followed resulted in a compromise, and an agreement to fund aspects of the scheme, at least until 2013 (DfE, 2010b). These changes are explored in more detail below, but first it is useful to describe the programme and its main achievements.

SSPs were local partnerships or 'families' of schools with dedicated staff working together to create a coherent structure of sporting opportunities for young people, with a specialist sports college at its hub.[6] Each partnership normally included eight secondary schools and their associated 'feeder' primary/special schools (approximately forty-five schools), with government funding largely focused on the employment of dedicated staff to manage and develop each partnership's activities. For example, each SSP had an overall, full-time manager (Partnership Development Manager, PDM); each secondary school had a School Sport Coordinator (SSCo), a teacher released from teaching for two days; and each primary school had a Primary Link Teacher (PLT), responsible for PE and released from teaching for twelve days per year to undertake the role. In addition to the funding supporting the staffing base, additional monies from the Big Lottery Fund were provided to 'kick start' additional out-of-hours sports activities designed to widen participation.

The programme was introduced over a seven-year period from 2000, and by 2007 included all schools in England. This implementation model means schools have been part of partnerships for very different amounts of time, which is important to bear in mind when analysing monitoring data on impact. Although each partnership was able to plan and implement its own programme of activities to suit its particular schools' location and intakes, the annual monitoring of their activities against specified targets seems to have curtailed, rather than supported, innovative practice, at least in the early years (Flintoff *et al.*, 2011).

One of the key evaluations of the SSPP was conducted by researchers at the Institute of Youth Sport at Loughborough University (Loughborough Partnership, 2008a,b,c). This was a six-year study that collected annual quantitative data from all partnerships, with more qualitative in-depth studies of a sample of individual partnerships carried out each year. Other evaluations of the programme include those conducted by Ofsted (e.g. 2011) and smaller, qualitative studies by individual researchers (e.g. Flintoff *et al.*, 2011; Smith and Leech, 2010). Few studies have attempted any longitudinal study of the development of partnerships (but see Flintoff, 2003, 2008; Flintoff and Cooke, 2005; Flintoff *et al.*, 2011).

The SSPP raised important questions about the nature, organisation and management of young people's PE and school sport opportunities, and who is best placed to manage and develop them. Organising and running extra-curricular sport teams and clubs have historically been an important part of the secondary PE teacher's role, and seen by many as one of the most positive aspects of the job (Armour and Jones, 1998). As a result, the SSPP has been welcomed more by primary than secondary schools, and its impact was more evident in the former and more variable in the latter. The new roles of SSCo and PDM presented PE teachers with very different challenges and required different skills from delivering curricular PE within one school. Moving outside the 'safety net' of one single school environment into strategic development work, and moving across a number of different schools and contexts was difficult for some teachers taking up such roles (Flintoff, 2003). Several features of the programme are worth noting:

- The programme allowed the building of local networks and opportunities around families of schools as the 'hub'.
- The fact that PE teachers were central to the decision making in each of the partnerships should have ensured that the activities that were developed were educationally sound and appropriate.
- The links between curricular PE and the programme were enabled by the dual positioning of SSCos as both teacher (three days a week) and coordinator (two days a week).
- Teachers' continuing professional development was an underlying element of the programme so that sustainable practice was built in.
- The programme included a focus on primary- as well as secondary-age children; arguably, this group has not always been well served by previous policies.

It is clear that the programme has produced some important gains for young people, particularly by increasing the range of opportunities to be physically active (Loughborough Partnership, 2008a,b,c). Big Lottery Funding has enabled partnerships to buy in coaches to deliver programmes, and the numbers of young people now taking part in two hours of high-quality PESS within and beyond the curriculum is impressive (as noted earlier). The impact of the programme on primary PE has been particularly substantial – a welcome but perhaps not surprising result, given that the generally poor state of primary PE has been a concern for the profession for some time. Many more pupils are taking part in intra-school (78 per cent) and inter-school competitive sport (48 per cent) (Quick *et al.*, 2010), although, as explored below, the coalition government views these figures as much too low.

The programme has significantly improved the time allocated to curricular PE, particularly in years 1–6; this does, however, remain very variable, both between schools and between year groups within schools. Whereas 84 per cent of pupils in 2009/10 received two hours of curricular PE (an increase from 44 per cent in 2003/4), this drops to 66 per cent and 62 per cent of years 10 and 11 respectively (Quick *et al.*, 2010). So, although there have been many gains, there is still much variety, with no formal entitlement to two hours of curriculum PE for *all* young people.

Similarly, although there has been a significant increase in the amount of after-school activities, it is clear that these have not catered for all young people. The six-year evaluation of the programme shows a consolidation of the place of traditional team sports at the heart of partnership programmes (although less traditional activities such as martial arts, cycling or orienteering, for example, have grown steadily in popularity) (Loughborough Partnership, 2008b). There is less evidence of innovation in non-mainstream sports and recreational activities. Simply offering more opportunities for competitive sport is unlikely to attract those young people who have in the past been excluded from positive physical activity experience (Flintoff, 2008). The evaluations show that young people from ethnic minorities, girls and disabled young people are under-represented in participation figures. As highlighted earlier, participation figures do not tell the full story; they tell us little about which youngsters are involved, and nothing about the nature of the pedagogy underpinning such opportunities.

Qualitative research (e.g. Flintoff, 2008; Flintoff *et al.*, 2011; Smith and Leech, 2010) gives some insight into these aspects. Both Flintoff and colleagues' (2011) and Smith and Leech's (2010) research show the way in which the government's evaluations of the programme, through the collection of participation figures, affected the way in which coordinators worked. Coordinators have focused on increasing the quantity of opportunities (for example, raising participation figures and time on timetable to the expected two hours) at the expense of considering the quality of learning opportunities and pedagogy used. In his critique of PESSYP, Kirk (2005) rightly points out the importance of using educational, task-orientated pedagogy, rather than one orientated towards sports performance, particularly for children's early learning experiences. In task-based pedagogy, success depends on doing the best you can, compared with 'ego'-orientated pedagogy, in which success depends upon being better than others. It is the former kind of pedagogy, he argues, that is needed to develop young people's lasting involvement in sport. Flintoff and colleagues' (2011) interview-based study with experienced coordinators from eight different sports partnerships in the north of England showed that, though they were aware of this, finding the right person to deliver inclusive, pedagogically appropriate sessions remained a challenge. The SSPP has sought to raise the quality of primary PESS through the use of SSCos or sports coaches working alongside primary teachers. Arguably, neither group is necessarily best placed to deliver PESS and the continuing professional development of teachers of primary-age children. SSCos are PE teachers, trained to work with secondary- (eleven to eighteen years) rather than primary-age children. Sports coaches have in-depth specialist knowledge of how to develop performance in their activity, but may have little experience of adapting this for, or working with, young children. Employing both groups to work with primary teachers to develop good practice risks the imposition of inappropriate pedagogies for younger children (Flintoff, 2003; Kirk, 2005). Providing inclusive learning experiences in PESS is increasingly challenging as school cohorts become more differentiated, reflecting the differential access of families to 'buy into' pre-school and out-of-school PE programmes and coaching (Evans and Davies, 2010). 'Pedagogies of difference' (Lingard, 2007) have never been more important for PESS, and yet are not always evident in current practice.

THE SCHOOL GAMES

The final policy discussed here is the School Games, a new structure to provide competitive school sport for young people across the schools in England. One way to try to disguise a significant cut in funding is to 'reinvent' a programme and call it something else. This is, in effect, what happened to the SSPP when the coalition government came to power in 2010 and introduced its 'radical' new approach to youth sport, centred on the 'new' School Games.[7] Using the same participation figures that the outgoing Labour government had used to herald the SSPP a success, Michael Gove, the incoming Secretary of State for Education for England, announced that a new approach to youth sport participation was needed to address the failure of the SSPP to get more young people engaged in competitive sport. As already noted, the outcry from head teachers and parents at the government's announcement that it were to cut the scheme resulted in some backtracking and compromise. Funds to support the full-time PDM and the twelve days of teacher release for the PLT have been cut, but some monies have been released to ensure every secondary school is funded to release a PE teacher for a day a week for coordinator work until the end of 2013. In addition, a new School Games Organiser (SGO), funded for three days a week, has been appointed to oversee the development and implementation of the new School Games.

The School Games is the government's new structure for competitive school sport, aimed at including young people of all abilities in years 3–13 in intra- and inter-school competitions (see Figure 6.1). Levels 1 and 2 will focus on opportunities at individual schools level, with Levels 3 and Level 4 providing opportunities for high performers to compete at county and national level. The programme will also specifically provide opportunities for disabled pupils at all levels through the School Games 'Project Ability'. Fifty schools across the country have been identified as 'hub' schools to provide a lead on this programme and are delivering bespoke training and providing local advice and guidance to SGOs about how to develop competitions for disabled youngsters, and to help the establishment and implementation of more local competitive opportunities for young people.

Nationally and locally, the School Games are being delivered through partnerships. At the national level, the policy is being led by the Department for Culture, Media and Sport, supported by the Department for Education, and involves Sport England, the British Paralympic Association and the Youth Sport Trust (managing the day-to-day support for schools). At a local level, the School Games will be delivered by schools, clubs, county sports partnerships and other local partners, with a local organising committee set up, chaired by head teachers, to oversee the county festivals. Schools sign up to be part of the School Games through their website (www.yourschoolgames.com), which provides a wealth of material to support the development of age-appropriate competitions in a range of sports, including some new

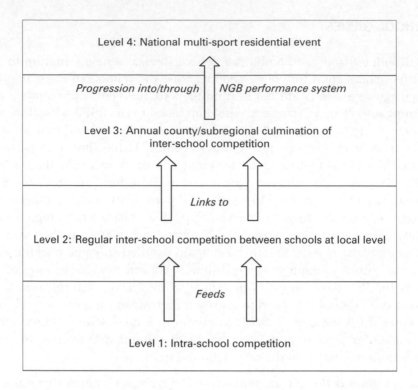

Figure 6.1 The School Games structure. Source: adapted from material on the School Games website (www.yourschoolgames.com).

activities specifically developed to be played by disabled and non-disabled pupils together. Alongside the School Games, each SGO is also encouraged to develop Change4life[8] clubs, based in schools and designed to increase physical activity levels in less active children. These focus on different kinds of activities to the School Games, including badminton, volleyball and fencing, for example, rather than the traditional competitive sports such as football or athletics, and specifically try to bolster an inclusive ethos in the clubs. Young people are centrally involved in the running and organising of these 'different' school sports clubs (see Canterbury Christ Church University, 2011).

A 'RADICAL' NEW APPROACH TO YOUTH SPORT?

It is too early to assess the impact of these initiatives against their supposed aim: to reduce the 'drop-off' of young people's participation in sport once they leave school. What is clear, however, is that the proposed new approach is far from radical. As this chapter has shown, a competitive sport discourse has dominated PESS for several decades, albeit challenged at different times to different extents by

164

more inclusive, progressive policies (Penney and Evans, 1999; Kirk, 2010; Tinning, 2011). In an Olympic and Paralympic year, with the Games in London, it is difficult to see how any other discourse could be prioritised. The important question remains, however: who benefits and who loses out from PESS constructed around competitive sport?

The last decade has seen a significant investment in PESS through the national PESSYP strategy. As is often the case, a change of government has brought with it a change in strategy and, importantly, a much reduced funding base. The demise of PESSYP, the dismantling of the SSPP and the introduction of the School Games in their place will have significant implications for young people's opportunities to be physically active. Who will be engaged in the School Games? Will Change4life really engage those youngsters previously uninterested in PESS? What other opportunities will be lost with the demise of the SSPP? These are important questions to ask of any new policy. A shift in policy relies heavily on the abilities and enthusiasm of the people involved in its day-to-day implementation, and the pedagogy underpinning the new provision. There has been a lot of talk about new policies, new structures, new opportunities, all designed to 'fix' the previous 'problems' of youth sport participation. There has been much less talk about pedagogy, learning and relationships, and even less about continuing professional development for teachers and practitioners charged with the responsibility of delivering new programmes (Department for Education and Skills and Department for Culture, Media and Sport, 2004, 2005). We need to attend to *how* we deliver, as well as *what* we deliver, in the new PE and youth sport opportunities. Pedagogy has been the 'absent agenda' in contemporary PESS debates (Penney and Waring, 2000). Teachers, sport development workers and others working with young people need support to engage in critical reflection about the nature of their pedagogy if we expect them to provide programmes capable of engaging the very different needs of today's young people.

LEARNING ACTIVITIES

1 Reflect back on your own experiences of school PE. How did these differ between primary school and secondary school? Think about:
   a the nature of the activities on offer;
   b who your teacher was, for example male or female, specialist or generalist;
   c the kinds of groupings that were used, for example mixed sex, ability based;
   d the nature of the pedagogy, for example didactic, problem-solving.

2 In groups of four or five, compare and contrast your experiences with the others.
  - What are the commonalities and differences in your experiences?
  - What do your discussions tell you about the social construction of PE?
  - Which children benefit and which lose out from this kind of construction of PE?
  - What changes would you propose to ensure that PE is inclusive of all young people?

NOTES

1. Originally called the PE and School Sport Club Links strategy (see Department of Education and Skills and Department for Culture, Media and Sport, 2003), this was an English strategy. Similar youth sport strategies exist in Wales (e.g. Dragon Sport) and in Scotland (The Active Schools Strategy).

2. The quality of the evidence showing impact has been effectively critiqued elsewhere (see Houlihan and Green, 2006; Smith and Leech, 2010).

3. This is interesting wording; unlike in Scotland, there has never yet been a definitive government commitment to two hours of PE within curriculum time in England. The wording 'expected' rather than 'will' allows schools to deliver much less than this if they so wish.

4. The PE and School Sport Survey published data collected from School Sport Partnerships, a central policy within PESSYP (a collection of secondary and primary schools working together to improve the opportunities for, and quality of, PESS opportunities for young people; see later for more information). Since 2007, all maintained schools were within a partnership, and 99.8 per cent of schools responded with data for the 2009/10 survey.

5. Eligibility for free school meals is one measure of socio-economic deprivation.

6. Specialist Sports Colleges were part of the former Labour government's wider 'specialist schools' initiative: maintained secondary schools in England which received additional funding from the Department for Education and Skills to raise standards in a particular subject area within their own school, in a local family of schools and in the community. The coalition government has stopped providing funding for this type of school, introducing new types of schools, such as academies and free schools.

7. A School Games structure had already been in existence for the previous five years as part of the SSPP.

8. Change4life is a Department for Health-sponsored national health strategy for England and Wales; see National Health Service (2012).

REFERENCES

Armour, K.M. and Jones, R.L. (1998) *Physical Education: Teachers' Lives and Careers*, London: Falmer.

Azzarito, L. and Solomon, M. (2005) 'A reconceptualisation of physical education: the intersection of gender/race/social class', *Sport, Education and Society*, 10 (1): 25–47.

Bramham, P. (2003) 'Boys, masculinity and PE', *Sport, Education and Society*, 8 (1): 57–71.

Anne Flintoff

Brown, D. and Rich, E. (2002) 'Gender positioning as pedagogical practice in physical education', in Penney, D. (ed.), *Gender and Physical Education: Contemporary Issues and Future Directions*, London: Falmer.

Canterbury Christ Church University (2011) 'Evaluation of the Change 4 Life School Sport Clubs programme: final report', www.youthsporttrust.org/downloads/cms/SPEARCCCU_-_Change_4_Life_SSCs_Final_Report_(Nov_2011)1.pdf

Carless, D. (2011) 'Negotiating sexuality and masculinity in school sport: an autoethnography', *Sport, Education and Society*, DOI: 10.1080/13573322.2011.554536

Clarke, G. (2006) 'Sexuality and physical education', in Kirk, D., Macdonald, D. and O'Sullivan, M. (eds.), *The Handbook of Physical Education*, London: Sage.

Coakley, J. and White, A. (1992) 'Making decisions: gender and sport participation amongst British adolescents', *Sociology of Sport Journal*, 9: 20–35.

Curtner-Smith, M.D. (1999) 'The more things change the more they stay the same: factors influencing teachers' interpretations and delivery of National Curriculum Physical Education', *Sport, Education and Society*, 4 (1): 75–97.

Department for Children Schools and Families (DCSF) (2008) 'PE and Sport Strategy for young people', www.education.gov.uk/search/results?q=Pe+and+youth+sport+strategy

Department for Culture, Media and Sport (DCMS) (2010) 'Plans for the legacy from the 2012 Olympic and Paralympic Games', www.culture.gov.uk/what_we_do/2012_olympic_games_and_paralympic_games/3427.aspx

DCMS (2012) *Creating a Sporting Habit for Life: A New Youth Sport Strategy*, London: Crown.

Department for Education (DfE) (2010a) *The Importance of Teaching: The Schools White Paper 2010*, London: Crown Copyright.

DfE (2010b) 'A new approach to school sports: decentralising power, incentivising competition and trusting teachers', press release, www.education.gov.uk/inthenews/pressnotices/a0071098/a-new-approach-for-school-sports

DfE (2011) 'The framework for the National Curriculum: a report by the expert panel for the National Curriculum review', www.education.gov.uk/publications/standard/publicationDetail/Page1/DFE-00135–2011

DfE (2012) 'Review of the National Curriculum in England: summary report of the call for evidence', www.education.gov.uk/publications/standard/publicationDetail/Page1/DFE-00136-2011

Department for Education and Employment (1999) *Physical Education: The National Curriculum in England*, London: Department for Education and Employment.

Department for Education and Skills and Department for Culture, Media and Sport (2003) *Learning through PE and Sport: A Guide to the Physical Education, School Sport and Club Links Strategy*, Nottingham: DfES Publications.

Department for Education and Skills and Department for Culture, Media and Sport (2004) *High Quality PE and Sport for Young People*, Annsely: DfES Publications.

Department for Education and Skills and Department for Culture, Media and Sport (2005) 'Do you have high quality PE and sport in your school? A guide to self-evaluating and improving the quality of PE and school sport', www.education.gov.uk/search/results?q=high+quality+PESS

Department of Education and Science (1991) *Physical Education for Ages 5–16 Years: Proposals to the Secretary of State of Education and Science*, London: HMSO.

Department of Education and Science (1992) *Physical Education in the National Curriculum*, London: HMSO.

Department of Education and Science (1995) *Physical Education in the National Curriculum*, London: HMSO.

Dyson, B. (2006) 'Students' perspectives of physical education', in Kirk, D., Macdonald, D. and O'Sullivan, M. (eds.), *The Handbook of Physical Education*, London: Sage.

Dyson, B., Griffin, L. and Hastie, P. (2009) 'Sport education, tactical games and cooperative learning', in Bailey, R. and Kirk, D. (eds.), *The Routledge Physical Education Reader*, London: Routledge.

Editorial (2011) 'National Curriculum review update', *Physical Education Matters*, 6 (3): 8–9.

Evans, J. (2004) 'Making a difference? Education and "ability" in physical education', *European Physical Education Review*, 10 (1): 95–108.

Evans, J. and Davies, B. (1986) 'Sociology, schooling and physical education', in Evans, J. (ed.), *Physical Education, Sport and Schooling: Studies in the Sociology of Physical Education*, London: Falmer.

Evans, J. and Penney, D. (1995) 'The politics of pedagogy: making a National Curriculum Physical Education', *Journal of Education Policy*, 10 (1): 27–44.

Evans, J. and Davies, B. (2006) 'Social class and physical education', in Kirk, D., Macdonald, D. and O'Sullivan, M. (eds.), *The Handbook of Physical Education*, London: Sage.

Evans, J. and Davies, B. (2010) 'Family, class and embodiment: why school physical education makes so little difference to post-school participation patterns in physical activity', *International Journal of Qualitative Studies in Education*, 23 (7): 765–784.

Evans, J., Davies, B. and Penney, D. (1996) 'Teachers, teaching and the social construction of gender relations', *Sport, Education and Society*, 1 (2): 165–183.

Fitzgerald, H. (2005) 'Still feeling like a spare piece of luggage? Embodied experiences of (dis)ability in physical education and school sport', *Physical Education and Sport Pedagogy*, 10 (1): 41–59.

Fitzgerald, H. (2006) 'Disability and physical education', in Kirk, D., Macdonald, D. and O'Sullivan, M. (eds.), *The Handbook of Physical Education*, London: Sage.

Fitzgerald, H. (2011) 'Drawing on disabled students' experiences of physical education and stakeholder responses', *Sport, Education and Society*, DOI: 10.1080/13573322.2011.609290

Fitzpatrick, K. (2011) 'Brown bodies, racialisation and physical education', *Sport, Education and Society*, DOI: 10.1080/13573322.2011.559221

Flintoff, A. (2003) 'The School Sport Co-ordinator programme: changing the role of the physical education teacher?' *Sport, Education and Society*, 8 (2): 231–250.

Flintoff, A. (2008) 'Targeting Mr Average: participation, gender equity, and school sport partnerships', *Sport, Education and Society*, 13 (4): 413–431.

Flintoff, A. (2011) 'Gender and learning in PE and youth sport', in Armour, K. (ed.), *Sports Pedagogy: An Introduction for Teaching and Coaching*, London: Pearson.

Flintoff, A. and Scraton, S. (2001) 'Stepping into active leisure? Young women's perceptions of active lifestyles and their experiences of school physical education', *Sport, Education and Society*, 6 (1): 5–22.

Flintoff, A. and Cooke, B. (2005) 'Playing to learn: out of school hours learning in PE and sport', *British Journal of Teaching Physical Education*, 36 (2): 43–47.

Flintoff, A. and Scraton, S. (2006) 'Girls and PE', in Kirk, D., Macdonald, D. and O'Sullivan, M. (eds.), *The Handbook of Physical Education*, London: Sage.

Flintoff, A., Fitzgerald, H. and Scraton, S. (2008) 'The challenges of intersectionality: researching difference in physical education', *International Studies in Sociology of Education*, 18 (2): 73–85.

Flintoff, A., Foster, R. and Wystawnoha, S. (2011) 'Promoting and sustaining high quality physical education and school sport through school sport partnerships', *European Physical Education Review*, 17 (1): 341–351.

Gard, M. (2006) 'More art than science? Boys, masculinity and physical education', in Kirk, D., Macdonald, D. and O'Sullivan, M. (eds.), *The Handbook of Physical Education*, London: Sage.

Harris, J. and Penney, D. (2002) 'Gender, health and physical education', in Penney, D. (ed.), *Gender and Physical Education: Contemporary Issues and Future Directions*, London: Routledge.

Hastie, P., Martinez de Ojeda, D. and Calderon Luquin, A. (2011) 'A review of research on Sport Education: 2004 to the present', *Physical Education and Sport Pedagogy*, 16 (2): 103–132.

Hickey, C. (2008) 'Physical education, sport and hyper-masculinity in schools', *Sport, Education and Society*, 13 (2): 147–161.

Houlihan, B. and Green, M. (2006) 'The changing status of school sport and physical education: explaining policy change', *Sport, Education and Society*, 11 (1): 73–92.

Hunt, J. (2012) 'Press release: four thousand community sport clubs to be created to drive a sporting habit for life', www.culture.gov.uk/news/media_releases/8762.aspx

Inchley, J., Mitchell, F. and Currie, C. (2011) 'Fit for Girls evaluation: interim report 2', www.sportscotland.org.uk/ChannelNavigation/Topics/TopicNavigation/Fit+for+girls/

Kay, T. (2006) 'Daughters of Islam: family influences on Muslim young women's participation in sport', *International Review for the Sociology of Sport*, 41 (3): 357–373.

Kirk, D. (1993) *The Body, Schooling and Culture*, Geelong: Deakin University Press.

Kirk, D. (1999) 'Physical culture, physical education and relational analysis', *Sport Education and Society*, 4 (1): 63–74.

Kirk, D. (2005) 'Physical education, youth sport and lifelong participation: the importance of early learning experiences', *European Physical Education Review*, 11 (3): 239–255.

Kirk, D. (2006) 'Sport education, critical pedagogy and learning theory: towards an intrinsic justification for physical education and youth sport', *Quest*, 58: 225–264.

Kirk, D. (2010) *Physical Education Futures*, London: Routledge.

Lingard, B. (2007) 'Pedagogies of indifference', *International Journal of Inclusive Education*, 11 (3): 245–266.

Loughborough Partnership (2008a) 'School Sport Partnerships: final annual monitoring and evaluation report: the Partnership Development Manager survey', www.lborowww.lboro.ac.uk/departments/ssehs/research/centres-institutes/youth-sport

Loughborough Partnership (2008b) 'School Sport Partnerships: final monitoring and evaluation report: the Primary Link Teacher survey', www.lboro.ac.uk/departments/ssehs/research/centres-institutes/youth-sport

Loughborough Partnership (2008c) 'School Sport Partnerships: the final evaluation and monitoring report: School Sport Coordinator surveys', www.lborowww.lboro.ac.uk/departments/ssehs/research/centres-institutes/youth-sport

Macdonald, D. (2002) 'Extending agendas: physical culture research for the twenty-first century', in Penney, D. (ed.), *Gender and Physical Education: Contemporary Issues and Future Directions*, London: Routledge.

Macdonald, D., Abbott, R., Knez, K. and Nelson, K. (2009) 'Taking exercise: cultural diversity and physically active lifestyles', *Sport, Education and Society*, 14 (1): 1–19.

National Health Service (2012) 'Change4life sports clubs', www.nhs.uk/change4life/pages/sports-clubs.aspx

Nelson, A. (2012) '"You don't have to be black skinned to be black": indigenous young people's practices', *Sport, Education and Society*, 17 (1): 57–75.

Nelson, A., Macdonald, D. and Abbott, R. (2010) 'The cultural interface: theoretical and "real" spaces for urban indigenous young people and physical activity', in Wright, J. and Macdonald, D. (eds.), *Young People, Physical Activity and the Everyday*, London: Routledge.

Nike/Youth Sport Trust (1999) *The Girls in Sport Partnership Project: Interim Report*, Institute of Youth Sport: Loughborough University.

Nike/Youth Sport Trust (2000) *Girls into Sport: Towards Girl-Friendly Physical Education*, Loughborough: Institute of Youth Sport.

Office for Standards in Education (2005) *Ofsted Subject Reports 2003/04 Physical Education in Secondary Schools*, London: Crown Copyright.

Office for Standards in Education (2009) 'Physical education in schools 2005/08: working towards 2012 and beyond', www.ofsted.gov.uk

Office for Standards in Education (2011) *School Sport Partnerships: A Survey of Good Practice*, London: Crown Copyright, www.ofsted.gov.uk/news/learning-lessons-school-sport-partnerships

O'Sullivan, M. and MacPhail, A. (2010) *Young People's Voices in Physical Education and Youth Sport*, London: Routledge.

Penney, D. (2001) 'The revision and initial implementation of the National Curriculum for Physical Education in England', *Bulletin of Physical Education*, 37 (2): 93–135.

Penney, D. (2002a) 'Equality, equity and inclusion in PE and school sport', in Laker, A. (ed.), *The Sociology of Sport and Physical Education*, London: Routledge.

Penney, D. (2002b) 'Gendered policies', in Penney, D. (ed.), *Gender and Physical Education: Contemporary Issues and Future Directions*, London: Routledge.

Penney, D. (2006) 'Curriculum construction and change', in Kirk, D., Macdonald, D. and O'Sullivan, M. (eds.), *The Handbook of Physical Education*, London: Sage.

Penney, D. and Evans, J. (1999) *Politics, Policy and Practice in Physical Education*, London: E and F N Spon.

Penney, D. and Waring, M. (2000) 'The absent agenda: pedagogy and physical education', *Journal of Sport Pedagogy*, 6 (1): 4–37.

Penney, D. and Evans, J. (2005) 'Policy, power and politics in physical education', in Green, K. and Hardman, K. (eds.), *Physical Education: Essential Issues*, London: Sage.

Penney, D., Clarke, G., Quill, M. and Kitchin, D. (2005) *Sport Education in Physical Education*, London: Routledge.

Qualifications and Curriculum Authority (QCA) (2007a) 'Physical education: programme of study for Key Stage 3 and attainment target', www.education.gov.uk/schools/teachingandlearning/curriculum/secondary/b00198952/pe/ks3/programme

QCA (2007b) 'Physical education: programme of study for Key Stage 4 and attainment target', www.education.gov.uk/schools/teachingandlearning/curriculum/secondary/b00198952/pe/ks3/programme

QCA (undated) 'The New Secondary Curriculum: what has changed and why?', http://dera.ioe.ac.uk/6564/

Quick, S., Simon, A. and Thornton, A. (2010) 'The PE and school sport survey 2009/10', www.education.gov.uk/publications/standard/publicationDetail/Page1/DFE-RR032

Scidentop, D. (1994) *Sport Education: Quality PE through Positive Sport Experiences*, Leeds: Human Kinetics.

Seidentop, D. (2009) 'Junior sport and the evolution of sport cultures', in Bailey, R. and Kirk, D. (eds.), *The Routledge Reader in Physical Education*, London: Routledge.

Smith, A. and Leech, R. (2010) 'Evidence, what evidence? Evidence-based policy making and School Sport Partnerships in north west England', *International Journal of Sport Policy*, 2 (3): 327–346.

Smith, A., Thurston, M., Lamb, K. and Green, K. (2007) 'Young people's participation in National Curriculum Physical Education: a study of 15–16 year olds in north-west England and north-east Wales', *European Journal of Physical Education*, 13 (2): 165–194.

170

Tinning, R. (2011) 'The idea of physical education: a memetic perspective', *Sport, Education and Society*, DOI: 10.1080/17408989.2011.582488

Waddington, I., Malcolm, D. and Cobb, J. (1998) 'Gender stereotyping and physical education', *European Physical Education Review*, 4 (1): 34–46.

Wright, J. and Burrows, L. (2006) 'Re-conceiving ability in physical education: a social analysis', *Sport, Education and Society*, 11 (3): 275–291.

Wright, J. and Macdonald, D. (2010) *Young People, Physical Activity and the Everyday*, London: Routledge.

Wright, J., Macdonald, D. and Groom, L. (2003) 'Physical activity and young people: beyond participation', *Sport, Education and Society*, 8 (1): 17–34.

Youth Sport Trust/Sport England (2009) 'The PE and Sport Strategy for young people: a guide to delivering the five hour offer', www.youthsporttrust.org/downloads/cms/PESSYP_5hr_flyer.pdf

CHAPTER 7

SPORT AND HEALTH

STEPHEN ROBSON AND JIM MCKENNA

Participation in sporting activity is often associated with improvements in health and fitness. Sport providers frequently extol the health benefits of taking part in regular physical exercise. Externalities of sport, physical activity (PA) and exercise have not been lost on politicians, policy makers, professionals and local communities, while the imminence of world-level sports events often sharpens their interest. Indeed, recent economic developments have created calls for the closer integration of services with common interests.

To this end, and with an eye on promoting improved public health and better individual health, Fineberg (2012) has called for a societal shift away from concerns for modifying 'health care systems' towards the development of effective and sustainable 'health systems'. This is all the more urgent given a recent Scottish analysis, suggesting that primary prevention centred on modifying health-related behaviours contributes up to four times as much to health outcomes as medically based secondary prevention (Hotchkiss *et al.*, 2011). Throughout this chapter we argue that the links between sport and health, notwithstanding the different perspectives about which is more important, need to be seen for how they can be best aligned towards this ultimate aim.

The chapter therefore examines how participation in different forms of sport and physical exercise can enhance individual well-being in a variety of ways. It also explores how professionals in the field can work in partnership to generate opportunities for people from all walks of life to enjoy the health benefits of sport. The chapter concludes by further developing (relative to earlier editions of this book) the use of new theoretical understandings about behavioural change, which can support both the sport development professional and the student alike.

172

KEY TERMS: HEALTH AND FITNESS

In many settings, the terms 'health' and 'fitness' are often used interchangeably, although they carry distinct meanings. These definitions are of long standing, which attests to their enduring characterisation, and bear repetition, if only to remind ourselves of what sport might contribute to the lives of participants. The distinction between fitness and health is an important one. It is most useful to think of fitness as a component of health, with health as an all-embracing term used to describe the individual's overall well-being. Various established definitions of health, including that of the World Health Organization, emphasise an integration of factors: health is not merely the absence of disease, but complete and optimal physical, mental, social and spiritual functioning. To quote Bouchard and colleagues (1990: 6–7), health is a

> human condition with physical, social and psychological dimensions, each characterized on a continuum with positive and negative poles; positive health is associated with a capacity to enjoy life and withstand challenges, it is not merely the absence of disease; negative health is associated with morbidity and, in the extreme, with mortality.

Therefore, experts consider health to be an all-embracing concept; it cannot be measured simply by objective physical criteria, but must also take into account an individual's subjective perception of his/her status. The concept of fitness is therefore but one, albeit important, dimension of health, and deals specifically with the capacity to perform given tasks, such as to perform work satisfactorily. Although fitness is conventionally thought of in terms of the capacity to achieve physical goals, which can be helpfully redefined as 'exercise capacity' (Mark and Lauer, 2003) most lay, or everyday, definitions of fitness accommodate ideas of mental fitness. For example, 'mental toughness' and other psychological factors such as commitment, motivation, coping with stress, resilience and so on now occupy a vital role in the lives of elite athletes, although the growing body of recent positive evidence associates these factors with exercise in more modestly achieving individuals. For others, the literature shows the positive effects of aerobic activity (which is the bedrock of many sports) on cognitive functioning across the life cycle (e.g. Vercambre et al., 2011). This offers another, perhaps overlooked, reason for promoting engagement with physically demanding forms of sport.

The physical aspects of fitness (speed, power, strength, endurance and flexibility) can be developed in elite performers to a high degree and they are specific to the particular demands of sport. Fitness can also be achieved by recreational sport participants to benefit individual health; for example, an older person taking up cycling may experience gains in endurance and leg strength and subsequently be able to undertake daily tasks with increased ease and vigour, while also avoiding the harmful outcomes of sedentariness. Recent data have shown how increased aerobic capacity improves cognitive functioning across the life course, which adds a further reason for promoting involvement in continuous, moderate-intensity forms of activity on most days of the week (Medina, 2008).

'Fitness' is clearly a relative term, and a problem is that it can be used ambiguously. It is shaped by individual needs and wants, but it is also dependent upon political, economic, social and cultural contexts. For example, compare a young Premier League footballer with a slight injury, unable to play on in a crucial Saturday fixture and described by his/her coach or physiotherapist as 'unfit', with the condition of a middle-aged smoker with obesity, discharged from hospital and described by doctors as 'fit' to return to work. The footballer is significantly fitter in general terms, but, weighed against his individual and team needs, has been declared unfit. This distinction leads to concepts of *health-related fitness*:

> an ability to perform daily activities with vigor . . . and demonstration of traits and capacities that are associated with a low risk of (movement restricting) diseases and conditions
>
> (Bouchard and Shephard, 1994: 81)

and performance-related fitness:

> Fitness necessary for optimal work or sport performance . . . [that] depends heavily upon motor skills, cardio-respiratory power and capacity, body size, motivation etc.
>
> (ibid.)

Individual fitness needs are personal and unique, and other than in the case of the competitive performer need not be compared between individuals. Consequently, sport development professionals should enable people at all levels of physical capacity to access the benefits of sport participation. To accrue the benefits of an active, sport-based lifestyle, individuals are thought to best support this behaviour by being self-determined, meaning that they engage with the behaviour because they want to, not because of the requirements of other coercive forces and agencies. Self-determination can be optimised by accenting three main themes: autonomy, competence and relatedness (Deci and Ryan, 1985). Minimising competitiveness by reducing opportunities for comparison with others seems to play an important role in achieving these three features for most recreational participants. This applies across the profile of body size, and the phrase 'exercise at every size' should be applied.

So, health is an all-embracing indicator or expression of a person's state of being, whereas fitness is one aspect of this which deals with capacity to perform tasks.

Neither is solely confined to physical condition, and a crucial contemporary issue is to understand the relative importance of physical activity behaviour over any risks that it might produce (Nelson *et al.*, 2007; O'Donovan *et al.*, 2010).

This leads to another confused area of terminology: behaviours and activities that develop aspects of health and fitness. In particular, the terms 'sport' and 'exercise' are frequently interchanged, whereas they have very different meanings both in behavioural science and in everyday life. We examine these below, while also introducing the concept of physical activity. A key theme of this chapter is to highlight the numerous ways in which sport development professionals can work to change many people's negative perceptions of both sport, and their potential engagement in it, through careful packaging, promotion and delivery.

KEY TERMS: SPORT, EXERCISE AND PHYSICAL ACTIVITY

> Of all the hoaxes perpetuated upon humankind, the most destructive is the one that puts forth the ludicrous claim that exercise is a good and positive thing
>
> (Roeben, 2001)

Such homilies to idleness, emphasising unwanted outcomes of PA such as injury, are acerbic reminders that for many people the notion of indulging in any activity creates negative motivation. Those with the responsibility for encouraging and enabling sport participation should therefore be familiar with the language or discourse of activity, and be able to articulate the different elements of sport and exercise to those in need of persuasion to take part. Equally, they need to be aware of an emerging set of reasons for encouraging engagement in sport. One new concept here may centre around the emerging evidence in 'inactivity physiology', which highlights the powerful effects of prolonged inactivity, such as accompany extended TV watching (Dunstan *et al.*, 2007; Katzymark *et al.*, 2009). Few of these effects seem to be undone by adopting additional activity, meaning that 'low activity' – and not inactivity – is the only meaningful counterpart to 'high activity'. Worse, recent evidence (Dickerson *et al.*, 2012) has suggested that the most harmful of these effects are experienced by the most overweight/obese individuals.

Recent estimates suggest that inactivity accounts for 3.5 per cent of the disease burden and up to 10 per cent of EU deaths. In the UK alone this equates to costs ranging from €3 billion to €12 billion (WHO, 2006). Yet just fourteen minutes per day can be a sufficient stimulus to add three years to life expectancy (Wen *et al.*, 2011). Notwithstanding the powerful effects of high-intensity training, it is unclear that this approach brings better adherence; worse, the broad sweep of the adherence literature suggests that it will only increase drop-out. This places a considerable value on reinforcing the message that sport distracts people from indolent behaviour, such as prolonged, unrefined 'electronic entertainment'. Indeed, in the English Premier League Health initiative 79 per cent of recruits were not initially meeting recommended PA levels, and almost 70 per cent of new recruits were sitting for harmful amounts of time per day, whereas after a soccer-based intervention one in four men had reduced their daily sitting to a low risk level (Zwolinsky *et al.*, 2012).

At this stage, it is useful to remind ourselves of definitions of sport, so that distinction from other aspects of PA can be clearly made. Notions of sport generally focus upon competitiveness and the presence of structured rules. Haywood and colleagues (1995: 42) outline the essential features of an activity that is a sport:

- a symbolic test of physical or psycho-motor skills
- a competitive framework which requires codified rules
- continuity and tradition in sporting practices.

Bouchard and Shephard (1994: 79), from the US perspective, link sport to wider concepts of activity: 'a form of physical activity that includes competition'. However, it is important to recall that some activities that are considered by their participants and administrators as sports do not sit comfortably within the US conceptualisation. 'New' games and cooperative sports have a significant role to play, and are often more welcoming to the reluctant or anxious participant. Therefore, similar issues may also play out in the fields of recreation and exercise.

Exercise is something that can be gained as a consequence of participating in certain sports, or it can be practised outside a sporting environment for its own sake. Exercise is usually seen to be an essentially structured form of activity, undertaken with particular (fitness-related) instrumental objectives in mind:

A form of leisure time physical activity . . . with a specific external objective, such as the improvement of fitness, physical performance or health (in which the participant is advised to a recommended mode, intensity, frequency or duration of such activity.

(Bouchard and Shephard, 1994: 78)

It follows logically that PA is an over-arching, generic concept, of which sport and exercise are two significant and meaningful forms. The idea of PA encapsulates the full range of major movements undertaken by a person, including those not subject to structure or form. Consequently, to paraphrase Bouchard and Shephard (1994: 77), PA comprises any body movement produced by skeletal muscles which results in energy expenditure above the resting state.

Clearly, this definition accommodates a wide range of actions not related to sport or formal exercise, but activity from which people can gain pleasure and fitness gains

176

such as gardening, walking, dancing or yoga. The sport development professional can promulgate the messages of the benefits of PA to further the cause of sport. This is acknowledged, for example, by the presence of a growing number of sport and physical activity teams in local authorities. These issues will be explored in detail later in the chapter; a summary of the benefits of PA, and sport in particular, identified in research, will help to set the scene for this discussion and provide a compelling discourse or rationale to motivate reluctant participants.

THE BENEFITS OF PHYSICAL ACTIVITY

Recent governmental initiatives in the area of health have placed an increasing emphasis upon the positive aspects of physically active lifestyles. Policy shifts throughout the 1990s and early in the new millennium reflected the growing evidence showing that individual activity-related gains were also shared societally. Primary and preventative health care policies were encouraged for economic, political and social as well as medical reasons. Reductions in the incidence of coronary heart disease, stroke and a wide range of other sedentary-related illnesses would reduce demands placed upon pressured health care budgets, while enabling individuals to play a more productive role in everyday life.

PA is a major issue for public and individual health. Regular engagement in moderately intensive activity has significant co-occurring health benefits, improving bone and functional health, reducing the risk of hypertension, coronary heart disease, stroke, diabetes, breast and colon cancer and falls, and helping to control weight. It can improve self-esteem, mood, sleep quality and energy, and reduce the risk of stress, depression, dementia and Alzheimer's disease. There is a growing body of evidence now showing that brain function is enhanced by each bout of physical activity (possibly through the action of brain-derived neurotrophin factor, which is released during activity and causes neuron growth in the brain).

In contrast, physical inactivity is recognised as a major independent risk factor for chronic non-communicable diseases. It is estimated to be the main cause globally for 21–25 per cent of breast and colon cancers, 27 per cent of diabetes and some 30 per cent of ischaemic heart disease burden. Lack of exercise contributes nearly 3.5 per cent of the disease burden and up to 10 per cent of deaths in the EU, annually costing the UK an estimated €12 billion (WHO, 2006). Despite these benefits and risks, millions of people the world over – including those living in what we wrongly label as the Third World – are not active enough to benefit their health and well-being (WHO, 2011).

Recent work has begun to identify the value of increments of fitness – typically determined through treadmill testing – for their specific value in altering health. They show both the health value of increasing exercise capacity and the consequences of losing capacity. The metabolic equivalent of task (MET) is a measure commonly used to express the energy expenditure related to physical activities, with sleeping typically equating to 0.9 MET. One recent US study (Lee *et al.*, 2011) followed over 14,000 men with a mean age of forty-four, over more than eleven years, showing that, for every 1 MET improvement in fitness, mortality was reduced by 15–20 per cent. Compared with men who did not exercise and lost fitness, men who maintained their fitness levels averaged a 30 per cent lower death rate. When men improved their fitness over more than eleven years, mortality decreases averaged 40 per cent; this effect was stronger than the effect of weight loss. In almost 6,000 women followed over eight years, for every 1 MET *increase* the risk of death from coronary heart disease *reduced* by 17 per cent, whereas for every 1 MET *reduction* the risk of death from coronary heart disease *increased* by 9 per cent (Gulati *et al.*, 2003; Peterson *et al.*, 2008). In another US male-only study, every extra 1 MET reduced annual health care costs by 5.4 per cent (Weiss *et al.*, 2004). However, the overall view of which is best is well summarised here:

> A curvilinear reduction in risk occurs for a variety of diseases and conditions across volume of activity, with the steepest gradient at the lowest end of the activity scale. Some activity is better than none, and more is better than some. Even light-intensity activity appears to provide benefit and is preferable to sitting still.
>
> (Powell *et al.*, 2011: 349)

A major challenge for providers of physical activities is to develop local awareness and to provide means for people to access activities suited to their needs, tastes and intensity preferences. This is true for sport development professionals, fitness and leisure centre managers and walks coordinators. The precise role of sport as a form of PA, with all of the attendant benefits, has not been as clearly defined as it might have been, although two Cochrane Reviews have called for more systematic research in this domain (Jackson *et al.*, 2005; Priest *et al.*, 2008). The next section concentrates on sport as a force for health gain, and offers practical ideas on how sport development professionals can exploit contemporary research.

THE HEALTH BENEFITS OF SPORT

To realise Fineberg's (2012) aspiration of a health system populated by healthy people it will be necessary to recognise and provide for all pertinent interventions and positive lifestyle choices. Fineberg (2012: 1020) calls for the population to attain 'the highest level of health possible'. The potential contribution of sport to individual and collective well-being, and therefore the ultimate accomplishment of this goal, has by no means been exhausted. This provides an opportunity to think

178

more broadly about sport's place in the PA milieu. Within this, there is a need to appreciate more keenly the negative connotations of sport participation, especially if we hope to see sport located more firmly in a health system which more readily embraces a culture of healthy living rather than curative intervention.

For many non-participants, sport is less a source of health gain than an activity ripe with the potential for physical injury and social embarrassment. Those with responsibility for the provision and promotion of sporting opportunities need to be aware of common – yet avoidable – perceptions regarding sport, and to be in a position to work towards overcoming the most negative of them. Changing the rules and officiating practice of sports may beneficially reduce rates of injury, yet there is also a need to address how different sports are portrayed and experienced. In some sports, or at least their local expression, active exclusion of minority groups may occur. More worrying is the institutionalised exclusion of especially young people in competitive sports, which often means excluding the youngest within an age cohort (Cobley *et al.*, 2009). It is hard to rationalise how these so-called 'relative age effects' can be condoned or endorsed, particularly by activities supported through the public purse.

Numerous sports are intensely physical and carry inherent risks of injury. To participants, the extreme physicality of such sports is attractive; to the majority of the population, this is inhibiting. Indeed, even the idea of acquiring an injury may be enough to dissuade people from engagement. Therefore, it is important to differentiate such notions of risk and to distinguish the more 'gentle' sporting forms that might encourage even the most timid. The nexus between formal sport and unconstrained, active recreation (Department of Health, 2011) is a prime site for such activities to be identified and promoted, tapping into sport's cultural dominance and broad appeal without the risks associated with more robust participation.

Many sports provide the full gamut of health benefits linked to PA. Improved understanding of the dose–response relationship of PA with health highlights that these benefits can be accrued, albeit to a lesser degree than regular participants, by 'weekend warriors' (Kruger *et al.*, 2007). Taking part also brings a wide range of social and psychological benefits. Many volunteers, paid officials and administrators consider themselves to be more rounded, accomplished individuals as a consequence of their roles in sport. Further, these individuals help to create traditions, customs and an 'atmosphere' that may attract and welcome newcomers or returners.

Naturally, each person's current health status and their disposition towards given activities will be highly influential in decisions about whether or not to take up any particular opportunity. The sport development professional or other promoter of an activity must identify the sections of the community to which the activity may be particularly suited or attractive. However, whatever the sport and the situation, the scope for health gains is vast. There are numerous population groups where inactivity prevails and where important physical activity benefits can be achieved.

Improvements to some or all of the five elements of fitness are intended or unintended outcomes of doing most sports. As has been stated, health gains do not have to be sought solely to improve athletic performance in a particular discipline. Physical fitness improvements can also enhance lost or diminished function, to those with any of the plethora of medical conditions affecting movement and daily living. Many conditions, such as diabetes or osteoporosis, may be prevented by physical activity programmes that address biological needs across the life course. For example, through life course epidemiology it is increasingly understood that osteoporosis is a disease of youth that becomes manifest only in older life. This underlines the need for sport promoters to engage with developments in epidemiology and medicine to better understand disease processes and to understand how PA can play a central role in primary prevention and in secondary prevention (once initial signs of problems occur).

The social and psychological gains to be found in sporting lifestyles should not be underestimated. Sport provides an ideal vehicle for individuals to express themselves in a variety of ways. Playing sport and affiliation to a club or team offer tremendous opportunities for improved self-esteem, socialising and community identity. However, sport can provide the means for social and psychological health gain in other ways.

High numbers of people fulfil vital administrative and leadership roles at all levels of sport, with no financial or other tangible reward. The estimated 2 million volunteers in English sport, including over 1 million individuals providing over 1.68 million coaching hours per week (North, 2009), have a multitude of motivations for engagement with their chosen sport. Reasons for giving up free time to perform bureaucratic and coaching functions are often expressed as 'helping with the kids', 'giving something back' and so on. Volunteers acknowledge the importance of their role – the majority of sports opportunities are founded upon good will – and volunteers experience enhancement of self-esteem and community solidarity. They may also enhance their level of social connectedness, which is another hitherto unvoiced health benefit (Berkman and Kawachi, 2000) of involvement with sport. Indeed, Bishop and Hoggett (1986) argue that the voluntary sector is where local democratic involvement is uniquely possible. Sport and leisure organisations can sometimes include those excluded elsewhere in the serious worlds of work, religion and politics. In other instances, people experiencing social isolation can tap into a vibrant network of friends by becoming involved in volunteering in sport. Indeed, Fineberg's (2012) 'ideal' health system comprises a commitment to equality that is a cornerstone of sport development philosophy:

treatment is applied without discrimination or disparities to all individuals and families, regardless of age, group identity, or place, and . . . the system is fair to the health professionals, institutions, and businesses supporting and delivering care.

(Fineberg, 2012: 1020)

This further highlights the case for inclusive sport to be seen as a core component of a reimagined health system which maximises the use of public funds and promotes healthier life choices for all, and which sees sport as a viable 'treatment' in the prevention of a range of conditions and the promotion of better public health. The case for the health benefits of sport is compelling, and researchers will doubtless continue to add to the growing body of impressive evidence. To optimise the value of this evidence and of the inevitable interconnectedness between sport and physical and mental activity, it makes sense for sport development and health professionals to work together more systematically. They can agree on at least three large target audiences: (i) those who spend long hours sitting, (ii) those who live inactive lifestyles and (iii) those who are already active and need to be supported to continue in this way. The next section examines how such initiatives can be realised.

PROMOTING THE PHYSICAL BENEFITS OF SPORT

In the USA a new public health initiative (2020 Impact Goals, Ford *et al.*, 2012) has been announced which can have profound implications for how sport is promoted. This approach has been adopted at least in part because attention on disease and ill-health has done little to change public health in the USA, and this issue also applies to the UK. The new approach – doubtless driven by concerns for cost cutting of national budgets – is based on the strong links between lifestyle behaviours and the clinical markers that so disengage non-scientists and ordinary people alike. Instead, and because of the strong and predictive link between additional health behaviours and clinical markers, attention has now fallen to promoting the health behaviours rather than pursuing misunderstood concepts of risk reduction. This presents an excellent opportunity for advocates to show how sport delivers on the public health agenda. Up to now, and the lack of published literature confirms this, showing changes in the clinical markers will have been too difficult for most people involved in sport promotion and delivery.

Here the essential idea can be summed by answering the question 'What's your score?' Scores are achieved according to how many 'Yes' answers result from five main questions. These are:

- Do you currently smoke?
- Do you do at least thirty minutes of at least moderate-intensity PA on five or more days per week?
- Do you consume fewer than twenty-two units of alcohol per week?
- Do you eat more than three portions of fresh fruit or vegetables per day?
- Is your height–weight ratio (body mass index, BMI) less than 25.1?

These same behaviours – even allowing for slightly different ways of assessing them – show progressive, incremental benefits for a host of markers of morbidity and mortality. These benefits occur in male and female adults across the life cycle. Indeed, the relationships have been shown to be predictive over anything from twelve months (Reis *et al.*, 2011) to twenty years (Liu *et al.*, 2012). In another large study, although women who adhered to a low-risk lifestyle had a low incidence of coronary events, only 3 per cent of the women in the study could sustain these four factors: (i) non-smoking, (ii) consuming a heart-healthy diet, (iii) maintaining a normal BMI and (iv) exercising daily (Stampfer *et al.*, 2000). Convincing general practitioners (GPs, family doctors) in the UK to adopt physical activity as a clinical intervention is one of the toughest challenges facing PA promoters. Let's Get Moving (Department of Health, 2009) outlines that 'treating' patients using physical activity is hugely cost-effective, to the extent that the National Health Service (NHS) could prevent thirty-eight heart attacks using PA for the cost of one drug-based intervention using statins. Despite this, the NHS favours the costlier therapy, and sport development professionals will need to exercise ever greater levels of creativity to appeal to health commissioners for PA funding.

Elsewhere the previous edition of this book reported the successful integration of sport into the wider physical education/physical activity agenda through the PE, School Sport and Club Links (PESSCL) strategy (later supplanted by the Physical Education and Sport Strategy for Young People, PESSYP) and School Sport Partnerships. Under the leadership of Partnership Development Managers, schools were exhorted to develop stronger school–community links to enable pupils to access structured sporting opportunities outside the curriculum as part of the 'five-hour offer' promoted by the government. Following the cuts announced in 2010, in recognition of the physical benefits of sport and the subsequent gains in academic performance, a significant number of School Sport Partnerships were retained under different funding regimes and often in different guises. To make community collaborations work more effectively in this new arrangement, teachers will need additional support, since they can otherwise be dominated by school-centred attitudes and behaviours (St Leger, 2004). This is where sport development's existing links and expertise can be exploited. Sport development professionals are accustomed to the notion of permeable boundaries rather than barriers and here they can be instrumental in ensuring that sport's potential as a tool for wider health gain can bear fruit.

182

The case for sport development to accommodate a more flexible concept of 'sport' – one which encompasses wider aspects of the Department of Health's (2011) model of PA modes – is strengthened by contemporary research into the link between PA and alcohol consumption. Recent evidence from the UK has shown that regular exercisers are more likely to exceed drinking recommendations (Poortinga, 2007). Indeed, even men's health initiatives that encourage heightened physical activity, such as the Premier League Health (Pringle *et al.*, 2011), have reported a similar trend. Their follow-up data provide preliminary numerical values on the strength of these relationships: increases in PA – typically resulting from playing regular football – were associated with a 40 per cent reduction in the likelihood of meeting alcohol recommendations. In contrast, not meeting alcohol recommendations reduced the likelihood of men meeting PA guidelines by only 7 per cent. This presents sport and PA promoters with a new and perhaps unexpected conundrum; so do examples exist of successful sport–PA crossover initiatives which resist inbuilt, subcultural predispositions towards unhealthy lifestyle choices?

Many UK local authorities have long since departed from the 'traditional' model of a sport development team focused solely on developing sport for its own sake. North Somerset Council, for example, has embedded sport development within a broader 'Go4Life' branding of its sports and active lifestyles section, and offers programmes such as Back to Sport 4 Life. Here, individuals and groups of friends are encouraged to resume a sporting activity from which they have lapsed or try a new mode of PA (North Somerset Council, 2012). Participants in such a programme are more likely to be exposed to positive lifestyle messages than those left to the caprices of sports club drinking cultures. Elsewhere, in North Wales, Wrexham County Borough Council's Swimming and Aquatic Development Officer's 'Why swim?' message consciously blurs the boundary between a recognised sport and its more recreational manifestations, outlining the fun, social and physical health benefits as well as the opportunity for competent swimmers to be able to take part in other aquatic disciplines (Wrexham County Borough Council, 2012). Weed and colleagues (2012), in their systematic review of literature related to the hoped-for sport/PA legacy of London 2012 are unequivocal that sport-only approaches are unlikely to have the desired effect of stimulating increased mass participation:

> The goal for physical activity participation policy and strategy will be to satisfy the desire to participate through providing physical activity (rather than sport) opportunities presented as fun community events or programmes, for which the achievement of a 'critical mass' of community engagement may be important.
>
> (Weed *et al.*, 2012: 80)

Sport policy and its implementation will need to recognise the growing evidence that higher participation will only be secured if providers adopt a very different stance to 'sport'. The next section therefore considers recent developments in this area of increasing interest to policy makers.

PHYSICAL ACTIVITY ON THE UK POLITICAL AGENDA

As the above section indicates, the arrival of the Conservative–Liberal Democrat coalition government in the UK in May 2010 heralded yet another significant shift in PA's political status and perceived worth. Previous editions of the book deal in detail with successive governments' attention to PA, highlighting milestone developments such as the Allied Dunbar National Fitness Survey and the Active for Life campaign. During Tony Blair's (1997–2007) tenure as Prime Minister the UK government's enhanced interest in sport and PA was apparent and included previously unmatched political support for the bid to bring the 2012 Olympic and Paralympic Games to the UK, along with the subsequent focus on a mass participation legacy that reached into every corner of the nation. The aforementioned 'five-hour offer', an attempt to ensure that every school pupil in the UK was able to access a total of five hours' curricular and extra-curricular physical education and school sport, emerged under Blair's successor, Gordon Brown. The final round of PESSYP participation data suggested that 'across Years 1–13, 55% of pupils participated in at least three hours of high quality PE and out of hours school sport during the 2009/10 academic year' (Department for Education, 2010: 2), although the veracity of these figures and therefore the success of the initiative were contested in other quarters. The suggestion seems to be, though, that heightened investment in sport-focused PA can lead to tangible gains. As has been shown, this comes at a fraction of the cost of medical interventions.

The previous edition discussed how, in order to achieve challenging mass participation targets, Sport England refocused its work away from traditional sport and in so doing rendered itself the *de facto* national PA agency for England. In keeping with the pace and apparently piecemeal nature of change in the PA and sport arenas, this was discontinued when the decision was taken to invest a greater proportion of National Lottery funding and accompanying expectations in the national governing bodies (NGBs) of sport. Through the Whole Sport Plan programme, a select number of NGBs became the focus of mass participation initiatives, thereby assuming a previously alien role as key agencies in the PA arena. Active People Survey figures (Sport England, 2012) indicate that the impact of the initial Whole Sport Plan cycle (2008–2011) had been negligible in terms of growing mass participation in most of the funded sports. Despite this a further four-year funding programme was announced (Sport England, 2011) which continued to locate much of the responsibility for enhancing grassroots sport (and therefore PA) participation with NGBs.

184

The transition from New Labour to the coalition was marked by further changes to the status of PA in the public health agenda. Although PA was not 'airbrushed' out of key central government documents it became subsumed in the obesity discourse which dominated many public health debates. Through initiatives such as Change4Life (NHS, 2012) the holistic message of physical activity allied to healthier eating was promulgated, but investment was relatively modest (e.g. Change4Life school sports clubs were funded to the tune of just over £8 million over a five-year period; the annual NHS budget is over £100 billion). Although arguments in favour of PA are almost universally accepted, the case for its status as a clinical intervention needs to be upgraded to justify the accompanying increase in investment. The need for the imaginative integration of PA into otherwise more specialised sport development work is as strong as ever.

CASE STUDY 7.1: THE STRATEGIC PHYSICAL ACTIVITY AGENDA IN KIRKLEES

Earlier editions of the book examined moves towards a more integrated relationship between mainstream sport development and broader PA work. This encapsulates a worthy determination to promote active lifestyles in their fullest but is also connected to the need to attract internal and external support essential for the survival of the service. As the resource base for sport and PA development continues to decline, the need for professionals to develop innovative partnerships is exacerbated. Previous editions cited projects such as the Middlesbrough GAP (Get Active on Prescription) Scheme, which at the time of writing had operated for almost twenty years, illustrating that it is by no means impossible for sport and PA developers to persuade clinicians of the benefits of alternative therapies to treat a range of conditions. Elsewhere in the UK there exists an example of just how extensive a PA partnership between local authority provision and public health care can become. Kirklees is a large metropolitan local authority in West Yorkshire. In line with a number of other councils it invested in a PA section as part of its wider Sport and Physical Activity Development Team provision. At the time of writing, the NHS and its relationship with a range of partner agencies were under review and subject to the prospect of sweeping change, added to which the structure of the local authority was in a state of flux brought about in no small way by the 2010 cuts. However, the principles underpinning the links between sport and health in Kirklees would be preserved. Sport and wider PA 'meet in the middle' through overlapping programmes hosted within the Sport and Physical Activity Development Team. Here the notion of a discernible boundary between sport and broader, recreational forms of PA is contested. Across these two areas of provision, members of the public are encouraged and enabled to embrace PA in all its forms. The key messages are that PA should be entered into consensually and that the mode of engagement can have a sporting focus without the threat of injury, violence or alienation evident in some competitive forms.

What is perhaps most striking about Kirklees Sport and Physical Activity Development is its strategic funding arrangement with the local NHS. Although the nature of this was liable to change dramatically as a consequence of NHS reforms, the commitment to the relationship was hoped to be secure. The Executive Director of Public Health for Kirklees had a joint role on behalf of the local NHS Primary Care Trust (PCT) and the council, and formally recognised the value of PA as an integral part of a much wider portfolio of public health interventions. The Sport and Physical Activity Development Manager, who oversees the Sport and Physical Activity Development Team, also occupied the part-time role of Obesity Portfolio Manager on behalf of the PCT for a period of time, helping to cement the relationship. The PCT entrusted very substantial funding to the Sport and Physical Activity Development Team and facilitated the creation of seventeen Physical Activity Development Officer posts. The bigger strategic picture reflects a shared commitment to reducing obesity through a more active Kirklees population. The Physical Activity Development Manager was able to use her substantial knowledge of the public health benefits of PA, coupled with a keen appreciation of clinical priorities and an ability to communicate in 'NHS-speak', to persuade NHS budget holders to contribute and enable pressured local authority resources to be stretched further. (A welcome by-product appears to have been the shoring up of core sport development activity through this joined-up approach.) PCTs were set to be abolished, and in Kirklees the responsibility and resources for public health would shift more markedly towards the local authority. The incoming regime included the instigation of Clinical Commissioning Groups (CCGs) with substantial purchasing power. It would therefore be necessary for the Sport and Physical Activity Development Manager to adopt a new professional language in order to demonstrate to CCGs how additional PA investment would enable them to meet their objectives, thus strengthening the unification of the worlds of sport and recreational PA in a fashion which will be the envy of many other providers.

Clearly, there are many other, equally diverse and successful initiatives in place around the UK. Sport development and healthcare professionals alike need to be aware of this vast body of work. Students intending to gain employment in these developing disciplines should engage with examples of good practice to assist in their efforts to become reflexive practitioners. Other tools to enable them to provide a high-quality service are also in place, including a growing body of academic research work and associated theoretical material. One example of this facilitates an understanding of how individuals are likely to respond to the stimuli provided by sport development promotional material, which, besides assisting practitioners, also enables students and scholars alike to appraise and evaluate existing initiatives.

Focusing on delivery

Few studies now question the predominantly positive links between PA, however it is derived, and health indicators. Attention is now falling to how this might be made a more common behavioural attribute. Emerging understanding of brain functioning is shedding light on why humans do what we do, as much as on why we do not do what is best for us. Importantly, and for the first time, developments in magnetic resonance imaging now allow a view – albeit that it is not yet fully understood what the images are showing – of the brain in action. One of the most important emerging understandings, summarised by the acronym MINDSPACE (Messenger, Incentives, Norms, Defaults, Salience, Priming, Affect, Commitments and Ego) (Cabinet Office/ Institute for Government, 2010), provided by this work is that much of human behaviour is driven by unconscious processes. Notwithstanding that decision making is still important, there are growing concerns to develop sporting environments that remove the need for even more decision making, especially around engagement, where the daily demands of ordinary life are high.

The science of willpower is helpful here (Baumeister and Tierney, 2011). This shows that willpower is a finite resource for any individual. Use this hypothetical sequence of events to consider how willpower may be quickly depleted: (i) get out of bed before 11 a.m., even though you have no job; (ii) resist alcohol and drink soft drinks instead; (iii) resist eating crisps in the bar with friends and (iv) resist watching more TV and go for a walk instead. At the end of such a day, and sequences of such days, is it surprising that there may be little left to complete job applications, iron a shirt and shine shoes in preparation for tomorrow's interview, let alone go out for a run or join in the local basketball pickup game? Indeed, when these other important tasks do not get completed, an individual with depleted willpower is likely to experience 'ego depletion'. Sequences of ego depletion eventually result in reduced motivation for subsequent attempts at behaviour change.

This raises the importance of positive environments which reduce the need for complex decision making that hinges on willpower. The practical value of this understanding is that engagement is best achieved when it is effortless – and as automatic – as possible. This explains, as an example, interest in posters to promote stair use (over escalators).

The literature regarding promotion of PA to healthy, community-dwelling adults has now grown so much that meta-analyses are now possible. One recent analysis (Conn *et al.*, 2011) has identified the delivery factors that are consistently linked with the best programme outcomes:

- project staff make the delivery ('training the trainers' was ineffective);
- promote standardised and specific exercise prescriptions, for example 10,000 steps per day, exercise at 60–80 per cent heart rate maximum for thirty minutes three times per week;
- emphasise behavioural techniques (exercise prescription, goal setting, self monitoring, PA feedback/consequences) throughout the delivery;
- deliver interventions direct to participants (rather than through posters, pamphlets or emails).

The five Rs of intervention

- *Recruitment*: promoting opportunities requires great care and skill to ensure that the right messages reach the right people. Proactive recruitment should be used when targeting sedentary people. A simple example is that of the sport development professional choosing to visit groups or individuals in person to promote programmes.
- *Retention*: in smoking research, and in the experience of sport development professionals working with sedentary people, high drop-out rates are commonly experienced. Shallow engagement can predict the likelihood of dropping

out completely. Consequently, close attention should be afforded to inactive individuals in terms of support and counselling, to identify and tackle risks of relapse.

- *Resistance*: increased 'prodding' by the service provider can lead to increased resistance to the messages encouraging positive behaviour change. Consistent with the findings of Conn and colleagues (2011), participants should be counselled to target small, manageable changes to their lifestyles. For example, a person who has recently taken up swimming may choose to set goals related to the distance swum, or, equally, may focus on basic attendances at the club as a measurable target.

- *Relapse*: clearly, the risk of this is a major issue, predominantly for individuals who are actively engaged. Sport development professionals should endeavour to 'recycle' relapsed participants, to enable subsequent attempts to undertake a sporting activity to 'stick'. Obviously, all delivery factors should be considered for their potential to initiate relapse. Talent development programmes may need to make substantial progress in this regard (Bailey *et al.*, 2009).

- *Recovery*: since behavioural change is 'a process rather than an immediate outcome' (Prochaska and Marcus, 1994: 162), 'recovery' – in sport development terms – involves shifting from a sedentary existence. Individuals who engage quite often but who can make a stronger commitment are more likely to 'recover'. As a consequence, inactive people may benefit from well-placed support and advice to enable them to progress, rather than being thrust into the potentially threatening environment of a sports activity from the outset.

A key principle to adhere to is appropriate 'treatment matching' to ensure that intervention by the sport development professional is in line with the individual's current readiness to change. If time and resources permit, one useful strategy is to help clients to progress by one stage per month. This can present new obstacles to successful progression, as the sport development professional must articulate this relatively complex information in such a way that it has meaning to the client.

Much of the foregoing, in terms of matching interventions to individuals' readiness to change, is already performed by sport development professionals, usually on a 'common sense' basis. Utilising a deeper and systematic understanding of the change process – by considering automatic brain processes as well as individual features of decision-making – can help to provide an enhanced service.

CONCLUSION

The over-riding message of this chapter is that sport has an integral role in improving public health. An understanding of the health benefits of specific sports enables the sport development professional to negotiate partnerships with health

188

care practitioners and to access a vast potential clientele. Sport can provide the impetus for sedentary people, often indisposed to structured exercise, to become active. It also does the very important work of sustaining activity for those who are already active.

Recent governmental policy moves have opened the door for work in this area to progress, although greater explicit political endorsement is desired. Strategic recognition of the health-enhancing properties of sport is a useful bargaining tool within and outside the host organisation. Many highly innovative and successful initiatives already take advantage of the opportunities provided by the link between sport and better health. An appreciation of academic research material, including theories addressing mechanisms of behaviour change, can assist with critical appraisal of initiatives, and can help practitioners to offer more relevant sports opportunities.

LEARNING ACTIVITY

With particular reference to growing mass participation in sport, review the work of a sport development organisation with which you are familiar. Write down at least three ideas for new initiatives which would (a) eliminate the negative elements of sport, (b) embrace the positive aspects of recreational physical activity and (c) ultimately encourage greater numbers of people to become active in sport.

REFERENCES

Bailey, R., Collins, D., Ford, P., MacNamara, Á., Martin, T. and Pearce, G. (2009) *Participant Development in Sport: An Academic Review*, Leeds: Sports Coach UK.

Baumeister, R. and Tierney, J. (2011) *Willpower: Rediscovering Our Greatest Strength*, London: Penguin.

Berkman, S. and Kawachi, I. (eds.) (2000) *Social Epidemiology*, Oxford: Oxford University Press.

Bishop, J. and Hoggett, P. (1986) *Organising around Enthusiasms*, London: Comedia Press.

Bouchard, C. and Shephard, R. (1994) 'Physical activity, exercise and health: the model and key concepts', in Bouchard, C., Shepard, R. and Stephens, T. (eds.), *Physical Activity, Fitness and Health: International Proceedings and Consensus Statement*, Champaign, IL: Human Kinetics.

Bouchard, C., Shepard, R., Stephens, T., Sutton, J. and McPherson, B. (eds.) (1990) *Exercise, Fitness and Health: A Consensus of Current Knowledge*, Champaign, IL: Human Kinetics.

Cabinet Office/Institute for Government (2010) *MINDSPACE: Influencing Behaviour through Public Policy*, London: Cabinet Office/Institute for Government.

Cobley, S., Baker, J., Wattie, N. and McKenna, J. (2009) 'Annual age-grouping and athletic development: a meta-analytic review of relative age effects in sport', *Sports Medicine*, 39: 235–256.

Conn, V., Hafdahl, A. and Mehr, D. (2011) 'Interventions to increase physical activity among healthy adults: meta-analysis of outcomes', *American Journal of Public Health*, 101 (4): 751–758.

Deci, E.L. and Ryan, R.M. (1985) *Intrinsic Motivation and Self-Determination in Human Behavior*, New York: Plenum.

Department for Education (2010) *PE and School Sport Survey 2009–10*, London: Department for Education.

Department of Health (2009) *Let's Get Moving – a New Physical Activity Care Pathway for the NHS: Commissioning Guidance*, London: Department of Health.

Department of Health (2011) *Start Active, Stay Active: A Report on Physical Activity for Health from the Four Home Countries' Chief Medical Officers*, London: Department of Health.

Dickerson, J.B., Smith, M.L., Benden, M.E. and Ory, M.G. (2012) 'The association of physical activity, sedentary behaviors, and body mass index classification in a cross-sectional analysis: are the effects homogenous?', *BMC Public Health*, 11 (926), DOI: 10.1186/1471-2458-11-926

Dunstan, D.W., Salmon, J., Healy, G.N., Shaw, J.E., Jolley, D., Zimmet, P.Z. and Owen, N. (2007) 'Association of television viewing with fasting and 2-hr post-challenge plasma glucose levels in adults without diagnosed diabetes', *Diabetes Care*, 30: 516–522.

Fineberg, H.V. (2012) 'A successful and sustainable health system: how to get there from here', *New England Journal of Medicine*, 366 (11): 1020–1027.

Ford, E., Greenlund, K. and Hong, Y. (2012) 'Ideal cardiovascular health and mortality from all causes and diseases of the circulatory system among adults in the United States', *Circulation*, DOI: 10.1161/CIRCULATIONAHA.111.049122

Gulati, M., Pandey, D.K., Arnsdorf, M.F., Lauderdale, D.S., Thisted, R.A., Wicklund, R.H., Al-Hani, A.J. and Black, H.R. (2003) 'Exercise capacity and the risk of death in women: the St. James Women Take Heart Project', *Circulation*, 108: 1554–1559.

Haywood, L., Kew, F., Spink, J., Capenerhurst, J. and Henry, I. (1995) *Understanding Leisure*, Cheltenham: Stanley Thornes.

Hotchkiss, J.W., Davies, C., Gray, L., Bromley, C., Capewell, S. and Leyland, A.H. (2011) 'Trends in adult cardiovascular disease risk factors and their socio-economic patterning in the Scottish population 1995–2008: cross-sectional surveys', *BMJ Open*, 1 (1): DOI: 10.1136/bmjopen-2011-000176

Jackson, N.W., Howes, F.S., Gupta, S., Doyle, J.L. and Waters, E. (2005) 'Interventions implemented through sporting organisations for increasing participation in sport', *Cochrane Database Systematic Review*, 18 (2): CD004812.

Katzymark, P., Church, T., Craig, C. and Bouchard, C. (2009) 'Sitting time and mortality from all causes, cardiovascular disease and cancer', *Medicine and Science in Sports and Exercise*, 41: 998–1005.

Kruger, J., Ham, S. and Khol, H. (2007) 'Characteristics of a "weekend warrior": results from two national surveys', *Medicine and Science in Sports and Exercise*, 39 (5): 796–800.

Lee, D.C., Sui, X., Artero, E.G., Lee, I.M., Church, T.S., McAuley, P.A., Stanford, F.C., Kohl, H.W. III and Blair, S.N. (2011) 'Long-term effects of changes in cardiorespiratory fitness and body mass index on all-cause and cardiovascular disease mortality in men: the Aerobics Center Longitudinal Study', *Circulation*, 124: 2483–2490.

Liu, K., Daviglus, M.L., Loria, C.M., Colangelo, L.A., Spring, B., Moller, A.C. and Lloyd-Jones, D.M. (2012) 'Healthy lifestyle through young adulthood and presence of low cardiovascular disease risk profile in middle age', *Circulation*, DOI: 10.1161/CIRCULATIONAHA.111.060681

Mark, D.B. and Lauer, M.S. (2003) 'Exercise capacity: the prognostic variable that doesn't get enough respect', *Circulation*, 108: 1534–1536.

Medina, J. (2008) *Brain Rules*, Seattle: Pear Press.

Nelson, M.E., Rejeski, W.J., Blair, S.N., Duncan, P.W., Judge, J.O., King, A.C., Macera, C.A., Castaneda-Sceppa, C. American College of Sports Medicine, American Heart Association (2007) 'Physical activity and public health in older adults', *Circulation*, 116 (9): 1094–1105.

NHS (2012) 'Change4Life', www.nhs.uk/Change4Life/Pages/change-for-life.aspx

North Somerset Council (2012) 'Back to Sport 4 Life', www.n-somerset.gov.uk/Leisure/Go4Life/getting+active/backtosport4life.htm

North, J. (2009) *The Coaching Workforce 2009–2016*, Leeds: National Coaching Foundation.

O'Donovan, G., Blazevich, A.J., Boreham, C., Cooper, A.R., Crank, H., Ekelund, U., Fox, K., Gately, P.J., Giles-Mutrie, B., Reilly, J.J., Saxton, J.M. and Stamatakis, E. (2010) 'The ABC of physical activity for health: a consensus statement from the British Association of Sport and Exercise Sciences', *Journal of Sports Science*, 28 (6): 573–591.

Peterson, P.N., Magid, D.J., Ross, C., Ho, P.M., Rumsfeld, J.S., Lauer, M.S., Lyons, E.E., Smith, S.S. and Masoudi, F.A. (2008) 'Association of exercise capacity on treadmill with future cardiac events in patients referred for exercise testing', *Archives of Internal Medicine*, 168: 174–179.

Poortinga, W. (2007) 'The prevalence and clustering of four major lifestyle risk factors in an English adult population', *Preventive Medicine*, 44 (2): 124–128.

Powell, K.E, Paluch, A.E. and Blair S.N. (2011) 'Physical activity for health: what kind? How much? How intense? On top of what?', *Annual Review of Public Health*, 32: 349–365.

Priest, N., Armstrong, R., Doyle, J. and Waters, E. (2008) 'Policy interventions implemented through sporting organisations for promoting healthy behaviour change', Cochrane Database of Systematic Reviews, Issue 3. Art. No.: CD004809, DOI: 10.1002/14651858.CD004809.pub3

Pringle, A., White, A., Zwolinsky, S., Smith, A., Robertson, S. and McKenna, J. (2011) 'The pre-adoption demographic and health profiles of men participating in a programme of men's health delivered in English Premier League football clubs', *Journal of Public Health*, 125 (7): 411–416.

Prochaska, J. and Marcus, B. (1994) 'The transtheoretical model: applications to exercise', in Dishman, R.K. (ed.), *Advances In Exercise Adherence*, Champaign, IL: Human Kinetics.

Reis, J.P., Loria, C.M., Sorlie, P.D., Park, Y., Hollenbeck, A. and Schatzkin, A. (2011) 'Lifestyle factors and risk for new-onset diabetes: a population-based cohort study', *Annals of Internal Medicine*, 155 (5): 292–299.

Roeben, S. (2001) 'The case against exercise', www.dribbleglass.com/articles/exercise.htm

Sport England (2011) *A Summary of Sport England's Strategy 2011–12 to 2014–15*, London: Sport England.

Sport England (2012) 'Active People survey 5', www.sportengland.org/research/active_people_survey/active_people_survey_51.aspx

St Leger, L. (2004) 'What's the place of schools in promoting health? Are we too optimistic?', *Health Promotion International*, 19 (4): 405–408.

Stampfer, M., Hu, F., Manson, J., Rimm, E. and Willett, W. (2000) 'Primary prevention of coronary heart disease in women through diet and lifestyle', *New England Journal of Medicine*, 343 (1): 16–22.

Vercambre, M.N., Grodstein, F., Manson, J.E., Stampfer, M.J. and Kang, J.H. (2011) 'Physical activity and cognition in women with vascular conditions', *Archives of Internal Medicine*, 171: 1244–1250.

Weed, M., Coren, E., Fiore, J., Wellard, I., Mansfield, L., Chatziefstathiou, D. and Dowse, S. (2012) 'Developing a physical activity legacy from the London 2012 Olympic and Paralympic Games: a policy-led systematic review', *Perspectives in Public Health*, 132: 75–80.

Weiss, J.P., Froelicher, V.F., Myers, J.N. and Heidenreich, P.A. (2004) 'Health-care costs and exercise capacity', *Chest*, 126: 608–613.

Wen, C.P., Wai, J.P.M., Tsai, M.K., Yang, Y.C., Cheng, T.Y.D., Lee, M.-C., Chan, H.T., Tsao, C.K., Tsai, S.P. and Wu, X. (2011) 'Minimum amount of physical activity for reduced mortality and extended life expectancy: a prospective cohort study', *The Lancet*, 378 (9798): 1244–1253.

WHO (2006) 'Gaining health: The European strategy for the prevention and control of non-communicable diseases', EUR/RC56/8, World Health Organisation, Copenhagen.

WHO (2011) *Scaling Up Action against Non-Communicable Diseases: How Much Will It Cost?*, Geneva, WHO.

Wrexham County Borough Council (2012) 'Why swim?', www.wrexham.gov.uk/english/leisure_tourism/sports_development/swimming/swimming.htm

Zwolinsky, S., Pringle, A., Daly-Smith, A., McKenna, J., Robertson, S. and White, A. (2012) 'Associations between daily sitting time and the clustering of lifestyle risk factors in men', *Journal of Men's Health*, doi.org/10.1016/j.jomh.2012.02.003.

Stephen Robson and Jim McKenna

CHAPTER 8

RESOURCES FOR DEVELOPING SPORT

PETER TAYLOR

INTRODUCTION

The resourcing of sport is contained within three major sectors of supply: the public sector, including central government, associated government agencies such as Sports Councils, and local government; the commercial sector, containing profit-seeking organisations; and the third sector, which includes in the UK a large and important voluntary sector, and also other non-profit organisations such as charitable trusts and other social enterprises.

Since the early 1970s there have been enormous changes in the financial landscape in sport. In the commercial sector there has been the impact of media and sponsorship on professional football, cricket, rugby, golf and other mainstream sports. This has taken place on both a national and a transnational scale and sport is usually cited as a key indicator of the processes of globalisation (see Horne, 2006). The emergence of a commercial health and fitness industry, based on private clubs, has witnessed a substantial growth in total turnover, based on increasing awareness of the benefits of active and healthy lifestyles. This has been mirrored by the development of fitness centres in conventional public sector sports centres, which has ensured continued growth in participation. The public sector at the local authority level is now divided, with most facilities still run by in-house management, an increasing number managed by non-profit trusts, and a substantial minority managed by commercial contractors.

This chapter provides an overview of some of the major resourcing issues in relation to the development of sport in recent times. It outlines key concepts to help understand the commercial, public and third sectors of the UK sports economy. It is no easy task to measure and assess the value of sports resources, as they include material resources such as capital and revenue, as well as human resources such as time, expertise and physical effort.

It is important to retain a firm grasp on the differences between the three main sectors involved in sport, as well as the economists' distinction between private, public and merit goods and services. Roberts (2004) argues that each sector possesses different capacities; they are driven by different motivations and, in policy terms, offer different discourses and rationales:

> these sectors are not just the alternative ways of providing much the same range of leisure goods and services. Each sector has its own 'engine', and the provisions that result are distinctively commercial, voluntary or public sector products.
>
> (Roberts, 2004: 8)

ECONOMIC IMPORTANCE OF SPORT

Standard macro-economics can measure the economic contribution of sport and leisure towards the gross domestic product (GDP), that is the total value of goods and services produced in the country. In England, the total value of consumer spending on sport in 2008 was over £21 billion, which was 2.5 per cent of consumer spending in the economy as a whole and more than double the equivalent figure in 1985 (Sport Industry Research Centre, 2009). Furthermore, the growth in consumer sport spending in this period was nearly twice the growth rate for all commodities in the economy. Sport-related employment in England was estimated to be over 421,000 jobs in 2003, or just under 2 per cent of total employment (Sport England, 2007). Three quarters of paid employment in sport in England is in the commercial sector, 12 per cent in the public sector and 11 per cent in the voluntary sector. In addition, it has been estimated that over 5.8 million adult volunteers work in sport, worth 720,000 full-time-equivalent paid workers (Sport England, 2003).

Figure 8.1 shows the main components of sport spending in the UK. Less than 40 per cent of consumer spending is on sports goods (clothing and footwear, equipment, publications and boats), whereas over 60 per cent of spending is on sport services (including sport gambling, sport TV, participant sports, sport-related travel, and health and fitness). Many of these subsectors are dependent on sports participation to sustain their growth, including not only membership subscriptions and admission fees but also sports clothing and footwear, sports equipment and sport-related travel.

Obviously, Figure 8.1 is dominated by consumption of commercial sector goods and services, because these are the ones to be measured in national income accounts. The extent to which participation is subsidised by government is not recorded in this figure, nor is the full extent to which third sector activity benefits sports

194

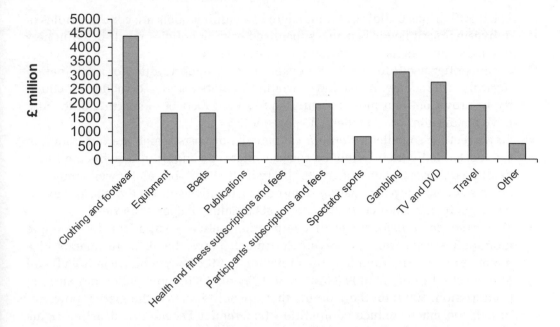

Figure 8.1 Components of consumer spending on sport in England, 2008 (Sport Industry Research Centre, 2009).

participants – with much of the labour in this sector being voluntary and therefore not paid for directly by members of voluntary sports clubs.

THE POLICY BACKGROUND

Governments may intervene in sports markets for a variety of reasons (Gratton and Taylor, 2000), including the following:

- To provide sufficient quantity of *public goods*. These are non-rival and non-excludable (i.e. one person consuming the good does not prevent another person from consuming the good, and no person can be excluded from consuming the good) and difficult to pay for in a normal market mechanism. An example is the pride many Britons felt when so many British elite sportspeople won medals at the London Olympics and Paralympics. In such cases the government intervenes in the market, by subsidy, direct provision or regulation, to guarantee an appropriate supply of public goods.
- To provide sufficient quantity of *merit goods*, which are considered to be of such merit to society that individual consumers are not to be trusted to pay for a sufficient amount, so the individual consumer meets only part of the costs, the remainder being covered by subsidy from central or local state budgets.

Local authorities building and managing swimming pools are good examples of delivering merit goods because subsidised pricing policies result in swimmers paying as little as half of the actual cost of the swim.

■ Public policy needs for *equity*, for example equal opportunities for participation regardless of income. As we have seen in Chapters 3 and 4, demands for equality in provision, and more recently equity with respect to sporting outcomes, have become important tenets of sports policy.

■ To correct for so called *externalities*: benefits or costs which are not traded in the market but which influence social welfare. Examples of benefits are lower health care costs because of greater participation in sport, and lower vandalism because of greater participation in more constructive sport activities; and external costs include higher health care costs because of sports injuries.

■ To correct for *imperfections* in competition between suppliers, for example monopolies legislation to prevent too much power being in the hands of a major supplier. An example is the prevention of the merger between BSkyB and Manchester United in 1999 (Gratton and Taylor, 2000; Monopolies and Mergers Commission, 1999) on the grounds that it would increase the market power of BSkyB too much, reduce competition for Premier League broadcasting rights and have adverse effects on the quality of UK football because of the consequent increase in inequality between clubs.

This wider consideration of the nature of economic resources suggests that one simply cannot ignore the scope of public sector involvement in sport development during a climate of greater economic accountability. New Labour's *Game Plan* (Department for Culture, Media and Sport and Cabinet Office, 2002) in Figure 8.2 suggests an overall public investment in sport in 2000 of £2.2 billion, comprising the following relative shares: central government 2 per cent, local government 87 per cent and National Lottery 11 per cent. Although lottery funding formally lies outside public expenditure, it is conventional to view it informally as a part of government expenditure, since the government decides what good causes lottery grants can be allocated to and directs much of the lottery distribution to its own programmes – see the later section in this chapter on the National Lottery. Another aspect of Figure 8.2 worth noting is that over half of local government expenditure in sport is paid for by the central government.

Variation in the estimation of sport expenditure is confirmed by equivalent figures in the Carter Report (Carter, 2005: 17), which suggests that for England: 'investment by central government = 11%; by local government = 67%; and by the National Lottery = 22%'. Such discrepancies may be accounted for by government funding for school sport sourced through the Exchequer and the New Opportunities Fund. As Carter (2005: 17) points out, it is difficult to compare UK levels of investment with other countries because nation states support sporting endeavours in very different ways.

196

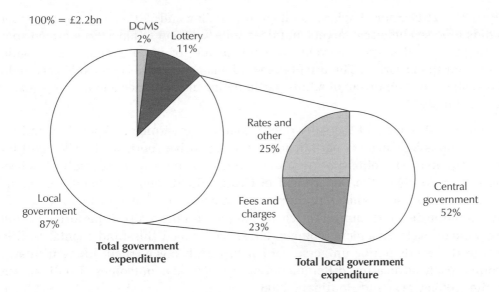

Figure 8.2 Estimated government and lottery expenditure on sport and physical activity, 2000 (Department for Culture, Media and Sport and Cabinet Office, 2002: 32). Total expenditure on sport estimated on the basis of lottery grants, Sports Council allocations, local government expenditure on leisure and recreation, education, sundry policing and grants to local clubs, sundry central government expenditure through departments such as the Ministry of Defence, Royal Parks and the prison service. Source: DCMS, Leisure Industries Research Centre, cited in *Game Plan* (Department for Culture, Media and Sport and Cabinet Office, 2002: 32), reproduced by courtesy of the Department for Culture, Media and Sport and of Sport England.

CENTRAL GOVERNMENT

Changing public sector finances have had a profound impact on those working in sport development. Since local government reorganisation in 1974, there have been periods of plenty and famine. Arguably two of the most significant changes have been the National Lottery (1994) – see later section – and New Labour's *Game Plan* (Department for Culture, Media and Sport and Cabinet Office, 2002). In response to *Game Plan*, Sport England, the main government agency responsible for sport in England, set ambitious participation targets for sport, which it has refined over the subsequent years. In 2008 (Sport England, 2008) it committed to targets of 1 million people doing more sport by 2012/13, a 25 per cent reduction in post-16 drop-off in at least five sports by 2012/13, a quantifiable increase in satisfaction by sports participants, and improved talent development systems in at least twenty-five sports. In respect of the main objective, participation in 2011/12 was 750,000 higher than in 2008/9.

The 2012–2017 Sport England strategy (Sport England, 2012a: no page number) avoids precise numerical targets, but does state 'we want to have transformed sport in England so that sport becomes a habit for life for more people and a regular choice for the majority'. The use of the word 'majority' in this context is very ambitious, since the proportion of adults participating in sport once a month was just 21 per cent in 2012.

Under New Labour and the subsequent Coalition government, Sport England has been responsible for mass participation in competitive sport, whilst UK Sport has been responsible for elite sport funding. Physical activity, more generally, has been the responsibility of the Department of Health (Sport England, 2008). The policy intention is to resolve the contradiction apparent in the drive for increasing mass participation in sport and more recent interest in elite sport at performance and excellence levels. Academic commentaries have noted this fundamental conflict within the sports policy universe, which in turn has generated different interest groups, each advocating different policy agendas and outcomes (Houlihan and White, 2002; Green and Houlihan, 2005).

Whether such policy tensions can be resolved depends ultimately upon sustained commitment from disparate partner organisations such as national governing bodies (NGBs), county sports partnerships (CSPs), local authorities and sports clubs. However, the policy ambitions for sport are undoubtedly threatened by the public expenditure cuts being implemented by the Coalition government. In the current budgets, the Department for Culture, Media and Sport faces a 24 per cent cut in real terms by 2014/15, including a 33 per cent cut for Sport England. The Department for Communities and Local Government faces 33 per cent cuts in real terms by 2014/15, including 28 per cent cuts in local government funding (HM Treasury, 2010). Sport is a discretionary rather than mandatory service provision by local authorities, so it can expect to suffer more than proportionate cuts in its subsidies.

CENTRAL GOVERNMENT RESOURCING OF EXCELLENCE IN SPORT

Central government funding of elite sportspeople has been transformed since the 1980s, when official policy was not to subsidise elite sportspeople. Now, UK Sport, the government agency for elite sport, funds selected sports through its World Class Performance Programme, in a four-year Olympic/Paralympic cycle. In the 2012 cycle, from 2009 to the London Games in 2012, twenty-eight sports were funded with a total of £247.2 million (UK Sport, 2012).

National governing bodies of sport are accountable for this elite funding by their performance in major competitions, particularly the Olympics. The 2013–2016 funding was announced in December 2012 and, although total funding has risen

198

by 12 per cent to £276.4 million, the number of sports funded has fallen to twenty-three. Five sports – basketball, handball, table tennis, volleyball and wrestling – have lost their World Class Performance funding, primarily because they did not perform well in the London 2012 Olympics and show no prospect of performing well in the Rio 2016 Olympics. Such is the harsh reality of contemporary accountability in government funding, which is understandable at a time of general public expenditure cuts.

Five other sports have suffered a decline in elite funding from UK Sport in the Rio cycle, whilst eighteen have had increased funding. Conspicuous among the latter are sports that did particularly well in the London Games, including amateur boxing (a 44 per cent increase), equestrian (34 per cent), gymnastics (35 per cent), rowing (20 per cent) and taekwondo (42 per cent). It is clear that funding for excellence in sport is as much a reward for recent performance as an investment in future performance.

CENTRAL GOVERNMENT RESOURCES FOR MASS PARTICIPATION

Policy issues of social inclusion, community development and equity are considered directly in Chapters 3 and 4 as well as motivation to engage in sport and physical activity (Chapter 7). For those actively involved in realising the ambitions set out by the government and Sport England, the main barrier to increased participation is often perceived to be more fundamental: more investment! This may be imagined in a number of forms, such as improved facilities, subsidised access, transport, improved leadership and coaching and a myriad more ways of investing in infrastructure.

Sport England's programmes are largely designed to promote mass participation. Recently their strategies have identified NGBs as the key agencies with which they will work (Sport England, 2008, 2012a). National governing bodies of forty-six sports are funded by Sport England and they have been required to include national participation programmes and targets in their whole sport plans. Furthermore, in recent years NGBs have been held accountable to these targets and some have suffered financial penalties when their participation targets have not been achieved. Sport England publishes progress reports for all NGBs funded by them, the latest being for 2011/12 (Sport England, 2012b).

The 2009–2012 period of NGB funding by Sport England totalled £438.6 million across forty-six sports. The 2013–2017 funding totals £494.1 million, a rise of 13 per cent. However, mainly because of falling participation numbers, some NGBs have had cuts to their Sport England funding for the new period – noticeably cricket, rugby union, rugby league, tennis and judo. Other sports have had significant increases in their NGB funding, for example archery, bowls, wheelchair basketball and wheelchair rugby. Furthermore, Sport England have taken £40 million of the total funding as a 'Reward and Incentive' fund for particularly successful NGBs in the new period.

In addition to NGB funding, Sport England has several other major funding programmes for mass participation, particularly 'Places People Play', a £150 million programme over three years. This programme includes 'Iconic Facilities', 'Inspired Facilities' and 'Protecting Playing Fields', three schemes for improving facilities; 'Club Leaders', a scheme to improve business skills in community sports clubs; 'Sport Makers', a programme to recruit, train and deploy 40,000 volunteers in sport; and 'Sportivate', a programme to attract teenagers and young adults to sport (Sport England, 2012c). Other Sport England funding programmes include a 'Small Grants Programme' for non-profit organisations, 'Sportsmatch' to match sponsorship funding, 'Inclusive Sport' for disabled participation, 'Active Colleges', and a 'Community Sport Activation Fund' for very local initiatives (Sport England, 2012d). All of this funding, however, will be directed from National Lottery monies, thus demonstrating that in practice the dividing lines between public expenditure and National Lottery funding are vague.

Sport England's call for what realistically is a sea change in participation rates up to 2020 may intensify current academic debates between sociologists, who emphasise controlling structures and society, and psychologists, such as Chelladurai (1985), who focus on individual agency, motivations and intentions. However, the renewed welfarist drive to attain genuine Sport for All may well flounder in an era of austerity and public expenditure cuts.

In terms of sport development during the past two or three decades, an increasing emphasis on individual choice and motivations has been accompanied by increasing efforts to persuade all groups in society to participate in sport. This tension between providing opportunities for all, whilst recognising that not all individuals will want to become involved, has been clearly articulated by academics such as Coalter (1998). Interestingly, although it has often been suggested that financial cost is the major barrier to greater participation, especially from the low participant groups, other research by Coalter for the Sports Council, over twenty years ago (Coalter, 1991), suggested that this is not always the case. Coalter and Allison (1996) threw a sharper focus on lifestyle and individual choice in terms of identifying reasons for low or non-participation.

The sometimes evangelical zeal of those agencies and organisations committed to sport must be understood in the context of an increasingly open and flexible culture, where individuals may exercise their choice to be indifferent or reject sport. Sports policy discourse is reminiscent of Victorian ideals of muscular Christianity, character building and moral development through sport (McIntosh, 1987). However, not everyone is convinced of the potency of government exhortations to play sport, volunteer, adopt healthy lifestyles and become good citizens.

200

The extent of the task of achieving step changes in the participation of the nation are highlighted by Sport England's 'Active People Survey'. Only 14 per cent of the adult population were found to take part once a week in sport and active recreation in 2006. Trend figures for once-a-week participation from the Active People Survey are shown in Figure 8.3. They demonstrate a flat period with no growth from 2008 to 2011, but a recent significant rise in 2011–2012, possibly attributable to the policy emphasis on sport, the inspiration of the London Olympics and Paralympics, and a generally increasing concern for health and body image.

LOCAL AUTHORITIES' RESOURCING OF SPORT

A key period of change in public sector sport centred on local government reorganisation in 1974. In the run up to 1 April 1974 many small authorities saw the opportunities for sports facility building on a comparatively grand scale, which was fuelled by a number of influences. First, councils that were about to be absorbed into much larger bodies grasped the opportunity to make political capital by spending on modern leisure facilities that had come into vogue. There was clearly a huge latent demand in local communities to be satisfied. This pragmatism coincided with a period of relative prosperity in local government which meant that budgetary provision on leisure as welfare was feasible. The Sports Council supported capital investment with modest 'pump priming' for projects. Consequently, there was a massive capital resource input concentrated in a comparatively short period of time.

The corollary of such expenditure on facilities was a concomitant increase in revenue budgets to run these new sport and leisure centres. Providing more comprehensive public sport and leisure services meant that the majority of ongoing

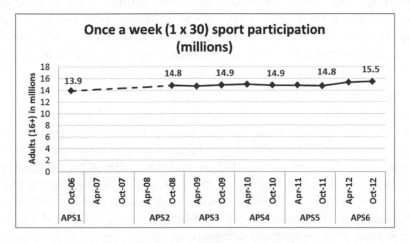

Figure 8.3 Sport participation in England (Sport England, 2012c).

expenditure was allocated to staffing. Sport and leisure are often described as 'a people business' and this emerging industry was generating job opportunities at all levels: from cleaners and catering staff to centre managers and directors of burgeoning new leisure services departments in town halls across the country.

The emphasis during the 1970s and early 1980s was spending on facilities. Policy drivers took the view that if good facilities were provided then local communities would take full advantage of them and so develop individual and collective sporting aspirations. The focus on local community facilities resulted in compromises in funding and provision of specialist facilities for elite athletes. For example, whereas many large urban conurbations had ambitions for major swimming and athletics facilities, local authority budgets were concentrated on the lower levels of the continuum. 'Sport for All' was the dominant policy discourse and the focus was clearly on mass participation.

As noted by Hylton and Totten in Chapter 4, this strategy of bringing *people to sport* proved to have serious limitations. Subsequent attempts to change direction during the mid-1980s by bringing *sport to people* were the epiphany of good practice in sport development as many understand it today. In UK local authorities this was the first time that budgets were dedicated to direct community sport interventions. This meant that leisure departments began to expand their remit beyond operational functions of facility management into realms of both generic and sport-specific development.

Resources for this expansion in outreach work came partly from within local authority budgets but also from central government funding through the Sports Council. This was substantially initiated by the promotion of Action Sport in response to urban unrest in the early part of the 1980s but there was also a clear determination on the part of many authorities to establish strong leadership in sport development. At its inception there was still a climate of relative affluence and making budgetary provision was not too onerous. However, the growth of both facility building and what was in effect an exercise in sports marketing, delivered by a growing band of teams and detached officers, began to falter as the pressure exerted by central government started to take its toll on local government finances.

In the early 1990s the introduction of compulsory competitive tendering (CCT), including the management of sports facilities, confirmed a new and tighter economic reality. The potential for savings in expenditure and growth in income encouraged 'managerialist' practices that focused on an improvement to the financial 'bottom line'. This was stimulated by real competition for the first time; less than two decades after the introduction of CCT, the Audit Commission (2006) estimated that 47 per cent of public sport and leisure facilities were managed by in-house local authority teams, 15 per cent by non-profit trusts and 10 per cent by commercial contract management companies.

202

Faced with real political and economic pressures, advances gained in less turbulent times in both facility and outreach sport development often froze or went into retreat from the early 1990s. The opportunities for access to sport were also constrained by other elements of government policy: the local management of schools and the National Curriculum, which were outlined in the Education Reform Act (1988); planning policy in relation to selling school playing fields; and the consequences of the teachers' industrial disputes of the late 1980s.

After a more generous economic climate in the first years of the twenty-first century, the financial crisis of 2008/9 heralded the current age of austerity. Public expenditure cuts are having severe consequences for all aspects of local authority sport provision, with closures of facilities increasingly common. Not all commentators, however, see this as an unqualified disaster for sport, because many of the facilities selected for closure are old, inefficient and under-utilised.

COMMERCIAL RESOURCES FOR SPORT

Irvine and Taylor (2001: 19) suggested that commercial leisure has become big business, and in 1998 it contributed 17.5 per cent of the UK economy. They defined commercial sports and leisure organisations as those concerned with generating profit. So commercial sport included all those resources for participation, equipment, clothing and footwear, and also involved spectating. Irvine and Taylor excluded costs of travel to sports venues, sports tourism and sports media, which they located in other areas of leisure. Even with a focus on just one sector of the sports industry, conceptual and ensuing problems of measurement abound.

Perfectly competitive markets, the ideal of nineteenth-century liberal economics, rarely exist; instead more restrictive market forms are the norm, where a few firms dominate production (oligopoly). Market structures such as oligopoly provide the business context for the operating policies of global companies such as Nike, Adidas and Reebok. However, they too are interested not only in global marketing, which includes sponsoring sports teams, sports celebrities, mega-sports events and sports stadia, but also in local initiatives such as talent development, training/coaching programmes and community-based junior sports initiatives.

Sponsorship

In sponsorship, as opposed to patronage, the sponsor seeks a commercial return from investing sponsorship money or in-kind help in an activity such as sport. The scale of sport sponsorship expenditure is difficult to measure, but IEG (2009) reports worldwide sponsorship expenditure as just over $41 billion in 2008, whereas Mintel (2006) reckons sponsorship expenditure in the UK to be £800 million in 2005. Sport typically takes most sponsorship expenditure – more than two thirds of the total in the USA according to IEG (2009) and 51 per cent in the UK according to Mintel (2006). Sponsorship is increasing in importance, partly because advertising is increasingly fragmented as the print, broadcast and internet media multiply. Sponsorship of a major event or sport ensures consistent and often conspicuous exposure across different media. Another factor, particularly in sport, is increased television coverage of major events.

Because of the benefits to both parties, sponsorship is typically seen as a commercial transaction. On the one side, it benefits sport and leisure organisations through revenue, services or resources from the sponsor, without which many events' financial viability would be threatened. Sponsorship can help to stimulate media coverage, and consequently increase attendance numbers. It can also help to attract major 'players' in sport and it can assist in bidding for events or other projects.

On the other side of the transaction, sponsorship benefits the sponsoring company in a number of ways and therefore complements other marketing and public relations activities. It increases publicity and hopefully benefits the company's image. It helps to improve the sponsor's relations with customers, employees and its supply chain (e.g. through corporate hospitality). It increases awareness of the sponsor's brands. And it may help to increase sales, market share and competitive advantage. However, all these benefits are difficult to measure in relation to specific sponsorship activity.

There are also costs to both parties. In particular the sponsor pays other 'leverage' marketing expenditure to realise the full marketing value of the sponsorship, and it bears the risks that star players either fail in their sport or fall from grace for other reasons. The sponsored organisations often devote considerable resources to servicing the sponsors' needs, such as ensuring that corporate hospitality arrangements are suitable, and that star players or performers are available for corporate occasions and publicity.

Commercial fitness

It would not be an exaggeration to say that the most important sector for maintaining sport and exercise participation in the UK in recent years has been the fitness industry, a large part of which is commercial. The Leisure Database Company estimates that, at a time of relatively static participation overall, the fitness industry has grown for the last ten years and is now worth £3.86 billion (69 per cent of which is in the commercial sector), serving a registered membership of 7.6 million people in 5,900 fitness facilities (Leisure Database Company, 2012).

The growth and quality of commercial fitness facilities have forced public sector sport and leisure facilities to compete, and it would not be unreasonable to say that this has improved the quantity and quality of fitness provision in the public sector. In fact the fiercest competition for members is now between the public sector and a new breed of low-cost commercial operators; both have demonstrated membership growth in the latest evidence (Leisure Database Company, 2012).

It is important to acknowledge the relevance of the fitness industry not only to tackling the health problems associated with obesity and the lack of physical activity, but also to the personal preferences of many participants for non-competitive activities as against traditional sports. More people in England now belong to fitness clubs than to voluntary sports clubs and, whilst many of the latter struggle to maintain members, the former continue to grow.

THIRD SECTOR RESOURCES FOR SPORT

The third sector in sport comprises not only voluntary clubs and their governing bodies, but also a relatively new breed of trusts formed to operate public leisure facilities. Trusts are non-profit social enterprises which consist largely of paid employees but which typically have a voluntary board of directors representing their communities and the local authorities they service.

Trusts and social enterprises

It was the introduction of CCT in the late 1980s which gave the stimulus for the development of non-profit trusts to bid for the management of local authority facilities. Many were started by former local authority sport managers, but over the ensuing decades some have grown to be large-scale operators, such as GLL, which manages 115 sports facilities for thirty different organisations.

The Audit Commission (2006) estimated that 519 sport and leisure facilities were managed by trusts – approximately 10 per cent of the total. Sporta, the umbrella organisation for leisure trusts, estimates that 30 per cent of public leisure centres are now operated by trusts (Sporta, 2012). Many trusts have charitable status and Taylor (2011) lists a number of advantages and disadvantages to this status. One of the most important advantages for local authorities is financial: charities can achieve considerable tax relief. Another major advantage is the management autonomy that trusts have, not being saddled with many of the bureaucratic procedures of local authorities.

Disadvantages of charitable trusts include the difficulty of access to capital resources; many sport and leisure trusts are dependent on local authority clients for capital funds. However, whatever the advantages and disadvantages, many local authorities have and are considering 'trustification' of their sport and leisure facilities' management.

Volunteers and voluntary clubs

The UK has a network of 110,000 community amateur sports clubs run by 1.5 million volunteers (CCPR, 2002: 3). Nichols (2001) draws a distinction between 'economic' approaches to measuring the voluntary sector in sport and the 'socio-cultural' approach adopted by Bishop and Hoggett (1986). The economic approach seeks to place a value on volunteering in sport. Sport England (2003) estimated there to be 5.8 million adult sports volunteers in England in 2002, contributing a total of 1.2 billion hours of volunteering. This is equivalent to 720,000 additional full-time paid workers in sport.

In their ground-breaking analysis of mutual aid in sport and leisure, Bishop and Hoggett (1986) acknowledge that the voluntary sector in leisure, the bulk of which is multi-functional sports clubs, is the unique home of enthusiasts who are prepared to volunteer time, energy and money towards their chosen leisure and sporting interests. The voluntary sector secures outcomes that commercial and public sectors fail to produce because it creates goods and services that are not economically profitable for the commercial sector and for which there is a lack of political consensus to provide through public expenditure. However, the voluntary sector is more than a residual; a central argument of Bishop and Hoggett's (1986) research designates the voluntary sector as the cradle of democratic processes in local communities and the lifeblood of active citizenship.

For Bishop and Hoggett and more recently Putnam (2000), joining a sports club is not simply a rational choice by the individual as a consumer; rather it involves membership and a sense of belonging to a key institution in a local community, and also opens up a 'community of interest' which may well extend beyond the local neighbourhood, thereby building up social capital. One only has to contact the Internet and sample, using search engines, the cornucopia of sporting websites. Each boasts its own pages and archives as well as links to related sites, other forums, chat rooms and personal blogs.

Whilst local politicians invested huge sums of money in building and staffing flagship sport and leisure centres in their areas, the volunteer workforce continued to supply the coaches, administrators, treasurers and club secretaries, without which most formal competitive sport provision would have disappeared. Increasingly, local authorities began to seek closer ties and develop partnerships with the voluntary sector, most notably clubs and community groups. Sport development workers with the remit to take sport to people through outreach working, and those required

206

to help young performers to fulfil their sporting potential, both worked ever more closely with the voluntary sector to achieve these aims.

Shibli and colleagues (1999) identified changes in sports volunteering, one of which was a move towards more payment for services. Initiatives such as Champion Coaching at a national level and a number of similarly organised local schemes helped to raise expectations amongst some volunteers in terms of more tangible recognition of their role, through pay. In common with other areas of voluntary work, distinctions between the volunteer and hourly-paid casual worker have become increasingly blurred. Many volunteers, especially those involved in coaching and coach education, have become accustomed to receiving payment for their services, although often the rates offered amount to little more than expenses and are used to convey token recognition for the work provided. National governing bodies, local authorities, Sport England and Sportscoach UK have continued to press for a greater recognition of the work of the voluntary sector and have recommended that coaching in particular should be rewarded financially where possible.

During the 1990s, pressures on capital expenditure, a declining revenue base and increasing expectations made an enabling role rather than a providing role a necessity for local authorities. Local authorities' sports providers were forced to reassess the vital role played by the voluntary sector and to involve them more in planning and work across the sport development continuum. The contemporary policy equivalent for the Coalition government is 'Big Society', which has a well-established base in sport. Local authorities have had to embed the role of the voluntary sector into a local and regional strategy for the comprehensive delivery of sporting opportunities. The need to consider all aspects and sectors is now politically essential rather than just desirable.

One major problem, according to Shibli and colleagues (1999), is that, with more expected of the voluntary sector in sport, any substantial decline in numbers could be very harmful. Unfortunately, there are signs that this may be happening as our leisure time declines and numbers in paid work continue to rise. Increasingly, it is not a matter of whether people possess skills and motivations to become involved in local clubs or in sport development initiatives but whether they have the time. The demographic increase in people aged over 50 appears to be a welcome development because traditionally this group has been heavily involved as sport volunteers, particularly as club administrators. However, older people too are attracted by a myriad of competing interests and leisure pursuits.

MAJOR EVENTS

Research by Gratton, Dobson and Shibli (2000, 2001) has confirmed that major international events tend to be of a 'one-off' nature, whereas annual national spectator events such as the FA Cup final, test match cricket and the Open golf championship generate the largest economic benefits for host locations. Such financial attractions and high-profile media coverage obscure the investment needed for large events. Nevertheless, the support for the successful bid to bring the Olympic Games to London in 2012 is demonstrable proof of government belief in the economic benefits of hosting the largest sports event in the world.

OLYMPIC AND PARALYMPIC GAMES

Hosting the Olympic and Paralympic Games is very resource intensive, but much popular commentary about the resources involved is misleading. The most important error is to conflate the sporting costs – building new sports facilities, hosting the Games – with the costs of generic infrastructure improvements such as transport, housing and other key aspects of urban redevelopment, and then claiming the total is 'the cost of the Games'. Clearly this is wrong and Preuss (2004) demonstrates emphatically that most of the costs of most Olympic and Paralympic Games are generic infrastructure improvements which have benefits far beyond sport and far beyond the period of the Games. Most of the sports capital expenditure is not just for the month or two of the Games; the assets will keep returning financial and social benefits for their lifetime.

Hosting the Olympic and Paralympic Games does not make a financial loss. Local organising committees for the Olympic Games (LOCOGs) typically make surpluses from the Games, which are divided between the host country, the National Organising Committee and the International Olympic Committee. The major revenues for LOCOGs are usally broadcasting rights, ticket sales and sponsorship. However, LOCOG revenues are not the major benefits of the Games; for these we need to consider social impacts such as the togetherness and goodwill stimulated by the Games; the environmental improvements to large areas of derelict and spoilt landscape; urban regeneration on a large scale; and the changed image of the host locations. To these in London's case we can add, at least hypothetically, the sporting legacy of increased participation inspired by the Games. This has yet to be proven, despite a promising uplift in participation figures for 2012.

Another major resource in the Olympic and Paralympic Games is the volunteers, in London's case the 70,000 Games Makers who made such a positive impression on all concerned. However, without wishing to take anything away from their achievement, concern can be expressed about the possible waste of potential of these 70,000 temporary volunteers. Some 120,000 people expressed an interest in volunteering at the London 2012 Games, and 240,000 applied. It is not clear what happened to the 170,000-plus who did not get a position; were they redirected into sports or other volunteering? And what has happened to the Games Makers: were

208

they left with only the memory of a great event or were any efforts made to capture them in more continual volunteering, in sport or elsewhere? Only six months after the Games did a web link appear from 'Games Makers' to 'Sport Makers', the programme to engage more volunteers in community sport. The problem with Games volunteers, good as they are, is that theirs is a one-off contribution to sport, but sport needs more regular volunteering.

THE NATIONAL LOTTERY

Since 1994, the National Lottery has transformed the resourcing of sport in the UK. The emergence of sport as one of the National Lottery's five good causes held the potential for a real change in the outlook for sport. Much of the future of the nation's plans for sport became inextricably linked to the emergent gambling habits of the population. As we have seen, the link between government policy and National Lottery funding is still very much evident, as many Sport England and UK Sport funding programmes are dependent on lottery funding.

Over £29 billion of National Lottery money has been given to good causes since it began in 1994. Out of the money raised, the distribution is as follows: 50 per cent to the winners as prizes; 28 per cent to good causes – a fifth of this goes to sport; 12 per cent to the government in lottery duty; 5 per cent to the ticket retailers; and 5 per cent to the operating company, Camelot (Department for Culture, Media and Sport, 2012). Sport, therefore, has benefited from the lottery by approximately £1.6 billion in the last eighteen years.

The original rules for the distribution of proceeds from lottery sales caused several important problems:

- None of the money designated for the Sports Lottery Fund was to be used for revenue purposes; the intention was to provide funding for a new wave of modern facilities and to refurbish older ones.
- Partnership funding of a minimum of 35 per cent of the cost of the project was to be provided by the organisation applying.
- The Sports Council, as distributing body, was not allowed to solicit bids and was expected to remain neutral in the allocation process.
- Funds provided by the lottery were intended to be new, additional resources, with no reductions in existing budgets.
- Grants could not be made to commercial enterprises.

To date, only the last of these rules has survived over the duration of the lottery and a much more pragmatic framework now exists. Many organisations struggled to reach the minimum 35 per cent level of capital funding. In addition, even if they could overcome such obstacles there was still the need for the project to provide a realistic business plan that could robustly predict a sustainable income and expenditure stream. There were issues around certain sectors of the community, typically disadvantaged, that were disenfranchised from the whole process.

Arguably the most significant and controversial change in the distribution of lottery funding to good causes is that there is clear directed distribution by government agencies, including all the home countries' sports councils. Most of the central government funding identified earlier – for mass participation, for excellence and also for the Olympics and Paralympics – is directed lottery funding. This calls into question the extent to which lottery funding is additional to, or a substitute for, central government spending on sport.

THE PROFESSIONALISATION OF SPORT DEVELOPMENT

During the past three decades there have been periods of substantial growth in full-time paid employment within sport development. Those working in the public sector have diverse roles to play in developing sporting opportunities. Growth in the commercial and voluntary sectors has been more difficult to chart. For example, increases in health, fitness and sport provision in the tourism and hospitality industry illustrate how difficult it is to quantify this dimension of the sport development industry. What is clear is that the human resource involved in all of these forms of sport development is a key factor in improving sport participation.

Within local authority settings, staff have experienced important changes with a strong emphasis on accountability, planning and cost-effectiveness. Different elements of everyday operation, dictated by the culture of efficiency, have contributed to a continual squeeze on both capital and revenue budgets. Effective sport development workers have had to develop skills and competencies to work in partnership with a range of others, both inside and outside sport. This has led to growing concern with training, education and qualifications. National governing bodies of sport, local authorities, public non-government agencies and higher education institutions all currently offer a plethora of courses and training opportunities, ranging from one-day seminars to postgraduate qualifications.

The drive towards professional status in sport development promises to raise standards of operation and improve service delivery, particularly in the public and third sectors. The emergence of the National Association of Sport Development (NASD) and its subsequent incorporation into the Chartered Institute for the Management of Sport and Physical Activity show the continued movement towards professional status, although it remains to be seen if the separate and distinct needs of the sport development professions will be developed within broader-based professional sport institutions.

210

SUMMARY

All three main sectors have a role and purpose in resourcing sport development in the UK. The commercial sector is both large and an important source of participation growth. The third sector is diversifying, particularly through the growth of charitable trusts, and still provides the core of organisation for competitive sport. The National Lottery is a major factor in supporting sport in the public and third sectors.

However, national public expenditure controls have determined that local government, as one of the key providers, is working in a stringent budgetary environment that requires a continual search for innovative ways of delivering existing and new services. Although the focus of resource management may be on finance, the importance of human resources in the sector is still very clear. Sport is still very much a people industry.

LEARNING ACTIVITIES

1 Name the three key sectors in sport and describe the main factors that make them different from each other.
2 How might sport's permissive status impact its development in austere times?
3 What reasons might governments have for funding sport development?

REFERENCES

Audit Commission (2006) *Public Sports and Recreation Services*, London: Audit Commission.
Bishop, J. and Hoggett, P. (1986) *Organizing around Enthusiasms: Mutual Aid in Leisure*, London: Comedia.
CCPR (2002) *Everybody Wins: Sport and Social Inclusion*, London: CCPR.
Carter, P. (2005) *Review of National Sport Effort and Resources*, London: DCMS.
Chelladurai, P. (1985) *Sports Management: Macro Perspectives*, Victoria: Sports Dynamics.
Coalter, F. (1991) 'Sports participation: price or priorities?', *Leisure Studies*, 12: 171–182.
Coalter, F. (1998) 'Leisure studies, leisure policy and social citizenship: the failure of welfare or the limits of welfare?', *Leisure Studies*, 17 (1): 21–36.
Coalter, F. and Allison, M. (1996) *Sport and Community Development*, Edinburgh: Scottish Sports Council.
Department for Culture, Media and Sport (2012) 'Distribution', www.culture.gov.uk/what_we_do/national_lottery/3393.aspx
Department for Culture, Media and Sport and Cabinet Office (2002) *Game Plan*, London: DCMS.
Gratton, C., Dobson, N. and Shibli, S. (2000) 'The economic importance of major sports events: a case study of six events', *Managing Leisure*, 5 (1): 17–28.
Gratton, C., Dobson, N. and Shibli, S. (2001) 'The role of major sports events in the economic regeneration of cities: lessons from six world or European championships', in Gratton, C. and

Henry, I.P. (eds.), *Sport in the City: The Role of Sport in Economic and Social Regeneration*, London: Routledge.

Gratton, C. and Taylor, P. (2000) *Economics of Sport and Recreation*, London: Spon Press.

Green, M. and Houlihan, B. (2005) *Elite Sport Development: Policy Learning and Political Priorities*, London: Routledge.

HM Treasury (2010) *Spending Review 2010*, Cm 7942, London: The Stationery Office.

Horne, J. (2006) *Sport in Consumer Culture*, Basingstoke: Palgrave Macmillan.

Houlihan, B. and White, A. (2002) *The Politics of Sport Development: Development of Sport or Development through Sport*, London: Routledge.

IEG (2009) 'Sponsorship spending', www.sponsorship.com/Resources/Sponsorship-Spending. aspx

Irvine, D. and Taylor, P. (2001) 'Commercial leisure: an international perspective', in Wolsey, C. and Abrams, J. (eds.), *Understanding the Leisure and Sport Industry*, Harlow: Pearson Education.

Leisure Database Company (2012) 'Fitness industry back in growth', www.theleisuredatabase. com/news/news-archive/fitness-industry-back-in-growth

McIntosh, P. (1987) *Sport in Society*, London: West London Press.

Mintel (2006) *Sponsorship, Special Report*, London: Mintel International Group.

Monopolies and Mergers Commission (1999) *British Sky Broadcasting plc and Manchester United plc: A Report on the Proposed Merger*, London: The Stationery Office.

Nichols, G. (2001) 'The UK voluntary sector: understanding the leisure and sport industry', in Wolsey, C. and Abrams, J. (eds.), *Understanding the Leisure and Sport Industry*, Harlow: Pearson Education.

Preuss, H. (2004) *The Economics of Staging the Olympics: A Comparison of the Games 1972–2008*, Cheltenham: Edward Elgar.

Putnam, R. (2000) *Bowling Alone: The Collapse and Revival of American Community*, New York: Simon & Schuster.

Roberts, K. (2004) *The Leisure Industries*, London: Palgrave Macmillan.

Shibli, S., Taylor, P., Nicholls, G., Gratton, C. and Kokolakakis, T. (1999) 'The characteristics of volunteers in UK sports clubs', *European Journal of Sports Management*, 6: 10–27.

Sport England (2003) 'Volunteering in England in 2002', www.sportengland.org/research/ research_archive.aspx

Sport England (2007) 'Economic importance of sport, England, 2003', www.sportengland.org/ research/economic_importance_of_sport.aspx

Sport England (2008) *Sport England Strategy 2008–2011*, London: Sport England.

Sport England (2012a) *A Sporting Habit for Life: 2012–2017*, London: Sport England.

Sport England (2012b) '30-month performance review for Sport England funded national governing bodies', www.sportengland.org/funding/ngb_investment/ngb_progress_ reports_2011–12.aspx

Sport England (2012c) 'Places people play: delivering a mass participation legacy from the 2012 Olympic and Paralympic Games', www.sportengland.org/research/active_people_survey/ active_people_survey_6.aspx

Sport England (2012d) 'Get funding', www.sportengland.org/funding/get_funding.aspx

Sport England (2012e) 'Sport participation factsheet: summary of results for England', www. sportengland.org/research/active_people_survey/active_people_survey_6.aspx

Sport Industry Research Centre (2009) *Sport Market Forecasts 2009–2013*, Sheffield: SIRC/ Sport England.

Sporta (2012) 'Community fitness, community sport, community culture', www.sporta.org/

Taylor, P. (2011) *Torkildsen's Sport and Leisure Management*, London: Taylor & Francis.

UK Sport (2012) 'Investment principles', www.uksport.gov.uk/pages/investment-principles/

CHAPTER 9

VOLUNTARY SPORTS CLUBS AND SPORT DEVELOPMENT

GEOFF NICHOLS

To understand the potential contribution to sport development of sports clubs run by volunteers, this chapter describes the characteristics of these clubs, the amount of sports participation they support, the challenges they face and the nature of 'management' in the clubs. The relationship to sport development work is then considered. The chapter thus provides sports development officers (SDOs) and students with an insight into clubs and how to work with them. It provides clubs with an insight into how to work with SDOs. It concludes with some broader considerations about the role and support of sports clubs led by volunteers.

The network of a large number of small sports clubs run by volunteers is a critical part of the sporting infrastructure in the UK. Volunteers support a similar structure in the Nordic countries, Denmark, Germany, Australia, New Zealand and Canada. They provide the opportunity for a large proportion of sports participation and the expression of active citizenship through volunteering. This type of civic activism epitomises, but far predates, the UK coalition government's aspirations for a Big Society.

Voluntary sector sports clubs, within their national governing body (NGB) structure, have developed in the UK since the second half of the nineteenth century. They have a long tradition of independence; however, they have developed in parallel with commercial sport and sports opportunities provided by local and central government, and continue to do so. Thus, although the structure of voluntary sector sport in the UK may appear very resilient, it has to adapt to change and the challenges this brings. These challenges include attracting, managing and retaining volunteers; attracting and retaining members; reacting to pressures to 'professionalise' in terms of emulating the management practices of the other sectors; reacting to the policy priorities of local and national government; and reacting to changes in legislation. These challenges are not unique to the UK.

Sport development professionals have to understand the nature of these clubs, what they are, what drives their volunteers, how they are 'managed' and the help they want. The independence of clubs means that working with them to deliver public policy objectives will require compromise with the club's own objectives and culture. Although the independence of clubs needs to be respected and understood, clubs may need to be helped to adapt to, or even survive in, changed circumstances.

WHAT IS A CLUB?

In a survey of Scottish clubs, Allison (2001) noted that a 'club' may be a single competitive team, a session in a sports centre led by a coach, a group of friends that maintain a regular booking in a facility or a single club with separate sections (a multi-sports club may have sections for each sport, or one large single sports club might have several clubs for different age groups). These difficulties of definition contribute to different estimates of the number of clubs between surveys (Nichols et al., 2004). For example, if a survey is conducted through NGBs of sport it will include only clubs affiliated to those NGBs. It will exclude clubs that do not affiliate because they do not want to compete in a league structure or see little benefit in affiliation. For example, a group who meet weekly to play badminton in a village hall may see no need to affiliate to Badminton England, or a university climbing club may not affiliate to the British Mountaineering Council. Even relying on NGB records is complicated by differences in club definitions over time, and the various national boundaries used to collate information. NGBs may cover any of England, Scotland, Wales and Northern Ireland, or a combination; and this may also change.

One also has to define a club run by volunteers. A membership association has been defined as 'a formally organized group, most of whose members – whether persons or organisations – are not financially recompensed for their participation' (Knoke, 1986: 2, in Tschirhart, 2006: 523). However, non-recompensed participation extends to volunteering to maintain the organisation. Some surveys of clubs, such as the Scottish Opinion Survey used in Reid's (2012) analysis of participation in clubs, have not made the distinction between clubs led by volunteers and clubs run commercially by paid staff. Others, such as the Sport and Recreation Alliance's surveys of clubs in 2009 (Taylor et al., 2009) and 2011 (Sport and Recreation Alliance, 2011a) included some clubs which were run for profit and so were probably not run by volunteers.

HOW MANY CLUBS ARE THERE AND IS THIS CHANGING?

As noted above, estimating the number of clubs depends on how a club is defined and measured. Table 9.1 shows the results of four surveys. The figures for UK

214

Table 9.1 Volunteer-led sports clubs in the UK

Survey sponsor	Voluntary sports clubs in the UK	Date	Area
Sports Council[a]	123,136	1995/1996	UK
Sport Scotland[b]	151,000	1999	Scotland
Sport England[c]	127,419	2002	England
SARA (formerly CCPR)[d]	101,426	2009	England

Sources: a, Sports Council (1996); b, Allison (2001); c, Taylor *et al.* (2003); d, information collected from NGBs to inform weighting of 2009 SARA club survey results.

Notes
SARA, Sport and Recreation Alliance.
a, b and c are discussed by Nichols *et al.* (2004).

sports clubs have in all cases but one been extrapolated from national surveys. An assumption is made that the ratio of clubs to population is similar across England, Scotland and the UK.

Surveys in 2002 and 2009 (Taylor *et al.*, 2003, 2009) both used telephone interviews of NGBs to estimate the number of clubs. These appear to show a reduction in the number of clubs of about 20% over this period. A reduction might reflect a trend towards more individualised sports participation, out of the club structure. This trend was identified between 1987 and 1996 (Coalter, 1999) and continued between 2005 and 2010. In this second period the biggest growth sports were athletics (including road running and jogging), gym and cycling, while golf, badminton, tennis, cricket, rugby union and rugby league all experienced a decline (Gratton *et al.*, 2011). A reduction in the number of clubs may also be caused by clubs merging. However, a close examination of the figures used in the 2002 and 2009 surveys shows ambiguities over NGBs' definitions of a club; the changing name or area of representation of NGBs (e.g. men's and women's NGBs merging), and the inconsistency of NGBs reporting by home nation, Great Britain or the UK. This leaves few sports in which one can confidently report a change between 2002 and 2009 using estimates collected from the NGBs. It seems probable that there has been a slight decline in numbers overall.

CLUB CHARACTERISTICS

The average club is very small, is run almost entirely by volunteers and has very limited resources, although this varies considerably between sports. These characteristics of clubs have implications for their capacity to contribute to sport development objectives.

Club surveys

The most recent information on sports clubs in the UK has been provided by surveys conducted for the Sport and Recreation Alliance in 2009 (Taylor *et al.*, 2009) and 2011 (Sport and Recreation Alliance, 2011a). Both surveys were completed online, promoted by governing bodies of sport and some county sport partnerships. In 2009, 2,991 clubs provided responses to questions about main sport and facility use and 1,975 clubs provided a complete set of responses, including full details of questions on income and expenditure. In 2011, 1,942 clubs responded, and 1,661 provided full financial data. In both surveys the overall results were weighted to reflect the distribution of clubs by sport in the UK. Weighting was necessary because the characteristics of clubs vary widely by sport. This procedure relied on NGB estimates of the number of clubs – which, as noted above, have limitations. Both samples over-represented clubs with Community Amateur Sports Club (CASC) status (which confers certain tax benefits) and with Clubmark accreditation. Clubmark is a Sport England licensing system for clubs with juniors. It requires clubs to develop policy documents, apply procedures such as risk assessments, appoint volunteer roles such as child protection officers and demonstrate the continuing professional development of coaches. Clubs have to reapply for Clubmark status every two years. CASC and Clubmark clubs would have found it easier to respond to the survey because these more formally organised clubs would be more likely to have the information to hand, and to be contacted through NGBs. An impact of this will be to overestimate club size in the sample. Despite the use of weighting, a comparison of the two samples has to be qualified by their different composition in terms of the numbers of clubs in each sport (for example, in golf and association football the 2009 survey contained thirty-two golf clubs and 204 association football clubs, whereas the 2011 survey contained eighteen and 124 respectively). However, this comparison is the best available. The 2009 survey categorised clubs as 'non-profit', 'profit-making', 'informal' and 'other'. Non-profit clubs represented 93 per cent of those in the complete sample of 2,991 clubs. This is the most common type of club, and the type that one would expect to be run by volunteers.

A further survey of regulatory burdens facing clubs (Sport and Recreation Alliance, 2011b), 'Red card to red tape', was commissioned by the new UK coalition government in 2010, specifically because it wanted to reduce regulatory burdens as part of its policy to promote a Big Society in which 'people come together to solve problems and improve life for themselves and their communities; a society where the leading force for progress is social responsibility, not state control' (Conservative Party, 2010: 1). This online survey was promoted to clubs through NGBs. From over forty-five sports, 1,401 clubs responded. The characteristics of clubs responding were not reported. Regulations were not presented as 'burdens' but clubs ranked their impact on a scale from 'very negative' to 'very positive'. Clubs could add qualitative comments.

216

Club size

The clubs are small. In 2011 the average club had 104 adult members, sixty-eight of whom participated in sport, and ninety junior members. The average number of members varies considerably by sport; see Table 9.2.

The selection of sports in Table 9.2 illustrates how some sports clubs are dominated by adults (e.g. golf, squash, bowls) and some by juniors (e.g. football, swimming, gymnastics/trampolining). It also shows how club size varies by sport. In this respect, golf is an outlier: the second biggest average club size by adult membership is sailing. Eleven per cent of golf clubs aimed to be profit-making, so are less likely to be run by volunteers. Third, the 2011 survey asked how many adult members participated in sport. From this one can deduce the number of adult members who do not participate in sport. Where there are few junior members, these non-participants are more likely to be social members – possibly former players who wish to remain affiliated with the club, and show how it meets a social function as well as allowing sports participation. In sports that have large numbers of junior members, these non-playing members will probably be involved in volunteering to support the junior teams.

The last observation from this table is the sports in which there appears to be a significant difference in membership between 2009 and 2011, such as sailing, tennis and bowls. This reflects the relatively small numbers of clubs representing any one sport in the two surveys, limiting the validity of a comparison between 2009 and 2011.

Table 9.2 Average club size by sport

Sport	All adult members 2011	Adult members: non-sport participating 2011	Junior members 2011	Adult members 2009	Junior members 2009
Golf	553	93	49	527	59
Sailing	242	61	53	340	74
Tennis	215	30	119	389	165
Squash	172	41	30	143	32
Bowls	103	25	2	167	4
Cricket	95	50	73	107	89
Football	79	44	147	95	167
Netball	34	4	28	33	32
Swimming	58	30	172	35	157
Gymnastics/ trampolining	26	11	149	21	171

Sources: Taylor *et al.* (2009); Sport and Recreation Alliance (2011a).

Club volunteers

The clubs are almost entirely dependent on the work of volunteers. Clubs have an average of twenty volunteers and only one paid staff member (most likely involved in coaching, grounds work or bar work). This is an extremely important character-istic. It affects the way the club is managed and operates (discussed below). The volunteers are involved in the club because it is an expression of their enthusiasm for the sport and of their affiliation to and identification with a social organisation, and to create the opportunity for themselves, their children and others to partici-pate. Volunteering is a leisure activity. Thus, unlike in the private or public sector of sports provision, volunteers are creating the opportunity for others to partici-pate; and the cost of participating in sport in a club is reduced by the efforts of the volunteers.

Fees and income

The average membership fee in 2011 was £83 for adults and £61 for juniors. Again this varies considerably: golf, £757; rowing, £201; cycling, £11. Thirty-five per cent of the average club income of £35,736 comes from membership fees. Twenty-two per cent comes from bar/catering/hospitality, but this is relevant only to clubs with their own facilities to generate this income. The average club surplus in 2010 was £1,092; just over £10 per member. So, clearly clubs do not aim to make a profit and just require enough income to keep running. However, they may not have reserves to meet major costs, such as facility maintenance.

Facility use

Only 21 per cent of clubs own playing facilities. Forty-one per cent hire them from local authorities, and 32 per cent from a school/college or university. This is important because clubs are reliant on public sector organisations to have access to facilities at the time, quality and cost they require.

A club typology

An analysis of the 2009 club sample clustered clubs by the degree of formality, resulting in three types of club (Nichols et al., 2012):

1 'Formal' clubs: these are bigger (average size 238 members) and more likely to have registration as CASC or a charity, and 48 per cent had Clubmark

218

accreditation. They are more likely to own or lease facilities, to have paid staff and to have a junior section.

2 'Semi-formal' clubs: these are smaller, with an average size of 113, and all have a junior section. Although they are unlikely to have CASC or charity status, 53 per cent of them have Clubmark accreditation. They do not own or lease playing facilities but hire them. They are less likely to have paid staff.

3 'Informal' clubs: these are very small; average size fifty-one. None has a junior section and few have Clubmark registration. They are very unlikely to have CASC or charity status. They hire playing facilities rather than owning or leasing them and are less likely to have paid staff.

Formality is driven by club size and Clubmark accreditation, which reflects junior membership. It is difficult to estimate the proportions of clubs in each of these groups because of the significant overestimation of Clubmark-accredited clubs in the 2009 sample. However, the typology is useful for sport development workers in identifying the type of clubs they want to work with and how these clubs might need help. For example, clubs with large junior sections but without their own facilities may need help to access facilities at a suitable time and cost. Clubs that own facilities may need advice in managing them or dealing with utility charges.

Previous research similarly found that clubs could be differentiated by formality (Harris and May, 2011; Harris *et al.*, 2009) but from a much smaller sample. Within this sample the more formal clubs were much more committed to policies consistent with the government's aspirations to expand club numbers and participation.

Formality is a useful dimension on which to place clubs to understand their reactions to change and challenges, discussed in more detail below. A comment based on impressions from the 2002 survey of volunteers in sport was that:

At one extreme are what might be termed traditional organisations, where informality of organisation is a proud culture and professionalisation is seen as a fundamental threat to this culture. These organisations are selective in their adoption of changes in response to the pressures. They often adopt pragmatic solutions to the resulting problems, such as key officers staying in their posts long past the time when they would have preferred to quit and multi-tasking reluctantly to ensure tasks are done, [but] not in the co-operative teamwork ethic of previously. They engage in crisis management but do not see it as that – instead it is perceived as a continuation of the 'mucking in' ethic, but with fewer volunteers. At the other extreme are organisations that have wholly embraced the need for professionalisation as a response to the pressures. They are more formal and managerialist in approach . . . These organisations are not immune to the problems brought about by the pressures reviewed above, but they are more likely to adopt formal procedures for dealing with them. These include paying for certain functions, including coaches . . . They are also more receptive to external assistance, particularly from NGBs and Sport England's Volunteer Investment Programme.

(Taylor *et al.*, 2003: 149–150)

CLUBS' CONTRIBUTION TO PARTICIPATION

A primitive estimate of clubs' contribution to participation, derived from the 2009 estimate of the number of clubs and the 2011 estimates of participating members, is that 6.9 million adults and 9.1 million juniors participate in sport in clubs in the UK. However approximate, this represents a lot of participation.

Reid (2012) was able to conduct secondary analysis of the Scottish Opinion Survey, which included questions on sports participation and club membership. This enabled an estimation of the percentage of participants in any one sport who were also members of a club for that sport – the inference being that the club was the organisation in which they participated. Unfortunately, the survey did not distinguish between commercial clubs, public sector clubs and clubs run by volunteers. (The latest round of Sport England's Active People survey did make this distinction, so offers the potential for more sensitive analysis.)

Reid found that the sports with the highest percentage of participants being club members were rugby, bowls, judo, martial arts, cricket, curling, golf, multigym/weight training and gymnastics. For all of these the percentage was over 60 per cent, except gymnastics, for which it was 54 per cent. The figures varied between men and women. The pattern for juniors was also different: judo and martial arts had very high club participation rates, whereas, of other sports, only shinty and gymnastics had over 50 per cent. Multigym/weight training is probably taking place in commercial facilities, but the survey does not show this.

Although this analysis can be developed from other surveys it shows that, as might be expected, the importance of club membership for participation varies across sports. This would have an implication if an SDO wanted to develop a particular sport. Another interesting, but as yet unexplained, finding was a considerable difference in the proportion of participants who are club members across Scottish local authority areas: between 53 per cent and 33 per cent. Thus the role of clubs in contributing to participation varied widely. A greater understanding of this would also inform SDOs' work.

CHALLENGES AND OPPORTUNITIES FOR CLUBS

Challenges and opportunities faced by clubs were researched in the 2002 Sport England survey (Taylor *et al.*, 2003; Nichols *et al.*, 2005), the 2009 (Taylor *et al.*, 2009) and 2011 Sport and Recreation Alliance (2011a) surveys and the survey of regulatory burdens facing clubs (Sport and Recreation Alliance, 2011b).

Recruiting new members was the challenge mentioned by the largest proportion of clubs (64 per cent) in the 2011 survey and 53 per cent mentioned retaining members. This is supported by a decline in adult membership levels by 11 per cent between 2008 and 2011, and junior membership by 8 per cent (bearing in mind the limitations of comparing the 2009 and 2011 club samples). This decline may reflect the impact of the financial recession, but may also reflect a long-term trend in participation in the type of sport these clubs cater for, as noted above, and the fact that both sports participation and volunteering have to compete more fiercely for individuals' time; lack of time was the first reason given in survey responses as a barrier to participating in either. Retaining and recruiting volunteers is mentioned across all surveys as a problem, and this reflects the same forces as recruiting members, but is amplified by the increasing complexity of volunteers' tasks.

Between 2008 and 2010 the average club surplus fell by 45 per cent, but the overall surplus is very small and 49 per cent of clubs still have a surplus of £200 or more. Accessing funds/sponsorship and generating sufficient income were the second and third most mentioned challenges by clubs. Clubs are financially resilient organisations, in that few carry any debts, and it is relatively easy to downsize operations. However, any expansion or redevelopment of facilities will require funds.

Increased facility costs were mentioned as a challenge by 58 per cent of clubs in the 2011 survey and this ability to obtain access to facilities at the time, cost and quality required was a frequent problem in the 'Red card' survey, which found that access to facilities was having a negative impact on 29 per cent of clubs (Sport and Recreation Alliance, 2011b). The 2010 'Red card' survey found that major burdens were the cost and time of gaining coaching qualifications; gaining funding; health and safety legislation; and complying with child protection legislation. This survey also identified several other regulatory burdens associated with tax, licensing, applying for charitable status, restrictions on use of school facilities out of school hours and other matters.

Prior to the surveys reported above, several related reviews of research had identified a broad range of challenges facing volunteer-led sports clubs. A 2010 report, *Volunteering in the European Union* (GHK, 2010), noted significant challenges faced by voluntary sports organisations across the EU. These included the recruitment and retention of volunteers, professionalisation of the voluntary sector (meaning requiring volunteers to adopt practices of management and service delivery comparable to those in the private or public sectors), reacting to legal and regulatory frameworks, the production of information on volunteering, achieving sustainable funding, managing a tension between state support and incorporating objectives of the state, achieving recognition for the work of volunteers, overcoming a prejudice towards voluntary engagement, and coping with a lack of a clear strategy in a fragmented political landscape (GHK, 2010: 254). The three most important concerns raised by sport organisations were the complexity and administrative burden of applying for subsidies, insurance and liability, and the low level of public funding (GHK, 2010: 256). The pertinence of these varies across nation states. Similar challenges have been noted in Australian clubs (Cuskelly *et al.*, 2006).

State intervention as assistance or a burden

A balance has to be struck between national and local government supporting clubs and imposing conditions on that support, which may be an additional burden to the volunteers.

Conditions for state support of NGBs cascade down to sports clubs. If clubs apply directly to local or national government for support, such as a lottery grant to improve facilities, conditions will be attached to this support which reflect the policy objectives of the funding organisations.

A review of the relationship between UK NGBs and the state (Green, 2008) noted that since Sport England became a distributing body for the National Lottery Sports Fund, introduced in 1994, the state has been able to increasingly influence the work of NGBs by imposing conditions on support. This has been clear in government policy strategies; for example, *A Sporting Future for All* required NGBs to modernise, professionalise, have policies to promote participation and excellence and 'commit themselves to putting fairness and social inclusion at the heart of everything they do' (DCMS, 2000: 20). The conditional support of NGBs was emphasised in Sport England's strategy for 2008–11, in which funding of NGBs was conditional on delivery of policy outcomes enshrined in Whole-Sport Plans; for example, developing a 'modern sports club network' in which opportunities for sports participation by young people will be made available in 'NGB-accredited clubs' (Sport England, 2008: 2). Further, 'Sport England will work with National Governing bodies to ensure that an accessible, modern, sports club structure is developed within each sport. This will drive up participation, improve satisfaction and retention and allow those with talent to fully develop' (Sport England, 2008: 3). An interesting implication for the role of NGBs is that they have to mediate the tension between meeting performance indicators imposed by Sport England and maintaining and channelling the enthusiasm of club volunteers, which is the driving force of clubs and without which the club structure would not exist.

A specific example of the impact of this on club volunteers is Clubmark accreditation, which, as outlined above, is a Sport England licensing system setting out broad criteria that junior clubs are expected to meet. Clubmark accreditation requires considerably more time and effort from volunteers. On the other hand it can be regarded as an opportunity to professionalise the management of the club to attract and retain junior members in a more competitive environment.

Opportunities

Pearce's (1993) study of volunteers identified a sense of 'martyred leadership' in which a few volunteers, contributing the majority of the work, had a pessimistic outlook. These are the key officers most likely to have responded to the surveys above, and this may result in an emphasis on challenges. However, the most commonly mentioned opportunities in the 2011 survey were securing grants, developing coaching skills and establishing links with local schools. The most polarised issue was coaching qualifications, which, while costly and time-consuming, and a requirement of Clubmark, can also enhance the service offered by the club.

MANAGEMENT OF SMALL VOLUNTEER-LED ORGANISATIONS

As well as the challenges perceived by sports clubs, development officers need to appreciate the distinctive nature of sports club management. Members of volunteer-led sports clubs can be thought of as people driven by and clustered together around a shared passion for their sport. Some will want to play, some will want their children to play and some will just want to support the club by volunteering, or to express an affinity for the club; but the organisation rarely has a clear set of aims and objectives, such as those embodied in Whole-Sport Plans, which NGBs have had to agree to as a condition of Sport England funding. This makes it harder to define the roles volunteers need to fill to allow the club to achieve these objectives. Roles tend to grow around long-standing volunteers; 18 per cent of volunteers in clubs contribute 62 per cent of the work (Nichols, 2005), and occupy key positions such as secretary, treasurer, chairperson and coach. The retention of these volunteers is critical to provide the structure in which others can volunteer; but these are the hardest roles to fill when a volunteer leaves. Within clubs there is a strong emphasis on informal personal relations, rather than formal roles defined in a hierarchical structure. Thus the way a club is managed will usually be quite different from organisations in the public or private sector (Schulz et al., 2011). Organisations led by volunteers typically have a flat management structure, with an ethos of egalitarianism (Pearce, 1993), but as social gatherings they will still have a strong status hierarchy.

IMPLICATIONS FOR SPORT DEVELOPMENT WORK

Sport development has been defined as:

> a process whereby effective opportunities, processes, systems and struc-
> tures are set up to enable and encourage people in all or any particular
> groups and areas to take part in sport and recreation or to improve their
> performances at whatsoever level they desire.
>
> (Collins, 2010: 4)

In other words, SDOs are 'fixers' of 'organisational weaknesses and strengths for promoting sport' (ibid.). This definition needs to be expanded to consider the objectives of development. As noted above, a development officer may wish to promote the objectives of central government, an NGB or local government, or any combination of these organisations.

Before further considering the implications for sport development work, it is worth summarising the challenges facing sports clubs led by volunteers. SDOs must have an appreciation of these to understand the type of help clubs might welcome.

These challenges include:

- recruiting and retaining members in a more competitive leisure market;
- recruiting and retaining volunteers;
- developing new volunteers to take the key roles in the club, required to keep it running;
- meeting the demands of Clubmark accreditation;
- gaining access to playing facilities at the cost, quality and time required;
- recruiting and training coaches up to the standard required by Clubmark;
- complying with legislation, including Health and Safety, child protection, licensing, charitable status and food hygiene standards;
- applying for funding, if the club wants to develop facilities.

Implications for sport development work are:

- Volunteers in clubs are motivated by a desire to support the club, participants and the sport. They do not want to spend any more time than is necessary on 'managing' the club to achieve these ends. Volunteering is a leisure activity; some volunteers may not even think of it as volunteering. Volunteers therefore welcome practical solutions to immediate problems.
- The nature of 'management' based more on relationships and the qualities of key individuals means that volunteers are more open to support and advice from people they trust and feel an empathy with, as having the interests of

the club at heart. For example, a local SDO who has built up a relationship with club officials, demonstrating a commitment to the sport and a track record of offering valuable advice, will be treated with more respect than a national Sport England officer who has had no previous contact. SDOs will need to identify the key individuals to work with in clubs. There is always a risk that, if those individuals leave, some time will need to be spent developing a new relationship.

■ Club volunteers are not in their role to support government policy, but they will recognise synergy between this and their aspirations for the club. Clubs have a strong tradition of independence. Sport development officers will need to identify synergy between the policy objectives of their funders and associated performance indicators, and at the same time recognise what the club wants to do. For example, from October 2011 county sport partnerships (CSPs) are the delivery mechanism for Sport England's Sport Makers programme, which aims to recruit 40,000 new volunteers to sport, inspired by the Olympic Games, and place some of them in sports clubs (Sport England, 2011). Funding has been devolved to CSPs, with targets specifying the numbers of volunteers placed. Placing these volunteers has synergy with clubs needing to recruit more volunteers, but to take part in the programme clubs will need to be convinced that the new volunteers will actually be of value to them. Similarly, if a club has aspirations to develop its junior section and improve its quality of sport coaching to attract the best juniors and feed them into its senior team, it may be very receptive to aiming at Clubmark accreditation.

■ The typology of clubs, based on degree of formality, suggests that SDOs will find it easier to work with clubs in the formal or semi-formal groups, as these are more likely to have the capacity to contribute to policy objectives and recognise synergy with them.

CASE STUDY 9.1: CLAIRE HOWE, SPORTS DEVELOPMENT OFFICER, KIRKLEES COUNCIL

Claire's core work is with sports clubs run by volunteers. She is part of the sports development team in Kirklees Council but part of her work is funded by a Sport England project across the five local authorities in West Yorkshire to coordinate volunteers in sport. Claire acts as a broker between volunteers and clubs, although she may also place volunteers in other sports opportunities, such as events. Clubs are a challenging placement because Claire has the least control over the volunteer's experience. A key part of this role is acting as a development officer for clubs. A club may approach Claire with a request for a volunteer. Claire will discuss with the club exactly how the volunteer will fit into the club and what s/he will do. This may involve helping the club recognise new opportunities; for example, to develop roles such as press officer, sending results to the local papers, or a website manager. She arranges a series of workshops for club officials. She will guide clubs on procedures, such as child protection, and check these are in place. So Claire's role is to build club capacity; at whatever stage of development they are at, 'it is to support them . . . confirm that they're doing the right thing or get them to improve'. Claire sees her role as 'developing the relationship with them, getting to know them . . . individual clubs, telling them that we're here as a sports development unit, the kind of things we can offer'. This means that clubs tend to come to Claire or the other SDOs with specific requests for help. The clubs can then be directed towards the more general development workshops. Attending these may be a condition of other support.

Volunteers may register directly on the scheme run by Claire or be passed on from other volunteer agencies. Claire will also discuss with the new volunteer his/her aspirations and the type of role s/he can expect to perform in the club, as they often have unrealistic expectations. She will arrange a general introductory workshop on volunteering and necessary training for specific roles, such as first aid, but will try to place the volunteer as soon as possible to maintain his/her enthusiasm. Having matched the volunteer to a club, Claire will introduce them and keep in touch with the club for eighteen months to make sure the placement has been successful.

Claire is able to build on contacts developed over ten years in this area. Clubs do not usually look outside the club for volunteers but Claire thinks they will approach her because they have built up a relationship with her. Her particular experience of working with clubs means that the work of the other four volunteer in sport coordinators across West Yorkshire might well be different.

This SDO example illustrates:

- The value of a personal relationship between Claire and the clubs, developed over some years. This is also used to place the volunteer in the club.
- A relationship of trust developed with the clubs. The clubs will approach the SDOs because they have confidence they will provide them with useful advice.
- A club development agenda that clubs are gently encouraged to take up by persuading them it is in their own interest.
- Recognising that each club has different development needs.
- Doing this job well takes a considerable amount of time.

FURTHER CONSIDERATIONS: THE BROADER PICTURE

Sport England requires NGBs to 'professionalise' and 'modernise' as a condition of being allocated public money, to spend in a way which will contribute to Sport England's policy objectives. Should similar conditions be imposed on sports clubs? Is a 'professional/rational-bureaucratic model of management' (Green, 2008: 105) suitable for small volunteer-led organisations which represent a clustering around enthusiasms (Hoggett and Bishop, 1985)? Promoting more 'professional' management practices to clubs, one has to be careful to retain, at the same time, the ethos of volunteering on which the club relies.

If volunteering becomes too onerous and demanding for the stalwart core volunteers who hold the club together, because they have to adopt more demanding and complex procedures – if it is no longer fun, as a leisure activity – the club will collapse. On the other hand, clubs are operating in a completely different environment from the nineteenth century, when the club structure was established. The demands on people's leisure time are much more competitive. People may be less willing to volunteer, as suggested in trends between 2001 and 2011 (National Statistics, 2011). If a higher proportion of the clubs' members view their relationship with the club as buying the provision of a service, and fewer regard them as an expression of a collective enthusiasm, requiring a collective endeavour, will clubs need to change anyway? Clubs may have to professionalise to attract members. The answer will vary between clubs. Those with strong support for their sport and little direct competition may be able to continue in the old model. Those in a more competitive leisure market, especially for junior participants, may need to adapt.

There is a paradox between the UK coalition government's aim of the state stepping back to allow the voluntary sector to develop and contribute to a Big Society, where the government claims that volunteering has previously been stultified, and at the same time wanting to be more directive in how volunteer-led organisations should manage themselves and what they should do. At the NGB level, NGBs have become more dependent on state funds since Sport England has been able to dispense them from the National Lottery, and this has paralleled their use by Sport England as policy tools. If government funding is reduced to allow NGBs to develop more independently, they cannot at the same time be expected to implement government policy. The same paradox holds at the level of the sports club. It has been claimed that 'voluntary action in Anglo-Saxon countries is still cast in a powerful *liberal* ideology that continues to celebrate voluntarism as autonomous and jealously defends its arm's length relationship from government' (Schofer and Fourcade-Gourinchas, 2001: 812). Hoggett and Bishop's (1985) seminal study of leisure organisations led by volunteers concluded that they represented a pluralist liberal society and should be encouraged for this reason. The recommendations of the 'Red card to red tape' report (Sport and Recreation Alliance, 2011b) were to remove regulative constraints, but a further implication is that, if the government is to respect and value the independence of sports clubs for its own sake, clubs cannot also be used as an instrument of policy.

The Big Society agenda has been criticised as coinciding with significant cuts in public expenditure (New Economics Foundation, 2010). These will affect the capacity of SDOs to support clubs, the number of SDOs employed and the charges paid by clubs to local authorities for facility use.

The infrastructure of a multitude of small sports clubs is a cultural heritage from the nineteenth and twentieth centuries. They were developed to meet a need for sports participation opportunities in a far less competitive leisure market, in which a spirit of amateurism and volunteerism predominated. Clubs with their own facilities, especially playing fields, acquired them when it was much easier to do so. These clubs still provide the structure of organisations in which the largest amount of formal volunteering takes place. Thus they facilitate civic activism, however much time people want to give to volunteering. Their existence provides the opportunity for people to become involved in volunteering by just contributing a little, but for their commitment to grow. For example, a parent of a junior participant might become involved to support his/her child's team, but develop to contribute to the club in a much more demanding role, possibly continuing well after his/her child has left. The structure that enables this volunteering to take place is maintained by the small proportion of volunteers that contribute most of the work. Is this structure a delicate cultural heritage that needs support to survive in changed times? Or will it continue to survive, irrespective of government policies?

LEARNING ACTIVITIES

1 If you are a member of a local sports club, how do its characteristics vary from the ones described in this chapter? What relationships does it have with local or national government and how does this affect how it operates? For example, does it hire local authority or school facilities, or has it applied for a grant or any other form of assistance? Where would you place this club on a scale of formality? What challenges and opportunities does this club face?

2 Read Sport England's 2008–11 strategy (Sport England, 2008) to identify the role of sports clubs run by volunteers in this. Do you think clubs can fill this role? Look at how the role of community sports clubs and NGBs have been developed in Sports England's 2012–17 strategy (Sport England, 2012).

3 Obtain the strategy of your local county sports partnership (CSP). This may be online, or you may have to ask for it. What are the roles of sports clubs run by volunteers in this? What will local SDOs need to do to persuade clubs to work with the CSP in achieving its aims?

4 Ask a local SDO if s/he is willing to discuss with your class his/her work with sports clubs. What are the SDOs aims? What support and advice do clubs want? How does the SDO achieve a balance between his/her aims and what the clubs want?

ACKNOWLEDGEMENT

Thanks to Claire Howe, Sports Development Officer, Kirklees Council, for providing an interview about her work for the case study in this chapter.

Geoff Nichols

REFERENCES

Allison, M. (2001) *Sports Clubs in Scotland*, Research Report No. 75, Edinburgh: sportscotland.

Coalter, F. (1999) 'Sport and recreation in the United Kingdom: flow with the flow or buck the trends?', *Managing Leisure*, 4 (1): 24–39.

Collins, M. (2010) *Examining Sports Development*, London: Routledge.

Conservative Party (2010) *Building a Big Society*, London: Conservative Party, www. conservatives.com/~/media/Files/Downloadable%20Files/Building-a-Big-Society.ashx

Cuskelly, G., Hoye, R. and Auld, C. (2006) *Working with Volunteers in Sport: Theory and Practice*, London: Routledge.

DCMS (2000) *A Sporting Future for All*, London: DCMS.

GHK (2010) 'Volunteering in the European Union', http://ec.europa.eu/sport/library/doc/f_studies/volunteering_final_report.pdf

Gratton, C., Rowe, N. and Veal, A.J. (2011) 'International comparisons of sport participation in European countries: an update of the COMPASS project', *European Journal of Sport and Society*, 8 (1–2): 99–116.

Green, M. (2008) 'Non-governmental organisations in sports development', in Girginov, V. (ed.), *Management of Sports Development*, London: Elsevier.

Harris, S. and May, T. (2011) 'Growing sport through clubs: understanding and respecting the heterogeneity of club types', presentation at Sport Volunteering Research network symposium, 7 April.

Harris, S., Mori, K. and Collins, M. (2009) 'Great expectations: the role of voluntary sports clubs as policy implementers', *Voluntas International Journal*, 20 (4): 405–423.

Hoggett, P. and Bishop, J. (1985) *The Social Organisation of Leisure*, London: Sports Council.

National Statistics (2011) 'Citizenship survey: April 2010–March 2011, England', www. communities.gov.uk/publications/corporate/statistics/citizenshipsurveyq4201011

New Economics Foundation (2010) 'Cutting it: the "Big Society" and the new austerity', www. neweconomics.org/publications/cutting-it

Nichols, G. (2005) 'Stalwarts in sport', *World Leisure*, 2: 31–37.

Nichols, G., Taylor, P., James, M., Garrett, R., Holmes, K., King, L., Gratton, C. and Kokolakakis, T. (2004) 'Voluntary activity in UK sport', *Voluntary Action*, 6 (2): 31–54.

Nichols, G., Taylor, P., James, M., Holmes, K., King, L. and Garrett, R. (2005) 'Pressures on the UK sports sector', *Voluntas*, 16 (1): 33–50.

Nichols, G., Padmore, J., Taylor, P. and Barrett, D. (2012) 'The relationship between types of sports club and English government policy to grow participation', *International Journal of Sport Policy and Politics*, 4 (2): 187–200.

Pearce, J. (1993) *Volunteers: The Organizational Behavior of Unpaid Workers*, London: Routledge.

Reid, F. (2012) 'Increasing sports participation in Scotland: are voluntary sports clubs the answer?', *International Journal of Sports Policy and Politics*, 4 (2): 221–242.

Schofer, E. and Fourcade-Gourinchas, M. (2001) 'The structural contexts of civic engagement: voluntary association membership in comparative perspective', *American Sociological Review*, 66 (6): 806–828.

Schulz, J., Nichols, G. and Auld, C. (2011) 'Issues in the management of voluntary sports organisations and volunteers', in Houlihan, B. and Green, M. (eds.), *Routledge Handbook of Sports Development*, London: Routledge.

Sport and Recreation Alliance (2011a) 'Survey of sports clubs 2011', www.sportandrecreation. org.uk/lobbying-and-campaigning/sport-research/sports-club-survey

Sport and Recreation Alliance (2011b) 'Red card to red tape: how sport and recreation clubs want to break free from bureaucracy', www.sportandrecreation.org.uk/sites/default/files/web/documents/pdf/Sport%20and%20Recreation%20Alliance-%20Red%20Card%20to%20Red%20Tape%20%28Full%20report%2C%20low%20res%29.pdf

Sport England (2008) 'Sport England strategy 2008–11', www.sportengland.org/about_us/what_we_do.aspx

Sport England (2011) 'Be a sporting hero', www.sportengland.org/about_us/our_news/sport_makers.aspx

Sport England (2012) 'Creating a sporting habit for life: a new youth sport strategy', www.sportengland.org/about_us/what_we_do.aspx

Sports Council (1996) *Valuing Volunteers in UK Sport*, Sports Council: London.

Taylor, P., Nichols, G., Holmes, K., James, M., Gratton, C., Garrett, R., Kokolakakis, T., Mulder, C. and King, L. (2003) *Sports Volunteering in England*, London: Sport England.

Taylor, P., Barrett, D. and Nichols, G. (2009) *Survey of Sports Clubs 2009*, London: CCPR.

Tschirhart, M. (2006) 'Nonprofit membership associations', in Powell, W.W. and Steinberg, R. (eds.), *The Nonprofit Sector: A Research Handbook*, 2nd edn, New Haven, CT: Yale University Press.

CHAPTER 10

SPORT DEVELOPMENT AND SPORT COACHING

JOHN LYLE (WITH THOMAS DOWENS)

'Sport development' is a term that has come to have meaning as a social service, a measure of progress in sport policy and practice, a professional rationale, and a form of engagement in sport. The term is both ubiquitous and insubstantial. However, any attempt at comprehensive genericism creates a lack of focus and interpretation of purpose that renders it almost worthless as a descriptor of function, and useful only as an occupational category. Much of the meaning and discourse about sport development is attached to the claims made for it (Coalter, 2007) but the 'picture' conjured up by the term is most often one associated with sporting activity in a learner, developmental or recreational context. Nonetheless, the term has a common usage that embraces all levels of sport participation, and increasingly, physical activity. The use of the term connotes a plethora of initiatives, personnel, social structures, aspirations and shared meanings.

The most familiar of these are the structures and pathways within each sport that allow participants to perform and progress at all levels from initiation to excellence; the more casual forms of sport that, taken in aggregation, might be termed community or recreation sport; and initiative-led forms of participation with specific social, educational or personal development objectives. Sport development embraces these activities and the policies, procedures, processes and personnel that are required for both facilitation and delivery. A common and taken-for-granted assumption is that sports participation itself is most often directed by and dependent on various forms of sport leadership, including sport coaching. This chapter adopts a critical and challenging approach to the assumption of a straightforward relationship between coaching and sport development.

Proposals for the professionalisation of coaching have a clear historical and developmental context (DCMS, 2002; Duffy *et al.*, 2011; sports coach UK, 2008; Taylor and Garratt, 2010), and the discourse is intended to embrace all forms of participation. It is further assumed that coaches play a significant role in the development of sporting talent (Martindale *et al.*, 2005), and that there is a particular link between successful coaches and their developmental profile (Gilbert *et al.*, 2006). This chapter goes beyond the initial, and perhaps obvious, assumption of a particular interrelationship between coaching and development to ask: (a) does the social agenda of much of grassroots sport development require a particular form of coaching; (b) is sport development adequately served by the 'quality' of coaching generally provided (Cassidy *et al.*, 2004); (c) does coach education currently provide sufficient preparation for achieving social and other objectives (Cushion *et al.*, 2003); and (d) does sport coaching exhibit characteristic features, and does sport development activity generally reach this threshold, with implications for professionalisation?

Since the previous edition of this book, the rationale for addressing these questions has not changed. Sport leadership is an essential, if not the most essential, element in the realisation of sporting activity. Indeed, it could be argued that much of the recyclable social capital of sport development (Adams, 2011) lies in the hands of coaches and other similar practitioners. An improved awareness of the dynamics of the relationship between coaches, coaching practice and sport development remains an appropriate aspiration. However, a greater awareness of coaching domains (Lyle, 2011a) and the emergence of models of participant pathways (Côté *et al.*, 2010) and coach development pathways (see North, 2009), and the relationship between them, have provided a much improved conceptual language for analysis, with some impact on coach education structures. This has been incorporated into the revised chapter.

Participation in sport is dependent to a greater or lesser extent on sport leadership, teaching, instruction or coaching. In so far as sport development is a process that is intended to lead to increased sport participation, more sustained participation or improved standards of performance, sport coaching (as a collective term) becomes an extremely important element of provision. However, sport coaching is a contested term in the sense that there are quite distinctive forms of coaching that can be associated with sport participation domains and contexts (Lyle and Cushion, 2010a; Trudel and Gilbert, 2006). The initial part of the chapter examines the definitions, concepts and expectations of coaching in each of these principal contexts (e.g. recreational/community, club/performance, excellence), and proposes a simple model of the association between coaching practice and developmental aspirations (Lyle, 2002). Sport coaching is treated as a problematic element of sport development in so far as it can be argued that many of the typical objectives of sport development are dependent on appropriate forms and quality of coaching leadership. Sport coaching must be interpreted not merely as a delivery behaviour, but as a process in which the coach increasingly adopts a strategic approach to the personal, organisational, environmental and technical factors that impact on performance. Thus sport development in performance or excellence sport involves the

John Lyle (with Thomas Dowens)

meta-strategic coordination of structures and systems at the level of the individual or team (Jones and Wallace, 2006).

Following an examination of definitional terms and the relationship between the concepts, sport development is examined as a 'ladder of opportunity' in the second part of the chapter, that is a staged, progressive pathway that young persons have to travel to move from initiation into sport to sustained participation and skilled performance (Lyle, 2004). The chapter examines critically how the incorporation of Long Term Athlete Development principles and participant development models into sport coaching and development may impact on a number of sport development imperatives (for example, competition between sports, early specialisation, team sports versus individual sports differences), and the implications for the balance between technical/performance development within a sport and other sport development objectives. In the final part of the chapter, the interdependency between coaching and environmental changes is demonstrated using a case study of a national representative team sport.

Sports policy is an ever-changing dynamic, within which sport development agencies, initiatives and objectives find support or are superseded by alternative structures and practices (Houlihan and Green, 2011). The most recent expression of this has been the refocusing of resources and energies around the 2012 Olympic and Paralympic Games in London, both as high-performance strategies and legacy-driven participation aspirations (McDonald, 2011). The demarcation of school-based sport development and elite sport (DCMS/DfEE, 2000) had been reinforced in 2008 with the publication of *Playing to Win: A New Era for Sport* (DCMS, 2008). This reinforcement of policy coincided with a change of government. The Conservative-led coalition dismantled the School Sport Partnership network that had been established (see Phillpots, 2011, for a description of this landscape), and replaced this with a 'School Games' policy emphasising competition sport in schools (see DCMS, 2012). The detail of the changes are less relevant to the purpose of the chapter than the realisation that policy and funding lead to structures and systems within which sports coaches 'service' participation and related developmental objectives. It cannot, or should not, be assumed that the changing nature of this participation landscape can be delivered unproblematically without attention to the most appropriate forms of sport leadership or coaching.

The UK government document *Game Plan* (DCMS/Strategy Unit, 2002) summarises the beneficial effects of sports participation. These range from social benefits, such as community development, social inclusion, urban regeneration and improved health, to more individual benefits, such as a sense of social, psychological and physical well-being, and the impact of successfully pursuing international sporting achievement. In order to achieve this, there is a considerable infrastructure of organisations, agencies, practitioners and initiatives (see McDonald, 2011: 376–377). Indeed, some of those deemed to be contributing might not think of themselves as sport developers (Hylton and Bramham, 2008). Providing the glue for this entire enterprise is a continuous stream of sport development strategic planning documents. However, there is a surprising dearth of material on development principles applied to sport, on programme evaluation, and on the impact of, for example, prescriptive versus facilitative interventions.

There may be a perception that the chapter has a critical tone. This seems almost inevitable when considering the contribution of sport coaching in the context of an absence of consensual rationales for intervention, the acknowledged barriers to development, the social deficit model of provision, and concerns over existing participation rates. Planning documents adopt sport coaching and other leadership roles as an 'ever present' common factor in sport development. However, the purpose of the chapter is to reinforce the danger of treating coaching as an unproblematic factor in the facilitation and delivery of sport development initiatives. At the same time, this requires an understanding about sport coaching concepts and the implementation of the coaching process. It would be simplistic but probably accurate to state that all sport coaching is a form of sport development. Key to the argument pervading the chapter is that sport development practitioners have not attended adequately to the role of the coach and the implications of differentiated practices in achieving sport development outcomes.

SPORT DEVELOPMENT AND SPORT COACHING: TOWARDS A DEFINITION

Inevitably we have to deal with the task of defining what is meant by sport development and sport coaching and establish why and in which ways sport development and sport coaching differ from other processes. Is everything that involves 'directed' sport participation to be considered sport development? In one sense the answer to the question is 'yes'. In engaging in sport, the purpose of the coach, teacher or instructor and the motives of the participants will be to produce better-quality, more skilled, increasingly successful, better prepared and/or more enjoyable participation. Nevertheless, it is not a helpful attempt at a definition simply to say that everything is sport development. Definitional frameworks are intended to provide, and should be measured against their capacity to provide, discrimination, criticality, substance, applicability and competence. This is no easy task since sport development is a policy space, an occupation, an intervention activity, and a 'concept'. Sport development is about purposive engagement in changing sports participation, behaviour or practice, but it should not be thought of as solely the prerogative of the practitioner.

In order to bring some boundaries to our discussion, the approach adopted here is to say that sport development is purposeful intervention to bring about more extensive, better-quality, more widely accessible sport participation and/or improved

John Lyle (with Thomas Dowens)

standards of performance. This can be sport specific, or multi-sport in focus. Intervention takes place at a number of levels – strategic facilitation, organisation and administration, and delivery – and is present at all levels and stages of participation, development and performance sport.

It would be a valuable first step to offer a catalogue of 'sport development categories' to bear in mind as an initial conceptualisation.

Sport development as the policy-led management of sport provision in the UK

This involves the system-wide facilitation of improved provision, within a set of political and sporting goals. Agencies involved are the Department for Culture, Media and Sport, the Department for Education, UK Sport, Sport England,[1] governing bodies of sport, local authorities, emerging regional sport governance organisations, specialist agencies (e.g. the Youth Sport Trust, sports coach UK) and so on. Issues include the extremely wide set of stakeholders, huge variation in interpretations of meaning and purpose, limited consensus on the interpretation of sport, management by control of the political agenda, and consequent funding. It is doubtful if this can be said to be a truly coherent system.

Sport development as de facto maintenance or improvement in sport participation within established avenues of transmission

This is generally to be found in sports clubs, representative sport and school sport. The continuous dynamic within sport (relative achievement, recruitment, growth, seeking competitive advantage) assumes developmental and progressive characteristics. This category is divided into two subsystems; first, developing and pursuing excellence in performance sport, and, second, the maintenance of activity in multi-level competition-led sport participation.[2] In each case there is inherently a competition for limited resources, and the application, partial or complete, of strategic development planning within sports.

Sport development as initiative-led intervention activity

Nationally directed, locally delivered intervention has characterised much of sport development in recent years (see Positive Futures, Active Schools, School Sport Coordinators, Step into Sport). Such initiatives are generally specifically targeted at non-participants, casual participants or those (primarily school children) who are expected to become non-participants. Social deficit or ethnic disadvantage ideologies influence provision and resources. The preferred transmission medium is partnerships involving local authorities, schools, governing bodies of sport and, increasingly, commercial providers.

Sport development as facility-led local authority provision (leisure centres, swimming pools, education facilities etc.)

The activities promoted, facilitated and scheduled within these facilities are often overlooked as a form of sport development. It is important to look at the development messages about sport participation, often unintended, that can be transmitted by such use. There is significantly more casual and recreational activity, and use by socially advantaged groups, despite inducements to other 'target' groups. Sporting activities are generally dominated by a fairly narrow range of popular sports.

Sport development as a stage of sport participation

Applied in a generic fashion, the term has come to be used for local authority, initiative-led and other grassroots activities that are characterised by their induction and preparatory or awareness motives. Most of this activity does not take place within competition sport structures. It may variously be considered a stage or level in the participation continuum.

Sport development as the consequence of related physical activity

The objectives of sport development (whatever we agree these to be) are often contributed to by other self-contained and other-directed forms of sport-related activity. Into this category can be placed physical education, professional sport, commercial sector fitness clubs and the play sector. Each of these, obviously some more than others, can be said to be contributing to the overall development of sport. Perhaps the most interesting characteristic is that none of these sectors is 'controlled' by those who devise mainstream sport development strategies.

Sport development as a descriptor of trends in the social sciences

Sport sociologists largely focus on the emergence of historical patterns and trends in sport: issues such as 'race', gender, social class, power relationships, commercialisation and globalisation. Such analyses generally deal with the consequences of more significant factors such as education, the family, resource control, transmission of the culture and so on. In addition, their focus is most often the media-dominated,

236

commercialised forms of activity. Sport development practice plays but a small role in such an analysis, and social scientists, when dealing with sport, should be encouraged to be more precise in their terms of reference.

The role of the coach is one that needs to be explored, particularly if the assumption that the coaching process and sport development are synonymous or symbiotic is to have any validity. To do this it is necessary to deal with the issue of definition and recent developments in the conceptual vocabulary about sport coaching. It would be helpful, therefore, if we could match classification systems for sport development and sport coaching. In doing so, the focus is on 'direct intervention/participation' forms of sport development, rather than sports policy or other socio-cultural descriptors of provision.

There is a good deal of debate about the specific definition of coaching (see Lyle, 2011b; Lyle and Cushion, 2010b) but this need not detain us. We should recognise, however, that there is some debate in the coaching literature (Lyle, 2011b) between all-embracing frameworks of coaching roles and more demanding definitions that would enhance a professional exclusivity. Lyle (2002) provides a thorough examination of the concept. In contrast, a recent report (MORI, 2004) used to scope the UK coaching population allowed individuals to classify themselves as coaches. There would appear to be a continuum between any form of leadership that is designed to lead or improve performance and a narrower conceptualisation of coaching in which there are boundary markers around competition, intensity of preparation and completeness of the coaching process.

The United Kingdom Coaching Certificate (UKCC) is a national endorsement process for certification in coach education (www.ukcoachingcertificate.org). The UKCC endorsement criteria (sports coach UK, 2004) conceived of the coaching role in five levels:

1 Assist more qualified coaches, delivering aspects of coaching sessions, normally under direct supervision.
2 Prepare for, deliver and review coaching session(s).
3 Plan, implement, analyse and revise annual coaching programmes.
4 Design, implement and evaluate the process and outcome of long-term/specialist coaching programmes.
5 Generate, direct and manage the implementation of cutting-edge coaching solutions and programmes.

This is a constantly shifting framework and the 'levels' have now been consolidated (for formal coach education) into four levels. This is exemplified in the most recent expression of the framework (see Duffy et al., 2011), based on the work of the European Coaching Council, which conceives of coaching in four domains – coach of beginner (child, junior, adult); coach of participant (child, junior, adult);

coach of talented individual (child, junior, adult); and coach of full-time/high-performance athletes – and in four roles: apprentice coach, coach, senior coach and master coach.

A further development has been the emergence of a coach development model (sports coach UK, 2009a). This conceives of coaching roles based on the sports participants' needs (more of which later). The 'model' allows for a pre-coaching status, before moving into one of four domains: children's coaching, participation coaching, performance development coaching and high-performance coaching. Within each of these domains is a recognition that coaches move through a continuum from novice to master.

It immediately becomes obvious that there are links between sports participants and coaching expertise/role and, as a consequence, that the practitioners within these roles are likely to be contributing differentially within the objectives of sport development. I tend to the belief that 'coaching' does not extend across the levels described, and that different labels are required for teaching, instructing and coaching. However, this does not impact on the basic argument about the match between role and development objective. An alternative is that 'coaching' is delivered by individuals who have different levels of expertise, but also operate within distinctive domains. Thus the sports facilitator, the sports teacher, the multi-skills coach, the sports club coach and the high-performance coach may be more useful role descriptors and framework than a 'level' of coach certification. This conceptualisation has the potential to enhance the compatibility between developed coaching expertise and specific sport development domains. However, this is not a current conceptualisation within the sport coaching policy community. The issue is one of professional boundaries and occupational growth. An all-embracing leadership definition provides a significantly more extensive magnitude of occupational presence but does not establish professional boundaries based on extensive and exclusive expertise.

A COMMON PURPOSE?

'Sport development' is a term that embraces a broad range of initiatives and activities. Figure 10.1 illustrates how the goals that are common to participation-led sport development are complementary to those of sport coaching. Sport coaching can perhaps be best conceptualised in three different forms or domains – participation, development and performance (Lyle, 2002; Lyle, 2011a; Lyle and Cushion, 2010b) – with a recognition that 'elite' sport produces a more limited sector within the latter category. These 'forms' are differentiated by their levels of preparation intensity, performance standards, competition involvement and development objectives, and the scope of the coaching process. The notion that coaching and coach education

238

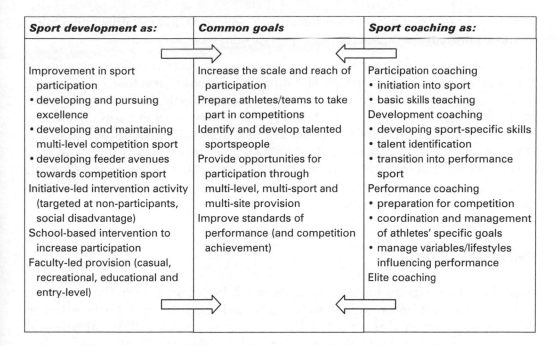

Sport development as:	Common goals	Sport coaching as:
Improvement in sport participation • developing and pursuing excellence • developing and maintaining multi-level competition sport • developing feeder avenues towards competition sport Initiative-led intervention activity (targeted at non-participants, social disadvantage) School-based intervention to increase participation Faculty-led provision (casual, recreational, educational and entry-level)	Increase the scale and reach of participation Prepare athletes/teams to take part in competitions Identify and develop talented sportspeople Provide opportunities for participation through multi-level, multi-sport and multi-site provision Improve standards of performance (and competition achievement)	Participation coaching • initiation into sport • basic skills teaching Development coaching • developing sport-specific skills • talent identification • transition into performance sport Performance coaching • preparation for competition • coordination and management of athletes' specific goals • manage variables/lifestyles influencing performance Elite coaching

Figure 10.1 Common goals between sport development and sport coaching.

must be considered within its domain-specificity was supported by Trudel and Gilbert (2006). Their categorisation of domains into recreational, developmental and elite has a self-evident match between coaching practice and the exigencies of the sporting context.

The *UK Action Plan for Coaching* (sports coach UK, 2006: 4) claims that coaches play a 'vital role in developing and increasing participation in sport, as well as in the attainment of international success'. The document goes on to identify what it terms the key principles and benefits underlying quality coaching:

- welcoming children and adults into sport;
- making sport fun;
- building fundamental skills in participants;
- improving sport-specific skills;
- developing fair play, ethical practice, discipline and respect;
- enhancing physical fitness and positive lifestyle;
- guiding children, players and athletes through the steps to improved performance;
- placing a high value on the development of the whole person; and
- keeping children, players and athletes safe in sport

(adapted from sports coach UK, 2006: 10).

This list of outcomes has a rather humanistic and 'participative' orientation but it would be difficult not to see this as a sport development agenda.

It is tempting to revert to the simplistic view that sports participation almost always involves a form of leadership to give it direction, purpose, structure, cohesion and quality. Such leadership may range from the less technically demanding animateur to the high-intensity coach of professional sportspersons. Sport participation on which development depends is therefore inextricably linked to sport coaching. However, the term 'development' also implies a process of change within a progressive structure. The implication from juxtaposing sport development and coaching is that there are some forms of coaching that are more or less appropriate for different sport development domains.

EMERGING ISSUES

One of the most significant developments in recent years has been the emergence of the multi-sport, multi-skills coach, particularly in primary school-aged sport activity. In so far as these coaches have tended to operate within initiative-led sport development and school-based interventions, their specificity (and, in some ways, non-specificity) of expertise provides an interesting exemplar of the need to match context, expertise and function. The demand for multi-skills, multi-sport coaches has emerged from an incremental insinuation of the Long Term Athlete Development (LTAD) model (Stafford, 2005), with its emphasis on the initial stages of development in which sports practice is less sport specific. This context emphasises variety (Sallis *et al.*, 2000). The principle is also reflected in the work of Côté and colleagues (e.g. Côté and Fraser-Thomas, 2007), who have studied athlete development stages and emphasised the 'early sampling' experiences of individuals who have sustained and extended their participation in sport. The inception of multi-skills academies and clubs was part of the government's all-embracing strategy for young people in sport, the National PE, School Sport and Club Links Strategy (PESSCL, and subsequently PESSYP) (see www.education.gov.uk/ for a historical perspective). The establishment of opportunities such as these has increased deployment flexibility across different sites and groups and provided the catalyst for the further employment of coaches and teachers.

The Sport England strategy document for 2008–2011 (Sport England, 2008) addresses the needs of the 'sport development system'. There is no doubt that coaches and coaching are viewed as a necessary step in achieving its ambitions: 'coaches and coaching play a critical role in the achievement of all three public outcomes – developing talent, improving satisfaction and encouraging participation' (Sport England, 2008: 3). Thus programmes such as the Community Sports Coaching Scheme, Recruit into Coaching and Coaching for Young People are a response to the need to recruit, train and deploy more coaches. We should note,

240

however, that many of the coaches are young people recruited within the school system, and many undertake leadership rather than coaching awards. There is a clear emphasis on the early stages of the athlete development ladder.

The term 'development coach' may seem to imply that it has a more direct relationship with sport development. However, the term applies to a sports domain that is characterised by being in the transition phase between becoming more fully committed to a sport, often recognised as having 'potential', and being prepared and ready to engage in performance sport. It is often considered to be synonymous with age-group sport but may be broader in its coverage than that. Development coaching provides an interesting example of the interplay between development objectives and coaching practice. The range of objectives within the domain may extend from pursuing excellence to retention of participants, and from growing the sport to the personal development of young people. The attainment of these sport development objectives is influenced greatly by sports coaches' practice. This phase is one in which there is considerable emphasis on talent identification and development. A report into talent development practice (sportscotland, 2004) demonstrated that the quality of coaching is a key factor. For example, talent identification and development is dependent on opportunity, provision structures and coaches' selection policies. Coaches who emphasise early specialisation and short-term gains necessary to achieve success at this stage may not be fostering the conditions likely to prepare athletes for subsequent optimal performance and lifelong participation.

The corollary of a complementarity between coaching domains and sport development is that coach education should focus on or emphasise particular competences. Sport coaching education/certification has traditionally neglected the pedagogical, delivery skills, and this may render such coaches less suitable for initiation-level demands in school-based interventions. However, it might be argued that the more episodic, short-horizon participation coaching requires 'direct intervention' or delivery skills, whereas the meta-strategic coordination and planning of the high-level performance coach (Bowes and Jones, 2006; Jones and Wallace, 2005) is redolent of the intensive programmes characteristic of that domain. As a picture gradually emerges of coaching roles with specialised functions and expertise being associated with specific domains, there is also potential for the 'wrong' forms of coaching to be adopted. This is generally thought to describe the deployment of (usually) higher-level sport-specific coaches whose emphasis on technical development and preparation for competition is assumed to be less suitable for the less committed beginner, for whom sport is often a means to achieving other benefits. Indeed, one of the drivers for the coach development model, with its multi-levels and multi-domains, and its relationship to the participant development model was to ensure that coaching education and practice reflected the particular development needs of participant populations.

PERFORMANCE PATHWAYS AND COACHING

In an earlier paper (Lyle, 1997) I pointed to the work of Hardman and Fielden (1994), who dismissed the mass participation–elite sport pyramid and spoke instead of a notional performance ladder. This idea of sport-specific performance ladders is now commonplace in sport development. The focus in provision of sporting opportunities has now moved to the comprehensiveness and appropriateness of the 'ladder of sporting opportunities'. At the level of the individual, the use of the term 'opportunity' implies both a redressing of entry-level exclusion barriers and a richness of provision that addresses variable abilities and motives. At a structural or system level, 'opportunity' implies ensuring that provision and delivery structures are in place to (a) ensure sufficient progression in terms of quantity, (b) provide transition mechanisms that ensure quality, (c) provide an element of 'inclusivity' or 'care' in tracking individuals and (d) develop the high-performance 'shop window' of the sport. It will be obvious that these disparate participant populations form the basis for a participant development model (sports coach UK, 2009b).

Performance pathways can be conceived of as 'stage models' (see Bailey *et al.*, 2011, for a review) or 'structural organisation'. The most significant example of the link between sport development and sport coaching has been the diffusion of the LTAD model (Stafford, 2005) throughout sports provision in the UK, and the extent to which this model has been adopted and incorporated into a governing body of sport policy and planning. The LTAD model is a form of long-term periodisation of an athlete's performance development in sport and appears to owe much to the East European systematic model for the development of high-level sport performance. The model describes the athlete's development as going through six stages: FUNdamentals, Learning to Training, Training to Train, Training to Compete, Training to Win, and Retaining (Stafford, 2005). The model is not without its criticisms (see www.sportdevelopment.info), which are centred on the absence of research support or impact evaluation data, a lack of clarity in the rationale for development (confusion between elite, retention, inclusion and understanding), and perhaps overestimating the potential for an integrated system across sports that eschews early recruitment or specialisation.

There is also a structural element to the performance pathway. This will be evident in each sport's arrangements for transition through school provision, local clubs, national clubs, age-group development squads, national squads and so on. The focus on the 2012 London Olympic and Paralympic Games has sharpened the focus on the development of elite potential. UK Sport has instituted a World Class Performance Programme with three levels: podium (realistic medal-winning capabilities), development and talent (www.uksport.gov.uk/pages/wc-performance-programme/; McDonald, 2011).

242

However, the most relevant issue here is that sport coaching levels or forms have become aligned with LTAD stages, perhaps most evidently in the *UK Action Plan for Coaching* (sports coach UK, 2006). The proposals create an alignment between LTAD stages and levels of coaching, and this is done by the coach's role function rather than coaching domain. The coach's development through the certification levels enables her/him to be most prepared for LTAD progressions. It is worth noting that the LTAD model assumes progression through performance levels, whereas this is not a principle of the UK Coaching Certificate. The language of Balyi's work (Stafford, 2005) has come to dominate the discourse about development, and coaching development has been termed Long Term Coaching Development. These linkages reiterate and emphasise the specificity of sport development and the consequent requirement to ensure that coaches are appropriately educated, trained and deployed to address the needs of each participant population. There is potential for inappropriate deployment. A common perception is that novice coaches are most often deployed with beginners in sport and that there is an over-emphasis on techniques and progression into competition rather than attention to fundamental motor patterns and personal development. At the elite level there are questions over fast-track recruitment into coaching, gender bias and the prioritising of medal winning over performer welfare and ethical probity.

The chapter goes on now to illustrate the relationship between sport development and the coaching environment by examining a case study of the development of Scottish volleyball (Case study 10.1).

CASE STUDY 10.1: SCOTTISH VOLLEYBALL: COACHING AND SPORT DEVELOPMENT

One of the key factors in establishing the success of the coach's endeavours in high-performance sport is the extent to which the coach is able to develop an environment that is supportive. This is a very direct example of the relationship between coaching and sport development. Such an environment is characterised by a pervasive climate of support for excellence in sport, an integrated and coordinated effort by national federations to focus on excellence, a provision and delivery structure designed to identify and develop talented performers, a specific programme for pursuing excellence within the national team framework, and the political and resource support of relevant government agencies.

This part of the chapter chronicles the development of the programme put in place to enhance performance and excellence in a relatively small national governing body (NGB), in the context of what were, at least initially, apparently unsupportive conditions. There is an attempt to identify the principles underpinning the programme. The content is based on the reflections of the National Team Coach, who was instrumental in driving through the required changes.[3] It examines the characteristics of the programme put in place to develop the senior men's national team and the adjustments made by the NGB of the sport to support this. It identifies a catalogue of key issues in support structures and coaching philosophy that will be of value in demonstrating the links between coaching at this level and 'sport development'.

Implementing the National Team Programme (NTP)

Background

In comparative terms, Scottish volleyball has played a modest role in Europe. Traditionally, the national team has occupied a place in the C division of European volleyball. Competition is divided into three divisions, with the A division featuring several of the world's top ten national teams. Although the national team had been established for many years and there is both a national league structure in place and also a significant presence in schools' curricula, it had become clear that progress was limited.

Despite the very considerable efforts of successive national team coaches, and a number of very committed performers, the volunteer status of the programme and the absence of a planned, resourced and concerted approach to developing performance and excellence had severely constrained progress. The introduction of ring-fenced funding from the Sports Lottery Fund, and the resulting initiatives, which enabled support programmes for targeted sports to be developed, provided an opportunity for a rethink in Scottish volleyball.

The challenge

In December 2000 a full-time professional High Performance Coach for Scottish Volleyball was appointed. At the same time, a performance target was established, specifying that the national team should reach the top eight of European B international competition within four years. At that time the Scottish Team was one of the top two sides in the C division and there were approximately sixteen to twenty different countries that could be placed in the B division. It was acknowledged that the target was ambitious and demanding, and would require a paradigm shift in attitude and practice from not only the players and staff in the programme, but all those more widely involved in Scottish volleyball.

Strategy

The first step was to identify the strategic objectives that would lead to improved performance. Three very simple targets were established for the players and the programme, and three targets for the organisation of Scottish volleyball, necessary to support the national team players. The targets set for the National Team Programme were for the players to become physically stronger, an increase in the volume of practice time and an increase in the number of competitive matches at the correct performance level. The Scottish Volleyball contextual targets were to establish stronger links between the NTP and the Division I national league clubs, the adoption of national team performance standards by the Division I clubs for national league play, and the establishment of a 'Team Scotland' concept.

This establishment of organisational/contextual or developmental targets was viewed as an essential element for the progress required. The strongly held belief was that there was little point in using the full-time coaching position to develop the NTP as a pocket of excellence in isolation from the rest of the Scottish game. If it were possible to achieve the desired change in the performance capacity of the team, it would only be with the active help and support of the Scottish Volleyball Association (SVA) and in particular the active participation of the Division I national league clubs. All of the countries that featured in the B and A bands of European play had substantially stronger domestic leagues than the one in Scotland; in fact most countries had professional leagues. This is significant because they provide consistent access to a higher and

John Lyle (with Thomas Dowens)

more intensive level of play, which in turn creates the demand for a higher quality of coaching input, strength and conditioning programmes and so on.

This part of the chapter considers the steps taken to build this supportive framework.

Communication issues

The key to achieving the contextual targets was creating a climate of positive communication between the NTP and Scottish Volleyball in general. The NTP was perceived to be elitist and isolated from the Scottish game by the majority of the coaches, players, members of the Executive Committee and so on who were not immediately involved with it. This lack of communication and consequent understanding could be attributed to the amateur status of the programme, and the lack of time available to the national team coaching staff. Members of the national team staff were in full-time employment, mostly in the education sector, and they were also extensively committed to club-level play. Therefore, there was a limited amount of time and energy available for national team work. This time was inevitably used to develop the players and the competition framework within the NTP. The resources required for an element of 'outreach' to involve the rest of Scottish volleyball in national team activities were simply beyond the capacity of the individuals concerned. The appointment of a full-time coach immediately changed that situation. The increased time resource was immediately deployed to improve all aspects of communication.

Action

A series of papers, reports and newsletters was written and circulated to as wide an audience as possible. The object was to raise awareness of all aspects of the NTP, to help identify the range of people who were involved, and to elicit support for the programme targets. This awareness raising was then supported by a series of one-to-one meetings with every coach of a national league Division I team. There were several purposes attached to the meetings, but in the first instance they were designed to establish a database of information about the personal details of the coaches and the training circumstances of their teams. The meetings were also used to identify areas where the national team coach, and the NTP could help the club teams.

It was evident that the SVA website could prove to be an invaluable resource for transmitting positive images and information about the NTP. A part of the site was devoted to the activities of the national team, and a series of articles entitled iNTouch was established. The iNTouch articles were used to explain and report on national team events, competitions and training camps, and were updated regularly. It was also felt that there was an overwhelming need to have a series of action photographs featuring Scottish players to add to the match reports. This was crucial to overcome the general perception that the Scottish game lagged behind the European version, and that Scottish players were physically disadvantaged. A programme to establish a library of such photographs was undertaken. Each of these initiatives was designed to create a positive image of the NTP, and of Scottish Volleyball.

Changing practice

A number of changes were required in the way that the players and clubs engaged in the game. Targets centred on increasing the volume of practice, increasing the number of matches played at an appropriate level, and the Scottish clubs adopting national team performance standards were viewed as complementary. Without doubt, the key to implementing these changes was enlisting the active support of the Division I club coaches. The dilemma arose from establishing a situation in which there were common standards of performance and a climate of mutual support between clubs and the NTP, yet at the same time acknowledging the uniqueness of each of the participating clubs, and their need to compete against and attempt to beat each other.

There were two clear schools of thought in evidence during National League play. One was orientated towards winning matches in any fashion, without regard to the performance criteria. The other recognised that being able to win matches consistently was dependent on operating to planned and measurable performance standards. This is simply a version of the process/product debate; that is, focus on the outcome (product) or focus on the method by which the outcome has been achieved (process). In reality, of course, both are required. Sustainable and consistent success cannot be achieved if the process is flawed, and therefore the process is crucial. At the same time there must be a product that is deemed worthwhile and is measurable, if the quality of the process is to be established. If the NTP was to benefit from the assistance of the clubs then the contribution of both approaches had to be established and worked towards.

Action

This position was achieved by the establishment of an initiative entitled the First Division Alliance (FDA). A number of projects were undertaken under the banner of the FDA, all of which received the unanimous support of the Division I coaches. The most significant was a series of performance clinics on specific aspects of the game. These were presented by Division I coaches and members of the national team staff recognised as having expertise in that aspect of the game. Topics for the clinics were selected by the national team staff conducting a statistical analysis of Division I club play, and comparing the results with the national team performances and the performances of European competitors in the B division. For many of the coaches involved this was the first set of objective performance criteria to which they had been exposed, and the statistical analyses and subsequent clinics met with enthusiastic support.

The FDA initiative was also fundamental in increasing the amount of practice time to which national team players had access. A regime of daily practice sessions had been established, for which local authority support was provided in the form of free access to specific facilities during the mid-day period when there was less demand on the facilities. However, access was limited in that it was available only to players from a limited geographical catchment, and who had time available mid-day. The FDA coaches agreed that players who were members of the national team squad could attend several different clubs during the week in order to increase the total volume of their practice time. This was a significant step, as none of the clubs involved practised more than three times per week, and most were limited to two nights for financial reasons. The potential problems associated with players moving from one club practice session to another were tackled in several ways: ensuring the highest standards of personal discipline from the players concerned; the national team coach attending club practices to assist the club coach; the sessions being focused on the needs of the club team as a priority; and the alignment of club playing standards to those of the national team over a period of time.

Support from the Scottish Volleyball Association

There were also a number of changes that required the sanction of the SVA itself. One change that was essential for the successful development of the national team performance targets was the active support of the SVA in adapting the national competition structures. One of the principal functions of any NGB is to develop and support the established national competition structures. All of the other functions of the NGB – youth development, officiating, coach education and so on – flow from this basic requirement. In Scotland the national league structures had been in place for a number of years and were well established. However, the standard of performance was significantly lower than the top levels of European play.

Action

Three major changes were introduced as a result of liaison between the NTP and the officers of the Scottish Volleyball Association. The first was to introduce a new competition, which was entitled the Power League. This event was scheduled for dates in the volleyball calendar that had been set aside for development purposes. The format of the competition was a series of single-day tournaments, leading to a final event. The normal rules of the game were applied to all matches. However, points in the Power League championship were awarded both for winning matches and also for achieving certain game points tallies. This encouraged both process and product thinking on the part of the match coaches. The Power League featured all the Division I clubs, but also included a team made up of players from the NTP who were seconded from their clubs for the duration of the event. This had the immediate effect of ensuring that the event was perceived as an essential part of the NTP, but also increased the level of competition by adding another strong team. Each of the national team staff was involved in coaching at the tournaments, and statistical analyses of game play were provided in all matches.

The second major development was to alter the structure of the National League to accommodate a series of play-offs at the end of the season. Traditionally, regular league play on a home and away basis had decided the outcome of the championship. This was changed to require the top four teams at the end of the round robin phase to play each other in a best-of-three match series for first semi-finals, and then the championship final. The best-of-three series had the added pressure of making the teams play matches on consecutive days. The reason for this was to highlight the need for improved match preparation and coaching. This was aided by good coaching practices such as video analysis, statistical analysis and rotational match-ups.

The third development was the introduction of a Player of the Year award. This was essential to encourage more active interest on the part of the players and the media in celebrating the success of the Scottish game and the players who participated in the national league.

In addition to the changes to the structure of the competitions, the SVA Referees Commission provided considerable support to the development of playing standards. It became obvious that increasing the volume and intensity of the competitions for the top players also placed a much higher level of pressure on the match officials and the standards of officiating. The Referees Commission established a programme of structured support and development for a core group of officials who were encouraged to participate in the key events and matches. Attention to enhanced officiating made a considerable contribution to the overall effort.

Summary

It is possible to identify a number of principles in the developments that took place:

- It is necessary to derive strategic performance objectives from the externally imposed performance targets.
- Changes in performance have to be accompanied by changes in supporting structures.
- A sense of ownership of the NTP was essential.
- It is important to establish an ideology of complementarity between process standards and product outcomes.

There were also a number of specific changes in competition and practice, designed to increase the volume and intensity of engagement by the players. Creating a coalition of all Division 1 coaches smoothed the way for many of the changes.

There is no doubt that a measurable shift in attitudes took place. The success of the overall change in attitude towards performance and excellence in the Scottish game is attributable to two main factors: a realignment of the perception of the primary aim of the Scottish Volleyball Association, and an acknowledgement by all of the top coaches in the game of the reality of the performance continuum concept. The primary aim of the Association has to be the development of the playing structures and the standards of performance. The significance of recognising this is that it provides a common purpose for their participation for all those who are involved. It acknowledges and allows for contributions in many different forms, and encourages opportunities for the different inputs to be fused into a coherent effort.

For the purposes of this chapter, the notable message was that the achievement of the coach's objectives was viewed as an issue of sport development. Performance improvements were perceived to be symbiotic with competition structures, common performance models and the recognition of a playing continuum to which all agencies were contributors.

CONCLUSION

Coaches can be thought of as 'service agents'; that is, they are capable (if fully trained and educated) of delivering services in response to specific sport development demands, whether school-based, club, high-performance or local authority programmes, and so on. Coaching is not context free. It may well be argued that it takes on meaning only in its social (and sporting) context, and indeed such a conceptualisation would be helpful in delineating roles, expertise and education. We have seen that a broad and inclusive definition of terms could describe intervention-led sport development as entirely dependent on sports coaches. Although this may have a headline value, it would be more useful to rely on the analysis described in this chapter to gain a much fuller appreciation of the links between them.

There seems little doubt that much of the sport development that is initiative led is focused on early stages of performance development and intended to address outcomes beyond participation itself; is not primarily competition focused; and is delivered by 'coaches' who operate in circumstances in which the fullest expression of the coaching process is not possible nor desirable. In the longer term it may not be helpful in terms of recruitment, education and professional development to conceive of a coherent, integrated continuum of coaching roles. For example, there is evidence to show that coaches operating in higher-level sport differ in their previous performance experience, motives, recruitment and aspirations from those whose role does not extend beyond participation coaching or 'teaching', and that they are generally recruited from within the playing/performing base of a sport

248

(Mallett, 2010). This, however, may not be the case for multi-sport coaches, with consequent implications for recruitment and, perhaps, the quality of delivery.

A number of questions were posed in the introduction, and the analysis within the chapter has provided us with a set of tentative responses. It does seem likely that the social agenda of many sport development initiatives requires a coaching approach that reinforces practices leading to retention, enjoyment and a form of sporting literacy that is transferable between sports. There is little doubt that this form of coaching requires a particular set of coaching skills (Lyle, 2002). However, it also brings with it potential for flexibility and multiple applications that are beneficial in sport development practice. Such a capacity may also present the coach with an increased range of employment possibilities.

Attention to the nature of the experience for the participant raises the issue of the 'quality' of the coaching episode or programme. Useful criteria here may be enjoyment, activity levels, sociability, success, achieving competence and so on. However, there has been little research work in this area. Enjoyment leads to 'coming back' (adherence) for the participation coach and this may be a simple but useful measure of perceived quality. However, it is also worth pointing out that there remains some doubt about the extent to which this form of engagement promotes sufficiently the competence, meaningfulness and commitment necessary for sustained participation. There may be alternative measures of quality related to the adequacy of the content in its sport-specific developmental context. The quality of the experience for the participant is strongly influenced by the quality of the coaching. Although this cannot be associated solely with certification, the evidence from the MORI (2004) report and from questionnaire surveys of coaches in Scotland (Lyle, 2009) confirm that there is a significant proportion of unqualified coaches operating at all levels of provision.

There is strong support for a significant level of domain specificity in coaching practice. A further question, therefore, is centred on the adequacy of coach education for providing levels of expertise that are commensurate with the demands of the context. The analysis suggests that there are quite specific coaching domains and that these describe different roles and functions. Coaching education is currently focused on levels of certification that are insufficiently orientated to these domains. The much-increased attention to participation development models, described earlier in the paper, and a more domain-specific coaching development model offer hope for improved population–domain matching.

The final question is that of professionalisation of coaching. To 'service' fully the complete range of sport development contexts, sport coaching requires a broad inclusive definition and a classification framework that embraces the barely-trained volunteer, the part-timer and the more highly trained, full-time professional coaches. This conceptualisation is too broad and is not conducive to the professionalisation of coaching. The academic development of sport coaching studies has made substantial progress in recent years. However, one of the gaps is the awareness of developmental stages in expertise, and the relationship of these to different roles both horizontally (responsibility within the same level of sport) and vertically (with increasing standards of performance). The breadth and scope of sport development tends to separate the coaching roles. This may be useful for sport development but not necessarily for the professionalisation of coaching and the establishment of a threshold status for entry to the profession.

As the chapter has shown, sport development and sport coaching have a symbiotic relationship. The distinctive forms of sport development and the sporting domains within which they occur create 'service leadership demands' from coaches and these in turn lead to distinctive roles, functions, and levels of expertise and education. It would be a mistake to treat sport coaching as an unproblematic element of sport development. In many ways the success of sport development is dependent on the capacity of the 'coach' and the coaching environment created.

LEARNING ACTIVITY

Identify and describe three sport development initiatives, perhaps school based, organised by a county sport partnership or local authority. Compare and contrast the roles of the 'coaches' or deliverers in these initiatives. Use a framework with criteria such as delivery challenges, particular skills, participant motives, characteristic qualifications and measures of effectiveness. Try to identify the particular features of the initiative that have impacted on the coach's role.

NOTES

1. This is intended to imply similar agencies in other 'home nations'. This principle applies throughout the chapter.

2. This sector is often referred to as the youth and adult club sector and comprises a significant swathe of sports participation in which there is a performance aspiration but whose participants are not part of that sport's 'fast-track' processes. It has often been considered to be a neglected sector (Keech, 2011).

3. The appointment of the National Team Coach was supported by an initiative of sportscotland, through Sports Lottery funding. The author was involved in an impact evaluation of this scheme for sportscotland, and the insights gained at that time, including multiple discussions with the coach himself, are reflected in this part of the chapter. The author acknowledges the contribution of sportscotland and the coach Thomas Dowens to the text.

250

REFERENCES

Adams, A. (2011) 'Sport development and social capital', in Houlihan, B. and Green, M. (eds.), *Routledge Handbook of Sports Development*, London: Routledge.

Bailey, R., Toms, M., Collins, D., Ford, P., MacNamara, Á. and Pearce, G. (2011) 'Models of young player development in sport', in Stafford, I. (ed.), *Coaching Children in Sport*, London: Routledge.

Bowes, I. and Jones, R.J. (2006) 'Working at the edge of chaos: understanding coaching as a complex, interpersonal system', *Sport Psychologist*, 20: 235–245.

Cassidy, T., Jones, R. and Potrac, P. (2004) *Understanding Sports Coaching*, London: Routledge.

Coalter, F. (2007) *A Wider Social Role for Sport: Who's Keeping the Score*, London: Routledge.

Côté, J. and Fraser-Thomas, J. (2007) 'Youth involvement in sport', in Crocker, P. (ed.), *Sport Psychology: A Canadian Perspective*, Toronto: Pearson.

Côté, J., Bruner, M., Erickson, K., Strachan, L. and Fraser-Thomas, J. (2010) 'Athlete development and coaching', in Lyle, J. and Cushion, C. (eds.), *Sports Coaching: Professionalisation and Practice*, Edinburgh: Churchill Livingstone.

Cushion, C., Armour, K.M. and Jones, R.L. (2003) 'Coach education and continuing professional development: experience and learning to coach', *Quest*, 55: 215–230.

Department for Culture, Media and Sport (DCMS) (2002) 'The Coaching Task Force: final report', www.culture.gov.uk/global/publications/archive_2002/sport_coach_task.htm

Department for Culture, Media and Sport (DCMS) (2008) *Playing to Win: A New Era for Sport*, London: DCMS.

Department for Culture, Media and Sport (DCMS) (2012) 'Creating a sporting habit for life: a new youth sport strategy', www.culture.gov.uk/publications/8761.aspx

Department for Culture, Media and Sport (DCMS/DfEE) (2000) *A Sporting Future for All*, London: DCMS/DfEE.

Department for Culture, Media and Sport (DCMS)/Strategy Unit (2002) *Game Plan: A Strategy for Delivering Government's Sport and Physical Activity Objectives*, London: DCMS/Strategy Unit.

Duffy, P., Hartley, H., Bales, J., Crespo, M., Dick, F., Vardhan, D., Nordmann, L. and Curado, J. (2011) 'Sport coaching as a "profession": challenges and future directions', *International Journal of Coaching Science*, 5 (2): 93–123.

Gilbert, W.D., Côté, J. and Mallett, C. (2006) 'Developmental paths and activities of successful sports coaches', *International Journal of Sport Sciences and Coaching*, 1: 69–76.

Hardman, K. and Fielden, C. (1994) 'The development of sporting excellence: lessons from the past', in Duffy, P. and Dugdale, L. (eds.), *HPER: Moving towards the 21st Century*, Champaign, IL: Human Kinetics.

Houlihan, B. and Green, M. (2011) *Routledge Handbook of Sports Development*, London: Routledge.

Hylton, K., and Bramham, P. (eds.) (2008) *Sports Development: Policy, Process and Practice*, London: Routledge.

Jones, R.L. and Wallace, M. (2005) 'Another bad day at the training ground: coping with ambiguity in the coaching context', *Sport, Education & Society*, 10: 119–134.

Jones, R.L. and Wallace, M. (2006) 'The coach as "orchestrator"', in Jones, R.L. (ed.), *The Sports Coach as Educator: Re-conceptualising Sports Coaching*, London: Routledge.

Keech, M. (2011) 'Sport and adult mass participation in England', in Houlihan, B. and Green, M. (eds.), *Routledge Handbook of Sports Development*, London: Routledge.

Lyle, J. (1997) 'Managing excellence in sports performance', *Career Development International*, 2 (7): 314–323.

Lyle, J. (2002) *Sports Coaching Concepts: A Framework for Coaches' Behaviour*, London: Routledge.

Lyle, J. (2004) 'Ships that pass in the night: an examination of the assumed symbiosis between sport-for-all and elite sport', in *Innovation in Cooperation*: *Proceedings of the 12th EASM European Sport Management Congress*, Ghent, Belgium: Publicatiefond voor Lichamelijke Opvoeding.

Lyle, J. (2009) 'Coaching in Scotland: a snapshot', paper presented at the ICCE Global Coaching Conference, Vancouver, Canada, November.

Lyle, J. (2011a) 'Sports development, sports coaching and domain specificity', in Houlihan, B. and Green, M. (eds.), *Routledge Handbook of Sports Development*, London: Routledge.

Lyle, J. (2011b) 'What is coaching and what is a coach?', in Stafford, I. (ed.), *Coaching Children in Sport*, London: Routledge.

Lyle, J. and Cushion, C. (eds.) (2010a) *Sports Coaching: Professionalisation and Practice*, Edinburgh: Churchill Livingstone.

Lyle, J. and Cushion, C. (2010b) 'Narrowing the field: some key questions about sport coaching', in Lyle, J. and Cushion, C. (eds.), *Sports Coaching: Professionalisation and Practice*, Edinburgh: Churchill Livingstone.

McDonald, I. (2011) 'High-performance sport policy in the UK: an outline and critique', in Houlihan, B. and Green, M. (eds.), *Routledge Handbook of Sports Development*, London: Routledge.

Mallett, C. (2010) 'Becoming a high-performance coach: pathways and communities', in Lyle, J. and Cushion, C. (eds.), *Sports Coaching: Professionalisation and Practice*, Edinburgh: Churchill Livingstone.

Martindale, R.J.J., Collins, D. and Daubney, J. (2005) 'Talent development: a guide for practice and research within sport', *Quest*, 57: 353–375.

MORI (2004) *Sports Coaching in the UK*, Leeds: sports coach UK.

North, J. (2009) *The UK Coaching Workforce*, Leeds: sport coach UK.

Phillpots, L. (2011) 'Sports development and young people in England', in Houlihan, B. and Green, M. (eds.), *Routledge Handbook of Sports Development*, London: Routledge.

Sallis, J.F., Prochaska, J.J. and Taylor, W.C. (2000) 'A review of correlates of physical activity of children and adolescents', *Medical Science of Sports and Exercise*, 32 (5): 963–975.

Sport England (2008) *Sport England Strategy 2008–2011*, London: Sport England.

sports coach UK (2004) 'UKCC endorsement criteria (Levels 1–3)', Paper 18, NCF, Leeds.

sports coach UK (2006) *UK Action Plan for Coaching. Consultation Draft: June 2006*, Leeds: sports coach UK.

sports coach UK (2008) *The UK Coaching Framework*, Leeds: Coachwise.

sports coach UK (2009a) 'Coach development model user guide', www.sportscoachuk.org/resource/coach-development-model-user-guide

sports coach UK (2009b) 'Participant development model user guide', www.sportscoachuk.org/resource/participant-development-model-user-guide

sportscotland (2004) *Talent Identification and Development: An Academic Review*, Edinburgh: sportscotland.

Stafford, I. (2005) *Coaching for Long Term Athlete Development: To Improve Participation and Performance in Sport*, Leeds: Coachwise.

Taylor, B. and Garratt, D. (2010) 'The professionalisation of sports coaching: definitions, challenges and critique', in Lyle, J. and Cushion, C. (eds.), *Sports Coaching: Professionalisation and Practice*, Edinburgh: Churchill Livingstone.

Trudel, P. and Gilbert, W. (2006) 'Coaching and coach education', in Kirk, D., O'Sullivan, M. and McDonald, D. (eds.), *Handbook of Research in Physical Education*, London: Sage.

CHAPTER 11

DISABILITY AND SPORT DEVELOPMENT

HAYLEY FITZGERALD

There are an estimated 650 million disabled people worldwide, approximately 10 per cent of the population.[1] Some people are born disabled whereas others acquire a disability at some point during their life (perhaps as a result of an accident or illness). In the UK the proportion of disabled people increases through the life cycle (Office for National Statistics, 2008). In recent years medical and techno-logical advancements have significantly improved the life expectancy of disabled people. However, it is worth noting that there are considerable disparities regard-ing the prospects and life chances of disabled people living in Western and Third World countries (Eide and Ingstad, 2011; Filmer, 2005). I believe these key facts are important to everyone in society and worth reflecting upon, so, if your first thoughts are that disability is irrelevant to you, I would encourage you to think again. For example, from a personal perspective it is likely that as you grow older you, your family or friends will be touched in some way by disability. As a result, disability may be something you, or the people around you, will have to adjust to living with. From a professional perspective, if you pursue a career in sport development you will work with many different kinds of people, including some disabled people. Indeed, in an era of inclusion it is expected that sport development practitioners will have the skills and commitment to adapt and rethink their practices in order to support disabled people in activities and programmes (Thomas and Smith, 2009).

Although contemporary expectations of sport practitioners towards working with disabled people have improved considerably, it should be recognised that this has not always been the case, as Guttmann explains:

> Unfortunately, society has failed so far to keep in step with the develop-ment of sport for the disabled . . . Although there has been an awakening of the needs of the disabled in recent years, there is still much to be desired.
>
> (Guttmann, 1976: 179)

Sir Ludwig Guttman is considered by many to be the founding father of disability sport through his pioneering work with people with spinal cord injuries (Brittain, 2010). Nearly thirty years ago he claimed that society was failing to adequately address and support sporting opportunities for disabled people. More broadly, during this time it was also recognised that disabled people were largely marginalised from society and often perceived as having no meaningful purpose in life (Hunt, 1966; Miller and Gwynne, 1972). This chapter will consider issues concerning disability and sport development and, in doing so, explore the extent to which contemporary society has been able to 'keep in step' with sport for disabled people. First of all, consideration is given to the notion of disability, a term often taken for granted but not fully understood. Disability is a contested concept and I provide an overview of two key models used to explain disability. For both of these models I also outline the implications they have for sport development practitioners. I then offer an overview of the structures and policies supporting sport for disabled people. I discuss the shift from a therapeutic rationale for provision to a targeted and mainstream focus. After doing this I provide three illustrative examples of how a number of organisations are attempting to work towards policy developments in disability sport. This chapter then considers the key challenges and barriers that disabled people experience when participating in sport. It is important that sport development practitioners are aware of these challenges in order that they can reflect on these issues when developing and initiating activities and programmes. The chapter ends by discussing the utility of taking a vantage point of disability to reconsider the inclusive and exclusionary practices of sport.

UNDERSTANDING DISABILITY WITHIN SOCIETY AND SPORT

Historically, disability has been understood in a number of ways, reflecting different social, cultural and political norms within society (Barnes *et al.*, 1999). In general terms, the notion of disability is used to signify impairment, activity limitation or participation restriction (World Health Organization, 2002). Definitions and understandings of disability often vary according to the organisational context and the purpose for which information is being collected (Purdam *et al.*, 2008). Although there are varied definitions and understandings of disability, two key models dominate; these are known as the 'medical model' and the 'social model' of disability. Both models continue to influence how disability is understood within society and each model has different implications for the way disabled people are positioned and perceived within sport.

254

Medical model of disability

Until recently, disability has been seen as a naturalistic form, defined and legitimised within medical terms. This medical model of disability was driven by a desire to diagnose and treat disabled people. Medical specialists sought to help disabled people fit in with 'normal' life (Barnes *et al.*, 1999). The medical influence on disabled people also provided the catalyst for other professionals to make judgements about their lives in relation to education, work and welfare. From the medical perspective, the disabled person is deemed to be deficient in some way and this limitation is considered the cause of his/her disability. Individuals are usually defined according to their physical (e.g. paralysis), learning (e.g. Down's syndrome) or sensory (e.g. visual or hearing) impairments. These kinds of labels often lead to negative views of disabled people; such individuals come to be regarded as unfortunate, useless, different and sick (Hunt, 1966). Consequently, under this model disabled people are often judged by what they cannot do, rather than what they can (Barnes and Mercer, 2003). Applying the medical model to delivering sport opportunities would first and foremost focus on the disabled person and his/her specific physical, learning or sensory limitations. These impairments would be deemed as restricting the disabled person from engaging in sport in the same manner as others around her/him. For example, not being able to perform a specific sport skill would be seen as a consequence of the individual's impairment limitation. Therefore, the inability to perform in the same way as non-disabled people is considered to be a problem with the disabled individual.

Social model of disability

In contrast to the medical model of disability, an alternative view has emerged that challenges its emphasis on personal tragedy. Disabled people developed the social model of disability to challenge the idea that disability is an individual problem that requires a cure. Instead, the social model supports the view that disability is an artificial and exclusionary social construction that penalises people with impairments; in Finkelstein's terms, disability is a form of social oppression (Finkelstein, 2001). Advocates of the social model draw a distinction between impairments and health conditions, and disability. As Barnes explains:

> Impairment is the functional limitation within the individual caused by physical, mental or sensory impairment. Disability is the loss or limitation of opportunities to take part in the normal life of the community on an equal level with others due to physical and social barriers.
>
> (Barnes, 1991: 2)

Supporters of the social model believe that people with impairments are disabled by a society that is not organised in ways that take account of their needs (Oliver, 1996, 2004). From a social model perspective, inaccessible buildings, the lack of accessible information, prejudicial attitudes and the lack of opportunities in sport are not problems located with the person with the impairment, but rather should be seen as forms of discrimination found within society. Applying the social model to delivering sport opportunities would focus on the ways in which sport assumes a non-disabled norm in its structure, organisation and delivery. It is this non-disabled norm that penalises and disadvantages disabled people participating in sport. For example, not being able to perform a specific sport skill would be seen as a limitation of the sport, or failure of the sport development practitioner to be flexible and account for the needs of disabled people. Using a social model approach to plan and deliver opportunities in sport would entail initially focusing on the environment, the nature of the resources and equipment available and possibilities of diverse activity options. Importantly, attention would not primarily be on the impairment of a disabled person. Adjustments, modifications or changes to activities might then be made for specific individuals or groups of people (including non-disabled participants).

The distinctive characteristics of the medical and social models of disability are illustrated in Table 11.1.

Although both models of disability remain useful tools for planning and developing sport opportunities, it should be recognised that they have limitations (see Goodley, 2011; Shakespeare, 2006). Indeed, Marks (1999: 611) suggests that 'Individual [medical] and social models of disability represent two sides of the same coin'. What Marks is suggesting here is that, by pathologising the body (the medical model) and focusing on structural issues (the social model), both models are implicated in failing to consider the individual beyond these restricted understandings. More recently, it has also been argued that focusing on a person's disability does not enable other important aspects of identity such as gender, ethnicity and social class to be sufficiently acknowledged and accounted for (Björnsdóttir and Traustadóttir, 2010; Connor, 2008). The way(s) in which disability is understood continue(s) to influence the organisation of sport for disabled people and associated policy developments. The next section outlines how many of the characteristics of the social model found in Table 11.1 are featured in contemporary organisational and policy developments focusing on disabled people and sport.

ORGANISATIONS AND POLICY SUPPORTING SPORT FOR DISABLED PEOPLE

Internationally within a sporting context, there is growing recognition that disabled people have a 'right' to sport. The United Nations Convention on the Rights

Table 11.1 Characteristics of medical and social models of disability

Medical model of disability	Social model of disability
Individual is seen as faulty	Individual is valued
Diagnosis of impairment defines the individual	Strengths are defined by individual and recognised by others
Medicalised assessment, monitoring and programmes are prioritised	Resources used to promote use of inclusive/ mainstream services and opportunities
Segregated and alternative services and opportunities developed	Training and professional development initiated to support inclusion
Normality strived for	Diversity welcomed
Society remains unchanged and assumes a non-disabled norm	Society evolves and positively recognises difference

of Persons with Disabilities (United Nations, 2006) explicitly expresses this, as do a number of international sporting organisations (International Council for Sport Science and Physical Education, 2003; International Disability in Sport Working Group, 2007). Beyond a sporting context, the rights of disabled people have also been acknowledged in recent anti-discrimination legislation (for example, the Equality Act 2010; see Government Equalities Office, 2010). The recognition of such rights continues to influence how sporting organisations plan and provide for disabled people. Within the UK, contemporary sport policy, particularly that relating to disability and sport, is initiated or implemented through a range of sport organisations. At a national level, these organisations include the home sports councils (such as Sport Northern Ireland and sportscotland), national governing bodies (NGBs) of sport and national disability sport organisations (NDSOs) (such as the English Federation of Disability Sport and Disability Sport Wales). These national bodies coordinate policy and strategic direction. Regional and local disability sport organisations (DSOs) affiliated to these organisations will often work towards national policies and priorities. Figure 11.1 illustrates the range of organisations involved in policy formation and the delivery of sport for disabled people.

Figure 11.1 reflects a contemporary approach to sport policy and provision for disabled people that supports a mainstreaming and inclusive approach. However, provision prior to the early 1990s was underpinned by a targeted approach that emphasised the need for different groups, particularly disabled people, to be supported in sport through separate provisions and opportunities. This provision was segregated and facilitated by rehabilitative organisations, residential institutions and other community-related organisations that promoted broader leisure interests (DePauw and Gavron, 2005). During this time it has been suggested that the then Sports Council (which had a UK remit) had limited interest in supporting disabled people in sport. In 1989, a review group established by the UK Minister for Sport

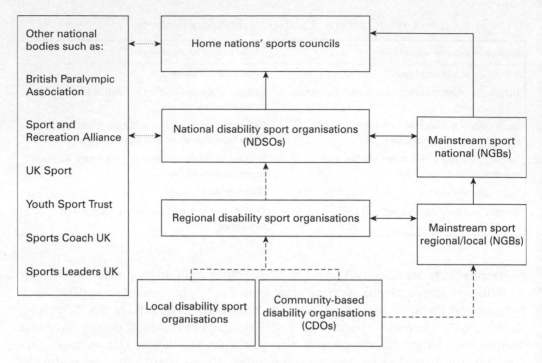

Figure 11.1 Organisations involved in developing and delivering sport for disabled people (adapted from Fitzgerald and Bass, 2007).

initiated the shift in sports policy towards a mainstream approach to sports provision for disabled people. The review group recommended that the Sports Council take action 'to ensure that the needs of disabled people are taken into account in all of its activities' (Minister for Sport's Review Group, 1989: 17). In 1993, the Sports Council (1993) published *People with Disabilities and Sport: Policy and Current Planned Action*, which outlined the change in policy direction towards mainstreaming. A key part of this policy was to move responsibility for the provision of sport opportunities for disabled people from NDSOs and DSOs to NGBs (Thomas and Smith, 2009).

Each home nation sports council has responded in a different way to the drive towards the mainstreaming and inclusion of disabled people in sport. For example, in 2006 Sport Northern Ireland initiated the *Disability Mainstreaming Policy*. This policy encourages organisations to work towards the goal of mainstreaming while at the same time it recognises that in some instances a 'twin-track' approach, which includes parallel provision, may be more appropriate. The policy aims are to ensure that people with disabilities:

Hayley Fitzgerald

- Are able to access and participate fully in the provision of facilities, goods, services and employment opportunities in sport and physical activity in Northern Ireland,
- Including young people and groups representative of those particularly vulnerable to exclusion, are fully and appropriately consulted by Sport Northern Ireland in future policy and programme development,
- Influence and inform future Sport Northern Ireland policy and programme development,
- Identify and implement positive action initiatives based on consultation and identified needs.

(Sport Northern Ireland, 2005: 1)

Responsibility for supporting the implementation of this policy was awarded to Disability Sports Northern Ireland. Disability Sports Northern Ireland developed its own *Policy Agenda 2006–2009* (Disability Sports Northern Ireland, 2006), which sought to review the provision of sport and physical activity opportunities for people with disabilities in Northern Ireland and made recommendations to various government agencies and sports organisations. The strategy for sport in Northern Ireland, *Sport Matters: A culture of lifelong enjoyment and success in sport* (Department of Culture, Arts and Leisure/Sport Northern Ireland, 2009), was developed in 2009. This strategy outlines targets around 'participation', 'performance' and 'places', and states that, 'by 2019, physically active lifestyles will be the "norm," regardless of age, gender, disability, ethnic or social background. The value of sport and physical recreation in contributing to improved health and community cohesion will be understood, accepted and supported' (Department of Culture, Arts and Leisure/Sport Northern Ireland, 2009: 26). These developments in Northern Ireland demonstrate how a national sports council and NDSO are both working to support disabled people in sport. As a result of these kinds of policy developments in each home nation, the contemporary complexion of sport for disabled people reflects support for provision through mainstream organisations and dedicated disability sport organisations. The sport development pathway for disabled people uniquely reflects this dual, or 'twin-track', purpose and is discussed next.

PARTICIPATION PATHWAYS IN SPORT FOR DISABLED PEOPLE

Like non-disabled people, disabled people have a range of motives and aspirations for participating in sport. Some disabled people may always be located in the same place on a participation pathway. For example, they may be interested in recreational level sport and motivated by social or health reasons. For other disabled people, the participation pathway can provide a structure that enables progression through different levels in sport. These disabled people may be more interested in competitive success and in this way strive to progress along their sport's participation pathway in order to reach a high level of performance. It is important to remember that motives for participation in sport will change over time and can shift from elite competition to one that focuses more on recreational interests. This means disabled and non-disabled people enter and leave participation pathways at different points and for various reasons. Within a participation pathway, disabled people have a range of participation opportunities; they may participate in:

- multi-activity – a variety of different sports (sometimes these opportunities are offered in clubs with a broader remit than just sport, e.g. Gateway Clubs, PHAB Clubs, youth clubs, Royal National Institute of Blind People clubs);
- mainstream sport – traditionally played by non-disabled people;
- mainstream clubs/teams/competitions;
- disability sport – played by disabled people as either an adapted version of mainstream sports (e.g. wheelchair basketball, blind football, and table cricket) or sports specifically developed for disabled people (e.g. boccia, goalball);
- disability sport clubs/teams/competitions.

As Figure 11.2 illustrates, disabled people can work towards different levels of participation and this may involve movement between mainstream and disability sport clubs, competitions and teams. For example, a disabled table tennis high performer could train with a local mainstream club and also play in their team. This person may also play in regional and national disability sport (table tennis) competitions.

These different levels and contexts of participation may initially seem confusing. However, utilising a social model approach could enable a practitioner to recognise and value individual choices. As part of this process it is important to discuss with disabled people their goals and preferences and the ways in which the player pathway can best facilitate these aspirations. The next section highlights a number of organisations and how they are working to support disabled people to participate in sport.

DISABILITY SPORT IN ACTION

The three case studies below (Case studies 11.1–11.3) illustrate disability sport in action. They include a number of organisations featured in Figure 11.1. Each case study also reflects the different contexts and levels of participation outlined in Figure 11.2.

260

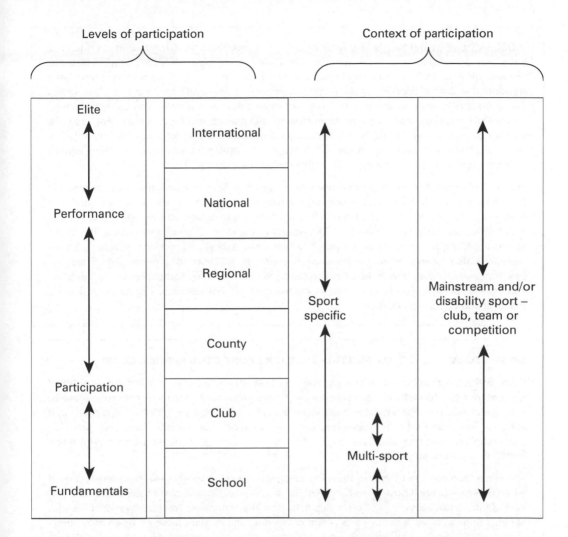

Figure 11.2 Player pathway.

CASE STUDY 11.1: NATIONAL MAINSTREAM GOVERNING BODY (THE SCOTTISH FOOTBALL ASSOCIATION)

Mainstream NGBs of sport are well positioned to promote sport for disabled people. They can support the development of strategic policy focusing on disability, establish player pathways, initiate programmes, offer support for elite athletes and develop coach education that addresses disability and inclusion.

Prior to 2005 the Scottish Football Association (SFA) was involved in a number of ad hoc disability football projects. In 2005, the SFA became the first Scottish governing body of sport to employ a dedicated disability officer. This post was created in partnership with Scottish Disability Sport

(SDS), McDonald's and Sports Match. Since 2005, at a grassroots level, footballing opportunities have been widened through the development of a number of programmes including fun festivals, the Schools Football Programme and Disability Soccer Centres. Competitive pathways have been developed and these support regular playing opportunities in leagues and at a club level. Teams can contest SDS National championships (five, seven and eleven a side). Throughout Scotland a range of football partnerships have been created with mainstream football clubs. For example, Lothian Special Olympics and Hibernian Community Foundation formed 'Lothian Hibernian', a team for players with learning disabilities. Through this partnership Hibernian Academy players conduct regular coaching sessions with Lothian Hibernian players.

International opportunities have also been expanded and Scotland now has a Scottish squad for cerebral palsy (CP) and under-nineteen learning disability. These teams play in world and European championships, home nations tournaments and international friendlies. Recently, the SFA hosted the European CP Football Championships and the Scottish team came fifth in the tournament. National squad training provides high-level tactical and technical coaching. Squad members also receive individual training programmes. In 2006, to support player pathway developments for people with disabilities the SFA set up a 'Coaching Footballers with a Disability' course. This six-hour course is offered to experienced and novice football coaches. It includes practical and workshop activities.

CASE STUDY 11.2: LOCAL MULTI-DISABILITY SPORT CLUB (FIRHILL CLUB)

Each disabled person has different aspirations, motivations and interests in sport. Some disabled people strive to achieve Paralympic success and others will be content to participate recreationally. A range of sporting opportunities need to be available that cater for different aspirations and abilities. For people who participate recreationally in sport, the benefits may focus more on socialising and meeting other people. These are key outcomes of sport and are particularly important for disabled people.

The Firhill Club was established in 1990. The catalyst for its development was the interest created when Glasgow Council hosted the European Special Games. Several of the founder members of Firhill Club remain actively involved in club activities. The club meets forty-five weeks of the year at Firhill Sports Centre, a multi-sports centre with indoor and outdoor facilities. Between seventy-five and 100 members attend each week and take part in a range of different sports including football, netball, badminton, table tennis and power lifting. The club caters predominantly for adults with learning disabilities and also includes some people experiencing behavioural problems and autism. Emphasis is placed on recreational participation, having fun and making a regular commitment to take part in sport. Less stress is placed on competitive sport and this means members do not feel pressured to perform only to win or be the best. Friends and family are encouraged to join in the various club activities. The club has been self-funded from the outset with members paying a subscription and an attendance fee. Eighty per cent of Firhill members travel by themselves using public transport; this supports independence and raises self-confidence. The majority of members travel five or six miles but there are some members travelling up to twenty miles to attend the club. The local authority provides minibus transport for the remaining 20 per cent of the Firhill members. Although the club ethos focuses on recreational participation in sport, pathways for more talented and ambitious athletes are well signposted and over the years several Firhill members have gone on to performance-level disability sport through national and international Special Olympics events.

262

Some people with disabilities enjoy participating in a range of sports and others have an interest in one sport. Sport-specific opportunities can be provided in mainstream clubs or dedicated disability sport settings. Establishing links between both types of provision enables disabled people to be supported by coaches with mainstream and disability sport expertise.

Red Star Athletic was founded in 1990 and meets the needs of athletes with disabilities within the Glasgow area. The club was established by a keen athlete, and qualified coach, working at a day centre for people with disabilities. A request was made by one of the attendees for a running club and Red Star Athletic was formed. Red Star Athletic is a self-funded voluntary sports club and has over fifty members, forty of whom are regular participants. The club meets twice a week throughout the year at East End Healthy Living Centre in Glasgow. Athletes participate in a number of disciplines including track, throws, jumps and wheelchair racing. The athletes are not differentiated by their disability and all train together for each event. Within training sessions, coaches are flexible to the needs of individual athletes and work to promote a fun ethos in order to improve athletic ability. The Red Star Athletic share track time with Shettleston Harriers (a mainstream athletics club). There is a reciprocal relationship between the clubs enabling some Red Star athletes to be included in Shettleston Harriers' training sessions. This means some Red Star athletes join Shettleston Harriers for occasional training sessions that are focused on a technique or skill relating to a specific discipline. At other times, Red Star athletes train on consecutive weeks with Shettleston Harriers. Pathways to elite athletics are signposted and many Red Star athletes have represented Scotland in World Championships, Paralympics, learning disability events and the National Special Olympics. For example, two members recently competed in the International Sports Federation for Persons with Intellectual Disability World Championships, and twenty-five competed in the Special Olympics 2009. Currently, two athletes are working towards selection for the Commonwealth Games. Three athletes have successfully competed at a national level in badminton, football and power lifting. One club member has gone on to undertake a university degree and master's and now works in sport development.

Each of these brief case studies provides an insight regarding how sports organisations are attempting to work towards the inclusion of disabled people in their programmes and activities. Although there are many positive developments such as these, it should be recognised that a range of enduring challenges continue to impact on the sports participation of disabled people. These are discussed next.

CHALLENGES TO PARTICIPATION IN SPORT BY DISABLED PEOPLE

As indicated at the beginning of this chapter, the prospects and life chances of disabled people have improved considerably in recent years. Even though this is the case, it is important to note that disabled people continue to experience inequalities in many different aspects of life, including education, employment, transport and health (Burchardt, 2003; Equality Commission for Northern Ireland, 2003; Fevre *et al.*, 2008; Lewis *et al.*, 2006). Disabled people experience a range of specific challenges when participating in sport; these include attitudinal, physical, structural, opportunity, support and representation barriers.

Attitudinal

Attitudinal barriers to participation in sport can include the attitudes of people in society towards disabled people or the attitudes of disabled people themselves. Research conducted by French and Hainsworth (2001) and Moran and Block (2010) found that stereotypical and negative attitudes of other people can influence the sport participation of disabled people. These attitudes include:

- parental and coach attitudes that assume young disabled people will have negative sporting experiences because of the risk of injury, lack of success, or being teased by peers (Anderson, 2009; Martin and Choi, 2009; Moran and Block, 2010);
- facility staff discouraging disabled people from accessing or participating in sport (French and Hainsworth, 2001; Sport England, 2001);
- sports facility users believing that disabled people should access separate facilities or programmes (French and Hainsworth, 2001);
- coaches/sport development practitioners believing that participants with a disability will be hurt and that the child's parents will take legal action (Moran and Block, 2010);
- coaches'/sport development practitioners' concerns that adapted equipment (e.g. walkers or artificial arms) will injure other players (Moran and Block, 2010);
- practitioners believing disabled people will be less motivated, skilled and competent in sport than non-disabled people (Beyer *et al.*, 2008; Brittain, 2004a).

For disabled people, a lack of confidence and self-esteem in relation to sport may also influence their attitude towards sport participation. This may be an outcome of a number of factors including:

- negative PE or sporting experiences as a young person (Brittain, 2004a,b; Goodwin and Watkinson, 2000);
- perceptions of sporting inferiority and feeling different (Anderson, 2009; Fitzgerald, 2005; Fitzgerald and Kirk, 2009);
- a change of circumstances relating to disability, including acquiring a disability (Smith and Sparkes, 2005, 2008).

264

Physical, structural and opportunity

Physical, structural and opportunity barriers are those barriers that prevent participation in sport for reasons that are not directly associated with a disabled person. These include:

- inaccessible facilities (English Federation of Disability Sport, 2010; Independent Research Solutions, 2003; Rolfe *et al.*, 2009);
- lack of information (Sport England, 2002);
- lack of programmes accessible to disabled people (Independent Research Solutions, 2003; Moran and Block, 2010);
- problems with transport (Beart *et al.*, 2001; Disability Rights Commission, 2002; French and Hainsworth, 2001; Independent Research Solutions, 2003; Macbeth, 2009; Stride, 2009);
- financial and time constraints (Sport England, 2001, 2002; Stride, 2009).

From a social model perspective, such physical, structural and opportunity barriers to participation in sport are examples of the ways in which society contributes to exclusionary practices that result in the lack of participation by disabled people.

Support

Murray (2006) and Buttimer and Tierney (2005) found that the lack of engagement in exercise or sport by disabled people could be attributed to insufficient support. Murray (2006) suggests support may be required to:

- establish what kind of sporting opportunities are available in a local area;
- access transport to and from sports venues;
- communicate with sports staff;
- provide financial support to buy sports equipment or pay membership/facility fees;
- provide a source of motivation for ongoing participation in sport.

This kind of support can come in many forms and may be needed before or while sport is undertaken. Research has demonstrated that family and friends can be key sources of moral support and assistance for sport participation by disabled people (Fitzgerald, 2005; Fitzgerald and Kirk, 2009; Murray, 2002). It has also been noted that during periods of transition, for example leaving school/college, more support is needed (Sport England, 2001). It has long been recognised that this is a testing time for people's commitment to participate; it should not be difficult to appreciate that it might be particularly hard for disabled people to maintain participation.

Representation

The print media has been accused of under-representing and misrepresenting images of disability (Swain *et al.*, 2005). Analysing images of disability in fifty-nine key PE texts, Hardin and Hardin (2004) found that, of the 2,455 images, only fourteen included a disabled person. Of these fourteen images, a high proportion (ten) depicted disabled people receiving assistance or help, and no images included disabled people in leadership roles. A similar absence has been recorded of disabled female athletes in women's sports and disability sport magazines (Hardin and Hardin, 2005; Hargreaves and Hardin, 2009). At an elite level, disabled athletes receive less media attention than non-disabled elite athletes. A number of studies have focused on the Paralympics and found limited newspaper coverage of athletes, events and results (Schantz and Gilbert, 2001). In two UK studies, Thomas and Smith (2003, 2005) found that the media often use medical terminology to describe Paralympians and their performances. More recently, Howe (2009) conducted ethnographic research exploring the culture of print media production by focusing on the 'community' of the newsroom at the Paralympic Games. This study found that, unlike coverage of mainstream sport, responsibility for covering the Paralympics favourably is given to journalists.

Hardin and Hardin (2003) argue that the limited media exposure of disabled athletes can result in these athletes believing they do not deserve to be respected as athletes in the same way as non-disabled athletes. In addition, the few athletes with disabilities who do gain media attention may be labelled 'super crips': 'Publishers love "super crip" stories – those that frame individuals with disabilities as "overcoming" their handicap' (Hardin and Hardin, 2003: 247). This can lead to resentment by people with disabilities who are attempting to lead 'normal' lives. Berger (2008) criticises this kind of positioning, concluding in his research that disabled people may, at different times, be both empowered and disempowered through their experiences and representations in sport.

CONCLUDING REMARKS

A combination of developments associated with legislation, policy and social model thinking have served as a catalyst for promoting a more inclusive society and sports community (Rioux, 2011). For the sporting profession, it is no longer acceptable to marginalise and ignore disabled people. Indeed, sport is working in positive ways to support disabled people; we now publicly celebrate Paralympic and other international disability sport successes. Increasingly, sports clubs engage in professional development around inclusion, and player pathways continue to evolve that support disabled people at all levels of participation. Although these developments are positive, I would agree with the sentiments of Guttmann (1976:

Hayley Fitzgerald

179), highlighted at the beginning of this chapter, that 'there is still much to be desired'. For example, there continues to be disparities in patterns of sports participation between disabled and non-disabled people. Moreover, disabled people are under-represented in key coaching, teaching and management roles in (disability) sport. The ongoing challenge for the world of sport is to continue to reconsider itself: how does sport perpetuate these inequalities and how can sport be a driver for positive change?

DePauw (1997) argues that one way sport can reconsider itself is to centralise discussions around disability. She believes: 'The lens of disability allows us to make problematic the socially constructed nature of sport and once we have done so, opens us to alternative constructions, and solutions' (DePauw, 1997: 428). That is, drawing on understandings of disability can offer a sport development practitioner an alternative vantage point to think about and reflect on the constitution and practices of sport. From this perspective, a practitioner may reflect upon a recently delivered activity session and consider the extent to which disabled participants were included or excluded. Similarly, practitioners could reflect upon plans relating to new initiatives, programmes, facility developments or policy. Here, questions could be asked regarding the assumptions made about the nature of these plans and the implications for the inclusion of disabled participants. For example, how would such plans marginalise, stereotype or enable disabled people? Through these reflections, practitioners are likely to develop an increased awareness of the non-disabled normalised assumptions dominating sporting practices (Barton, 1993, 2009). More importantly, they will be better equipped to work towards the alternatives and solutions advocated by DePauw. Of course, such solutions will help many people, not just disabled people, to have rewarding and enjoyable sporting experiences.

LEARNING ACTIVITIES

Review the current sports plan or policy of one NGB (these can often be found on the governing body's website). Then consider the following:

1 Identify one area of work the NGB is planning to undertake to support the sporting needs of disabled participants and outline the NGB's reasons for focusing on this particular area of work.
2 What 'levels' and 'contexts' of participation does the plan or policy address (see Figure 11.2)?
3 Identify two areas of work within the plan or policy that demonstrate a social model approach to disability and explain why this is the case.
4 What advice would you offer to the NGB to improve its plan or policy regarding disabled participants?

NOTE

1. This is a global estimate based on partial data available. It should be acknowledged that within specific national contexts there are often different measures of disability (see Purdam *et al.*, 2008).

REFERENCES

Anderson, D. (2009) 'Adolescent girls' involvement in disability sport: implications for identity development', *Journal of Sport and Social Issues*, 33 (4): 427–449.

Barnes, C. (1991) *Disabled People in Britain and Discrimination*, London: Hurst and Co., in association with the British Council of Organisations of Disabled People.

Barnes, C. and Mercer, G. (2003) *Disability*, Oxford: Blackwell Publishers.

Barnes, C., Mercer, G. and Shakespeare, T. (1999) *Exploring Disability: A Sociological Introduction*, Cambridge: Polity Press.

Barton, L. (1993) 'Disability, empowerment and physical education', in Evans, J. (ed.), *Equality, Education and Physical Education*, London: Falmer Press.

Barton, L. (2009) 'Disability, physical education and sport: some critical observations and questions', in Fitzgerald, H. (ed.), *Disability and Youth Sport*, London: Routledge.

Beart, S., Hawkins, D., Stenfert, K., Roese, B., Smithson, P. and Tolosa, I. (2001) 'Barriers to accessing leisure opportunities for people with learning disabilities', *British Journal of Learning Disabilities*, 29 (4): 133–138.

Berger, R.J. (2008) 'Disability and the dedicated wheelchair athlete: beyond the "Supercrip" critique', *Journal of Contemporary Ethnography*, 37 (6): 647–678.

Beyer, R., Flores, M.M. and Vargas-Tonsing, T.M. (2008) 'Coaches' attitudes towards youth sport participation with Attention Deficit Hyperactivity Disorder', *International Journal of Sports Science and Coaching*, 3 (4): 555–563.

Björnsdóttir, K. and Traustadóttir, R. (2010) 'Stuck in the land of disability? The intersection of learning difficulties, class, gender and religion', *Disability and Society*, 25 (1): 49–62.

Brittain, I. (2004a) 'Perceptions of disability and their impact upon involvement in sport for people with disabilities at all levels', *Journal of Sport and Social Issues*, 28 (4): 429–452.

Brittain, I. (2004b) 'The role of schools in constructing self-perceptions of sport and physical education in relation to people with disabilities', *Sport, Education and Society*, 9 (1): 75–94.

Brittain, I. (2010) *The Paralympic Games Explained*, London: Routledge.

Burchardt, T. (2003) *Social Exclusion and the Onset of Disability*, Case Report 21, York: Joseph Rowntree Foundation/ESRC. Available from http://sticerd.lse.ac.uk/dps/case/CR/CASEreport21.pdf

Buttimer, J. and Tierney, E. (2005) 'Patterns of leisure participation among adolescents with a mild intellectual disability', *Journal of Intellectual Disabilities*, 9 (1): 25–42.

Connor, D.J. (2008) *Urban Narratives: Portraits in Progress – Life at the Intersections of Learning Disability, Race and Social Class*, New York: Peter Lang.

Department of Culture, Arts and Leisure/Sport Northern Ireland (2009) *Sport Matters: A Culture of Lifelong Enjoyment and Success in Sport*, Belfast: Department of Culture, Arts and Leisure/Sport Northern Ireland.

DePauw, K.P. (1997) 'The (In)Visability of DisAbility: cultural contexts and "sporting bodies"', *Quest*, 49 (4): 416–430.

DePauw, K.P. and Gavron, S.J. (2005) *Disability Sport*, Champaign, IL: Human Kinetics.

268

Disability Rights Commission (2002) *Survey of Young Disabled People Aged 16–24*, London: Disability Rights Commission Research and Evaluation Unit.

Disability Sports Northern Ireland (2006) *Policy Agenda 2006–2009: Achieving Equality in Sport and Physical Activity*, Belfast: Disability Sports Northern Ireland.

Eide, A.H. and Ingstad, B. (eds.) (2011) *Disability and Poverty: A Global Challenge*, Bristol: Policy Press.

English Federation of Disability Sport (2010) *Satisfaction of Disabled People in Sport: Results from Active People Surveys 1, 2 and 3 and Satisfaction with the Quality of the Sporting Experience Survey*, Loughborough: English Federation of Disability Sport.

Equality Commission for Northern Ireland (2003) *All Aboard: The Experience of Disabled People Using Transport in Northern Ireland. A Case Study Report*, Belfast: Equality Commission for Northern Ireland.

Fevre, R., Robinson, A., Jones, T. and Lewis, D. (2008) *Insight: Work Fit for All – Disability, Health and the Experiences of Negative Treatment in the British Workplace*, Cardiff: Equality and Human Rights Commission.

Filmer, D. (2005) 'Disability, poverty, and schooling in developing countries: results from 11 household surveys (December)', World Bank Policy Research Working Paper No. 3794, http://ssrn.com/abstract=874823

Finkelstein, V. (2001) 'The social model repossessed', www.leeds.ac.uk/disability-studies/archiveuk/archframe.htm

Fitzgerald, H. (2005) 'Still feeling like a spare piece of luggage? Embodied experiences of (dis)ability in physical education and school sport', *Physical Education and Sport Pedagogy*, 1 (10): 41–59.

Fitzgerald, H. and Bass, D. (2007) 'Disability, Sport and Exercise', in Merchant, J. Griffin, B. and Charnock, A. (eds.), *Sport and Physical Activity: The Role of Health Promotion*, Hampshire: Palgrave Macmillan.

Fitzgerald, H. and Kirk, D. (2009) 'Physical education as a normalising practice: is there a space for disability sport?', in Fitzgerald, H. (ed.), *Disability and Youth Sport*, London: Routledge.

French, D. and Hainsworth, J. (2001) 'There aren't any buses and the swimming pool is always cold! Obstacles and opportunities in the provision of sport for disabled people', *Managing Leisure*, 6 (1): 35–49.

Goodley, D. (2011) *Disability Studies: An Interdisciplinary Introduction*, London: Sage Publications.

Goodwin, D.L. and Watkinson, E.J. (2000) 'Inclusive physical education from the perspectives of students with physical disabilities', *Adapted Physical Activity Quarterly*, 17 (2): 144–160.

Government Equalities Office (2010) *Equality Act 2010: What Do I Need to Know? A Summary Guide to Your Rights*, London: Government Equalities Office.

Guttmann, L. (1976) *Textbook of Sport for the Disabled*, Aylesbury: HM+M Publishers.

Hardin, B. and Hardin, M. (2003) 'Conformity and conflict: wheelchair athletes discuss sport media', *Adapted Physical Activity Quarterly*, 20 (3): 246–259.

Hardin, B. and Hardin, M. (2004) 'Distorted pictures: images of disability in physical education textbooks', *Adapted Physical Activity Quarterly*, 21 (4): 399–413.

Hardin, M. and Hardin, B. (2005) 'Performance or participation . . . pluralism or hegemony? Images of disability and gender in Sports 'n' Spokes magazine', *Disability Studies Quarterly*, http://dsq-sds.org/article/view/606/783

Hargreaves, J.A. and Hardin, B. (2009) 'Women wheelchair athletes: competing against media stereotypes', *Disability Studies Quarterly*, 29 (2), www.dsq-sds.org/article/view/920/1095

Howe, P.D. (2009) 'From inside the newsroom: Paralympic media and the "production" of elite disability', *International Review for the Sociology of Sport*, 43 (2): 135–150.

Hunt, P. (ed.) (1966) *Stigma: The Experience of Disability*, London: Geoffrey Chapman.

Independent Research Solutions (2003) *Barriers to Participation in Culture, Arts and Leisure: Final Report*, Coleraine: Independent Research Solutions.

International Council for Sport Science and Physical Education (2003) *Young People with Disabilities in Physical Education/Physical Activity/Sport in and out of Schools: Technical Report for the World Health Organisation*, Geneva: World Health Organisation.

International Disability in Sport Working Group (2007) *Sport in the United Nations Convention in the Rights of Persons with Disabilities*, Boston, MA: International Disability in Sport Working Group.

Lewis, A., Parsons, S. and Robertson, C. (2006) *My School, My Family, My Life: Telling It Like It Is. A Study Detailing the Experiences of Disabled Children, Young People and Their Families in Great Britain in 2006*, Birmingham: Disability Rights Commission.

Macbeth, J.L. (2009) 'Restrictions of activity in partially sighted football: experiences of grassroots players', *Leisure Studies*, 28 (4): 455–467.

Marks, D. (1999) 'Dimensions of oppression: theorising the embodied subject', *Disability and Society*, 14 (5): 611–626.

Martin, J.J. and Choi, Y.S. (2009) 'Parents' physical activity: related perceptions of their children with disabilities', *Disability and Health*, 2 (1): 9–14.

Miller, E.J. and Gwynne, G.V. (1972) *A Life Apart: A Pilot Study of Residential Institutions for the Physically Handicapped and the Young Chronic Sick*, London: Tavistock Publications.

Minister for Sport's Review Group (1989) *Building on Ability: Sport for People with Disabilities. Report of the Minister of Sport's Review Group 1988/89*, London: Minister of Sport's Review Group.

Moran, T.E. and Block, M.E. (2010) 'Barriers to participation of children with disabilities in youth sports', *Teaching Exceptional Children Plus*, 6 (3), http://escholarship.bc.edu/education/tecplus/vol6/iss3/art5

Murray, L. (2006) *Sport, Exercise and Physical Activity: Public Participation, Barriers and Attitudes*, Edinburgh: Ipsos MORI.

Murray, P. (2002) *Hello! Are You Listening? Disabled Teenagers' Experience of Access to Inclusive Leisure*, York: Joseph Rowntree Foundation.

Office for National Statistics (2008) *Population Trends (No. 134)*, London: Office for National Statistics.

Oliver, M. (1996) *Understanding Disability: From Theory to Practice*, Basingstoke: Macmillan.

Oliver, M. (2004) 'If I had a hammer: the social model in action', in Barnes, C. (ed.), *The Social Model of Disability: Theory and Research*, Leeds: Disability Press.

Purdam, K., Afkhami, R., Olsen, W. and Thornton, P. (2008) 'Disability in the UK: measuring equality', *Disability and Society*, 23 (1): 53–65.

Rioux, M.H. (2011) 'Disability rights and change in a global perspective', *Sport in Society*, 14 (9): 1094–1098.

Rolfe, D.E., Yoshida, K., Renwick, R. and Bailey, C. (2009) 'Negotiating participation: how women living with disabilities address barriers to exercise', *Health Care for Women International*, 30 (3): 743–766.

Schantz, O. and Gilbert, K. (2001) 'An ideal misconstrued: newspaper coverage of the Atlanta Paralympic Games in France and Germany', *Sociology of Sport Journal*, 18 (1): 69–94.

Shakespeare, T. (2006) *Disability Rights and Wrongs*, London: Routledge.

Smith, B. and Sparkes, A. (2005) 'Men, sport, spinal cord injury, and narratives of hope', *Social Science and Medicine*, 61: 1095–1105.

Smith, B. and Sparkes, A. (2008) 'Changing bodies, changing narratives and the consequences of tellability: a case study of becoming disabled through sport', *Sociology of Health and Illness*, 30 (2): 217–236.

Hayley Fitzgerald

Sport England (2001) *Disability Survey 2000 Young People with a Disability and Sport, Headline Findings*, London: Sport England.

Sport England (2002) *Adults with a Disability and Sport National Survey 2000–2001*, London: Sport England.

Sport Northern Ireland (2005) *Disability Mainstreaming Policy (December)*, Belfast: Sport Northern Ireland.

Sports Council (1993) *People with Disabilities and Sport: Policy and Current Planned Action*, London: Sports Council.

Stride, A. (2009) 'We want to play football', in Fitzgerald, H. (ed.), *Disability and Youth Sport*, London: Routledge.

Swain, J., French, S., Barnes, C. and Thomas, C. (2005) *Disabling Barriers – Enabling Environments*, London: Sage.

Thomas, N. and Smith, A. (2003) 'Pre-occupied with able-bodiedness? An analysis of the British media coverage of the 2000 Paralympic games', *Adapted Physical Activity Quarterly*, 20 (2): 166–181.

Thomas, N. and Smith, A. (2005) 'The "inclusion" of elite athletes with disabilities in the 2002 Manchester Commonwealth Games: an exploratory analysis of British newspaper coverage', *Sport, Education and Society*, 10 (1): 49–67.

Thomas, N. and Smith, A. (2009) *Disability, Sport and Society*, London: Routledge.

United Nations (2006) 'Convention on the rights of persons with disabilities', www.un.org/disabilities/convention/conventionfull.shtml

World Health Organisation (2002) *Towards a Common Language for Functioning, Disability and Health*, Geneva: World Health Organisation.

CHAPTER 12

RESEARCHING AND EVALUATING SPORT DEVELOPMENT

JONATHAN LONG

If you are anything like me there is no shortage of people around you who are only too happy to pontificate on sport. Their confidence is based in the knowledge that they are expert because of their experience. There is, of course, some truth in that, but, strange to say, there are lots of other experts disagreeing with them. Inevitably there are gaps in their knowledge and some of the things they take for granted as being true are based on belief rather than evidence. Unless those working in sport can produce something more compelling by way of evidence, sport is bound to lose out in the policy arena. What is needed to try to ensure that our policy and professional practice are well informed is good-quality research, but we are operating in what has been an under-researched field.

Clearly things are changing. The expansion of sport-related courses in universities has meant a growing academic body engaged in research. Alongside that, the enormous datasets provided by the Active People survey and other large-scale surveys (see below) have helped to satisfy the need for basic data on participation patterns, but that still leaves gaps in knowledge about the reasoning that underpins that (non-)participation and even bigger gaps in appreciating the broader social, economic and political processes at work. Just as Hylton and Totten in Chapter 3 raise issues around the evidence base for understanding inequality, policy makers criticise sport and leisure professionals for basing arguments on inadequate research evidence.

When the contribution that sport makes to achieving a range of social goals has been addressed by the government (in the UK), it has been unconvinced by the research base. Like several writers in the field (e.g. Allison and Coalter, 1996; Glyptis, 1989; Long and Sanderson, 2001), the report of Policy Action Team 10 (1999: 37) to the Social Exclusion Unit, although favourable, concluded that there

272

is little 'hard' evidence of the social costs and benefits involved. The subsequent Game Plan strategy for sport and physical activity observed:

> The greatest challenge in assessing the state of sport and physical activity has been the lack of reliable data . . . although this does not invalidate the case for action, it weakens our ability to develop evidence-based policy interventions.
>
> (Department for Culture, Media and Sport/Strategy Unit, 2002: 21)

It is therefore not surprising that when Sport England produced a research strategy it noted the need to 'strengthen the evidence base for decision-making in sport at all levels and . . . put in place a coherent framework for sports research that is responsive to the wider social policy agenda' (Sport England, 2005: ii). In support of this, Sport England and UK Sport have set up the Value of Sport Monitor, which identifies research demonstrating the benefits of sport.[1] Nonetheless, more recently the Centre for Social Justice (2011: 13) still felt that 'further research is required to enable us to understand how sport programmes can most effectively contribute to social policy goals'.

Many sport development professionals seem to mistrust research, perhaps because it is seen to be conducted by 'outsiders'. The intention here is to give 'insiders' some guidelines for conducting good-quality research. It should be fairly evident that researchers think about the research enterprise differently depending upon the challenge being addressed. Those who want to improve the performance skills of athletes tend to go about their research in a rather different way from those who are picking up the concerns of developing sport for all (Hylton and Totten, Chapter 3) about the need to understand inequality. These various research communities may use the same techniques, they may use different techniques or they may use the same research techniques in different ways. Clearly it is impossible to provide recipes for what to do in all possible circumstances, so this chapter is about ways of thinking and exploring, and it will also provide leads for finding out more detailed information from elsewhere.

In line with that approach, the next section emphasises the need to be clear about the problem to be addressed and the information needed to do that. Without this clear specification, vagueness will threaten the validity of the research, so researchers are constantly exhorted to be critical thinkers. This does not mean criticising anyone and anything, but carefully analysing arguments and propositions to see whether they stand up under scrutiny (see Bowell and Kemp, 2010, for some guidance). The chapter then emphasises the value of assessing what previous research has to offer and considers some of the issues associated with different styles of research (questionnaires, interviews, observation and evaluation are featured here). That leads to a case study of projects conducted in India and Africa for Comic

Relief (Coalter with Taylor, 2010). The chapter concludes with an encouragement to always question the research being conducted and to consider how the findings can best be put to use; just as it is important to be critical in our analysis of what we research, it is important to be critical about how we research.

IDENTIFYING WHAT YOU NEED

Irrespective of the particular techniques used, research in this area may come in different forms, for example:

- audits of people's needs or current provision;
- market research to establish people's attitudes and behaviour;
- feasibility studies to test the viability of some proposed provision;
- project evaluation to assess the success of an initiative;
- forecasting future demands or behaviours.

The crucial thing is to plan these carefully, dissecting the research challenge in order to identify what needs to be done. There are some people who take this advice too far and use 'planning' as a way of procrastinating to avoid doing the research, but it is important not to jump in and start gathering data without proper preparation. The two watchwords typically associated with good research are *systematic* and *rigorous*, but this should not underplay the contribution of creativity, intuition and empathy.

Ouseley's (2001) report into the ethnic divisions in Bradford suggested that community cohesion might be helped by good sports provision. Research might be needed to support projects by informing what they do, but the more challenging task is to assess whether the sports projects have achieved what was expected. So where would you start if you had to do the research that would assess the benefits?

Some important principles:

1 Define key terms – it is important to be precise about what you are investigating. Can sport be taken to encompass leisure and recreation? Are you interested in sports facilities or projects?
   What is meant by social cohesion and how can it be assessed?
2 Narrow the focus – break big problems such as this down into more manageable chunks.
   You might decide to examine whether those involved in a sports project have more social contact with people from other ethnic groups than people who are not.
3 Decide what evidence you will need.

274

How would you measure social contacts? Do you need a quantitative measure or is this an occasion when qualitative data would tell you more?

4 Question the (potential) findings.

If there does prove to be a relationship it may be because of some other factor; for example, those involved in the project are younger than those who are not and they may have more extensive social networks as a result.

At the same time as working out what you need, you should also be sensitive to whom it is for. Whom are you trying to inform/convince? Sometimes it may be research purely for yourself in that you feel you need to know something to let you do your job better. Alternatively your line manager may require the information for shaping departmental practice, or it may be to support sporting arguments in the face of challenges or doubts from potential partners in health, education or regeneration, or it may be for the council or board to decide on policy and priorities, or it may be for course tutors. This is more than just a question of presenting results in different formats, though that may indeed be crucial; we need to recognise that different kinds of research are likely to be more appropriate for different audiences. I am certainly not suggesting here that you 'fix' your findings in order to satisfy these different audiences, but you need to be alert to what kind of evidence they are likely to believe.

To make your research effective it is important to understand the policy context and work out which are the main 'drivers', what is the local context and who are the key stakeholders. For example, as the sporting imperative shifts from medals to participation to regeneration to inclusion to health to forestalling riots to a new policy issue, the research questions will need to change too.

However you resolve these issues, you should consider the ethical implications of your research to make sure that people do not suffer harm or distress that they would not be subjected to if it were not for the research project. This, of course, is not a hard and fast rule as there may be some greater good that outweighs any apparent unfairness to these individuals. The institution you work in or for may require you to get formal ethical approval for the research before you start. Whether or not that is the case, you should listen to your own conscience and consider carefully the consequences of conducting the research in the way you intend.[2]

USING EXISTING KNOWLEDGE

Despite the concerns about gaps in our research knowledge, there is a lot of information already in existence that might go some way to satisfying many research needs. For example, when we conducted a systematic review for Sporting Equals and the 'home' sports councils on the supposedly under-researched subject of black and minority ethnic communities in sport and physical recreation, we identified over 100 pieces of directly relevant research over a ten-year period in the UK alone and more than 230 further related pieces that might play a part in informing policy (Long *et al.*, 2009). Whatever the search, the studies identified may contain data collected to represent the national picture or have been conducted in another part of the country or even overseas. So evaluate carefully whether you need to collect your own data or those sources will suffice. Some research may be done entirely as a desk study reviewing such data/literature; alternatively, this might be one element in a larger whole. Box 12.1 gives examples of datasets that are available in the UK.

However, you need to ask yourself several questions before accepting the findings into your report/assessment:

- Were their categories for age and so on the same as you are interested in?
- How useful were the questions they actually asked?
- Is it reasonable to expect the patterns revealed by a national survey or one done in some other part of the country to be the same as the area you are involved with?
- Have things changed since that research was conducted?

BOX 12.1 MAJOR UK SOURCES OF EXISTING DATA

- Taking Part: a home interview survey of (non-)participation in culture and sport in England. Conducted for the Department for Culture, Media and Sport since 2005/6 with a sample of *c*. 29,000 per year. Allows sport participation to be considered in the context of a wider range of leisure activities. www.culture.gov.uk/what_we_do/research_and_statistics/4828.aspx

- Active People: a telephone survey conducted on behalf of Sport England to record participation in sport and recreational physical activity. Initially it had an extremely large national (England) sample of *c*. 350,000 to give 1,000 in each local authority. More recently it has had an annual sample size of approximately 180,000 – probably the largest sports participation survey in the world. www.sportengland.org/research/active_people_survey. aspx

- General LiFestyle Survey (GLF): a survey by the Office for National Statistics of some 15,000 people aged sixteen and over in Great Britain, providing a picture of households, families and people living in Great Britain. Its predecessor, the General Household Survey, included questions on sport in 1973, 1977, 1980, 1983, 1987, 1990 and 2002. Those questions have been accompanied by others on leisure/arts/social activity/holidays, though the mix has varied. http://data.gov.uk/dataset/general_lifestyle_survey

- Living Costs and Food Survey (LCF): previously separate as the Family Expenditure and National Food Surveys. Diaries kept by people aged sixteen and over in more than 5,000 UK households a year provide data on all aspects of expenditure and income, including 'recreation and culture', which is sub-divided into many categories and subcategories. www. esds.ac.uk/government/efs/

QUESTIONNAIRE SURVEYS

For many people it is the questionnaire survey that is synonymous with social research. Undoubtedly a useful tool if well constructed and administered, unfortunately it is commonly misused. I have often heard it said that any fool can design a questionnaire. Unfortunately many do, but the basic skills can be easily acquired (see, for example, de Vaus, 2002; Long, 2007; Oppenheim, 2000).

A few years ago the Carnegie Research Institute was approached by a local authority undertaking its Best Value review of the parks service. What the council needed was information on people's patterns of use and assessment of the different elements of provision, not just as a 'one-off', but to provide a baseline for future assessments. This is typical territory for questionnaire surveys, but different styles were used for different constituencies of interest (e.g. some were looser with more open questions than others and were administered in different ways). We did all of these 'in house' apart from a home interview survey of residents aged sixteen and over, which was conducted for us by a market research company. Our team administered a site survey of the users of three parks; distributed postal questionnaires to sports clubs, allotment holders and councillors; conducted a telephone survey of the secretaries of tenants' and residents' associations; and distributed questionnaires in eighteen schools. Interestingly, the lowest level of response came from the councillors, who have other arenas to voice their views. Let's consider now some of the issues we had to address then.

At the outset, consider the key issues in designing a questionnaire survey:

- Who is meant to answer the questionnaire? How will they be identified and selected? Who might get left out or refuse?
- Will there be enough willing respondents to give confidence in the findings?
- What questions should be asked?
- How should they be worded?
- And the big one at the end: do the data justify the conclusions?

The first two relate to sampling; the second two to questionnaire design. It would be unfortunate, to say the least, if your research report were to be dismissed because it was found to be based on twenty people you happened to bump into at the weekend. Whether you consider it an art or a science, at its most basic, sampling here is about selecting a subset that can be accepted as being representative of the entire set of people or facilities or schemes that is of interest in the research. In most circumstances, more is better, in terms of the confidence the findings will command. Ignore the siren calls of those who try to suggest the sample has to be some constant percentage of the population; it is the absolute size of the sample that is more important (de Vaus, 2002).

Questionnaire surveys may take many forms:

- *Site surveys*, conducted at the stadium or sports centre, by definition cover participants only, so the majority of the population who are non-participants are ignored. However, not all non-participants are potential participants anyway.
- *Street surveys* are a quick and easy way of gathering data, but it is unclear who the respondents represent, as some sections of 'the public' are very unlikely to be included.
- *Home interview surveys* are more expensive, but can be more representative of the whole population. Of course, those involved in sport and recreation activities may be out doing those activities, so the interviewer has to call back, taking even more time.
- *Telephone surveys* can reach large numbers quickly and make direct data entry to the computer easy. With more and more households not having a landline it is harder to compile a suitable list from which to select the sample. Although market research companies are refining methods of sample selection, for most people reading this it will probably be difficult unless there is something like a membership list available. People are also getting increasingly suspicious of 'cold calls' and it can be hard to establish rapport.
- *Postal questionnaires* can be very useful to accommodate a wide geographic spread, but often have very low response rates, which can call the findings into question. The response can be improved by an accompanying letter explaining the importance of the study; offering a reward; sending reminders; providing a reply-paid envelope.
- *Electronic questionnaires*, if delivered by email, are much like postal questionnaires. Alternatively, if they are web based they are dependent on the 'right people' finding them. However, they can be linked directly to a database/spreadsheet, thereby avoiding the errors that might occur as someone in the research office enters data from the questionnaire into the computer.

It should be fairly obvious that, with these different styles of survey, not only does the cost vary, but so too do likely sample sizes, the number of questions that can be asked and the detail sought.

When it comes to designing the questionnaire itself, the key is to understand what you want to know. Without that kind of critical reflection, there is a danger that questions will not reach those key issues at stake, there will be completely unnecessary questions wasting the time of the respondents or, just as bad, there will be too few questions to allow a proper examination of the issues at stake. The advice to avoid questions that are ambiguous (e.g. Do you *train* and *play* sport at school) or leading (suggesting a particular response) or hypothetical (the 'what if?' questions) is good for the most part, but not so easy to follow. It can be difficult for the questionnaire designer to spot questions s/he has written that are leading people to

278

answer in a particular way, so it is useful to have fresh eyes to review the questions. The general principle has to be to give people the chance to report as accurately and honestly as possible what they do and think.

It is worth examining the questions used by other people doing related research. This can give useful ideas, and if the questions are replicated it may be possible to compare findings.[3] Doing this should introduce you to careful wording and useful classifications, and give you an appreciation of how to balance different types of question to help both the researchers and the respondents.

Using closed questions (people select from a predetermined set of responses) makes it much easier to handle the resultant data, with matched numerical codes simply entered into a spreadsheet or database. However, this does mean that the researcher's view of the world is being imposed on the research; open questions that invite a free response give respondents more chance for self-expression. Typically those responses are then assigned to categories in preparation for statistical analysis, but they may be treated as qualitative data.

Rather than asking people what they might do in the future, it is better to ask them what they have actually done, but then it is necessary to consider how accurately people can recall what happened at different times in the past. Consider the implications of imperfect memory for the following challenges that might be of interest to researchers: asking them as they leave the sports centre what they have done on that visit; asking them what they have done in the past four weeks or twelve months; asking adults what they did while they were at school. It is generally assumed that the more recent the memory the more detailed the recall, but this is not always the case.

In studies of participation, one of the key variables is the frequency of that participation. Researchers have to tread carefully here. For a start, much sports participation is seasonal, so when the question is asked can be crucial. Terms such as 'rarely', 'occasionally' and 'frequently' are not very helpful, as they can mean different things to different people (and to the same person in the context of different activities). It is important once again to consider what needs to be known. It might be the number of people who participate, the number of participant occasions (tickets sold), or the percentage of the population who (do not) participate. The following forms are frequently used:

- Have you taken part in [gymnastics] in the past day/month/year?
- How many times have you taken part in the past day/month/year?
- Do you take part in [gymnastics]
    - Daily
    - At least once a week
    - At least once a month
    - At least once a year

- Less than once a year
- Never

When asking for the details of participation, rather than asking about normally/usually it is better to ask about a specific occasion; 'normally' the most recent or favourite/best.

Sport psychologists in particular are keen to explore people's attitudes and beliefs, typically using some kind of scaling technique. Collectively known as psychometric scaling, this basically means trying to put numbers on what is going on in people's heads (typically 1–5 or 1–7, but there is considerable variation). The two most commonly used approaches involve:

rating (say) a youth programme on a set of bi-polar scales (e.g. flexible/rigid; friendly/unfriendly) – the *semantic differential*;
asking people to assess the extent to which they agree or disagree with a series of statements – *Likert scaling*.[4]

The key consideration here is whether individual items and composite scales measure what they are supposed to. To do that they have to be unambiguous so that everyone understands them in the same way.

Read a book about questionnaire design and it will stress the need for a pilot exercise. There are good reasons for this. For a trial run there is no need to involve large numbers of people, but it is useful to check that others understand the questions in the way that was intended when they were written. At the same time the categories given for answers to closed questions can be checked, as can the flow and sequencing of the questionnaire as a whole. It also makes sense to check the link to the spreadsheet/database that will store the coded responses.

You need to consider whether your survey instruments will be administered by an interviewer or self-administered. Although it is not always possible or even sensible, my normal preference is to use interviewers to ask the questions, but of course they have to be good at their craft; a bad interviewer can severely damage the research. Interview staff should be able to encourage participation by people who would otherwise not bother to respond, encourage people to take the exercise seriously and clarify any confusion about the meaning of the questions. Apart from cost and convenience, one of the main arguments in favour of self-administered questionnaires is that people may feel more able to give honest answers in more anonymous circumstances.

There is no point in having a carefully designed questionnaire if the interviewers are casual in the way they administer it, are not rigorous in the selection of respondents or are off-hand in the way the questions are asked and recorded.

280

IN-DEPTH INTERVIEWS

Questionnaires are good at gathering data to reveal basic patterns in a standardised format. On the other hand, questionnaires can seem regimented and restricted in the way they seek to compartmentalise people and knowledge. They may also recreate knowledge in the image of researchers' preconceptions, with standard questions packaged in standard configurations leading to constrained outputs through fixed categories. Some interviews may similarly be very structured but based around more open (less easily quantified) questions. In this section I am concerned with more flexible forms of interviewing designed to gather qualitative data to advance our knowledge of how people understand what happens in and around their lives. The central idea is that people should be given the chance to explain what is important to them.

That was why, although we did use questionnaires among club officials and spectators, when we were investigating the nature and extent of racism in sport we used one-to-one interviews with players and group interviews with match officials (Long et al., 1995, 1997, 2000). Our assessment was that we would be able to find out much more about people's experience of racism and their own attitudes by talking with them rather than asking them to respond to a standard questionnaire. Racism is such a sensitive subject that asking brusque, direct questions may mean people (white or black) will not give a natural response. Some people think that African Caribbean and Asian players are too ready to blame racism for all their problems. Far from it in our research; it was only because we were talking with them for some time that they became sufficiently confident to discuss such experiences. To my mind this vindicated the decision to use this way of gathering data because we found out things we would not otherwise have done.

Some people like a fairly structured approach, whereas others want it to be as free-flowing as possible (Bell, 2011; May, 2001). Of course, having no structure at all can be very disconcerting for respondents. Clearly you need some idea of what your research is trying to achieve, especially if research is being conducted to a tight timescale. Consequently, most people use an interview schedule to provide a framework. The basis for the questions may come from 'brainstorming', a literature review or preliminary discussions with 'experts' and other contacts. Instead of standard wording, the interviewer frames questions that slot naturally into the flow of the conversation, and typically tries to use the language of her/his respondent. In large part the reason this research approach is referred to as being 'in-depth' lies with the follow-up questions used to get beyond the initial response. These do not have to be complicated or clever, just something that gives the message that more information would be helpful. Some of the principles that apply in questionnaire design are equally appropriate here: group questions together in blocks and work out logical sequences, learn your 'script', but be prepared to be flexible.

Trial runs are as important to pilot this kind of interview as they are with questionnaires and other research approaches. You need to know how to introduce the various topics in such a way that you will get a full, honest and informative response from the person you are interviewing. The 'trick' is to get people to talk freely about what they think are the most important aspects of what you are examining without going off at a tangent; the interviewer then acts as a guide. Unlike the questionnaire survey, the analysis is not a separate stage that follows the data gathering; a lot of analysis has to be done during the interview so that you know how to direct it most profitably.

Interview technique

Some researchers think that questionnaires are a bit inquisitorial. It has been suggested that we should try to escape the authoritarian approach of questionnaire surveys in which all the power rests with the researchers, and establish a more equal relationship so that the experience is less like an inquisition. Some researchers believe that the relationship between researcher and respondent is so crucial to the success of the research that they should be carefully matched, according to sex, ethnicity, age and so on. In part this is because of the importance of empathy (the ability to put oneself in the shoes of another) in this style of research.

This process of empathy also helps in designing the interview by imagining what would make you most forthcoming in your responses were you being interviewed. In that position I would want to feel comfortable and able to relate to the interviewer and be reassured they would be non-judgemental. Good interviewers give the impression of being good listeners, but also carefully guide and draw out. They manage not to hurry respondents, giving them plenty of time to develop their answers, and also probe beyond the initial responses to get at underlying reasons.

These interviews will normally, but not necessarily, be longer than questionnaires; an hour is not unusual, and sometimes longer. So it is important to select the venue carefully so that the respondent feels comfortable and can give her/his full attention to the interview.

Given the importance typically ascribed to the way in which people 'construct' the world, it is important to have an accurate record of what they said. Although some may be cautious, most people do not object to the interview being recorded as long as it has been explained to them how their comments will be used. Removing the need to scribble notes all the time offers the interviewer the major advantage of being able to concentrate on what is being said and guiding the interview. Through the course of the project this may result in hours of recordings. What then? I like to have full transcripts, but not all researchers have the energy (or staff) for that.

Jonathan Long

There may be occasions when you feel it would be inappropriate to record the interview in any way at the time (perhaps you are talking with a young person on the project about their encounter with the police last night). As full an account as possible then has to be written soon afterwards, which is a surprisingly difficult thing to do.

For those who are phobic about numbers, this kind of interviewing may seem an easy alternative. It may be a rewarding alternative, but not an easy one. Understanding statistics may be difficult, but they at least provide a formal procedure to follow; take the right steps and an answer is delivered. Processing and analysing the qualitative data from in-depth interviews is less straightforward. So it is good to ask at the outset how all the information that is going to be so diligently collected from respondents will be examined in the context of existing/emerging theories and analysed. Whatever happens, you will almost certainly have to be selective and reduce the amount of data that you have while classifying it in some way. Although some qualitative researchers are horrified by the prospect, there are several software packages to assist in the task of analysing qualitative material; they serve to organise, retrieve and relate large amounts of data.

OBSERVATION

Observation can be used to gather quantitative data (e.g. number of times a player receives abuse or encouragement), but is probably more commonly associated with qualitative data (e.g. about the way people react to stress or how they generate team spirit even on a losing run). Although this can be a particularly revealing way of doing research (after all, seeing is believing), its findings are often dismissed by decision makers as inferior knowledge. Researchers who use observation as their preferred approach tackle this in one of two ways. The first is to try and devise a robust framework intended to convince people that the process is objective. The second is to insist that their aim is to use observation to understand the subjective experience. Whereas some want to draw on concepts and categories from established theory to guide their analysis and reporting, others insist on the blank slate: going into 'the field' with a completely open mind.

McCall and Simmons (1969: 3) rather grandly suggest that participant observation involves 'repeated genuine social interaction on the scene with the subjects themselves as part of the data gathering process'. The extent to which the researcher becomes immersed in the activity can vary considerably. (Note: it has been argued that it is not possible to be a non-participant observer, as any observation will have some impact on the observed.) Gans (1962) identified three different stances that can be adopted (others identify more; the point is to recognise that there is no single way to 'do' observation):

- observer – present, but apart;
- participate, but as a researcher;
- participant – temporarily abdicates study role.

The methodology was originally devised by social anthropologists going into unfamiliar surroundings (e.g. among tribes they considered to be 'primitive') and trying to explain how that society/culture operated. However, more recently people have used it in their own 'lifeworlds' on the basis that it is there that they have the best chance of working out how the world works (e.g. Blackshaw, 2003). So the observation may be conducted in the immediate setting of the project/team the researcher works with anyway (Holt and Sparkes, 2001), with other similar projects/teams or a less familiar environment such as the committee structure. Participant observation is also used when people might be motivated to distort what they do when questioned (e.g. using drugs to improve performance, drinking behaviour or sexual encounters). Moreover, it allows the researcher to examine structures not recognised by those taking part, and hence not accessible through questionnaires or interviews.

You might be well advised not to follow my example in this case. I had a moment of brilliant insight that led me to try to do some participant observation to find out why the kind of spectator violence frequently experienced at football matches rarely occurred at rugby league games even though both are essentially masculine, working-class sports. Trying to observe why something is not happening is not the easiest challenge to set yourself. Equally, although observing children playing may be the best way of getting a window into their world, spending a lot of time watching the play area in the local park may mean that others start watching you with suspicion.

Those who have not come across participant observation may be forgiven for wondering just how hard it can be to go and watch what is happening. Well, it is much harder than it initially sounds, as it involves trying to make sense of everything around you, picking out the key aspects and turning all that into a set of generalisations. However, it can be very fruitful. As a research methodology, participant observation conventionally tends to be considered very much a qualitative approach, but can in fact use a suite of techniques (Gans, 1962) such as:

- using and observing at local facilities;
- attending meetings, gatherings and the like;
- informal visiting to friends and neighbours;
- formal and informal interviewing;
- special informants;
- day-by-day observation.

284

In addition to deciding whether they are there to observe or participate, those doing participant observation have a decision to make about whether to declare their position as a researcher. Not to do so may be seen as deceitful and unethical, whereas broadcasting the role may mean that people alter the way they would normally behave. Either way, the researcher has to find a role to play so that s/he has something to do rather than just look conspicuous. When the researcher is not operating in her/his usual environment, s/he has to find a way 'in' and then win trust and establish relationships so that people feel comfortable with this newcomer around. This is especially important if the research is into something like the use of drugs to improve performance. The best data are likely to come if rapport is established. Irritatingly for those who have been successful in doing this, they have sometimes been criticised for excessive rapport and 'going native' to such an extent that they no longer think like a 'proper' researcher. Some are so concerned at jeopardising their relationships in the field or changing the direction of behaviour that they consider it wrong to ask questions. Writers in this field do nearly all agree, though, that the researcher should adopt a low profile and not pass moral judgements on those around them.

One of the things that worries some who use participant observation is that the people they have worked with intensively may not be typical of wider populations, thus preventing generalisations. If your interest is purely in your team, project or committee structure, this hardly matters. However, even if that is so, you cannot be there all day every day, so some sampling is inevitable, as it is with any style of research.

Participant observation does seem to highlight ethical issues, most obviously over whether it is legitimate to do covert research by not telling people they are being observed for research purposes. Then, when 'in the field', the researcher has to decide to what extent s/he can intervene in what is happening when the research is intended to study the people encountered, not the consequences of the researcher's own actions. Even if people have been informed, when it comes to reporting, it may prove difficult to write without betraying confidences.

Critics suggest that participant observation produces neither reliable nor valid data, as it may simply recycle hearsay and is subject to observer bias because it depends on the personal observation and interpretation of someone who may have 'gone native' and suspended their critical faculties. Moreover, it can be difficult to draw inferences that warrant generalisation and provide proof of a causal link (two highly prized functions of research) and there is no shortage of ethical dilemmas to address. Do not despair; there are advantages in using participant observation. Its proponents argue that in practice it is less likely to be biased, unreliable or invalid because it provides more internal checks. Being in the field for a long time allows information to be checked, emerging explanations to be tested and unsatisfactory explanations discarded. The research can be very flexible (not the hypothesis–data–test tramway) which makes it more responsive to the data than the imposed systems of 'scientific' research. It allows researchers to get really close to the realities of social life.

See Box 12.2 for an overview of issues to take into consideration when planning what kind of research to use.

BOX 12.2 ASKING QUESTIONS OF YOURSELF

You cannot afford to be mechanical in your research. Always ask yourself questions to make sure you are not taking things for granted.

So you want to do a questionnaire survey . . .

Why?

- How are you going to phrase the questions?
- Open/closed/scales?
- Has someone already worked out how to do that?
- How many questions do you need?
- Why are you including each question?
- Will your respondents be able to understand them?
- Who is going to answer the questionnaire?
- How many? ⎫
- How are you going to select/identify/reach them? ⎬ What are the consequences?
- Whom do they *really* represent? ⎭
- Have you arranged necessary access?
- Why should they take part?
- Can you do anything to improve response rates?
- Do you need special approval to question children?
- Are you sure you do not need to ask the questions directly, face to face?
- If it is a postal survey, do you think many people will reply?
- Whom will your pilot be administered to?
- How will you code the responses?
- How are you going to analyse the data?
- Are pie charts really enough?

So you want to do in-depth interviews . . .

Why?

- What questions will you use?
- What makes them 'in-depth'?
- What kinds of follow-up questions could you use?
- Have you got the language right?
- How structured will it be?
- Is this different from a questionnaire?
- Who are going to be your respondents?

286

- Why will they agree to take part?
- Whom do they represent/speak for? Really?
- Can you interview children on this topic?
- Do you need police clearance?
- How can you practise interviewing?
- Are you going to transcribe your interviews?
- How will you process the data?
- How will you analyse it rather than just write it down?
- How will you demonstrate that the data are real and really did come from your respondents?
- How will you present the data?

So you want to do some observation . . .

Why?

- Will you declare your purpose? To everyone?
- How will you find your subjects, get 'in' and be accepted?
- What will you do while observing in order to fit in?
- Are you entitled to 'spy on them'?
- What behaviour do you expect to observe?
- What will you actually record?
- How will you know what is important and what is not?
- How will you record it?
- How much time will you have to spend there to be sure you *know* what is going on?
- How will you analyse and make sense of your observations?
- How will you present this to others so that they are persuaded by what you say?

So you want to use multiple approaches . . .

- Often a good idea, but do you need to?
- What will one approach get you that the others will not?
- Can you combine the data you get from different approaches?

EVALUATION

Evaluation is not a technique or even an approach in its own right, but a challenge that may draw on a range of different kinds of research. Particularly strongly associated with policy research, it typically tries to assess the impact or effect of some intervention. Given this, it has been of considerable interest to the sports councils (e.g. Coalter, 2002; Sport England, 2001). Some evaluations have enormous financial resources available (though probably never enough in the eyes of the researchers), but many more are small-scale projects (Robson, 2000). At this more modest level, Nichols (2005) makes use of the 'realistic evaluation' principles proposed by Pawson and Tilley (1997) when examining the contribution of sports-based projects to reducing crime.

The most common kind of question that an evaluation is expected to address is 'Has a change occurred?' If it can be demonstrated that change has occurred it is then important to assess whether that can be attributed to the intervention or is the result of other factors. Both policy makers and practitioners will also be interested in what made it work (or stopped it from working) and whether it represents value for money.

Ideally, to assess change there should be some measure of how things were before the project started and then clear measures of performance used to see what has changed by how much by the end of the project. Assessments at various stages during the project would also be useful to track progress and allow feedback. Assessments some time after the project can be used to find out how long the benefits last. It may be possible to avoid the need for all these sets of data by asking people involved with the project to assess retrospectively what change there was (e.g. whether they are physically more or less active now as a result of their involvement), though that requires a further assessment of the validity and reliability of the data produced.

It is difficult to find appropriate quantitative measures of many of the things that currently interest people responsible for sport projects: skills, confidence, deviance, teamwork, community cohesion and so forth. Unfortunately, many have therefore thrown their hands up in the air in despair and given up the evaluation exercise, relying instead on anecdotal evidence. If valid and reliable quantitative measures are available, all well and good; otherwise the challenge is to work out what does constitute 'evidence'.

Few people doubt that sport can produce social benefits, so pointing out that someone has grown from being a youngster 'at risk' to an Olympic medallist does not get us much further forward. What we need to know is to what extent such benefits occur and if there is a direct causal link. So what is needed is a more rigorous analysis of all the people involved and a careful consideration of any counter examples. That might allow us to work out why there should be the different outcomes.

Coalter (2002) encourages a distinction between three different types of outcomes (and a fourth might be added). *Sporting outcomes* are such things as improved performance or increased participation; *intermediate outcomes* are the impact on the individuals taking part, such as improved health and well-being; *strategic outcomes* are the wider impacts, such as lower levels of crime in the community; and *process outcomes* relate to how the goals were achieved, such as the success of partnership working. The other key considerations for policy makers are the efficiency of the project (e.g. number of people involved per pound), whether it is effective (e.g. whether it really does deter people from anti-social behaviour) and, sometimes, who benefits (equity).

288

Coalter (2002, 2007) is also quite insistent that any evaluation exercise should be conducted against the aims of the project (of course, different people may see different aims for the project). However, the task may not be just to assess change within a single project, but to compare one with another. Although that suggests using identical methods of evaluation in each project, doing that might be inappropriate if they have rather different aims.

Probably the two biggest problems facing evaluation exercises are identifying suitable indicators and establishing cause (see Case study 12.1). In an example I have used elsewhere (Long, 2007), if we want to know whether health has improved as a result of an active lifestyles project, would it be best to measure the number of visits to local doctors, the number of prescriptions dispensed, individual blood pressure or cholesterol levels, or self-reported health? Which of those offers the best indicator depends on the underlying assumptions about what constitutes the link between activity and health. Making those explicit also helps to deal with the second problem. Just because the health of someone involved in the project improves, it may not have been their increased activity (always assuming the project was successful in increasing activity levels) that caused it. For example, their health may have improved because they changed job and experienced less stress, or they got a job as the economic climate improved so they earned the income to allow a better diet, or they gave up smoking because their best friend died of cancer. The change may also have more to do with positive social interaction with the person running the project and the other participants. If this was part of a major national evaluation these personal experiences might not be enough to distort the overall picture, but in small-scale evaluations they can be crucial. Setting out clearly at the start what the presumed links are between physical activity and health not only clarifies what the expected outcome should be, but also helps identify the most appropriate kind of evidence (some refer to this as establishing logic models).

In an environment that extols the virtue of evidence-based policy, and in which the Treasury looks to hold tight the purse strings of public expenditure, there is greater and greater pressure on sports projects to demonstrate the benefits accruing from their actions, and that wherever possible this should be done in financial terms. This has led to a revisiting and refinement of research techniques that involve more flexible forms of cost–benefit analysis in order to recognise the social contribution of the many things not given a value by being bought and sold in the marketplace. These use various techniques to assign a value in pounds (or whatever your local currency) to some of the outcomes from (in our case) sports initiatives, perhaps in terms of health, crime or congestion.

Led by the Cabinet Office, government departments and a network of non-governmental organisations (including the New Economics Foundation, Charities Evaluation Services, the National Council for Voluntary Organisations and New Philanthropy Capital) have enthusiastically been exploring the use of social return on investment (SROI). Part of the political agenda here is to allow third sector organisations to shift thinking away from being seen as a drain on public funds because of the grants they consume, towards recognising their net contribution to the common good. For example, Nevill and van Poortvliet (2011: 6) have estimated that for every £1 invested in one sport project '£7 of value is created for the state and the local community', largely through reductions in crime.

The SROI Network produced for the Cabinet Office (2009) a guide to SROI that can be found on the web. This tries to emphasise SROI as a process rather than the mechanical application of a set of formulae. In its model the various stakeholders are brought together to agree the main outcomes (e.g. reduced crime or improved health) and how they result from the inputs (resources) and outputs (deliverables). This is what the SROI Network refers to as an impact map or a theory of change or logic model. Key indicators are then selected to show whether outcomes have happened, the necessary data are gathered and a monetary value is assigned. The guide offers examples of how this can be done, though the messiness of most sports projects will undoubtedly complicate the real world application.

In one of the worked examples provided in the SROI Guide, the main outcomes are in the form of health and social benefits to those taking part in the scheme, just as there might be in a community sport project. Because the health benefits are calculated on the basis that fewer encounters will be necessary with health professionals, they amount to over £80,000, whereas the social benefits of residents making new friends and spending more time with others through the group activities of the project were calculated to be worth less than £500. Adherents of Putnam's social capital thesis (e.g. Putnam, 2000) who promote the value of social connectedness might argue that something aspiring to assess the social return might look to establish a better balance.

If these procedures were being used to guide a project's internal deliberations around alternative 'what if' scenarios, all well and good, but the Guide is quite clear that organisations should use these 'findings' in the competition for funding. On the other hand, as the Charities Evaluation Services (2011) observe on their website:

> it would be a very unwise funder who made funding decisions simply on the basis of one number. It is also not recommended that you use the ratio to compare different organisations. They will be working with different users with different needs, and will have made different judgements in calculating their ratio.

Being responsible, the producers of the Guide enjoin users not to make inflated claims, to conduct sensitivity tests (what difference would it make if we assume

290

this rather than that?) and to make the whole process as transparent as possible so that the calculations can be open to public scrutiny.

In line with this belief that the cultural sector needs to use the tools and concepts of economics to fight its corner in a competitive policy environment, a former colleague reviewed the procedures suggested in the Green Book that is produced by the Treasury (HMT, 2003) and assessed how appropriate they might be for valuing culture (O'Brien, 2010). He favoured contingent valuation methods, in part because of the point just made about the limitations of SROI 'when making comparative funding decisions, particularly across different forms of culture' (O'Brien, 2010: 41). So what is contingent valuation? It is based on getting both users and non-users of a service to state their preferences (how much they would be prepared to pay for a service) in an imaginary marketplace. The idea is that this should take into account:

- what users say it is worth to them;
- the value people place upon having it there for them to use if they wanted to or for others to use now or in the future;
- the value people get from the existence of a cultural good or service, even if they have no direct involvement with it (e.g. the pride people might feel in their local community from knowing that it has a nationally recognised project delivering sporting opportunities to disadvantaged youngsters).

Not surprisingly there is no shortage of critics of this approach as well, not least because of the difficulty people have in making hypothetical decisions about how much they would be prepared to pay.

Most commonly, the challenge for evaluation exercises is to assess whether a project was successful in delivering what it said it would, or to calculate how much of something has been delivered and what it is worth. However, taking its lead from Pawson (2006), the Centre for Social Justice (2011), as indicated above, has tried to shift the emphasis to *how* sport programmes can do this.

Of course, project evaluation is an intensely political exercise. Whatever nice words surround the exercise, people and processes are being judged, and project funding may be dependent on the outcome. It is often seen to be a major advantage to engage external evaluators, as they will be seen by others as being relatively dispassionate with no particular axe to grind. The downside is that they lack the accumulated knowledge belonging to existing staff that can play such an important part in interpreting data about outcomes and processes. Ideally, both project workers and participants should be integrally involved in a collaborative enterprise. In such politically charged environments, evaluators need to be able to recognise arguments driven by vested interest and then to have the confidence in the quality of their research to defend their findings. Appreciating the difficulty of providing research evidence to demonstrate positive outcomes, one of the project teams in a study for the Department for Culture, Media and Sport (Long *et al.*, 2002) had decided that the best way to ensure future funding was to let decision makers 'see it with their own eyes' by inviting them to an open evening each year.

CASE STUDY 12.1: SPORT FOR DEVELOPMENT IMPACT STUDY

Background

Fred Coalter was commissioned by UK Sport and Comic Relief to assess whether 'sport contributes to the personal development and well-being of disadvantaged children and young people'. With his colleague John Taylor, he worked in conjunction with six sport for development organisations that were being funded by Comic Relief in India and Africa to help them gather the necessary data (Coalter with Taylor, 2010):

- Magic Bus, Mumbai, India
- Praajak and Railway Children, Kolkata, India
- Elimu, Michezo na Mazoezi (EMIMA), Dar-es-Salaam, Tanzania
- Kamwokya Christian Caring Community (KCCC), Kampala, Uganda
- The Kids League, Gulu, Uganda
- Sport Coaches Outreach (SCORE), South Africa

The programmes were all delivering 'sport' in different ways: outdoor activity camps; transport to sports facilities; football/netball (two projects); sport and other activities to develop life skills and raise awareness of HIV and AIDS; training for sports leaders.

A series of in-country training workshops were conducted with each organisation to develop survey methods and questionnaires. This approach was adopted for a number of reasons: it enabled relatively standardised comparisons between the organisations; most people working in the organisations did not have the necessary expertise to conduct robust and comparable qualitative research; a survey approach enabled technical support to be provided by email in addition to the periodic visits to the projects.

The research

Although they all went under the banner of sport for development, there were big differences between projects in terms of their context and what was offered, making it difficult to know just what was being measured. The research approach had to be one that was sensitive to different circumstances and could work 'on the ground'. Therefore, part of Coalter's role as the research consultant was to help them work out a programme theory; that is the various components, mechanisms and cause/effect relationships that it is presumed produce the outcomes the projects were trying to deliver. To do that, workshops were run at each project with a view to formulating precise and realistic programme outcomes that the project workers could subscribe to, alongside some common elements for all projects to measure: perceived self-efficacy and self-esteem among the young people engaged in the projects.

Because of the interest in the impact of participating in the programmes, the research was based on a longitudinal design. The idea was that the same people would complete the questionnaire

---

before they got involved in the project and after they had finished so that an assessment could be made of what had changed. The report is transparent in providing information on where there were any differences between the intention and the practice. For example, the first phase of data gathering may have been at the beginning of the project, but respondents could have been involved with the programme as a whole for some time by then; equally the 'after' questionnaires were sometimes gathered over a period of a few months. This is the nature of real world research, but it can leave you not quite measuring what you thought you were measuring. This was complicated further in projects where sport was just part of what was being offered to participants, so it was not clear whether any identified change was attributable to sport or to something else they were doing at the same time. And of course it was not always possible to get all those who had done the first questionnaire to do the second.

There were variations on the standard model. In two projects, questionnaires were also administered to a 'control group' of the same age who were not participating in the project. In another project, the experiences of participants were so disparate that the questionnaire was abandoned in favour of individual interviews. Coalter was keen to limit what is known as 'social desirability bias'. This is the tendency of respondents to say what they think the researcher wants to hear or which will make them sound good. This form of bias might reasonably be expected to be increased if the questions are being asked by people familiar to the young people, but it was not always possible to avoid this.

One of the big challenges was to strike a balance between individual projects, identifying measures useful to them and allowing some comparability between projects. For the most part, organisations found it difficult to define their programme outcomes precisely, but through discussion with people involved in each of the projects self-efficacy and self-esteem were identified as core concepts. 'Self-efficacy' relates to an individual's perception of her/his ability to achieve a task and is closely related to the notion of resilience; 'self-esteem' relates to an individual's assessment of her/his self-worth. Each project team was provided with a suite of questionnaires that they modified in discussion with Coalter to take account of their participants' ability to deal with certain questions.

Findings

Typically, sport for development programmes assume they are working with people who are deficient in some way and that sport is going to make good this deficit (see also Mwaanga, Chapter 14 in this edition). In practice, the majority of respondents scored within what is considered the 'normal' range. All projects recorded an increase in self-esteem scores, but for only one project was this statistically significant; self-efficacy scores showed more variation between projects. Coalter concluded that the data did 'not indicate that the programmes had a systematic and strong impact on gender-related attitudes' (Coalter with Taylor, 2010: 93). Overall, Coalter was unable to isolate a specific 'sport effect' and it was not the case that all individuals, or even all projects, moved in the same direction.

MAKING USE OF THE FINDINGS

So the brilliant research project has been completed: what next? If it was to inform your own practice, you need to show that you can learn the lessons of your research. If it was done for almost any other purpose, the findings have to be communicated to others. I was about to suggest that you have to find the best way to present the research, but, just as you had to be aware during the research that people react differently to what they encounter in everyday life, so they will respond in different ways to what you produce. The implication is that it may be necessary to use more than one format depending upon your audience. Those who share your new-found enthusiasm for research may be prepared to read a lengthy report, but board members or the council may want no more than two or three sides of A4, and the media probably less. Within some professional cultures a slide presentation is expected, whereas in others people will be bored by 'yet another' PowerPoint presentation.

Within the reporting there are alternative ways of presenting data too; for example:

- extended arguments for your peers who crave the detail and want to be reassured that you are alert to the subtleties of the problems they have to grapple with;
- tables of figures for the data hungry;
- diagrams for those who respond better to visual representations;
- direct quotes for those who like the original voices to show through;
- short, topical thought pieces for the media (and politicians).

Once again, people respond in different ways and they may not even be consistent in this. In my own case:

- I feel quite comfortable dealing with large tables of figures, but sometimes feel that researchers let the numbers take over from the reality.
- I respond to diagrams and figures, but feel frustrated by the lack of precision and detail in the commonly produced pie charts, and question graphics in newspapers and magazines that hide the true nature of the data behind the impact message.
- I like to read what reflective respondents have had to say, but sometimes wonder why certain quotes have been selected in preference to all the others.

The tone of your research report needs to suit your audience, and this is often a tough challenge (see Fairbairn and Winch, 2011, for advice).

FINDING OUT MORE

Useful sources of further information about doing research are those by Long (2007) and Gratton and Jones (2010), but there are several other useful guides and introductions. The main point to bear in mind is that, whichever books you use, you should not try to follow them slavishly, but use them to give you ideas and help you to think through the various issues associated with your research.

294

There are also several good web-based sources, such as the one set up by the Higher Education Academy Network for hospitality, leisure, sport and tourism to provide a gateway to useful research resources (www.heacademy.ac.uk/hlst/resources/researchgateway).

LEARNING ACTIVITIES

Imagine a research challenge to satisfy the needs of your employer or your course. The challenge now is to plot what the research will look like. When you do this for real it helps if it is done in conjunction with reading the available literature.

1   Try to write as precisely as possible what you aim to find out. (Some people like a more open, exploratory approach, but when time and finances are limited this can be risky, and you must still have some idea about why you are going to invest so much effort in the enterprise.)
    a   You could start with a word cloud and then begin to link the words together so that some order appears.
    b   Define precisely the key concepts you intend to use (e.g. sport, development, well-being).
    c   Having written the general aim, you may find it easier to write a series of questions you want to answer rather than the 'objectives' you more commonly see referred to in research methods texts.
2   Now you need to plan how you will get the necessary information to allow you to resolve those questions. Using your favoured spreadsheet, database, word-processing package or piece of paper, draw a simple table with four columns.
    a   In the first column put each of your research questions;
    b   in the second, the information you need to allow you to address the question (what information will tell you about offending behaviour, self-confidence or health?);
    c   in the third, the possible sources of such information (you need to consider issues of access and sampling here);
    d   in the fourth the means of gathering the data (survey, observation etc.).
    This should suggest alternative research paths, some of which you should begin to appreciate are better than others.
3   Review the kinds of question in Box 12.2, and prepare your arguments to explain why the routes you eventually choose from column 1 to column 4 (in Learning activity number 2) are suitable for addressing your research aim.

NOTES

1. The Value of Sport Monitor is available online: www.sportengland.org/research/value_of_sport_monitor.aspx

2. I am lucky; where I work I can always get advice on these tricky issues. If you lack that immediate support you may have guidelines issued by a professional association, or you can find information on a relevant website. I try to adhere to the principles of the Social Research Association, which also address the safety of the researcher: www.the-sra.org.uk/sra_resources/research-ethical/ethics-guidelines

3. In the UK the Survey Question Bank contains the questions used in publicly funded surveys: www.surveynet.ac.uk/sqb/

4. Although the term tends to be applied to any such exercise, it more properly refers to a set of statements (items) reflecting a concept such as competitiveness or orientation to fair play, and it is the composite (reflected in the summed values for all items) that is the Likert scale.

REFERENCES

Allison, M. and Coalter, F. (1996) *Sport and Community Development*, Edinburgh: Scottish Sports Council.

Bell, J. (2011) *Doing Your Research Project*, 5th edn, Maidenhead: Open University Press.

Blackshaw, T. (2003) *Leisure Life: Myth, Masculinity and Modernity*, London: Routledge.

Bowell, T. and Kemp, G. (2010) *Critical Thinking: A Concise Guide*, 3rd edn, London: Routledge.

Cabinet Office (2009) 'A guide to social return on investment', www.sroi-uk.org/publications-uk/cat_view/29-the-sroi-guide-2009

Centre for Social Justice (2011) 'More than a game', www.centreforsocialjustice.org.uk/client/downloads/20110523_CSJ_More_than_a_Game_web.pdf

Charities Evaluation Services (2011) 'Social return on investment', www.ces-vol.org.uk/index.cfm?pg=494&gclid=CLmnkPf7i60CFVBTfAod_x-umw

Coalter, F. (2002) *Sport and Community Development: A Manual*, Edinburgh: sportscotland.

Coalter, F. (2007) *A Wider Social Role for Sport*, London: Routledge.

Coalter, F. with Taylor, J. (2010) 'Sport-for-development impact study', www.uksport.gov.uk/pages/research-and-publications/

Department for Culture, Media and Sport/Strategy Unit (2002) *Game Plan: A Strategy for Delivering the Government's Sport and Physical Activity Objectives*, London: Cabinet Office.

Fairbairn, G. and Winch, C. (2011) *Reading, Writing and Reasoning: A Guide for Students*, 3rd edn, Maidenhead: Open University Press.

Gans, H. (1962) *The Urban Villagers*, New York: Free Press.

Glyptis, S. (1989) 'Public sector sport and recreation initiatives for the unemployed in Britain's inner cities', in Bramham, P., Henry, I., Mommaas, H. and van der Poel, H. (eds.), *Leisure and Urban Processes: Critical Studies of Leisure Policy in Western European Cities*, London: Routledge.

Gratton, C. and Jones, I. (2010) *Research Methods for Sports Studies*, 2nd edn, London: Routledge.

HMT (2003) *The Green Book: Appraisal and Evaluation in Central Government*, London: HMT.

Holt, N. and Sparkes, A. (2001) 'An ethnographic study of cohesiveness in a college soccer team over a season', *Sport Psychologist*, 15 (3): 237–259.

Long, J. (2007) *Researching Leisure, Sport and Tourism: the Essential Guide*, London: Sage.

Long, J. and Sanderson, I. (2001) 'The social benefits of sport: where's the proof?', in Gratton, C. and Henry, I. (eds.), *Sport in the City*, London: Routledge.

Long, J., Tongue, N., Spracklen, K. and Carrington, B. (1995) 'What's the difference: a study of the nature and extent of racism in rugby league', http://repository.leedsmet.ac.uk/main/view_record.php?identifier=5461&SearchGroup=Research

Long, J., Nesti, M., Carrington, B. and Gilson, N. (1997) 'Crossing the boundary: a study of the nature and extent of racism in local league cricket', http://repository.leedsmet.ac.uk/main/view_record.php?identifier=4825&SearchGroup=Research

Long, J., Hylton, K., Welch, M. and Dart, J. (2000) 'Part of the game: an examination of racism in grass roots football', www.leedsmet.ac.uk/ces/lss/kioreport.htm

Long, J., Welch, M., Bramham, P., Hylton, K., Butterfield, J. and Lloyd, E. (2002) 'Count me in: the dimensions of social inclusion through culture and sport', report to the Department for Culture, Media and Sport, http://repository.leedsmet.ac.uk/main/view_record.php?identifier=2879&SearchGroup=research

Long, J., Hylton, K., Spracklen, K., Ratna, A. and Bailey, S. (2009) 'Systematic review of the literature on black and minority ethnic communities in sport and physical recreation', www.sportingequals.org.uk/resources.php?resources_ID=1#anchor

McCall, G.J. and Simmons, J.L. (eds.) (1969) *Issues in Participant Observation*, Reading, MA: Addison-Wesley.

May, T. (2001) *Social Research*, Buckingham: Open University Press.

Nevill, C. and van Poortvliet, M. (2011) 'Teenage kicks: the value of sport in tackling youth crime', www.laureus.com/files/Teenage%20Kicks_Report_FINAL.pdf

Nichols, G. (2005) 'Reflections on researching the ability of sports interventions to reduce youth crime: the hope of scientific realism', in Hylton, K., Long, J. and Flintoff, A. (eds.), *Evaluating Sport and Active Leisure for Young People*, Eastbourne: Leisure Studies Association.

O'Brien, D. (2010) 'Measuring the value of culture', report to the Department for Culture, Media and Sport, www.culture.gov.uk/images/publications/measuring-the-value-culture-report.pdf

Oppenheim, A.N. (2000) *Questionnaire Design and Attitude Measurement*, 3rd edn, London: Continuum.

Ouseley, H. (2001) *Community Pride Not Prejudice*, Bradford: Bradford Vision.

Pawson, R. (2006) *Evidence-Based Policy: A Realist Perspective*, London: Sage.

Pawson, R. and Tilley, N. (1997) *Realistic Evaluation*, London: Sage.

Policy Action Team 10 (1999) 'Arts & sport', report to the Social Exclusion Unit, DCMS, London.

Putnam, R.D. (2000) *Bowling Alone: The Collapse and Revival of American Community*, New York: Simon & Schuster.

Robson, C. (2000) *Small Scale Evaluations*, London: Sage.

Sport England (2001) *Performance Measurement for the Development of Sport: A Good Practice Guide for Local Authorities*, London: Sport England.

Sport England (2005) *A Strategy for Sports Research, 2005 to 2008: Towards Evidence Based Decision-Making in Sport*, London: Sport England.

de Vaus, D. (2002) *Surveys in Social Research*, 5th edn, London: Routledge.

CHAPTER 13

SPORT DEVELOPMENT AND THE OLYMPIC AND PARALYMPIC GAMES

VASSIL GIRGINOV

The link between sport development and the Olympic Games is not as obvious as it may seem and has been the subject of vigorous academic and political debates. The Olympics were revived in their modern form with the explicit aim of using sport for the betterment of the world. However, throughout the history of the Olympic movement, concerns have regularly been voiced about the widening divide between mass and elite sport, the excessive commercialisation and spectacularisation of the Games. Thus, questions about what sports should be promoted and how the lofty universal Olympic ideas should be pursued deserve more thorough examination. The sport development promise of the 2012 London Olympic Games bears very little resemblance to this event's humble beginning in 1896, and the two previous Games hosted by the same city in 1908 and 1948. However, despite conceptual and organisational transformations and the political and economic challenges, over the years the Olympics have grown in popularity and potential to use sport to affect social change.

This chapter examines the contested relationship between sport development and the Olympics by engaging with the Games' capacity to shape the domain of sport development and vice versa. This is a multi-faceted and mutually constructive relationship, and one that is not given but needs to be established and maintained both at conceptual and practical levels. The chapter first interrogates the Olympics as a developmental project promoting universalised visions of the ideal human being and conceptualises sport development. It then analyses the constitutive ideological, economic and organisational elements of the relationship between the Games and sport development. Finally, this relationship is located within six core sport development processes, and the need to leverage the social, economic and legitimising powers of the Olympics, as well as to affect the developmental design of the Games, is discussed.

THE OLYMPIC GAMES AS A DEVELOPMENTAL PROJECT

The Olympics–sport development nexus cannot be meaningfully understood before the nature of the Games and sport development are established. The Olympic Games represent a practical manifestation of Olympism, which is a philosophy of social reforms underpinned by a philosophical anthropology advocating an idealised vision of the human being and a just society. According to Coubertin (1936), Olympism is a philosophy of social reform that emphasises the role of sport in world development, international understanding, peaceful coexistence, and social and moral education. At the heart of this new type of education were a number of fundamental values and aspirations which form the essence of Olympism: those for education, international understanding, equal opportunities, fair and equal competition, cultural expression, independence of sport and personal excellence embodied in the modern Olympic Games.

Olympism was formally articulated in 1894, and it was not only original and comprehensive in terms of the scope of social change anticipated, but highly altruistic, optimistic and controversial as well. What distinguishes the Olympic Games from all other international sport events and institutions is the explicit pursuit of social values. Olympism, therefore, claims the status of a social, political and educational ideology. Any such ideology necessarily appeals to a philosophical anthropology – an idealised conception of the human being towards which the ideology strives in its attempted social reproduction of the individual. Olympism offers an answer to the fundamental question of philosophical anthropology 'what is a human being?' by implicitly and explicitly seeking to reconcile different societies' distinct political anthropologies and their images of the exemplary citizen.

Olympism was not conceived in an ideological vacuum, and was heavily influenced by a number of intellectual and material sources including the ancient Greek heritage, philosophical ideas of the Enlightenment, the English educational system and the emerging spirit of industrial capitalism and internationalism. As a body of knowledge, Olympism is rooted in a powerful view of reality (i.e. ontology), propagating the existence of a world of universal truth beyond all boundaries of language, nation, culture, religion, class, gender and history. However, this ontology, as MacAloon (1992: 15) observed, 'is only one among many ontologies organizing the experience of peoples of the world today'. This observation raises the question whether it would be possible to unite the vastly culturally diverse sport practices of the world into a coherent representation, and whose representation that would be.

The significance of Olympism as a worldview for sport development is threefold. First, it promotes a universalised and idealised image of the exemplary citizen. Second, it creates the institutions responsible for achieving this ideal: the International Olympic Committee (IOC) and National Olympic Committees (NOCs). Finally, it offers the main instruments for accomplishing its mission:

athleticism and education. However, as Mangan (2000) and Tranter (1998), among others, have convincingly demonstrated, athleticism was an ideological model of dominant social groups to be diffused downwards through class and gender. Similarly, Popkewitz (1990) reminds us that education, the other main technique for spreading the Olympic ideas, is not neutral and universal, but a socially constructed ideological institution in a world of inequality.

The Olympic Games and the philosophical anthropology on which they are premised, therefore, have been conceived and promoted as a developmental project. This project is based on normative ideas about what constitutes the ideal citizen, calls for creating the institutions designed to promote it, and prescribes the main instruments for achieving its ideals. The history of the Olympics offers ample evidence that political regimes from all persuasions – from capitalists to dictators and communists – have tried to appropriate the Olympic ideology in order to advance their visions of the world and particular forms of citizenship (Hoberman, 1984; Senn, 1999). Recently, Price (2008), reflecting on the geopolitical changes in the world and the growing power of the Olympics as a global media event, has raised the issue of the brutal competition that occurs to appropriate the Olympic platform by a variety of groups and powers in society. He argues that increasingly the Olympics have been hijacked by all kinds of groups – from terrorists to local activists and international pressure alliances – to advance political and commercial messages. As Price (2008: 239) expressed it: 'media events become marked by efforts by free riders or interlopers to seize the opportunity to perform in a global theatre of representation'. When those loosely coordinated efforts are added to much more sophisticatedly orchestrated national political campaigns promoting certain ideologies, the Olympic message of social change becomes blurred and is often lost. The point is that, although the hijacking of the Olympic platform can certainly incite the wrong sentiments and behaviours, at the same time it can offer the opportunity for less powerful groups in society, including those with sport development concerns, to have their voices heard by the authorities and to place issues on the political agenda.

Despite political, economic and ethical controversies, the Olympic Games have evolved from a small (mostly) European occasion dominated by a Western male, aristocratic elite, with ill-defined participation rules, unspecified duration and independence from governments, to an unrivalled global phenomenon involving 205 countries and heavy public support. The 2008 Beijing Olympics cost US$2.4 billion to organise, were followed by a worldwide audience of 4.3 billion people, sold 6.5 million tickets and involved some 1,000,000 volunteers across China (IOC, 2008a). Today, the power of the Olympics is such that cities vie to host the Games, kings, presidents and other dignitaries attend the IOC sessions for the election of the host city, billions of people watch them, top brands pay hundreds of millions of dollars to be associated with the five Olympic rings, stock markets react positively to the announcement of the Games' next location, and millions of young people around the world dedicate years of their lives to pursuing the Olympic dream.

The Olympic Games belong to a special category of mass ceremonies or liminal events, such as royal weddings, moon landings or presidential inaugurations, that possess celebratory and cohesion-building character, and bring together performers and spectators into an organic whole. As a performance category, the Olympics have a great symbolic power derived from the four most semantically and functionally significant genres that constitute them: spectacle, festival, ritual and games (MacAloon, 1984). Moreover, sport has been associated with great equalising powers because in the sporting arena competitors are judged on their performance and not on traits such as ethnicity, gender and class. The Games also represent sites where different discursive constructions – personal, place, sport or national – take place: successful athletes become instant celebrities, ordinary cities are branded as international tourist destinations, less well-known sports receive global exposure and whole nations assume heroic identities. Those socially constructed images have the capacity to mirror, sustain or challenge the position of individuals and groups in society (Hogan, 2003). In addition, the Olympics have the potential to mobilise public support and investments on an unprecedented scale, hence their capacity to transform the lives of various communities, cities and sport organisations. In short, the symbolic, discursive, equalising, legitimising and transformative character of the Olympics makes them hugely politically significant and practically relevant in general, and to the field of sport development in particular. Gold and Gold (2008) observed that London is one of a series of Olympic cities that have used the Games as a catalyst for urban regeneration and wider positive change in the country. The Olympic Games represent a global normative developmental project, which promotes universal visions of the ideal citizen who is to be moulded by means of sport and education.

Like the Olympic Games, sport development also represents an inherently normative project carried out in the name of certain goals. Typically, sport development projects prescribe how a particular form of intended development is to be achieved and what its outcomes should be. Sport development has been defined as 'a process of inspiring and engaging people, while learning and creating opportunities for participation in sport and enhancing personal and social well-being' (Girginov, 2008: 282–283). Sport development, therefore, is not a static goal but an ideal and a moving target.

Conceptually, sport development can be understood as a unity of three interrelated meanings: a vision, a process of social change and a practice. As a vision, sport development aims to ensure a progressive and sustainable change by establishing frameworks and policy instruments in the field to be promoted locally, nationally or internationally. Hylton and Bramham (2008) point out that ultimately any vision of development should engage with social justice. Considered as an agent of social change, sport development takes place through six main mutually constructive processes (Girginov, 2008). These are: (i) vision setting or getting sport development issues on the political agenda at international, national and local levels; (ii) governance; (iii) 'un-doing' or overcoming a perception of what one is not; (iv) 'be-coming' or the construction of personal and group identities, as well as space and place meaning construction; (v) leveraging the opportunities presented by the implementation of various global, national and local visions; and (vi) learning (i.e. development as a cognitive enterprise). The final section examines more specifically how these six processes are related to the Olympic Games. When conceived as practice, sport development is concerned with the planning, operations and outcomes of various interventions. Adams (2008) argued that the focus of sport development here becomes creating social capital and empowering people.

THE OLYMPIC GAMES' INTERPRETATIONS OF SPORT DEVELOPMENT

Since the Olympics represent a normative project promoting particular visions, it follows that multiple interpretations of sport development would be possible. This renders the Games' relationship with sport development always evolving and contested. At the heart of this relationship is an inherited duality of the Games: on one hand, they celebrate human excellence, which is exclusive and governed by strict organisational rules and scientific methods; on the other, they aspire to promote a sport, which is inclusive irrespective of class, gender, religion, ethnicity and ability. The UK Sport (2010: 2) current 'No Compromise' policy illustrates this point, as it is very explicit in its philosophy and objectives:[1]

> No Compromise can be summarised as our commitment to reinforce excellence, support talent, challenge under-performance and reject mediocrity. In practice, this means sports that consistently develop medal-winning athletes can be rewarded with stable, ongoing funding at the level needed to at least sustain the standard of excellence attained. Conversely, funded sports that fail to reach agreed benchmarks in both performance and programme development run the risk of having our investment reduced or removed.

Sporting excellence, therefore, is not only a matter of aspiration, but of possibilities and control as well, which makes pursuing it very challenging for less well-off groups in society. Forty per cent of Team GB athletes who competed at the 2008 Beijing Olympic Games came from private schools and 65 per cent were university students (BUCS, 2008). The ethos of sporting excellence is explicitly premised on the exercise of control over the athlete and runs counter to that of sport development, which is concerned with empowering people and sport for all. The notions of empowerment and equality form a central plank of the UK government's plans

302

to use the London 2012 Olympics to inspire a generation of young people and the whole country to be more physically active (DCMS, 2007).

As the history of the Olympic movement demonstrates, it never successfully managed to resolve the elite/mass duality and to produce a balanced picture of sport. This duality has been interpreted rather simplistically through the metaphor of the pyramid in which sport development represents the foundation that leads to the Olympic podium, and elite success serves to draw new participants. As early as 1913 the fifth Olympic Congress expressed concerns over the growing divide between mass and elite sport, and the Games' preoccupation with the latter at the expense of the former (Coubertin, 1936). Those concerns continued to dominate the agenda of the highest Olympic forum ever since, and, as the Olympic movement has become more democratic and transparent, they are even more pronounced today (Girginov and Hills, 2009; Lekarska, 1986).

Although the Games epitomise sport in general, it should be noted that their relations with different sports have always been ambiguous. This is an important issue as the symbolic, discursive, equalising, legitimising and transformative powers of the Olympics would have very different expressions when applied to various sports. Moreover, it would appear that there is a negative causal relationship between sport development and Olympic success. Evidence suggests that, when Olympic athletes fail to deliver the medals expected from them, the public funding for their sports gets cut and, as a consequence, grassroots development programmes suffer the most (Girginov and Hills, 2009; Green, 2007; Houlihan and Green, 2009). Therefore, the IOC, which owns the Olympic Games, has always actively interpreted the field of sport and the role of the Games in it by including or excluding sports from the Games' programme (Georgiev, 1996). The place of different sports on the Olympic programme is not a given; it has to be established in contestation with many other sports and is subject to regular reviews by the IOC. These highly selective determinations about which particular sports are to be directly associated with the Olympics have been informed by three main considerations: ideological, economic and organisational.

The Olympic Games' ideological interpretations of sport are multi-layered and have undergone a series of transformations – from sport as a cultural expression of Western civilisation, to a means for capital accumulation, and currently to sport as a developmental tool. Until the early 1950s the Games were clearly a Western domain and indigenous or non-capitalist forms of sport were deemed 'uncivilised' and kept out of the programme. The most enduring ideological interpretation of sport has been along the lines of 'amateur' and 'professional', which was finally abandoned at the 1992 Barcelona Games when multi-millionaire basketball stars and professional tennis players were allowed to compete alongside full-time students and office workers. The excessive commercialisation of the Games in the 1990s and 2000s attracted significant criticism about their real mission. In order to compensate for the capitalist excesses of the Olympics since the beginning of the 2000s, increasing importance has been afforded to the Games as a developmental tool to be used to create a lasting sport legacy in the host city and country (Girginov and Hills, 2008).

The Games' economic interpretations of sport are also varied, but are essentially rooted in an understanding and packaging of sport as a form of entertainment and passive consumption (Tomlinson, 2005). The economic potential of the Games was not unleashed until the 1980s and was achieved by turning the Olympic ideals and symbols into an intellectual property and a trade mark. This allowed for the world-wide sale of broadcasting and sponsorship rights of the Olympics (Preus, 2004). For example, golf was reinstated in the 2016 Games after a 126-year absence mainly because of its potential to bring in leading commercial brands and ready television audiences, both of which guarantee significant economic revenues for the Olympic movement. Increasingly, Olympic merchandise and tickets have also proved a stable stream of income to Games organisers (IOC, 2008a). As the symbolic, economic, legitimising and media power of the Games grew, they became an important source of income for the sports on the Olympic programme and sport development in general. The IOC provided NOCs, international sport federations (IFs) and various sport initiatives with US$311 million for the 2009–2012 quadrennial, which is 27 per cent up on the previous sport aid budget (IOC, 2009a). However, the current IOC formula for distribution of the revenue generated through the sale of global sponsorship and broadcasting rights, which allocates 92 per cent back to sports and NOCs and retains 8 per cent for the IOC, did not happen without fierce feuds between the IOC, NOCs and IFs (Barney *et al.*, 2004). With enhanced economic power came the ability of NOCs and IFs to directly influence sport development nationally and locally through a range of policy instruments such as earmarked funding for programmes, provision of specialist facilities and training.

The Games' organisational interpretations include value judgements and social constructions about what constitutes a 'global, 'appealing', 'priority' or 'inclusive' sport and an 'eligible athlete'. The Olympic programme has always been a highly contested terrain on which different ideologies, commercial and public interests have been haggling for recognition. The London 2012 Games featured twenty-six Olympic sports and nineteen Paralympic sports. However, the deaf athletes, who constitute the greatest number of the people with disabilities, are not part of the Paralympic Games. This is because the International Committee of Sports for the Deaf (CISS) could not agree with the International Paralympic Committee (IPC) on the terms and conditions of participation and runs its own Deaflympics. Furthermore, from the 2016 Rio de Janeiro Olympics, two new sports – golf and rugby – will join the programme at the expense of other contenders such as softball, squash, baseball, karate and roller sports. The leaders of these two international governing bodies were very quick to praise the massive boost which joining the

Olympics will provide for the development of their sports (McCullagh, 2009). In contrast, capoeira is a traditional Brazilian sport which is practised globally but stands virtually no chance of inclusion. It is worth noting that, despite advances, women continue to be under-represented at the Olympics; that the Paralympic Games, which provide both a source of inspiration and a forum for millions of people to participate, started to be jointly organised with the Olympic Games in only 1988; and that the number of countries that win Olympic medals is still very low relative to the global spread of sport. Definitions of national, gender, ability and eligibility represent important constructions which bear significant implications for sport development locally, as they serve to regulate access to sport. Moreover, elite sport policies around the world prioritise the development of sports nationally according to their ability to win Olympic medals (Houlihan, 2009). Collins (2008) examined the elite/mass sport duality in the UK context and demonstrated that ensuring the conducive socio-economic environment needed to promote equitable sport development is far more politically complex and uncertain than the national kudos and feel-good factor generated by winning an Olympic medal, which has always been far more appealing to the political establishment.

Table 13.1 shows a summary of the media, economic and organisational potential of selected sports on the Summer Olympic Games relative to the medals won by UK athletes and adults' sport participation rates in the UK. The choice of sports is deliberate, as it includes two popular participation activities (football and swimming), two well-established elite sports with limited participation base (boxing and cycling) and two under-developed sports (handball and volleyball). Three important points could be drawn from the information presented. First, the sport development strategies of the IFs of two sports, boxing and handball, depend to a great extent on the revenue allocations from the Games, which make up 63 per cent and 23 per cent of their respective budgets. It is worth mentioning that the sport movements in most of the fifty-three African countries rely almost entirely on Olympic dividends. At the same time, although the cost of organising one day of competition for football is the highest (US$276,788), FIFA gets less than 1 per cent of the revenue generated. This discrepancy is a reflection of the varying commercial viability of different sports. For example, the football governing body, FIFA, runs its own World Cup and does not rely on Olympic receipts. Second, significant discrepancies exist between the media popularity of certain sports (e.g. volleyball and swimming) and participation in those sports in the UK in particular. What is more, the huge success of Team GB in Beijing 2008 in cycling and swimming has failed to translate in increased participation and there has been a decline in the take-up of swimming and volleyball (Sport England, 2011). The high number of television hours and newspaper articles dedicated to Olympic sports (see Table 13.1) should not distract from the fact that the £16,245,000 BBC broadcast of 548 hours of the Beijing Olympics in the UK devoted 97 per cent of the coverage to four sports (athletics, swimming, gymnastics and cycling) and only 3 per cent to the

Table 13.1 Selected sports and their relations with the Olympic Games, Team GB success and adults' sport participation in the UK

Sport		Boxing	Cycling	Football	Handball	Swimming	Volleyball
On Olympic programme	Men	1904	1896	1900	1972	1896	1964
	Women	2012	1984	1996	1976	1912	1964
Olympic revenue (% of IF's total budget)		63	17	0.3	23	16	n/a
Cost to organise one day ($US)		68,493	128,359	276,788	78,946	309,319	97,871
TV coverage (hours)		477	399	746	366	884	1,003
National federations		190	158	196	147	190	201
Articles		300	546	633	176	1425	248
Countries with medals		44	54	6	6	19	6
Team GB medals at Beijing		3	14	0	0	6	0
UK participation 2009–2010 (30 mins 3 times/week)		No change	No change	Decrease	n/a	Decrease	Decrease

Sources: IOC (2005) and Sport England (2010).
Note: Data refer to 2004 Athens Games unless otherwise specified.

remaining twenty-two sports (National Audit Office, 2010). Third, the significant organisational cost of Olympic sport raises legitimate questions about the main priorities of sport development and the political vulnerability of those priorities. It has been estimated that the £9.3 billion for organising the 2012 London Games could have paid for free participation in all leisure centres in the UK for eight years. Furthermore, between 2007 and 2010, the UK sport development priorities markedly changed three times: from sport for good (i.e. the use of sport for tackling social problems), to sport for sport's sake (i.e. sport as a means of personal development), to now more competitive schools sport with its emphasis on competitive individualism (DCMS, 2012).

In summary, the needs of sport development, as a project for social change, are very different from those of developing sporting excellence as promoted by the Olympic Games. The assumption that an elitist forum, such as the Olympics, will automatically inspire generations of people to become physically active, even when backed by dedicated participation strategies, has been challenged by a number of commentators and never established empirically (Cashman, 2006; Coalter, 2010; Collins, 2010; Rowe et al., 2004; Weed et al., 2009). The dichotomy between sport development and the Games is eloquently expressed by a senior official at the Atlanta 1996 Olympic Games who contended that the Olympics are not a welfare programme but a business venture. The important analytical point is that the sport development potential of the Olympics can be properly understood only in relation to specific communities and sports, and the meaning they attach to this event.

KEY SPORT DEVELOPMENT PROCESSES AND THE OLYMPICS

The symbolic, legitimising and economic powers of the Olympics should not be considered as given, but have to be established and maintained in practice. Sport development promoters can learn a lesson from the world of business by being more creative and better at leveraging the potential powers of the Olympics. For example, global Olympic sponsors, in addition to the amounts they pay for the exclusive rights to associate their products with the five rings, invest three to five times as much to activate this association. It is true that asymmetrical power relations exist between the Olympics and the development of various sports, and that the sport policy community in most countries is loosely organised and not powerful enough. However, recently the Olympics have increasingly been framed within the notion of sustainable development, which suggests that there are real benefits to be gained by the field of sport development through shaping the course of Games' legacies (IOC, 2010a). This is because at the heart of both sustainability and development is an expressed concern with social justice, participation, democratic governance and distributing social and economic benefits equally and fairly across society.

Chalip (2006: 112) has argued for social leverage of mega sporting events, and observed that 'the purpose of studying event leverage is to identify and explore event implementations that can optimise desired event outcomes'. Although such an approach clearly combines a strategic with tactical focus and directs attention to the process of event implementation, it tends to overlook a key factor: the conceptual and structural designs of the Olympics. Unless the fundamental principles of sport development become ingrained in the design of the Olympic Games, this event will remain concerned with elitist interests. The current developmental logic promoted by the Olympic Games moves from an IOC framework, to Games organisers' vision, to local delivery. A true commitment to sport development requires reconsidering this logic. It needs to start with locally informed development strategies, which are supported by the Olympics through a developmental design of the Games based on sustainable principles. The city of Amsterdam's approach to the Olympics provides evidence that this is possible. Amsterdam 2028 is a nationwide campaign designed to consult all segments of Dutch society on their developmental needs and aspirations and to explore how an Olympic bid for the Games in 2028 could help the country become a better and juster place to live (NOC, 2008).

The rest of this section interrogates how the key sport development processes – (i) vision setting; (ii) governance; (iii) 'un-doing' or overcoming a perception of what one is not; (iv) 'be-coming' or the construction of personal and group identities; (v) leveraging the opportunities presented by the implementation of various global, national and local visions; and (vi) learning – can be integrated within the Olympic Games with a view to both better leveraging their powers and influencing their design.

The first key sport development process concerns vision setting or getting issues on the political agenda at international, national and local levels. Three examples with different design and implementation implications illustrate this process. An essential element of the concept of sustainable sport development concerns its relationship with the environment. The IOC recognised the negative environmental impacts of the Games and sport practice in general, and has put in place a global strategy, 'Agenda 21' (IOC, 1992). This strategy is designed to inform thinking and practice in the field and has since been refined and expanded. It involves global initiatives such as the partnership between the IOC and the United Nations Environment Programme (UNEP) in organising the World Conference on Sport and the Environment. The ninth edition of this conference took place in 2011 in Doha, Qatar, on the theme of 'Playing for a Greener Future'. At a practical level, specific instruments have been developed to help implement environmental requirements into reality. The *Sustainable Sport and Events Tool Kit* (International Academy of Sport Science and Technology, 2009) gives sport organisations the tools required to incorporate sustainability organisationally and to plan and execute sustainable sport events, and was used in the planning and delivery of the 2010 Vancouver

308

Winter Olympics. London 2012 also adopted its own environmental concept, *Towards a One Planet 2012* (LOCOG, 2009), which permeates every concept and action undertaken in the name of the Games. It should be noted, however, that neither of these documents acknowledges the institutional dimension, or the governance of sustainability, which is the second key sport developmental process.

An example of placing sport developmental issues on the political agenda at national level is the UK government's use of the Paralympic Games to affect wider social change in society. For the first time in history, the UK government placed sport development for people with disability on the policy agenda, making politically and economically explicit the link between social equality, urban regeneration and sport development (DCMS, 2009).

Similarly, at local level, the five Olympic boroughs of east London, where the Games were held, have made explicit the link between sport development and urban regeneration. More specifically, the five boroughs' Olympic strategy explicitly addresses inequality in its various forms including housing, health, education and employment, and sets the overcoming of these inequalities in the next twenty years as a precondition for any advances in sport development (HBSU, 2009). Collins's (2010) examination of sport development policies in the UK provides convincing support for the link between social equality and sport development. The three examples show that setting sport development visions is not only a long-term process, but one that is uncertain and contingent on many factors. The change of UK government in 2010, from Labour to a Conservative–Liberal Democrat coalition, has resulted in a marked shift in sport development Olympic legacy priorities. All sport participation targets and some of the key mechanisms for their delivery were abandoned and replaced with a new strategic legacy framework (Cryer, 2011).

The second key process of governance of sport development is critical, as it provides the systems and policy instruments to guide and steer collective actions towards a consensus amongst various parties concerned in achieving the long-term visions. It is premised on the ideas of public participation, mandate for action and accountability. The notion of governance was first introduced in the Olympic Charter in 2004 (IOC, 2004) and further spelled out in *Basic Universal Principles of Good Governance of the Olympic and Sports Movement* (IOC, 2008b), but it is not yet clear how it will be applied to the design and running of the Games. The scope of the IOC's Olympic Games Impact Manual covers only the economic, socio-cultural and environmental areas of sustainable development, but not its institutional one, and makes no reference to governance (IOC, 2009b). Four main modes of governance of Olympic sport development legacy that involve exchanges between the state, market and society have been identified in relation to the 2012 London Games: coercive, voluntarism, targeting and framework regulation (Girginov, 2012). However, commentators have expressed concerns that the main modes of governance have been very state-centred, and popular and local participation has been afforded only a marginal role (MacRury and Poynter, 2009).

At the heart of sport development, as indeed of any development, is the process of 'un-doing' or overcoming a perception of what one is not. Changing perceptions is critical because development in its various forms necessarily involves a change in subjectivity. A prime illustration of this process is the first main promise of the UK government's Olympic legacy plan for disability sport (DCMS, 2009). The plan is underpinned by a strong commitment of the government to make a fundamental shift in society's perceptions about people with disability. It envisages that, by 2025, disabled people in Britain should have the same opportunities and choices as non-disabled people, and be respected and included as equal members of society (DCMS, 2009). The use of the Paralympic Games to influence attitudes and perceptions is based on four main strategies: working with media organisations, achieving high standards of access and inclusion at Games-time, connecting the UK with the Games and implementing innovative educational programmes in the UK and abroad.

Similarly, China used the 2008 Beijing Games to completely overhaul the inadequate image and organisation of its health system. The Chinese state launched a comprehensive nationwide public health programme including four key strands: improved capacity in traditional medical services required for hosting the Olympics, a strengthened public health system (i.e. disease surveillance, risk management and health emergency response), an enhanced living environment, and increased health awareness among athletes, visitors and residents through successful health education and campaigns (Dapeng, Ljungqvist and Troedsson, 2010).

The five Olympic host boroughs' strategy provides another illustrative example of real issues that have to be overcome before any meaningful gains in sport development can be delivered. To secure the strategic framework vision, by 2015, the host boroughs and their partners need to 'undo' a challenging list of specific 'undesirables' including unemployment (put 120,000 more residents in jobs), lack of education (ensure that 99,000 residents have a qualification), poverty (lift approximately 21,000 children from living in poverty), under-achievement (ensure that 1,800 more children achieve five A*–C GCSEs, including maths and English), inactivity (ensure that 25,000 more adults do weekly physical activity) and anti-social behaviour (ensure that 44,000 fewer people are affected by burglaries) (HBSU, 2009). Overcoming sport under-development is closely intertwined with the process of assuming a new role, identity and activity, and place meaning, which is discussed next.

The fourth main process in sport development is 'be-coming' or the construction of personal and group identities, as well as space and place meaning construction. The history of the Olympic Games provides ample evidence for the workings of this process and suggests that this is a social construction process involving a range of struggles. Parent (2008) identified three types of changes brought about by mega events which are related to sport development: individual, infrastructural and policy and planning. The sport development emphasis of Games organisers between the 1970s and 1990s was mainly on building infrastructure and raising general awareness about the importance of sport (Poynter and MacRury, 2009). The Olympics, however, have also been successfully used to shape space and place meaning. As Wainwright and Ansell (2008: 183) note, 'essentially, sport development is an encounter between people and place that takes place in and through space'. For example, Barcelona used the 1992 Games to refashion the city as a tourist paradise, while Beijing 2008 Olympics were perceived as an opportunity to transform this city into a capital for a twenty-first-century power. London also projected the 2012 Games as a catalyst for transformation but only of its east part. The lack of clear focus on London as a place has earned Olympic organisers criticism from various corners including its citizens (Fussey *et al.*, 2011).

The implications for sport development are that it is necessary to comprehend 'be-coming' not simply as a one-dimensional process or a move from one destination to another, but as a process involving objective conditions and subjective perceptions of those affected by development. Development is a subjective category and different people will interpret it differently depending on their life experiences, education and culture. Critical here is the role of discourse in shaping action and the institutions who promote it. The former prescribes what development is whereas the latter ensures that the sport development norms are reinforced and adhered to. As London and previous Games hosts' practices demonstrate, sport development projects have always been located within broader political agendas and visions of citizenship. The UK government has been very explicit in its Olympic ambitions with regard to transforming the younger generation: 'we will transform the lives of young people through sport' (DCMS, 2008: 3). The plan is to use the London Olympics to cultivate a range of characteristics in young people so they become not only physically active but better citizens as well. To that effect, a specific policy instrument that was employed by LOCOG is the 'Inspire' programme, which also bridges the gap between elitism and wider participation. It was created to officially recognise outstanding non-commercial sport, as well as other projects and events inspired by the Games. 'Inspire' promotes a discourse about how organisations should operate and how individuals should act (www.london2012.com/inspire-programme). The 'inspired person' therefore, is not simply an active sportsperson, but one who is creative, sharing and with leadership qualities, as only the very best are recognised and given the 'Inspire' badge. Building on the success of the Beijing Olympics, the Chinese government designated 8 August of each year as China's National Fitness Day. Thereby, fitness becomes transformed from a personal issue to one of national importance and people are expected to take action.

The fifth sport development process concerns leveraging the opportunities presented by the implementation of various global, national and local visions. It links with the first process of establishing visions and their implementation by highlighting the role of various institutions, and brings together sport developers and those being developed. It is impossible to provide a comprehensive picture of the sport development leverage of previous Olympics, but several studies offer useful analyses in this regard (Cashman, 2006; Chalip and Leyns, 2002; Gold and Gold, 2010; Weed, 2009). London offers the advantage of witnessing the sport developmental leverage of the Olympics in practice and allows several conclusions to be drawn.

For the first time in history an Olympic host country has embarked on a concerted nationwide programme of leveraging the opportunities presented by the Games through an unprecedented mobilisation of public energy. As the former Secretary for Culture, Media and Sport (DCMS) and Olympic Minister, Tessa Jowell (2006), stated: 'There is nothing inevitable or god-given about the legacy of the 2012 Games, it was up to those involved to make it and create it'. The social, economic and sporting leverage of the Olympics was conceptualised within the notion of legacy. The UK government undertook the ambitious task of ensuring a UK-wide legacy of the 2012 Games formulated in six specific promises and a comprehensive delivery strategy (DCMS, 2007). The government's eighty-page action plan *Before, During and After* (DCMS, 2008) offers a road map for implementing the six (including disability; DCMS, 2009) substantial promises in order to leverage various opportunities presented by the Games. It is important to note the institutional dimension of leverage, which comprises eleven government boards designed to develop different aspects of 2012's legacy. The leveraging action of the state at national level is carried out by a mix of public, private and charitable agencies, all of which were initiated and heavily regulated by the state. Eight new institutions with specific leverage remit emerged: the Olympic Delivery Authority (ODA), the Sport Legacy Delivery Board (SLDB), the Government Olympic Executive (GOE), the Commission for Sustainable London (CSL), the Legacy Trust, the London Employment and Skills Task Force (LEST), the Host Boroughs Strategic Unit (HBSU) and Podium, the tertiary and higher education unit for the Games. The GOE is closely involved with the Sport Legacy Delivery Board, which is made up of senior representatives from seventeen public and voluntary organisations including eight government departments and agencies.

The institutional picture of leveraging actors at regional and local level is truly complex and diverse, as almost every local authority, school, higher education institution and chamber of commerce in the UK has some sort of plan for making the most of the Olympics. Clearly the sport, economic and cultural typographies of Olympic leverage will vary significantly across the UK (Walton *et al.*, 2008) and will be contingent on past experiences, organisational and economic capacities and

312

political will. The point is that the sport development leverage of the Games is constructed by people and organisations. This entails that the sport development community needs to engage with the Games from the outset and to ensure a place at the decision-making table by employing a range of strategies including advocacy, lobbying and direct action. Although the institutionalisation of sport development leverage implies a degree of prescribing and controlling human conduct, it also means greater power in relation to Games owners and organisers. Although the multitude of sport development legacy promoters will have different interests, collectively they possess much greater bargaining power and are in a position to significantly affect the developmental and sustainable designs of the Games.

The final sport development process sees development as a cognitive enterprise and involves learning. Since sport development is not a static goal but a moving target, it follows that there is a great deal of learning taking place on the part of both developers and developed. The critical issue here is to ensure the right balance and constant interplay between professional and lay knowledge. The former is promoted by various institutions with development agendas, whereas the latter is largely in the form of tacit knowledge residing in the heads and experiences of sport participants. The power relation between professional and lay knowledge tends to be asymmetrical, as it is often assumed that professionals know better than the lay person how development should occur. This is a very problematic proposition, which can be counter-productive and usually leads to meeting the targets of various agencies instead of the developmental needs of communities.

Olympic-related sport development learning can take many different shapes and forms. Historically, prominence has been given to various educational programmes, but more recently the IOC has put in place a formalised knowledge-transfer process designed to capture the experiences of every Games organiser and pass them on to the next host city (IOC, 2009b). The transfer of knowledge includes not only operational information about running the Games but strategies for promoting sport in general and how to measure and sustain its legacies in particular. Other forms of learning and knowledge creation include various sport leadership training and volunteering schemes, conferences, research, and academic courses and publishing. The main challenge for sport developers is how to capture, store and share the knowledge created so it can be internalised and acted upon by individuals and organisations in the field, and turned into a productive force.

A Centre for British Teachers Education Trust Report (Graver *et al.*, 2010) provides a comprehensive review of fifty-two educational programmes operated across the Olympic Games, Commonwealth Games and FIFA World Cup since 1992, but similar programmes had existed prior to 1992. The broader political aim of recent Olympic education programmes has been to ensure that all children in the world have equal access to education. For example, one third of all UK schools (8,000) participated in the 'send my friend to school' 2010 campaign designed to win the support of the Prime Minister for the 1GOAL programme, committing governments around the world to improve access to education. As Graver and colleagues (2010: 21) observed:

> the projects arising from and created by mega events are not in themselves the valuable lasting legacy for education – rather it is the change in attitudes, values and approaches, the increased opportunities, and the greater sense of engagement with education among the wider community.

The Athens 2004 educational programme had very practical implications as it was supported by the appointment of the Greek government of over 3,000 physical education teachers (Grammatikopoulos *et al.*, 2005). Particularly ambitious was the Beijing 2008 educational programme, which aimed to engage some 400 million children and 500 model schools across China. London 2012 also established its own Get Set programme for schools, college and local authority education providers across the UK. This is more than an educational programme for three- to nineteen-year-olds; it also provides resources, membership of a nationwide network of 16,500 schools, engagement with enterprise, culture, creativity and internationalism, and recognition from the Games organisers. In addition to that, for the first time a leading academic publisher (Routledge: www.routledgeonlinestudies. com/) has commissioned over forty Olympic-focused special issues of journals from a wide range of disciplines. A similar coordinated approach will ensure that the Olympics are interrogated not only from a social science perspective, but from a variety of perspectives, thus generating new knowledge. Moreover, studies on the local and national leveraging of the Games will yield valuable insights into sport development (Bell, 2010; Sadd and Jones, 2008, 2009). Table 13.2 summarises the mutual relations between the six core sport development processes and the Olympic Games.

CONCLUSIONS

This chapter has conceptualised the Olympic Games as a developmental project and examined its relevance to the field of sport development. The gist of the argument has been that, although the Games and sport development are underpinned by two different philosophies, a great deal of synergy is still possible. The main rationales behind this claim are the democratisation of the Olympic Games process from the bid to the delivery stage, and the critical role of governments and the public sector in general. After the Salt Lake City Winter Olympics scandal in 1999, which exposed corruption and unethical and undemocratic practices within the Olympic movement, it became apparent that the existing growth and spectacle model of the Olympics could no longer be sustained. As a result, the IOC has

314

Table 13.2 Mutual relations between sport development and the Olympic Games

Key sport development processes	Olympic Games help sport development to:	Sport development affects Olympics' design by:
Placing issues on political agenda	Make explicit the link between the Games, equality and sport development Establish global environmental and organisational standards to be followed locally	Working with bid and organising committees to ensure local sport development priorities get political recognition Advocacy and lobbying at local and national level Establishing local development practices to be shared globally
Governance	Assert its autonomy Establish sustainability as a guiding principle Promote public participation and accountability Build national consensus on sport development policies	Ensuring a balance between public and private interests Participating in Games Committees Establishing local accountability frameworks
Overcoming perceptions	Address prejudices and change old identities Identify forms of inequality and address them	Placing sport under-development on Games organisers' agenda
Constructing identities	Construct personal, social and place meanings Use global discourses to affect identity construction	Promoting images of people, sports and places to be supported by the Games Tackling sports under-development
Leveraging opportunities	Develop plans for leveraging social, cultural and sporting potential of the Games Forge public–private partnerships Gain global exposure	Providing means to tackle wider social issues Offering a collective bargaining voice Introducing new architectural and technological designs of facilities and equipment
Learning: social, organisational	Generate, share and disseminate knowledge Promote public awareness about sport Develop personal dispositions for sport	Initiating various educational programmes Ensuring local/lay knowledge is given a voice Collecting and sharing empirical evidence

actively sought to change this model by using the Games to promote a wider social agenda in the host city and country. Since the beginning of the 2000s the IOC has added developmental assurances, as well as promoting a positive legacy, to the political, economic and security guarantees required by governments wishing to host the Olympics (IOC, 2007). At the same time, the Games would not have been possible without huge public investments. This is true even for the much publicised profitable capitalist 1984 Los Angeles Games, which had received a state subsidy of $75 million. This requires governments not only to justify that those investments go well beyond the sixteen days of spectacle and leave lasting improvements for the host communities, but to be accountable for them as well. The UK government committed £9.3 billion of public money to the staging of the 2012 London Games and put in place a comprehensive strategy for leveraging the social, cultural, sporting and economic opportunities presented by them as well as an accountability framework.

In reconsidering the link between sport development and the Olympics, and in line with the main thrust of this book, three main conclusions can be drawn. First, as policy, sport development entails making politically and economically explicit the link between urban regeneration and sport development. A key task here is to address inequality in its various forms through advances in education, health, social cohesion, housing and urban regeneration. Although the Olympics should not be considered as the magic wand capable of solving long-standing structural problems, the sport development community and Games organisers have to make sure that all plans clearly address those issues. The five Olympic host boroughs in London provide an illuminating example that this is possible. Second, as a process of personal and social change, sport development needs to capitalise on the potential of the Olympics to unleash the creative potential of different groups for addressing sport-specific issues, such as raising awareness, participation, building self-esteem and skills, and developing programmes and networks. The developmental potential of the Olympics and sport allows the changing of personal and public perceptions through the creation of relevant discourses, as well as the active leveraging of this potential both to make the most of the Games and to influence their design. However, the institutionalisation of development poses a danger of promoting normative discourses representing the interests of the most powerful groups in society. Therefore, participation and accountability, as fundamental principles of sustainable development, have to be established from the outset and followed through. Finally, as a set of practices, sport development and the Olympics need to systematically integrate sustainable thinking in the delivery of sport services and programmes. Furthermore, better measures can be implemented to utilise various educational, health and cultural initiatives as a context for sport development. Education and culture in their various forms are largely responsible for creating the dispositions needed for sport participation as well as the sites where the practice of sport can take place. However, the relationship between the Olympics and sport development has to be mutual. A mutually constructive relationship necessitates not only an effort on the part of the sport development community to utilise the opportunities presented by this event, but a change in the design of the Games, so they can actively promote sport development.

1 Study three existing 'Inspire' projects concerned with different forms of sport development available at www.london2012.com/get-involved/inspire-programme/index.php

2 Use the six key processes in Table 13.2 to analyse what mutual relations have been established between those projects and the Games in terms of values, inclusion, governance and sustainability.

NOTE

1. UK Sport is the government agency responsible for elite sport in the UK and international sport development.

REFERENCES

Adams, A. (2008) 'Building organisational and management capacity for the delivery of sport development', in Girginov, V. (ed.), *Management of Sport Development*, Oxford: Butterworth-Heinemann.

Barney, R., Wenn, S. and Martyn, S. (2004) *Selling the Five Rings: The International Olympic Committee and the Rise of Olympic Commercialism*, Salt Lake City: University of Utah Press.

Bell, B. (2010) 'Building a legacy for youth and coaching: champion coaching on Merseyside', in Collins, M.F. (ed.), *Examining Sports Development*, London: Routledge.

BUCS (2008) 'Over half of Team GB from the university sector', www.bucs.org.uk/news.asp?section=000100010002&itemid=1499

Cashman, R. (2006) *The Bitter-Sweet Awakening: The Legacy of the Sydney 2000 Olympic Games*, Sydney: Walla Walla Press.

Chalip, L. (2006) 'Towards social leverage of sport events', *Journal of Sport & Tourism*, 11 (2): 109–127.

Chalip, L. and Leyns, A. (2002) 'Local business leveraging of a sport event: managing an event for economic benefit', *Journal of Sport Management*, 16 (2): 132–158.

Coalter, F. (2010) 'The politics of sport-for-development: limited focus programmes and broad gauge problems?', *International Review for the Sociology of Sport*, 45 (3): 295–314.

Collins, M. (2008) 'Public policies on sports development: can mass and elite sport hold together', in Girginov, V. (ed.), *Management of Sports Development*, Oxford: Butterworth-Heinemann.

Collins, M. (2010) 'From "sport for good" to "sport for sport's sake": not a good move for sport development in England?', *International Journal of Sport Policy*, 2 (3): 381–391.

Coubertin, P. (1936) 'The unfinished symphony', *Olympic Review*, 32–34.

Cryer, J. (2011) 'Introduction to sports development', www.sportdevelopment.org.uk/index.php?option=com_content&view=category&layout=blog&id=54&Itemid=66

Dapeng, J., Ljungqvist, A. and Troedsson, H. (eds.) (2010) *The Health Legacy of the 2008 Beijing Olympic Games*, New York: World Health Organisation.

DCMS (2007) *Our Promise for 2012: How the UK Will Benefit from the Olympic and Paralympic Games*, London: DCMS.

DCMS (2008) *Before, During and After: Making the Most of the London 2012 Games*, London: DCMS.

DCMS (2009) *London 2012: A Legacy for Disabled People*, London: DCMS.

DCMS (2012) *Creating a Sporting Habit for Life*, London: DCMS.

Fussey, P., Coaffee, J., Armstrong, G. and Hobbs, D. (2011) *Securing and Sustaining the Olympic City: Reconfiguring London for 2012 and Beyond*, Ashgate: Farnham.

Georgiev, N. (1996) *Analysis of the Olympic Programme 1896–1996*, Lausanne: IOC.

Girginov, V. (ed.) (2008) *Management of Sports Development*, Oxford: Butterworth-Heinemann.

Girginov, V. (2012) 'Governance of London 2012 Olympic Games sport legacy', *International Review for the Sociology of Sport*, 47 (5): 543–558.

Girginov, V. and Hills, L. (2008) 'The 2012 London Olympic Games and participation in sport: understanding the link', *International Journal of the History of Sport*, 25 (14): 2091–2116.

Girginov, V. and Hills, L. (2009) 'The political process of constructing a sustainable London Olympics sports development legacy', *International Journal of Sport Policy*, 1 (2): 161–181.

Gold, J. and Gold, M. (2008) 'Olympic cities: regeneration, city rebranding and changing urban agendas', *Geography Compass*, 2 (1): 300–318.

Gold, J.R. and Gold, M.M. (eds.) (2010) *Olympic Cities: City Agendas, Planning, and the World's Games, 1896–2016*, 2nd edn, London: Routledge.

Grammatikopoulos, V., Tsigilis, N., Koustelios, A. and Theodorakis, Y. (2005) 'Evaluating the implementation of an Olympic education program in Greece', *International Review of Education*, 51 (5–6): 427–438.

Graver, A., Cammiss, L., Charlton, C. and Plantak, J. (2010) *What Lasting Educational Benefits Can Be Created from Mega Events? Literature Review*, Reading: CfBT Education Trust.

Green, M. (2007) 'Olympic glory or grassroots development? Sport policy priorities in Australia, Canada and the United Kingdom, 1960–2006', *International Journal of the History of Sport*, 24 (7): 921–953.

HBSU (2009) *Olympic and Paralympic Legacy: Strategic Regeneration Framework*, London: HBSU.

Hoberman, J. (1984) *Sport and Political Ideology*, London: Heinemann.

Hogan, J. (2003) 'Staging the nation: gendered and ethnicized discourses of national identity in Olympic opening ceremonies', *Journal of Sport & Social Issues*, 27 (2): 100–123.

Houlihan, B. (2009) 'Mechanisms of international influence on domestic elite sport policy', *International Journal of Sport Policy*, 1 (1): 51–70.

Houlihan, B. and Green, M. (2009) 'Modernisation and sport: the examples of UK Sport and Sport England', *Public Administration*, 87 (3): 678–698.

Hylton, K. and Bramham, P. (2008) 'Models of sports development', in Girginov, V. (ed.), *Management of Sports Development*, Oxford: Butterworth-Heinemann.

International Academy of Sport Science and Technology (2009) *Sustainable Sport and Event Tool Kit*, Lausanne: AISTS.

IOC (1992) *Olympic Movement's Agenda 21: Sport for Sustainable Development*, Lausanne: IOC.

IOC (2004) *Olympic Charter*, Lausanne: IOC.

IOC (2005) *Olympic Programme Commission Report to the 117th IOC Session*, Lausanne: IOC.

IOC (2007) *Olympic Charter*, Lausanne: IOC.

IOC (2008a) *Beijing Olympic Games Marketing Report*, Lausanne: IOC.

IOC (2008b) *Basic Universal Principles of Good Governance of the Olympic and Sports Movement*, Lausanne: IOC.

IOC (2009a) *Where the Action Is: 2009–2012 Quadrennial Plan*, Lausanne: Olympic Solidarity.

IOC (2009b) *Technical Manual on Olympic Games Impact*, Lausanne: IOC.

IOC (2010) *Shaping the Future: IOC Interim Report 2009–2010*, Lausanne: IOC.

Jowell, T. (2006) 'What social legacy of 2012?', speech at the Fabian Fringe in Manchester, 27 September, http://fabians.org.uk/events/event-reports/what-social-legacy-of-2012

318

Lekarska, N. (1986) *Tenth and Eleventh Olympic Congresses: Comparative Studies and Essays*, Sofia: Sofia Press.

LOCOG (2009) *Towards a One Planet 2012*, 2nd edn, London: LOCOG.

MacAloon, J. (1984) 'Olympic Games and the theory of spectacle in modern societies', in MacAloon, J. (ed.), *Rite, Drama, Festival, Spectacle: Towards a Theory of Cultural Performance*, Philadelphia, PA: ISHI.

MacAloon, J. (1992) 'Sport, science, and intercultural relations: reflections on recent trends in Olympic scientific meetings', *Olympika: The International Journal of Olympic Studies*, 1: 1–28.

McCullagh, K. (2009) 'Golf and rugby sevens will both be on the programme for the 2016 and 2020 Summer Olympic Games, after winning the approval of the International Olympic Committee in a vote today', www.sportbusiness.com/news/170676/rugby-and-golf-win-ioc-approval-for-olympics-inclusion

MacRury, I. and Poynter, G. (2009) *London's Olympic Legacy: A 'Thinkpiece' Report Prepared for the OECD and Department for Communities and Local Government*, London: University of East London.

Mangan, J.A. (2000) *Athleticism in the Victorian and Edwardian Public School: The Emergence and Consolidation of an Educational Ideology*, London: Frank Cass.

National Audit Office (2010) *The BBC's Management of its Coverage of Major Sporting and Music Events*, London: NAO.

NOC (2008) *Olympisch Plan 2008*, Amsterdam: NOC.

Parent, M. (2008) 'Mega sporting events and sports development', in Girginov, V. (ed.), *Management of Sports Development*, Oxford: Butterworth-Heinemann.

Popkewitz, T. (1990) 'Whose future? Whose past? Notes on critical theory and methodology', in Guba, E. (ed.), *The Paradigm Dialog*, London: Sage.

Poynter, G. and MacRury, I. (eds.) (2009) *Olympic Cities: 2012 and the Remaking of London*, Farnham: Ashgate.

Preus, H. (2004) *The Economics of Staging the Olympics: A Comparison of the Games 1972–2008*, Cheltenham: Edward Elgar.

Price, M. (2008) 'On seizing the Olympic platform', in Price, M. and Dayan, D. (eds.), *Owning the Olympics: Narratives of New China*, Ann Arbor: University of Michigan Press.

Rowe, N., Adams, R. and Beasley, N. (2004) 'Driving up participation in sport: the social context, the trends, the prospects and the challenges', in Sport England (ed.), *Driving Up Participation: The Challenge for Sport*, London: Sport England.

Sadd, D. and Jones, I. (2008) 'Implications and issues for London site residents', *London Journal of Tourism, Sport and Creative Studies*, 1 (1): 22–29.

Sadd, D. and Jones, I. (2009) 'Long-term legacy implications for Olympic Games', in Raj, R. and Musgrave, J. (eds.), *Event Management and Sustainability*, Wallingford, UK: CABI.

Senn, A. (1999) *Power, Politics and the Olympic Games*, Champaign, IL: Human Kinetics.

Sport England (2010) *Active People*, London: Sport England.

Sport England (2011) *Active People-5*, London: Sport England.

Tomlinson, A. (2005) 'The commercialisation of the Olympics: cities, corporations, and the Olympic commodity', in Young, K. and Wamsley, K. (eds.), *Global Olympics: Historical and Sociological Studies of the Modern Games*, Oxford: Elsevier.

Tranter, N. (1998) *Sport, Economy and Society in Britain*, Cambridge: Cambridge University Press.

UK Sport (2010) *Performance Investment Guide*, London: UK Sport.

Wainwright, E. and Ansell, N. (2008) 'Geographies of sports development: the role of space and place', in Girginov, V. (ed.), *Management of Sports Development*, Oxford: Butterworth-Heinemann.

Walton, H., Longo, A. and Dawson, P. (2008) 'A contingent valuation of the 2012 London Olympic Games', *Journal of Sports Economics*, 9 (3): 304–317.

Weed, M. (2009) *A Review of the Evidence Base for Developing a Health and Physical Activity Participation Legacy from the 2012 Olympic Games*, London: Department of Health.

Weed, M., Coren, E., Fiore, J., Mansfield, L., Wellard, I., Chatziefstathiou, D. and Dowse, S. (2009) *A Systematic Review of the Evidence Base for Developing a Physical Activity and Health Legacy from the London 2012 Olympic and Paralympic Games*, London: Department of Health.

CHAPTER 14

INTERNATIONAL SPORT AND DEVELOPMENT

OSCAR MWAANGA

Despite long-held beliefs concerning the capacity of sports participation for promoting holistic health and well-being, it is only in the last decade or so that a concerted effort has been seen to (re)mobilise sports to achieve broad human and social development goals, whether this be for deprived communities of high- or low-income countries (Kidd, 2008; United Nations, 2003). This global awakening to sport's capacity to contribute to achieving development goals is apparent through the rapid increase in numbers of dedicated initiatives aimed at addressing specific aspects of under-development. For example, at the time of writing this chapter, the International Platform on Sport for Development and Peace had officially registered 2,146 individuals and 141 projects involved in the sport for development and peace (SDP) movement. Additionally, there were 366 organisations worldwide that had officially registered with the same platform – an estimated 100 per cent growth compared with 2008 (also see evidence of this proliferation through other activities such as conferences and online debates on the website for the International Platform on Sport for Development and Peace: www.sportanddev.org). However, given that many SDP initiatives operating within low-income countries have limited Internet access, it is safe to state that there may be many unaccounted for initiatives. For instance, only eleven of the over ninety SDP initiatives operating in Lusaka (Zambia's capital) are registered with the platform website. Notwithstanding such omissions, this global intensification of SDP activity is now recognised as an emerging sector, an academic field of study and a global social movement (Kidd, 2008). Indeed the SDP movement's alignment with the United Nations Millennium Development Goals (MDGs)[1] signals this global nature; and, although, of course, sport is unable to achieve the MDGs alone, nevertheless it is considered a potentially valuable component in addressing global development challenges (SDP IWG, 2008).

As a consequence of this, SDP initiatives have been, and are, linked to multilateral institutions, such as the United Nations Office of Sport for Development and

Peace (UNOSDP) and the United Nations Children's Fund (UNICEF); international non-governmental organisations (NGOs); governmental bodies, such as the Norwegian Confederation of Sport and Olympic Committee (NIF); international corporations, such as Nike; local community-based organisations (CBOs); and national NGOs, such as the Zambian-based EduSport Foundation.[2] Additionally, academic institutions, including the University of Toronto, Southampton Solent University and the Interdisciplinary Centre of Excellence for Sports Science and Development at the University of the Western Cape, for instance, are considered as being SDP organisations. This stakeholder innumerability has tended to overpopulate the SDP policy terrain, thus leading to wide-ranging interpretations of the meaning of sport and development in this context. Levermore and Beacom (2009) therefore emphasise the need to differentiate between the various interpretations of the sport and development relationship.

In an attempt to critically map the emerging field of SDP, this chapter aims to achieve three primary objectives. First, the chapter provides a two-tier (Global Northern and Southern)[3] account of the historical factors that have shaped and continue to shape the SDP movement. Second, it examines the meaning of sport and development, aiming to critically unpack the discourses[4] framing sport, on the one hand, and development, on the other. As an alternative development approach within SDP, postcolonial theory together with the indigenous sub-Saharan cultural philosophy of Ubuntu is examined as constituting a counter-argument to the selected dominant development discourse of modernisation, which is assumed to underpin the global SDP movement. The Zambian-based EduSport Foundation, in being partly framed by Ubuntu, is discussed in order to highlight how an alternative development discourse could influence SDP policy and organisational processes (Broodryk, 1997; Louw, 1995; Shutte, 1993).

This chapter's critique is essentially informed by three primary sources of material; the first is the recent body of work in critical sociology of sport and development (see Darnell, 2010; Hayhurst, 2009; Jarvie, 2011; Lindsey and Gratton, 2012; Nicholls *et al.*, 2011; Tiessen, 2011). Second, the chapter is informed by empirical data obtained from research focusing upon the sport (dis)empowerment of people living with HIV/AIDS (PLWHA) in Zambia (Mwaanga, 2012). The final primary source material is my prolonged involvement in the SDP movement, as both an activist and a practitioner.

SDP AND THE UNITED NATIONS

In passing Resolution 58/5 the United Nations (UN) officially recognised sport as a formidable tool in achieving peace, health, education and economic developmental objectives (United Nations, 2003). However, despite its delayed recognition, formal acknowledgement of sport as a fundamental right for all was actually outlined much earlier by various entities within the UN family (Beutler, 2008). Indeed in 1978 the United Nations Educational, Scientific and Cultural Organisation's International Charter of Physical Education and Sport described sport and physical education as a 'fundamental right for all' (Beutler, 2008). Furthermore, Beutler (2008) asserts that as far back as 1959 the international community had recognised sport as a fundamental right through the Declaration on the Rights of the Child. Nonetheless, when compared with other human rights fostered at the UN level, arguably the rights to play and to participate in sports and physical education are essentially forgotten, especially in light of the limited actions deriving from these international recognitions.

However, a drive towards concrete directive policy actions came in July 2002, when the Secretary-General convened a United Nations Inter-Agency Task Force on SDP whose mandate was to review activities involving sport within the United Nations system. The Task Force aimed to promote a more systematic use of SDP activities, particularly at the community level, as well as to generate greater support for such activities among governments and sports-related organisations (Beutler, 2008). Concerning the necessity of the latter mission, the Task Force compiled and published *Sport for Development and Peace: Towards Achieving the Millennium Development Goals* (United Nations Inter-Agency Task Force on Sport for Development and Peace, 2003). The report found that well-designed sports-based initiatives can be practical and cost-effective tools to achieve objectives in development and peace (hence desirable for governments). Additionally, the report spells out that the aims of SDP activities under the jurisdiction of the UN should be the promotion and use of sport as an intervention for the achievement of international development and peace-building objectives. As a consequence, the UN Resolution 58/5, entitled 'Sport as a Means to Promote Education, Health, Development and Peace', was passed and followed by the proclamation of 2005 as the International Year of Sport and Physical Education.

SDP AND THE GLOBAL SOUTH

Given the paucity of alternative voices in a field framed by Western hegemony (Darnell, 2010), the historical role of the Global South in shaping SDP remains a predominantly untold story. Without doubt, the impetus of the globally defined SDP movement has partly been inspired by the spirited advocacy emanating from the Global South, particularly in sub-Saharan Africa (SSA) (Mwaanga, 2010). Within the SSA context the Zambian-based EduSport Foundation has led activism focusing on the use of sport to build young people's awareness of and education on the dangers of HIV and AIDS. Thus, the work of EduSport is particularly relevant to MDG number 6, which calls for the halting and reversal of the spread of HIV and AIDS.

Indeed SSA is more heavily affected by HIV and AIDS than any other region in the world, with an estimated 22.9 million people living with HIV – around two thirds of the global total of those living with the disease (UNAIDS, 2010). Additionally, the social and economic consequences of the AIDS epidemic are widely felt, not only in the health sector but also in education, industry, agriculture, transport, human resources and the economy in general. Thus the AIDS epidemic in SSA continues to devastate communities, rolling back decades of development progress (UNAIDS, 2010). It comes as no surprise, then, that the majority of early SDP work in SSA was heavily linked to the HIV and AIDS epidemic; indeed at present over 50 per cent of SDP initiatives operating within SSA have not departed from this initial tendency, if only because of necessity.

Like all people in SSA, the indigenous leaders of the SDP movement within the Global South have themselves been affected directly by the HIV and AIDS scourge. Their involvement within the SDP movement constitutes a larger movement, or what the former South African President Thabo Mbeki called the African Renaissance, wherein African people are leading the way in overcoming the challenges confronting them as a continent. This Renaissance perspective on SDP also recognises the little-known African SDP activists who provided leadership for many young people in SSA: Clement Chileshe (Sport in Action, Zambia), Dr Cyprian Maro (EMIMA, Tanzania), Saa Moses Lamin (Youth in Action, Sierra Leone) and Yomi Kuku (Search and Groom, Nigeria), to mention but a few. In Zambia, for example, the sustained grassroots activism inspired the inclusion of SDP within the Zambian government's fifth National Development Plan, the development of the first National Diploma in sport studies and the development of world-renowned SDP programmes, such as the Kicking AIDS Out approach (see www.kickingaidsout.net).

UNPACKING THE MEANING OF SPORT IN SDP

Definitions of sport are diverse and range from the narrow – for example, Coakley (2001: 20) defines sport 'as a type of organised physical activity or exercise that involves the use of relatively complex physical skills, competence or intense effort' – to the broad, such as that used by the Sport for Development International Working Group (SDP IWG, 2008: 1), defining sport as 'all forms of physical activity that contribute to physical fitness, mental well-being and social interaction, such as play, recreation, organized or competitive sport, and indigenous sports and games'. The former definition, narrowly focused on organised sport and exercise, is common in the SDP research literature, most likely because it suits the measuring of certain key initiative outputs, such as participation (Kidd and Donnelly, 2007). This definition, of course, neglects the considerable amount of traditional and informal play and games participated in within the SDP context. Given that SDP is a cross-cultural phenomenon it would be useful to adopt a more comprehensive and

324

inclusive definition, such as the one used by the SDP IWG, incorporating all forms of sport, physical activity and exercise. By and large, the above definitions have clear implications: if a narrow definition is chosen, one neglects those activities that marginalised groups such as women and PLWHA may consider as sport. On the other hand, adopting a broad definition becomes a problem as it forces one to perceive sport as being a vague and ambiguous set of activities. In terms of SDP this then leads to a whole host of problems, including the challenges of measuring initiative impacts. Coalter's (2007) conceptualisation of sport, wherein sport is deemed a collective noun referring to a wide range of processes, social relationships and presumed physical, psychological and sociological outcomes, does not fully solve this quandary but does bring to the fore new paths for further deliberation.

Furthermore, it is recognised that individual interpretations of the sport experience are subjective. As Grant (2001: 790) asserts, 'each person responds to [the sport experience] in different ways'. It is argued that underpinning myriad interpretations of the sport experience there will be found different and sometimes conflicting discourses. These discourses may be divided into two categories: the competitive and non-competitive sport discourses (Dionigi, 2004).

The competitive discourse construes sport as performed within specified performance standards and with the participant following required limitations and imposed conditions. Sport at this level may also be performed for financial gain. In many SDP target communities, competitive sport is seen as a male domain wherein masculine-related attributes, such as power, aggression, intense physical effort, winning, domination and strength, are emphasised and reified.

The non-competitive or alternative sport discourses downplay competition and other masculine attributes in favour of promoting friendship, camaraderie, fun and keeping fit and healthy through participation. For example, the Positive and Kicking programme that promotes sport for PLWHA in Zambia focuses on social and recreational aspects of sport, and physical fitness and enjoyment through shared participation, rather than on the fierceness of competitive sport. Coakley (1994: 870) refers to 'carefully controlled competition': competition that 'is controlled to the point that participation focuses on fellowship and pride in their own physical skills in addition to outcomes'. Coakley (2001) asserts, moreover, that there is potential for marginalised groups to embrace the friendly and fun side of sport and to resist the dominant competitive ideology underlying the mainstream.

It is imperative to note that 'the competitive ideology that is embedded in mainstream sport in Western society is not inherently positive or negative; it depends upon how it is interpreted and practiced by individuals' (Dionigi, 2004: 19). In others words, competitive sport is not inherently unsuitable in this respect; however, knowledge of the hegemonic competitive discourse may be useful in the designing of SDP activities, particularly because it presents dual and contradictory empowerment opportunities (Dionigi, 2004; Mwaanga, 2012). For example, the

EduSport Go Sisters programme uses competitive football both to experience and to demonstrate presumed male attributes such as strength, power, physical aggression and strong bodies; however, in certain instances it uses football to counter those same male attributes and promote what are portrayed as culturally inferior (female) attributes, such as emotions during play. The latter has been interpreted by many scholars as resistance to the male-dominated domain (Coakley, 1994). Given this, it is reasonable to suggest that competitive sport creates a platform for cultural challenges against hegemony to occur, liberating the marginalised (in this case girls and women) through opportunities to exercise personal and collective power (Mwaanga, 2003).

UNPACKING THE MEANING OF DEVELOPMENT IN THE SDP CONTEXT

In SDP policy circles the meaning of the concept of development is often assumed and thus rarely critiqued. This is strange since, as a topic of study, development has been treated to a barrage of contested conceptualisations (Desai and Potter, 2008). What is development? Who is developing? How do we measure it? These questions will never be definitively answered, as the very nature of 'development' is a term with no ontological reality; rather it is a social construction. It is a term created to understand and measure human productivity in an evolving modern and postmodern world (Sidaway, 2008). Distinguishing between 'developed' and 'developing' traditionally relies on a Western perspective; that is, the majority of developmental discourses often use language whose Western origins ultimately define the parameters of SDP rationality. Kothari and Minogue (2002: 12) elucidate a simple yet profound conceptualisation of development as constituting 'an idea, an objective and an activity'. Accordingly, when we examine SDP as an activity or set of activities we are effectively engaging with an underpinning idea, theory or philosophical worldview which frames those developmental activities. However, as mentioned earlier, what constitutes development as an idea or theory is disputed territory.

The next section unravels modernisation as one of the hegemonic ideas of development, before countering it with postcolonial theory. It should be noted that the aim of this examination is not to discredit Global Northern ideologies, but merely to highlight the dangers of basing SDP practice entirely and solely on any one perspective, irrespective of others. Thus, this analysis is helpful in so far as it helps us to speculate maturely on how SDP would be framed based on alternative, or balanced hybrids of, ideological perspectives. As stated earlier, owing to the paucity of SDP initiatives underpinned by non-Global Northern developmental perspectives the section ends with an examination of the sub-Saharan African human development philosophy of Ubuntu, together with the influence it exerts on the practice of one Zambian indigenous SDP organisation.

DOMINANT DISCOURSE OF DEVELOPMENT IN THE SDP PROJECT

Although the failures in traditional development have been attributed to an over-reliance on Western development discourses, SDP as a new development approach remains strongly influenced by modernisation as one dominant development theory (Kingsbury *et al.*, 2008; Kothari and Minogue, 2002). This is not to dismiss the existence of other Global Northern development theories but, as Kingsbury and colleagues (2008) argue, most of the Western development theories (for example, neo-liberalism, modernisation, interventionism and structuralism) overlap to varying degrees, being differentiated only by slight nuances. For the purpose of this analysis, with the aim of examining the underpinning development ideas of SDP, it is sufficient, then, to outline the modernisation perspective on development.

Generally speaking, modernisation is a process whereby societies move from a clear starting point to a definite end point (Kingsbury *et al.*, 2008). Such developmental thinking implies a binary understanding of the world, distinguishing between the less desired (developing, traditional) and the more desired (modern, civilised) society. As Inglehart (1997: 5, cited by Girginov, 2008: 4) observes, modernisation 'enabled a society to move from being poor to being rich clearly in a prescriptive manner.' Some of the ingredients stipulated by modernisation theory to stimulate development within more 'backward' countries included increasing aid, prompting free trade and foreign direct investment, as well as building widespread infrastructure (Simon and Narman, 1999). The crucial stimulus for development within modernisation prescriptions, then, was generally economic growth (Willis, 2005). A way out of this perceived 'backwardness' according to the logic of modernisation, then, is the adoption of and commitment to ideas and values of the 'successful' Global North, which 'will push aside the cultural obstacles of traditionalism' (Webster, 1990: 192).

> The evolution of societies occurs as traditional behaviour patterns give way under the pressure of modernization. While these pressures built up gradually within Western societies, 'developing' countries . . . can be exposed to them from outside. That is, they can be helped along the road to modernity with the assistance of the developed countries whose ideas and technologies can be introduced and diffused throughout these poorer countries.
>
> (ibid.: 53)

This view on development compels Global Northern countries to proactively 'assist' the poor countries in the latter's attempt to become modern. It therefore becomes an economic and moral necessity for the West to continue and intensify development interventions following the end of the colonial era. Clearly, this approach has been reproduced in SDP.

It is argued here that, within SDP practice, Global Northern approaches and voices remain privileged, seeing Northern approaches to development as being superior, civilised and further developed than those of the South (Darnell, 2007; Levermore and Beacom, 2009). Moreover, the North is perceived as the civiliser of the South. This led Frey (1988: 69) to conclude that 'sport assists in the transition from a traditional, agrarian society to an urbanized, modern/industrialized one', or, borrowing from Elias and Dunning (1986), it can be asserted that the Global North positions itself as the 'civiliser' of the Global South, using SDP as the means for this civilising process. Two examples from the author's experiences in SDP can help illustrate this argument. First, innovative SDP approaches initiated in the Global South are usually trivialised, or, if regarded favourably, are therefore not properly attributed to their initiators. For example, it has taken close to a decade for Northern Kicking AIDS Out (KAO) network members to publicly and officially acknowledge that the KAO approach was originally pioneered by the EduSport Foundation (Mwaanga, 2001). Cassidy and colleagues (2001) summarise this well when they submit that local knowledge, especially stemming from the Global South, has no place in the colonial and imperialistic developmental project. Second, given that the majority of SDP leaders are from the Global South, it is astonishing how so little is heard from them in comparison with their counterparts of Northern descent, such as the leaders and founders of Right to Play (RTP) and Matare Youth Sport Association (MYSA).

Girginov (2008) argues that 'development' is not only a social construction but equally serves as a constructor, specifically because it can create its opposite of under-development, thus carrying a specific power. Indeed, for the majority of the world's population, who live in the Global South, the word 'development' is a constant reminder of their supposed self-deficiencies (Esteva, 1997). Some commentators have often questioned the assumption held that development can occur in a unilinear and homogenous manner in distinct stages and with little cultural and contextual variation (Willis, 2005). They perceive development as being related to power configurations and therefore assert that true 'development can only take place when domination is reduced; development is not a matter of moving through stages as the modernists would suggest' (Frey, 1988: 80). The following section, accordingly, examines the alternative development theory of post-colonialism as counteracting mainstream Northern perspectives.

POSTCOLONIAL THEORY: AN ALTERNATIVE DEVELOPMENT DISCOURSE IN SDP

Postcolonial theory, as assisting alternative development discourses, centres its argument on questions of (imperialistic) knowledge and power (Childs and Williams, 1997). Within the development context, postcolonial theory asks: How can development as a discipline persist when derived from a discourse in which all knowledge has been gained from a single narrative, that of the colonial power (Kothari and Minogue, 2002)? The fact that SDP is devised in the Global North and implemented in the Global South implies that Global Northern perspectives of development heavily dominate SDP discourse and practice (Darnell, 2007). For example, despite the fact that the majority of SDP initiatives are implemented in the Global South, the two UN offices for the SDP movement are located in the Global North (New York and Geneva).

Post-colonial theory, then, is a specific intellectual discourse that consists of reactions to and analyses of the cultural legacy of colonialism (Hall, 2007; Victoria, 2007). Postcolonialism is useful because it focuses on the continuation of colonialism, albeit through the different or new relationships concerning power and the control/production of knowledge (Sharp, 2008). Colonialism involves the interruption and the destruction of native culture by European imperialism (Smith, 1999). Gilbert and Tompkins (1996) urge that the debate about and understanding of postcolonialism must be less a chronological construction of post-independence and more a contest of colonial discourses, power structures and social hierarchies still existent despite so-called independence. The above understanding of postcolonialism implies structural domination, then: a system of oppression whereby the dominant discourse privileges white, patriarchal knowledge and deems knowledge stemming from non-whites inferior (Darnell, 2007). Thus postcolonialism touches on one of the central issues within development: the concept of power and how it shapes developmental thinking and policy (McKay, 2004).

Of particular concern to postcolonialism is the way in which the Global South, within international (as well as SDP) literature and the media, is portrayed in a negative, derogatory and stereotypical manner (McEwan, 2002; Said, 1978). To redress these concerns the development thinking required by the Global South involves the inclusion of more local, indigenous understanding, to radically disrupt entrenched systems of (Northern) knowledge. The critical essence of postcolonial ideas (within the SDP project) entails *destabilising* entrenched Northern ways of thinking, thereby creating a space for marginalised groups to speak and produce alternatives to hegemonic discourse(s). The leading Zambian indigenous SDP NGO EduSport applies the sub-Saharan African worldview of Ubuntu to guide its programming, and in this respect somewhat counters Westernisation. For example, SDP initiatives predominantly aimed at behaviour change (to promote self-confidence and self-esteem) constitute a developmental thinking which elides the contextual realities of why 'development' is required in the first place. Arguably SDP approaches such as these deaden the critical awareness of initiative participants vis-à-vis the globally located sources of their marginalisation. This happens in several ways. For example, two of Africa's most heavily populated slums (Matare and Kebera in Kenya), being focal points for numerous internationally recognised

SDP initiatives, are never understood in terms of how sport could be used as a platform for collective resistance to Northern hegemonic practices that have failed to deliver development in these communities. Instead, sport and SDP activities are used to promote life skills which can only lead to partial individual empowerment, particularly as the root causes of underdevelopment, such as resource deprivation and limited opportunities, are never addressed. Accordingly, the Kicking AIDS Out programme in Matare focuses on teaching the ABC[5] of HIV and AIDS, which is based on the assumption that what young people need to prevent infection is basic knowledge and information, irrespective of contextual factors. This approach ignores research clearly stating that socio-economically disadvantaged people are highly vulnerable to HIV infection (Sydnes, 2000). In addition, poor nutrition and frequent exposure to other diseases also make the poor more prone to developing AIDS when first infected with HIV; such vulnerability cannot be overcome only through the ABC approach.

With this said, however, some still see sport as a potential vehicle to allow for resistance against dominant political structures (Jarvie, 1991). The Black Power salute at the 1968 Olympics highlights how the symbolic defiance of Tommie Smith and John Carlos was a significant display of the potential of sport to resist dominant political structures that marginalise and discriminate. Indeed, within colonial Africa, Wagg (1995: 34) highlights how football 'was wrested from European control and used by the African population to assert their new urban identity'.

SITUATING THE UBUNTU PHILOSOPHY IN SDP: THE EXAMPLE OF EDUSPORT

The scarcity of alternative development perspectives within SDP discourses and its ensuing practices is apparent (Levermore and Beacom, 2009). Therefore, in addition to closely examining the Ubuntu cultural philosophy in relation to EduSport initiatives, this section sets out initially to address the question: Why is there a paucity of global Southern discourses within the contemporary SDP movement? However, it is necessary to place here a caveat: because there are few examples and studies openly advocating the inclusion of global Southern discourses within the SDP movement, this examination of Ubuntu will be rather descriptive than expansive; the following analysis should be understood within this context.

A glance at the EduSport Foundation website (www.edusport.org.zm) highlights a number of unique organisational tenets; for example, the initial aims of EduSport were to try and match its daily work with the values and ideals as expressed in the organisation's vision and mission statement. However, this aspect of EduSport seems to have eluded many Global Northern academics who have researched this and similar indigenous SDP organisations in SSA. Three aspects relevant to this debate stand out. First, EduSport's organisational mission statement is framed

330

within the empowerment framework: 'To empower communities through sport'. It is important to note that this paradigm focus is towards how sport can help increase important resources and influence in the wider society for particular marginalised groups. This is a holistic approach that does not solely focus on behavioural change interventions. Second, by adopting an empowerment philosophy EduSport further situates its work within the holistic human and social development framework. This is in line with the UN Declaration on the Right of Development (1986), and therefore challenges the predominant notion that economic growth is the sole determinant of a nation's well-being. Accordingly, the Declaration reads:

> *development* is a comprehensive economic, social, cultural and political process, which aims at the constant improvement of the well-being of the entire population and of all individuals on the basis of their active, free and meaningful participation in development and the fair distribution of benefits.
>
> (UN Declaration on the Right of Development, 1986)

Finally, EduSport adopts the SSA philosophy of Ubuntu as the organisational philosophy whose primary focus is the people; indeed EduSport programmes are 'centred on the interests and needs of the people we serve' (www.edusport.org. zm). Clearly, this over-arching purpose of EduSport is a crucial part of the organisation and hence why its relevance ought to be captured in any research on the organisation.

It has been argued that the privileging of Global Northern forms of knowledge leads to the systematic marginalising of other forms. Indeed Sharp (2008) posits that forms of knowing other than that which is known by Global Northern thinkers are marginalised by them, who refer to such other forms of knowledge as myth or folklore. Thus the Northern academic wishes to know the marginalised person's experience, but not through the latter's own knowing, which is seen as inadequate by the self-professed expert (Lindsey and Grattan, 2012). Given this, hooks (1990) and McKay (2004) correctly question the Northern academics' engagement with 'the other': to truly engage with the marginalised or colonised 'other', they argue that an academic would need to decentre him/herself as the expert (see also Joanne, 2008). Indeed, hooks (1990) underscores this notion in suggesting that within Global Northern societies only academics are privileged as custodians of the 'truth'. As suggested, the SSA sport for development subject becomes subordinated and only known through the representations of Global Northern academics. hooks concludes that the relationship between the academic and the marginalised subject is as follows:

> No need to hear your voice when I can talk about you better than you can speak about yourself. No need to hear your voice. Only tell me about your

pain. I want to know your story. And then I will tell it back to you in a new way. Tell it back to you in such a way that it has become mine, my own. Re-writing you I write myself anew. I am still author, authority. I am still colonizer the speaking subject and you are now at the centre of my talk.

(hooks, 1990: 241)

Arguably, Global Northern academics who are willing to position themselves as co-learners and co-inquirers with research subjects are better positioned to appreciate and capture alternative discourses, such as the SSA philosophical worldview of Ubuntu.

Ubuntu

Ubuntu's meaning and its implications, like other philosophical perspectives, are highly contested (Broodryk, 2002). Nonetheless there is much consensus on the roots of Ubuntu, such as that 'it is an ancient African worldview with roots deeply anchored in the traditional African way of life' (ibid.: 56). Bhengu (1996: 10) defines Ubuntu as 'the art of being a human being'. This common African aphorism is often translated as 'a person is a person through other persons' (Ramose, 1999: 49). This aphorism identifies its central concept, Ubuntu, which variously means 'humanity' or 'humanness' (Shutte, 1993). At the core of the Ubuntu worldview, then, is the ideal of being with others: that humans should relate to one another with respect and compassion (Broodryk, 2002). Louw (1995) presents dialogue as both a fundamental element and a means for negotiating the art of being human through being with others. He argues that dialogue exposes the characteristic of conduct as prescribed by Ubuntu. Through inspiring us to expose ourselves to others and encounter the difference of their humanness, Ubuntu thus informs and enriches our own humanness (Sindane, 1994). 'To be human is to affirm one's humanity by recognising the humanity of others in its infinite variety of content and form' (Ramose, 1999: 193). This philosophical approach is difficult to translate; however, by applying dialogical approaches EduSport strives to recognise and respect the diversity and richness of the humanity encountered in its projects' target groups (women and girls, youths, PLWHA). As a personal reflective development task, EduSport programme members of staff, volunteers and partners (including researchers) are challenged to develop their own humanness through rich encounters with the programme target groups.

The emphasis on 'the other' and 'otherness' is an especially prominent feature in the Ubuntu worldview, entailing the centrality of relationships for the individual. Unlike the Western philosophical worldviews, such as neo-liberalism, wherein the individual's development interests rule supreme, and others within a society are regarded as a means to individual ends and not ends in themselves (Prinsloo, 1996), the Ubuntu worldview emphasises that an individual's existence is possible only through relationships with others. This aspect of Ubuntu is emphasised in several EduSport programmes. For example, the Go Sisters programme (girls' empowerment through sport) stresses and builds upon the relationship orientations of the African sisterhood in its attempt to facilitate the empowerment of socio-economically marginalised girls in six of Zambia's nine provinces. The Go Sisters are encouraged and supported to build family-like bonds and to do things together outside programme times. According to Louw (1995), the Ubuntu perception of the other is adjustable and open-ended; therefore it acknowledges that the other is always in the process of becoming a complete human being. Thus 'Ubuntu' denotes both a state of being and of becoming (Broodryk, 1997). As a process of self-realisation through others, Ubuntu enhances one's self-realisation (ibid.: 5–7). This is an important notion which situates EduSport's application of Ubuntu vis-à-vis collective empowerment, focusing on a particular community's mutual support to actualise its members' potential and improve the control of their lives within their given cultural context (Wallerstein, 1992). The relationship emphasis of Ubuntu also requires that one welcome and appreciate participation in a community as a key aspect of becoming an Ubuntu individual. In the Ubuntu worldview, Descartes's asocial 'I think, therefore I am' is replaced with 'I participate, therefore I am' (Shutte, 1993: 47). To link this to the EduSport approach, then, the idea of bringing Northern experts into Southern communities for short periods of time, not allowing full integration and participation in the realities of the everyday lives of the target groups and also their wider community, goes against the grain of Ubuntu and sound community development (see Hylton and Totten, Chapter 4 in this edition).

Christianity has influenced Ubuntu in its contemporary understanding. Indeed, many sub-Saharan Africans also follow the Christian religion. Consequently, EduSport is both a Christian and an Ubuntu organisation. With this said, Ubuntu and its application within EduSport is not flawless. Some have challenged Ubuntu on the grounds that its emphasis on collectivism can easily derail into an oppressive communalism (Teffo, 1994). Louw (1995) concurs but still maintains that true Ubuntu incorporates dialogue, that is, that Ubuntu should incorporate both relations and distance. It preserves the other in his/her otherness, in his/her uniqueness, without letting him/her slip into the distance (Shutte, 1993). If the ideals of Ubuntu are the destination, then dialogue is the transport to that end. In EduSport, Ubuntu is perceived as a work in progress so that, in situations when its principles are compromised, social meetings (called Indabas) are convened in order for the community members to discuss the continued fostering of Ubuntu. Indabas are also common in SSA's wider socio-cultural context, as they also occur at weddings and funerals, for instance.

Louw (1995: 8) makes a thoughtful defence of the philosophy by stating that, like others, 'Ubuntu is a given, but clearly also a task'. Ubuntu is primarily an ethical ideal, that is something that still needs to be realised; however, encouraging examples already exist (Shutte, 1998: 20). Within the EduSport context it is not strange to hear how a community football team contributed money to buy food for needy team members or to buy a coffin for a deceased member of the local community. In sum, the words of two Global Northern volunteers presented as a contrast conclude this discussion. The first is a Right to Play (RTP) volunteer on his way to work in SSA:

> My mission is to train, to empower, and to help bring a sense of dignity back to these people.
>
> (quoted in Darnell, 2007: 560)

The second is a Northern volunteer who has just completed a work placement in an EduSport community in Zambia:

> Coming and working as a community sport coach in Zambia has made me find myself in the struggle of others. I didn't know I had this much empathy before I travelled to Africa. I made my players' daily struggle my own.
>
> (Education through Sport Foundation, 2006: 3)

This partly highlights, on one hand, the stereotypical view of Global Southern communities as non-functional and, on the other, the unexpected encounter with the Ubuntu worldview as a learning experience.

CONCLUSION

This chapter maps the emerging field of SDP through three primary objectives:

1 to provide an account of the historical factors that have shaped and continue to shape the SDP movement;
2 to deconstruct the meaning and discourses associated with sport and development;
3 to critique modernisation as one of the dominant development discourses framing SDP, and to use postcolonial thinking together with the indigenous sub-Saharan cultural philosophy of Ubuntu as alternative examples of development perspectives.

Notwithstanding the leadership role that the UN provided to drive SDP towards concrete directive policy actions in line with the MDGs, it was recognised that the historical account of SDP was based on limited Global Northern narratives,

334

indicative of the hegemonic position of the Global North in the SDP movement. This is a historical account, critiquing as it does the misrecognition of the role played by Global Southern SDP activists at the end of the last century. The changes in the wider socio-political climate of SSA that were interpreted from an African Renaissance perspective recognise the role played by SSA activists and NGOs in shaping the global SDP movement. Additionally, the scourge of HIV/AIDS that ravaged SSA in the 1990s was identified as being the impetus for the development of the SDP movement in SSA. An attempt to provide a two-tier historical account is part of a destabilisation of Global Northern hegemony in framing SDP. It is argued that a more balanced narrative will impart new clarity of the SDP movement.

Second, it is argued that the multiplicity and ambiguity around conceptions of sport and development present one of the most important challenges for understanding SDP. Indeed, both sport and development were unravelled as social constructions framed within Global Northern discourses. In terms of sport, the limited global applicability of defining sport 'as a type of organised physical activity or exercise that involves the use of relatively complex physical skills, competence or intense effort' (Coakley, 2001: 20) was critiqued, but its usability for monitoring and evaluation is recognised. Conversely, the broad definition of sport adopted by the SDP IWG is cross-culturally advantageous but limited in terms of policy application. Moreover, the two competing discourses that frame sport – competitive (dominant) and non-competitive (alternative) – were examined in the light of SDP. Resistance to the dominant discourse that frames Global Northern sport was shown to be crucial for social transformation for target SDP groups and communities.

Sport for development and peace, as a movement, has the potential to carry home its goal of development, but not when carried on the wings of a single hegemonic Global Northern development paradigm. Looking to alternative paradigms can further unique contributions that SDP can make to failed traditional international development ways of working. Indeed, the philosophy of Ubuntu, with its real uptake within SSA, was suggested as not only an alternative to dominant conceptions of development but in fact, in some sense, the very antithesis of hegemonic Global Northern development paradigms. To see progress in the current SDP movement, this notion of a goal of development can be reached only through a truly democratically imbued process, whereby those at the receiving end of SDP initiatives negotiate their own initiatives; thus these initiatives would truly correspond to the people's hopes and wishes but equally retain a hybridity for global relevance. Only in this way may one pronounce the beginnings of any kind of development, not only for those people, but for all.

CASE STUDY 14.1: GO SISTERS

Go Sisters is a programme run under the auspices of the EduSport Foundation. Go Sisters uses sport to facilitate empowerment through providing education, leadership, mentorship and small business support to socially disadvantaged girls and women in Zambia. The programme aims to contribute to the achievement of Millennium Development Goal (MDG) number 3 – promoting gender equity and empowerment – within the Zambian context by increasing the number of girls and women in the target communities adopting leadership roles at community and district levels. The programme firmly embeds the principles of EduSport, which include finding development niches from within the local culture. Indeed, Go Sisters as a programme embodies African sisterhood as being a means to promote collective approaches to addressing gender inequality within the local context.

More specifically, the programme focuses on advocacy and empowerment through training girls and women in leadership, life skills and promotion of women's sport as a vehicle for gender-related development. The formation of action teams and community committees allows female peer leaders to take on positions with decision-making responsibilities, with support both from their parents and from the wider community being seen as fundamental in this process. Boys and men are included in the programme since it is generally agreed that without their involvement an understanding of gender inequalities and the changes hoped for will be partial and indeed only superficial. The programme is holistic not only in this respect, however; Go Sisters addresses both individual and cultural (as well as structural) barriers to empowerment. To address the individual level of empowerment (psychological empowerment), employment and skills development is seen within the programme as being imperative for the achievement of MDG 3. On the collective empowerment front, moreover, the programme joins with other programmes for women and girls to advocate for women's and girls' empowerment. Using the 'peer leader' approach, the programme builds a sustainable network of female role models who lead and inspire younger generations of female leaders. Peer leaders organise themselves into Action Teams, that is self-managed organising committees, supported by the EduSport staff, to devise and lead educational and sports programmes for their communities.

Achievements of Go Sisters to date (www.edusport.org.zm):

- Go Sisters is now active in sixteen communities in Lusaka, thirteen schools and five communities in Southern Province and six schools in Western Province of Zambia.
- It has trained 998 peer leaders in four sports codes, sport administration, event management, facilitation, HIV and AIDS awareness, sexual reproductive health and human rights.
- Thirty-two community action teams have been established, with 252 youths (240 girls and young women) involved in organising sports training, sports leagues, tournaments and special events, and life skills workshops for their local school or community. The established community action teams are able to organise events with minimum supervision.
- There are 550 peer leaders classed as 'very active', leading at least one training session per week or organising a monthly workshop with their model team.
- Of the 513 peer leaders surveyed after the workshop, 66 per cent felt that their confidence, leadership skills and ability to stand up for themselves had increased.
- Of the peer leaders surveyed, 79 per cent believed that Go Sisters had given them a sense of purpose in life.
- Since being in the programme, 164 female peer leaders have adopted other leadership roles (e.g. school head girl, class monitor, Sunday school teacher, praise team lead person and

prefect).

- Approximately 10,000 children and youths have been reached in regular sport and play (over 65 per cent are girls), as each peer leader actively engages with approximately eighteen young people in each peer-leading session.
- Ninety-five per cent of parents surveyed agree that the Go Sisters programme is good for their community and their daughters and therefore support further participation.
- It has held fifty-five workshop and training camps, where rights awareness has been central.
- Forty-eight trainers of trainers (thirty-one female) have been trained and are supporting peer leaders and action teams to run workshops and create sporting opportunities in their local communities.
- A further 20,000 children and youths have been reached through sports festivals and events, thus increasing awareness of HIV and AIDS, sexual reproductive health and gender equity.
- The Go Sisters team and trained peer leaders are trained to conduct interviews and questionnaires to monitor and understand the programme's dynamics. This information supports the external evaluation of the programme and enables the team to use evidence to advocate policy changes needed to further empower girls and women.
- Ninety-six school and two higher education scholarships have been distributed, enabling active female peer leaders to continue to study or go back to school in order to complete their secondary education.
- Four internships have taken place, giving valuable work experience opportunities.

LEARNING ACTIVITIES

Go to www.sportanddev.org/ and answer the following questions:

1 What is sport for development and peace?
2 Name three SDP projects on the website.
3 Describe the aims of one of your three projects.
4 What do you see as the strengths and weaknesses of your project?

NOTES

1. The United Nations Millennium Development Goals (MDGs) are eight goals that all 191 UN member states have agreed to try to achieve by the year 2015. The United Nations Millennium Declaration, signed in September 2000, commits world leaders to combat poverty, hunger, disease, illiteracy, environmental degradation and discrimination against women. The MDGs all have specific targets and indicators. The eight MDGs are:

   - to eradicate extreme poverty and hunger;
   - to achieve universal primary education;
   - to promote gender equality and empower women;
   - to reduce child mortality;
   - to improve maternal health;
   - to combat HIV/AIDS, malaria and other diseases;
   - to ensure environmental sustainability; and
   - to develop a global partnership for development.

The MDGs are interdependent; all the MDGs influence health, and health influences all the MDGs. For example, better health enables children to learn and adults to earn. Gender equality is essential to the achievement of better health. Reducing poverty, hunger and environmental degradation positively influences, but also depends on, better health (www.who.int/topics/millennium_development_goals/about/en/index.html).

2. EduSport Foundation is an indigenous SDP organisation founded by the author in 1999. As leader of the EduSport Foundation at the time, the author co-pioneered the development of initiatives such as Kicking AIDS Out and Go Sisters (the latter uses sport as a tool for girls' empowerment). Incidentally, Kicking AIDS Out is now also a network of organisations that are involved in addressing community problems by means of sport.

3. This way of referring to countries is extremely contentious in the academic and policy communities. As applied in this chapter the 'Global South' is not just another name for the 'South' or the 'developing world'. The term denotes a community of people at different geographical locations who experience a common set of problems – problems which emanate, by and large, from deep inequities of power within and between nations (UNDP, 2004).

4. A discourse can be defined as a system of ideas or knowledge linked to a specific text which is used to identify and legitimise the privileging of power of one person over another (Fairclough, 1992).

5. ABC is an initialism representing Abstinence, Be faithful and Condomise as the core essence of HIV/AIDS education.

REFERENCES

Beutler, I. (2008) 'Sport serving development and peace: achieving the goals of the United Nations through sport', *Sport in Society*, 11 (4): 359–369.

Bhengu, M.J. (1996) *Ubuntu: The Essential of Democracy*, Cape Town: Novalis Press.

Broodryk, J. (1997) *Ubuntuism as a Worldview to Order Society*, unpublished doctoral dissertation, UNISA, Pretoria, South Africa.

Broodryk, J. (2002) *Ubuntu: Life Lessons from Africa*, Tshwane, South Africa: Ubuntu School of Philosophy.

Cassidy, L., Good, K., Mazonde, I. and Rivers, R. (2001) 'An assessment of the status of the SaniBasarwa in Botswana: regional assessment of the status of the San in Southern Africa', Report Series No. 3 of 5, Legal Assistance Centre (LAC), Windhoek.

Childs, P. and Williams, P. (1997) *An Introduction to Post-colonial Theory*, London: Longman.

Coakley, J.J. (1994) *Sports in Society: Issues and Controversies*, 5th edn, St. Louis, MO: Mosby-Year Book.

Coakley, J.J. (2001) *Sports in Society: Issues and Controversies*, 7th edn, St. Louis, MO: Mosby-Year Book.

Coalter, F. (2007) *A Wider Social Role for Sport: Who's Keeping the Score?*, London: Routledge.

Darnell, S.C. (2007) 'Playing with race: right to play and the production of whiteness in development through sport', *Sport in Society*, 10 (4): 560–579.

Darnell, S.C. (2010) 'Power, politics and "sport for development and peace": investigating the utility of sport for international development', *Sociology of Sport Journal*, 27: 54–75.

Desai, V. and Potter, R. (2008) *The Companion to Development Studies*, 2nd edn, London: Hodder Education.

Dionigi, A.R. (2004) *Competing for Life: Older People and Competitive Sport*, unpublished PhD thesis, University of Newcastle, NSW.

Education through Sport Foundation (2006) *Quarterly Report on Positive & Kicking*, Lusaka: EduSport Secretariat.

Elias, N. and Dunning, E. (1986) *Quest for Excitement: Sport and Leisure in the Civilizing Process*, Oxford: Basil Blackwell.

Esteva, G. (1997) 'Development', in Sachs, W. (ed.), *The Development Dictionary*, London: Zed Books.

Fairclough, N. (1992) 'Discourse and text: linguistic and intertextual analysis within discourse analysis', *Discourse & Society*, 3 (2): 193–217.

Frey, J.H. (1988) 'The internal and external role of sport in national development', *Journal of National Development*, 1: 65–82.

Gilbert, H. and Tompkins, J. (1996) *Post-colonial Drama: Theory, Practice, and Politics*, New York: Routledge.

Girginov, V. (2008) 'Management of sports development as an emerging field and profession', in Girginov, V. (ed.), *Management of Sports Development*, Oxford: Elsevier.

Grant, B.C. (2001) 'You're never too old: beliefs about physical activities and playing sport in later life', *Age and Society*, 21 (6): 777–798.

Hall, S. (2007) 'The West and the rest: discourse and power', in Gupta, T.D., James, C.E., Maaka, R.C.A., Galabuzi, G.-E. and Anderson, C. (eds.), *Race and Racialization: Essential Readings*, Toronto: Canadian Scholars Press.

Hayhurst, L.M.C. (2009) 'The power to shape policy: charting sport for development and peace policy discourses', *International Journal of Sport Policy*, 1 (2): 203–227.

hooks, b. (1990) 'Marginality as a site of resistance', in Ferguson, R. (ed.), *Out There: Marginalization and Contemporary Cultures*, Cambridge, MA: MIT.

Jarvie, G. (1991) 'Sport, popular struggle and South African culture', in Jarvie, G. (ed.), *Sport, Racism and Ethnicity*, London: Falmer Press.

Jarvie, G. (2011) 'Sport, development and aid: can sport make a difference?', *Sport in Society*, 14 (2): 241–252.

Joanne, S. (2008) *Geographies of Postcolonialism: Can the Subaltern Speak?*, Glasgow: Sage Publications.

Kidd, B. (2008) 'A new social movement: sport for development and peace', *Sport in Society*, 11: 370–380.

Kidd, B., and Donnelly, P. (2007) *Literature Review for Sport for Development and Peace*, Toronto: Sport for Development and Peace International Working Group (SDP IWG).

Kingsbury, D., McGillivray, J. and Clarke, M. (2008) *International Development: Issues and Challenges*, London: Palgrave Macmillan.

Kothari, U. and Minogue, M. (2002) *Development Theory and Practice: Critical Perspectives*, Basingstoke, UK: Palgrave Macmillan.

Levermore, R. and Beacom, A. (2009) *Sport and International Development*, Basingstoke, UK: Palgrave.

Lindsey, I. and Gratton, A. (2012) 'An "international movement"? Decentering sport-for-development within Zambian communities', *International Journal of Sport Policy and Politics*, 4 (1): 91–110.

Louw, D.J. (1995) 'Decolonization as post modernization', in Malherbe, J.G. (ed.), *Decolonizing the Mind*, Pretoria, South Africa: Research Unit for African Philosophy, UNISA.

McEwan, C. (2002) 'Post colonialism', in Desai, V. and Potter, R.B. (eds.), *The Companion to Development Studies*, London: Hodder Education.

McKay, J. (2004) 'Reassessing development theory: modernisation and beyond', in Kingsbury, D.J., Remenyi, J., McKay, J. and Hunt, J. (eds.), *Key Issues in Development*, Basingstoke, UK: Palgrave Macmillan.

Mwaanga, O. (2001) *Kicking AIDS out through Movement Games*, Olso: Norwegian Development Agency.

Mwaanga, O. (2003) *HIV/AIDS At-Risk Adolescent Girls Empowerment through Participation in Top Level Football and EduSport in Zambia*, unpublished MSc thesis, Institute of Social Science, Norwegian University of Sport and PE, Oslo.

Mwaanga, O. (2010) 'Sport for addressing HIV/AIDS: explaining our convictions', *Leisure Studies Association*, 65: 61–67.

Mwaanga, O. (2012) *Positive and Kicking: Sport Empowerment for People Living with HIV/AIDS in Zambia*, unpublished PhD thesis, Leeds Metropolitan University, Leeds, UK.

Nicholls, S., Giles, A.R. and Sethna, C. (2011) 'Perpetuating the "lack of evidence" discourse in sport for development: privileged voices, unheard stories and subjugated knowledge', *International Review of the Sociology of Sport*, 46: 249–264.

Prinsloo, E.D. (1996) 'The Ubuntu concept of caring', paper presented at a nursing profession conference, UNISA, Pretoria, South Africa.

Ramose, M.B. (1999) *African Philosophy through Ubuntu*, Harare: Mondi Books.

Said, E. (1978) *Orientalism*, London: Routledge.

SDP IWG (2008) *Right to Play Publication. Harnessing the Power of Sport Development and Peace: Recommendations to Governments*, Toronto: Right to Play.

Sharp, J. (2008) *Geographies of Postcolonialism*, London: Sage Publications.

Shuttle, A. (1998) 'African and European Philosophising: Senghor's "Civilisation of the Universal"', in Coetzee, P.H. and Roux, A.P.J. (eds.), *Philosophy from Africa: A Text with Readings*, Johannesburg: International Thomson Publishing.

Shutte, A. (1993) *Philosophy for Africa*, Rondebosch, South Africa: UCT Press.

Sidaway, J. (2008) 'Post-development', in Desai, V. and Potter, R. (eds.), *The Companion to Development Studies*, 2nd edn, London: Hodder Education.

Simon, D. and Narman, A. (1999) *Development as Theory and Practice: Current Perspectives on Development and Development Cooperation*, London: Addison Wesley Longman.

Sindane, J. (1994) 'Ubuntu and nation building: South African governmental White Paper on social welfare', www.gov.za/whitepaper/index.html

Smith, L.T. (1999) *Decolonizing Methodologies: Research and Indigenous Peoples*, London: Zed Books.

Sydnes, A.K. (2000) 'Aids angår oss alle', *Tidsskrift for Norsk Psykologforening*, 37: 1099–1100.

Teffo, J. (1994) *The Concept of Ubuntu as a Cohesive Moral Value*, Pretoria, South Africa: Ubuntu School of Philosophy.

Tiessen, R. (2011) 'Global subjects or objects of globalisation? The promotion of global citizenship in organisations offering sport for development and/or peace programmes', *Third World Quarterly*, 32 (3): 571–587.

UNAIDS (2010) 'UNAIDS report on the global AIDS epidemic', www.unaids.org/globalreport/Global_report.htm

UNDP (2004) *Forging a Global South: UN Day for South–South Cooperation*, New York: UNDP.

United Nations (2003) 'Sport as a means to promote education, health, development and peace', Resolution 58/5, adopted by the General Assembly, New York.

UN Declaration on Right to Development (1986) 'Annex: declaration on the right to development', www.un.org/documents/ga/res/41/a41r128.htm

United Nations Inter-Agency Task Force on Sport for Development and Peace (2003) *Sport for Development and Peace: Towards Achieving the Millennium Development Goals*, Geneva: UN.

Victoria, L. (2007) *Making Development Geography*, London: Hodder Education.

Wagg, S. (1995) *Giving the Game Away: Football, Politics and Culture on Five Continents*, London: Leicester University Press.

340

Wallerstein, N. (1992) 'Powerlessness, empowerment and health: implications for health promotion programs', *American Journal of Health Promotion*, 6: 197–205.

Webster, A. (1990) *Introduction to the Sociology of Development*, 2nd edn, Houndmills, UK: Macmillan.

Willis, K. (2005) *Theories and Practices of Development*, London: Routledge.

INDEX

344

346

353

355